CRAFTING POETRY ANTHOLOGIES IN RENAISSANCE ENGLAND

The printed poetry anthologies first produced in sixteenth-century England have long been understood as instrumental in shaping the history of English poetry. This book offers a fresh approach to this history by turning attention to the recreative properties of these books, both in the sense of making again, of crafting and recrafting, and of poetry as a pleasurable pastime. The model of materiality employed extends from books-as-artefacts to their embodiedness – their crafted, performative, and expressive capacities. Publishers invariably advertised the recreational uses of anthologies, locating these books in early modern performance cultures in which poetry was read, silently and in company, sometimes set to music, and recrafted into other forms. Engaging with studies of material cultures, including work on craft, households, and soundscapes, *Crafting Poetry Anthologies in Renaissance England* argues for a domestic Renaissance in which anthologies travelled across social classes, shaping recreational cultures that incorporated men and women in literary culture.

MICHELLE O'CALLAGHAN is Professor of Early Modern Literature and Culture at the University of Reading. Her books include *The 'Shepheards Nation': Jacobean Spenserians and Early Stuart Political Culture, 1612–1625* (2000), *The English Wits: Literature and Sociability in Early Modern England* (Cambridge University Press, 2007), and *Thomas Middleton, Renaissance Dramatist* (2009).

CRAFTING POETRY ANTHOLOGIES IN RENAISSANCE ENGLAND

Early Modern Cultures of Recreation

MICHELLE O'CALLAGHAN

University of Reading

CAMBRIDGE
UNIVERSITY PRESS

University Printing House, Cambridge CB2 8BS, United Kingdom

One Liberty Plaza, 20th Floor, New York, NY 10006, USA

477 Williamstown Road, Port Melbourne, VIC 3207, Australia

314–321, 3rd Floor, Plot 3, Splendor Forum, Jasola District Centre, New Delhi – 110025, India

79 Anson Road, #06–04/06, Singapore 079906

Cambridge University Press is part of the University of Cambridge.

It furthers the University's mission by disseminating knowledge in the pursuit of education, learning, and research at the highest international levels of excellence.

www.cambridge.org
Information on this title: www.cambridge.org/9781108491099
DOI: 10.1017/9781108867412

© Michelle O'Callaghan 2020

This publication is in copyright. Subject to statutory exception and to the provisions of relevant collective licensing agreements, no reproduction of any part may take place without the written permission of Cambridge University Press.

First published 2020

A catalogue record for this publication is available from the British Library.

Library of Congress Cataloging-in-Publication Data
NAMES: O'Callaghan, Michelle, author.
TITLE: Crafting poetry anthologies in Renaissance England : early modern cultures of recreation / Michelle O'Callaghan.
DESCRIPTION: New York : Cambridge University Press, 2020. | Includes bibliographical references and index.
IDENTIFIERS: LCCN 2020020903 (print) | LCCN 2020020904 (ebook) | ISBN 9781108491099 (hardback) | ISBN 9781108792202 (paperback) | ISBN 9781108867412 (epub)
SUBJECTS: LCSH: Literature publishing–Great Britain–History–16th century. | Anthologies–Publishing–Great Britain–History–16th century. | English poetry–Early modern, 1500–1700–History and criticism. | Books and reading–Great Britain–History–16th century.
CLASSIFICATION: LCC Z326 .O33 2020 (print) | LCC Z326 (ebook) | DDC 070.5/79094109031–dc23
LC record available at https://lccn.loc.gov/2020020903
LC ebook record available at https://lccn.loc.gov/2020020904

ISBN 978-1-108-49109-9 Hardback

Cambridge University Press has no responsibility for the persistence or accuracy of URLs for external or third-party internet websites referred to in this publication and does not guarantee that any content on such websites is, or will remain, accurate or appropriate.

Contents

List of Illustrations	*page* vi
Acknowledgements	vii
Note on the Text	ix
Introduction	1
1 Books in Process: *Songes and Sonettes* and *Paradyse of Daynty Devises*	20
2 Household Books: Richard Jones, Isabella Whitney, and Anthology-Making	73
3 'To the Gentleman Reader': Re-creating Sidney in the 1590s	114
4 '*Impos'd designe*': *Englands Helicon* and Re-creative Craft	150
5 *A Poetical Rapsody*: Francis Davison, the 'Printer', and the Craft of Compilation	193
Conclusion	228
Bibliography	231
Index	244

v

Illustrations

1 *A Gorgious Gallery, of Gallant Inventions,* title-page,
   British Library, shelfmark c57 d49.   *page* x
2 British Library, Add. MS 4900.   71
3 *The Phoenix Nest* (1593), pages 90–1. British Library,
   shelfmark Huth 42.   164
4 *Englands Helicon* (1600), sig. L3v–L4r. British Library,
   shelfmark c39 e48.   164
5 *Englands Helicon* (1600), sig. Y3r. British Library,
   shelfmark c39 e48.   185
6 *Englands Helicon* (1600), sig. Y3v. British Library,
   shelfmark c39 e48.   186
7 British Library, MS Harley 280, fol. 104r.   198
8 British Library, MS Harley 280, fol. 105v.   202

Acknowledgements

Like the anthologies that are its subject, this book would not have been possible without the work of many hands, eyes, and ears and has been long in the making. Much of the research undertaken for this study was funded initially by a British Academy Small Grant for a pilot project that would eventually result in *Verse Miscellanies Online*, co-edited with Alice Eardley and funded through a British Academy Research Development Award. This digital project benefited from the assistance of Jonathan Gibson, James Cummings, Pip Willcox, and Miguel Vieira. Additional research on anthologies and further development of the digital edition was supported by a Leverhulme Research Project Award for a project led by Abigail Williams to augment *Digital Miscellanies Index*. Research for Chapters 1 and 2 benefited from my involvement in projects on women and the poetry of complaint funded by the Australian Research Council and the Marsden Fund, Royal Society of New Zealand, led by Rosalind Smith and Sarah Ross, respectively. Sections of an earlier draft of Chapter 2 appeared in '"My Printer must, haue somewhat to his share": Isabella Whitney, Richard Jones, and Crafting Books', *Women's Writing*, 26 (2019), 15–34, in a special issue on 'Early Modern Women Writers and the Question of Transmission', edited by Paul Salzman.

Many have read drafts, discussed ideas, proffered advice, or provided information at various stages: Katherine Acheson, Rebecca Bullard, Alice Eardley, Joshua Eckhardt, Andrew Gordon, Phillipa Hardman, Elizabeth Heale, Chloë Houston, Jenni Hyde, Una Mcilvenna, Steven Matthews, Mary Morrissey, Patricia Pender, Jennifer Richards, Sarah Ross, Paul Salzman, Lisa Sampson, Rosalind Smith, Adam Smyth, Peter Stoneley, Mathew Thomson, Nicola Wilson, and Sue Wiseman. Thanks should also go to the two anonymous readers for Cambridge University Press. Librarians at the Bodleian, British Library, and the Folger Shakespeare Library also have been very helpful.

viii *Acknowledgements*

The preliminaries before books tell many stories. The acknowledgements I have written over the years have told of the birth of children, their play, and family commitments. As always, Mathew has given excellent advice when it really mattered. Grace and Joseph are now at university – Grace proofread drafts and discussed Chartier, and Joseph asked sharp questions about what was different from my earlier books. Final drafts were written in their empty rooms as I followed the sun around the house. During the writing of this book, my parents died within six weeks of each other – this book is dedicated to their memory.

Note on the text

All conflations of u/v and i/j have been modernised and signatures given in Arabic numerals throughout to avoid confusion with the verso. Titles of anthologies retain the spelling of the first edition except when a subsequent edition is referred to explicitly.

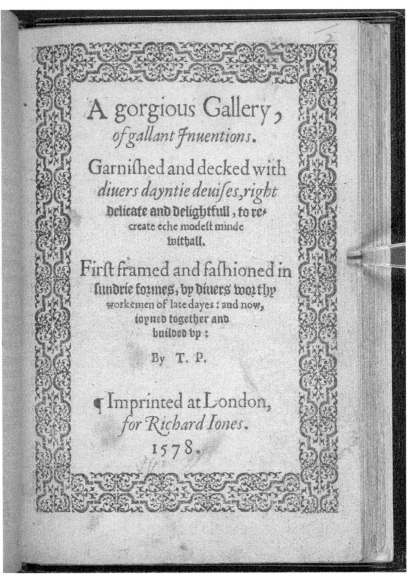

Figure 1 *A Gorgious Gallery, of Gallant Inventions*, title-page, British Library, shelfmark c57 d49.

Introduction

The title-page framing *A Gorgious Gallery, of Gallant Inventions* sets in play an architectural metaphor of the book that imagines this poetry anthology as a type of building (Figure 1). It is an apt place to begin, since the title-page's self-reflexive exposition of the spatiality of the book brings into focus the materiality of literary culture, a field of enquiry that has preoccupied early modern scholarship over past decades and informs this study.[1] If we cast our eyes down the title-page, attention shifts from metaphors describing the book-as-artefact to those accounting for the processes of making. 'First framed and fashioned in sundrie formes' by skilled artisans, 'divers worthy workemen' over time, this *Gorgious Gallery* has now been 'joyned together and builded up' in the anthology offered to its readers. On display is a language of poetic craft that is thoroughly grounded in the artisanal worlds of the sixteenth century. It is this understanding of craft that directs my account of the poetry anthologies that were made – and remade – in the second half of the sixteenth century in England, a period when the book trade was framing and fashioning an array of textual material in response to diverse and expanding markets for vernacular literature. The word 'craft' in the medieval and early modern period was semantically rich, bringing together imaginative, material, and technical processes with crafted objects, human agents, and the trades.[2] All books are

---

[1] See, for example, James Daybell and Peter Hinds, eds., *Material Readings of Early Modern Culture: Texts and Social Practices, 1580–1730* (Basingstoke: Palgrave Macmillan, 2010); Patricia Pender and Rosalind Smith, eds., *Material Cultures of Early Modern Women's Writing* (Basingstoke: Palgrave Macmillan, 2014); Elizabeth Scott Baumann and Ben Burton, eds., *The Work of Form: Poetics and Materiality in Early Modern Culture* (Oxford University Press, 2014); Kate Orden, *Materialities: Books, Readers, and the Chanson in Sixteenth-Century Europe* (Oxford University Press, 2015); Tara Hamling and Catherine Richardson, *A Day at Home in Early Modern England: Material Culture and Domestic Life, 1500–1700* (New Haven: Yale University Press, 2017); Adam Smyth, *Material Texts in Early Modern England* (Cambridge University Press, 2018).
[2] According to the *Oxford English Dictionary* (hereafter *OED*), the field of meaning of 'craft' narrows after the sixteenth century, when usages such as II 2 c, 'Human skill, *art* as opposed to *nature*' and 3c

I

Introduction

crafted, and yet, because poetry anthologies are, by definition, compiled, they necessarily foreground the processes through which they are 'joyned together and builded up'. Craft is integral to understanding the work of form in printed anthologies. It explains how the gathering, selecting, and conjoining of lyric material was an embodied practice that required manual work, technical skill, and literary judgement. Methods for compiling textual material were, of course, skills taught in Renaissance schoolrooms and underpinned humanist culture, from the assembly of commonplace books to practices of imitation.[3] Printed poetry anthologies provide an opportunity to understand how humanist methods for compiling books were adopted and adapted within the milieu of the printing house.

The role of poetry anthologies in shaping vernacular lyric cultures has long been understood and studies before mine have turned to the cultural work of the book trade to elucidate this process.[4] That said, critical attention has largely been confined to *Songes and Sonettes* and its publisher, Richard Tottel.[5] The activity of others involved in anthology production, and indeed other poetry anthologies first printed in the sixteenth century, remains very shadowy and our view of the field necessarily attenuated. This study turns to those booksellers, printers, and their associates engaged in anthology production in the second half of the sixteenth century in order to understand how the form of the anthology was shaped within the 'productive matrix of the printing house', to borrow Helen Smith and

---

(in the concrete sense), 'A work or product of art', fall away. On craft in medieval literature and Renaissance poetics, see Lisa H. Cooper, *Artisans and Narrative Craft in Late Medieval England* (Cambridge University Press, 2011); Rayna Kalas, *Frame, Glass, Verse: the Technology of Poetic Invention in the English Renaissance* (Ithaca: Cornell University Press, 2007); Pamela H. Smith, 'In the Workshop of History: Making, Writing, and Meaning', *West 86th*, 19 (2012), 4–31.

[3] M. B. Parkes, *Scribes, Scripts and Readers: Studies in the Communication, Presentation and Dissemination of Medieval Texts* (London: Hambledon Press, 1991), chapter 3; Jeffrey Todd Knight, *Bound to Read: Compilations, Collections, and the Making of Renaissance Literature* (Philadelphia: University of Pennsylvania Press, 2013), 5–9; Angus Vine, *Miscellaneous Order: Manuscript Culture and the Early Modern Organization of Knowledge* (Oxford University Press, 2019), Introduction.

[4] Elizabeth W. Pomeroy, *The Elizabethan Miscellanies: Their Development and Conventions*, University of California English Studies 36 (Berkeley: University of California Press, 1973); Wendy Wall, *The Imprint of Gender: Authorship and Publication in the English Renaissance* (Ithaca: Cornell University Press, 1993); Arthur Marotti, *Manuscript, Print, and the English Renaissance Lyric* (Ithaca: Cornell University Press, 1995).

[5] Recent book-length studies and essay collections addressing *Songes and Sonettes* include J. Christopher Warner, *The Making and Marketing of Tottel's Miscellany, 1557: Songs and Sonnets in the Summer of the Martyrs' Fires* (Farnham: Ashgate, 2013); Stephen Hamrick, ed., *Tottel's Songes and Sonettes in Context* (Farnham: Ashgate, 2013).

Introduction 3

Louise Wilson's phrase.[6] Where this study also differs from previous scholarship is in its argument that the poetry anthology is defined by its recreative properties. When publishers framed anthologies they invariably drew on the Horatian commonplace that valued poetry, a form of eloquence, for its capacity to give 'profit and pleasure', to quote Tottel's preface before *Songes and Sonettes*.[7] In doing so, particular weight was given to poetry's delightful qualities within this equation, that which is pleasant to the mind and senses. The title-page to *Gorgious Gallery*, echoing that of *Paradyse of Daynty Devises*, advertised that it was 'decked with divers dayntie devises, right delicate and delightfull, to recreate eche modest minde'. Recreate meant to refresh and reinvigorate the mind through the senses by engaging in pleasurable pastimes. The recreational properties of literature have received comparatively little attention in early modern studies.[8] Yet, this was the century when leisure increasingly gained cultural credibility and discourses of recreation and treatises on various pastimes proliferated. Publishers of anthologies, along with others in the trade, were engaged in producing a body of vernacular poetry for use within wide-ranging domestic cultures of recreation. We should remember that pastimes were not restricted to the elite; those in work enjoyed 'small but regular doses of daily or weekly leisure' when, for example, ballads might be performed.[9] Anthologies collected poems that moved between elite and non-elite cultures challenging any straightforward identification of poetry-as-pastime with courtliness.[10] The galleries and other spaces framing anthologies may be places for courtly pastimes, but the variety of verse these books gathered included ballads alongside the songs and sonnets.

---

[6] Helen Smith and Louise Wilson, 'Introduction', in *Renaissance Paratexts* (Cambridge University Press, 2011), 9.

[7] *Songes and sonettes, written by the right honorable Lorde Henry Haward late Earle of Surrey, and other* (Q1, 1557), fol. 1b.

[8] *OED*, 4b. On poetry as recreation, see Katharine Craik, *Reading Sensations in Early Modern England* (Basingstoke: Palgrave Macmillan, 2007), especially chapters 1 and 2; Lori Humphrey Newcomb, *Reading Popular Romance in Early Modern England* (New York: Columbia University Press, 2002); Robert Matz, *Defending Literature in Early Modern England: Renaissance Literary Theory in Social Context* (Cambridge University Press, 2000).

[9] Peter Burke, 'The Invention of Leisure in Early Modern Europe', *Past and Present*, 146 (1995), 136–50; see also Alessandro Arcangeli, *Recreation in the Renaissance: Attitudes towards Leisure and Pastimes in European Culture, c. 1425–1675* (Basingstoke: Palgrave Macmillan, 2003).

[10] See, for example, Matz's identification of poetic recreations with aristocratic cultures of leisure, *Defending Literature*, 13.

4 Introduction

Attending to the recreational properties of poetry anthologies has consequences for how we understand the material cultures of books, as well as other print formats, like the ballad. If we return to the metaphor of the gallery, which in this period described a covered structure for leisurely walking, then it opens out the anthology as a tangible and sensory space that gives scope for recreating one's mind and body.[11] This recreative metaphor of the book-as-gallery points to a model of materiality that extends from books-as-artefacts to their 'embodiedness' – their 'communicative, performative, emotive, and expressive capacities'.[12] To understand these capacities I draw on the concept of affordance, as set out by Caroline Levine, to describe the 'potential uses or action latent' in forms, including 'materials and design', and how they can be carried 'across time and place', accruing changing 'meanings and values'.[13] Recreative affordances locate anthologies in early modern performance cultures which gave scope for experiencing poetry at leisure – read, silently and in company, sometimes set to music, and recrafted into other forms. Poetry anthologies and the poems they collect have often been implicitly or explicitly identified with the male domains of the Inns of Court, universities, and other homosocial milieux, and the emphasis placed on how they fashioned gentleman authors and readers.[14] Once we bring recreation into play, then what becomes visible – and audible – are the ways in which these anthologies were also located in the company of women, and so take us to the mixed gendered household. The early modern household encompassed diverse socio-economic and cultural functions, from education to recreation, and was differently articulated across the social spectrum. The boundaries of the household were highly porous, continually opening out on to other arenas, from the shop to the court.[15] Because it was so 'shifting, and malleable', the household was 'more open to being differently inhabited or used'.[16] In this study, I turn to the household as a site

[11] *OED*, I, 'A covered space for walking in, partly open at the side, or having the roof supported by pillars.'

[12] On the 'embodiedness' of objects as 'active agents', see Leora Auslander, 'Beyond Words', *American Historical Review*, 110 (2004), 1017.

[13] Caroline Levine, *Forms: Whole, Rhythm, Hierarchy, Network* (Princeton University Press, 2015).

[14] See, for example, Elizabeth Heale, 'Misogyny and the Complete Gentleman in Early Printed Poetry Miscellanies', *Yearbook of English Studies*, 33, (2003), 233–47; Jessica Winston, *Lawyers at Play: Literature, Law and Politics at the Early Modern Inns of Court, 1558–1581* (Oxford University Press, 2016).

[15] Hamling and Richardson, *A Day at Home*, chapter 5.

[16] Patricia Fumerton, *Unsettled: the Culture of Mobility and the Working Poor in Early Modern England* (University of Chicago Press, 2006), 54. See also Wendy Wall, 'Introduction: In the Nation's Kitchen', in Wall, *Staging Domesticity: Household Work and English Identity in Early Modern Drama*

The Work of Form

where the recreative affordances of poetry anthologies were practised and accrued meaning and as a *topos* that can help us to comprehend the malleability of Renaissance anthologies.

By bringing household recreations into focus as one of the lenses through which the craft of poetry anthologies can be understood, my aim is to tell alternative histories of vernacular poetry in early modern England. The cultural role of the Tudor poetry anthologies has frequently been understood in terms of popularising the 'courtly makers', from Sir Thomas Wyatt and Henry Howard, Earl of Surrey, to Sir Philip Sidney. The history of a vernacular lyric tradition becomes one which has its origins in an aristocratic scribal culture that then undergoes a process of dissemination to wider reading publics through printed anthologies, establishing a canon of English poetry that extends from Wyatt and Surrey through to Sir Philip Sidney, Edmund Spenser, and William Shakespeare. Anthologies made up of ballads and other more lowly verse forms, such as *A Handefull of Pleasant Delites* and *A Gorgious Gallery, of Gallant Inventions*, are often written out of or marginalised within this cultural narrative.[17] By including those 'minor' anthologies and 'lesser' verse forms, like the ballad, alongside major works and canonical writers, it becomes possible to tell other histories of the domestication of literary culture in the English Renaissance that are more open to a wider social and cultural range of participants and practices. Rather than employing a top-down model of literary influence, this study explores the productive and dynamic exchanges between non-elite and elite cultures. Even if we take *Songes and Sonettes* as a starting point, the dialogue in its pages between courtly makers and ballad makers discloses an ongoing creative exchange between elite and non-elite poetic forms resulting in a 'Renaissance' that is heteroglot and as much part of the printing house and household as it is of the humanist study and court.

The Work of Form

The poetry anthology as a class of books was still being worked out in the early modern period, a process that continued well into the eighteenth

---

(Cambridge University Press, 2002) and 'Introduction: the Order of Serving', *Recipes for Thought: Knowledge and Taste in the Early Modern Kitchen* (Philadelphia: University of Pennsylvania Press, 2016).

[17] For example, Steven W. May, 'Popularizing Courtly Poetry: Tottel's Miscellany and its Progeny', in *The Oxford Handbook of Tudor Literature, 1485–1603*, edited by Mike Pincombe and Cathy Shrank (Oxford University Press, 2009), 418–31; Matthew Zarnowiecki, *Fair Copies: Reproducing the English Lyric from Tottel to Shakespeare* (University of Toronto Press, 2014).

6   Introduction

century and beyond.[18] *Crafting Poetry Anthologies* concentrates on those books first published in the second half of the sixteenth century because this is the period when vernacular poetry anthologies emerged as a recognised and recognisable type of printed book. I would argue that the poetry anthology had a distinct form. In the only detailed survey of the early anthologies, *Elizabethan Miscellanies, their Development and Conventions*, Elizabeth Pomeroy concludes that, because of their diverse 'length, purpose, composition, structure, and audience', the Tudor anthologies cannot be said either to establish or to utilise a clearly defined set of conventions.[19] It is the case that anthologies do not constitute a discrete print genre, and instead share features with other types of books, most notably, in this period, commonplace and music books.[20] Even so, I would argue that they were a recognisable type of early modern book. Part of the conceptual difficulty may result from assuming anthologies must conform to abstract and totalising models of formal coherence in order to be understood as a distinct type of book. Instead, we need to understand form as practised and to turn our attention to technologies for making books.

Poetry anthologies emerge out of medieval practices of *compilatio* used to organise textual matter into books. The aim was to make knowledge more accessible by imposing a scheme or structure that would enable the incorporation and organisation of selected exemplars. In the words of M. B. Parkes, 'To think became a craft.'[21] There were many models and techniques available in the Renaissance for organising textual matter shared across manuscript and print. Commonplace books, which arrange selected material under topics or heads, are one of the most recognisable products of compilation practices.[22] The affordances of poetry anthologies are shared with commonplace books – poetic matter is framed and designed for use and reuse, to be carried away and put to other purposes. Yet, while poetry anthologies borrowed and adapted organisational methods from commonplace books, they are less systematic and more varied in their modes of arrangement and material forms. One of their key marketing points is typically the variety of poems and authors anthologies collect for

---

[18] See Anne Ferry, *Tradition and the Individual Poem: an Inquiry into Anthologies* (Stanford University Press, 2001); Joshua Eckhardt and Daniel Starza Smith, 'Introduction', in *Manuscript Miscellanies in Early Modern England*, edited by Eckhardt and Smith (Farnham: Ashgate, 2014), 1–16.
[19] Pomeroy, *Elizabethan Miscellanies*, 116–21.
[20] On this feature of miscellanies, see Adam Smyth, *'Profit & Delight': Printed Miscellanies in England, 1640–1682* (Detroit: Wayne State University Press, 2004), 2.
[21] Parkes, *Scribes*, 37.
[22] Mary Thomas Crane, *Framing Authority: Sayings, Self, and Society in Sixteenth-Century England* (Princeton University Press, 1993), chapter 1; Vine, *Miscellaneous Order*, chapter 1.

The Work of Form

the delight of readers. The language used alludes to the value and pleasures attributed to *copia* as a generative and transformative principle of nature, God's handiwork, and expressed in the *florilegium* motif of the healthful properties of the recreative garden. This is not to imply that anthologies were idiosyncratic, unsystematic collections. Instead these are deliberately composite volumes whose 'miscellaneous order', to use Angus Vine's phrase, results from the sundry organisational schemes employed to allow for the expression of variety and to give scope for recreation.

One place where the idea of the anthology as a type of book slowly begins to take shape is in the paratext. Prefaces, titles, and other apparatus bring into focus the work of publishers and the printing house in moulding the meaning of books and guiding readers in how they could be comprehended and used.[23] An obvious mechanism through which booksellers described the type of book on offer was the title-page. Buyers typically first encountered this page independently from the rest of the book as a sheet fixed to a post or pasted to a wall where the bookseller advertised the products on offer. The title-page offered an opportunity to classify the book, its form and contents, and other significant features.[24] Once bound with the other pages, it helped to guide readers in their 'approach not only to the text in question but to the experience of reading, and of interpreting the world beyond the book'.[25] What do the titles of the early poetry anthologies say about the way publishers, readers, and the wider culture were beginning to understand these types of books? It is the case that not all the titles given to poetry anthologies use the same conventions. Nonetheless, these books so often are framed in similar ways that what emerges are shared, if not monolithic, organisational concepts. Whereas Tottel settled on a title that concentrated on poetic forms and authors, both known and unknown – *Songes and Sonettes of Henry Haward, Earl of Surrey, and other* – the majority of other publishers of sixteenth-century poetry anthologies opted for titles that figure the embodied spatiality of the book as a gathered, composite object or meeting-place. Architectural and garden metaphors bring into play *florilegia* or *anthologia* traditions, in which the compilation is depicted as a gathering of choice flowers or other delightful matter: *The Court of Venus, A Handefull of*

---

[23] On the cultural role of publishers in shaping the meaning of books, see Zachary Lesser, *Renaissance Drama and the Politics of Publication* (Cambridge University Press, 2004); Kirk Melnikoff, *Elizabethan Publishing and the Makings of Literary Culture* (University of Toronto Press, 2018).

[24] Michael Saenger, *The Commodification of Textual Engagements in the English Renaissance* (Aldershot: Ashgate, 2006), 38.

[25] Smith and Wilson, 'Introduction', 6–7.

8   Introduction

Pleasant Delites, Paradyse of Daynty Devises, A Gorgious Gallery, of Gallant Inventions, Brittons Bowre of Delights, The Phoenix Nest, The Arbor of Amorous Devices, and *Englands Helicon.*[26] Courts, paradises, galleries, bowers, arbours, helicons, and even the phoenix's nest direct attention to the recreative space of the book in simultaneously conceptual and material terms. The physical structures of the book have been organised in such a way as to give readers mental scope and to guide their passage through the variety of poetic matter offered in the volume.[27] *A Poetical Rapsody* (1602) similarly announces its status as a compiled book since 'rhapsody' describes a 'sowing together or conjoining of those Poems and verses..., which before were loose and scattered'.[28] The poetic matter these books conjoin is cast in the form of devices, inventions, or delights, terms that describe the *techne* of crafted form, both material and imaginative, as a process, a method of devising or framing, which specifically affords reading experiences that are defined in terms of pleasure and use.

As the title of this book indicates, I opt for the term anthology rather than miscellany to describe the books under discussion. It should be said from the outset that neither miscellany nor anthology was a term used in the sixteenth and early seventeenth century to describe these books.[29] Even so, although there may not have been one word, but many to describe these books in this period, this does not necessarily mean that compilers and publishers were not aware of the kind of books they were making.[30] While arguably miscellany and anthology are interchangeable terms, my use of the latter term is intended to keep in mind the reliance of these books on methods of compilation. Titles that employ *anthologia* motifs, since they belong to this broader category of *compilatio*, of course, are not particular to poetry anthologies. Instead, this vocabulary announces that the book has been compiled by editorial agents out of other textual matter.

---

[26] On this phenomenon, see Randall Anderson, 'Metaphors of the Book as Garden in the English Renaissance', *Yearbook of English Studies*, 33 (2003), 248–61.

[27] Ferry, *Tradition*, 24. On spatial metaphors of commonplace culture, see Vine, *Miscellaneous Order*, 45.

[28] Philemon Holland, *The Philosopie, commonlie called the Morals written by the learned philosopher Plutarch* (1603), sig. zzzzz6v. See also Piers Brown, 'Donne, Rhapsody and Textual Order', in *Manuscript Miscellanies*, ed. Eckhardt and Smith, 39–55.

[29] On the history of the term 'miscellany', see Eckhardt and Smith, 'Introduction', 1–10; Barbara Benedict, *Making the Modern Reader: Cultural Mediation in Early Modern Literary Anthologies* (Princeton University Press, 1996), 4.

[30] While I broadly concur with Zarnowiecki's point that 'there was no one activity that all these printers and poets were pursuing', I would argue that it is not only authors, but also publishers who 'recognize this condition of reproducibility – multiplicity – and begin to exploit its potential', *Fair Copies*, 24, 46.

The Work of Form

The printed compilations put out in 1600 all have very similar titles – *Bel-vedére or the Garden of the Muses, Englands Helicon, Englands Parnassus* – yet two are commonplace books, compiled of textual extracts organised into sections by topic, whereas *Englands Helicon* is a collection of pastoral poems that is not divided into sections. All are compilations; however, the textual matter these books collect and the way this material is framed, although closely related, can be distinguished. Collections of devotional texts, in particular, also frequently used *florilegia* metaphors of the book as garden or as a nosegay: Thomas Becon's *A pleasaunt newe nosegaye full of many godly and swete floures, lately gathered by Theodore Basille* (1542), Josias Nichols's *A spirituall poseaye contayning most godly and fruictfull consolations and prayers to be used of all men in the time of sickenesse and mortalitie as at all times else, Gathered out of the sacred Scriptures* (1573), and Nicholas Breton's *A smale handfull of fragrant flowers selected and gathered out of the lovely garden of sacred scriptures, fit for any honorable or woorshipfull gentlewoman to smell unto* (1575). Publishers used titles to position their books in relation to other products within their own stock and a wider market. Shared motifs advertised shared properties with other types of books, not only commonplace books but also printed songbooks and devotional works. The title given to *Paradyse of Daynty Devises*, for example, given the biblical associations of this garden, knowingly advertises its affiliations with the type of scriptural gathering that flourished in this period.

Poetry anthologies resembled other types of books because they are related within the broader category of *compilatio* and because publishers chose to highlight these shared uses for their customers through the paratext. The malleability attributed to printed anthologies is often identified as a property carried over from scribal cultures in which poems were 'inherently malleable' and made and remade within the pages of manuscript miscellanies.[31] We do need to be aware, however, that malleability is not 'an *inherent* quality, but ... a *transitive* one', as Adrian Johns has said of the fixity attributed to print, one that is realised as it practised and 'acted upon by people'.[32] Malleability is therefore dependent on compilation practices shared between manuscript and print, in other words, how anthologies were made and used. Publishers, and others involved in their

---

[31] See, for example, Marotti, *Manuscript, Print*, 135.
[32] Adrian Johns, *Nature of the Book: Print and Knowledge in the Making* (Chicago University Press, 1998), 19. Wall moves between an inherent and practised concept of malleability in *Imprint of Gender*, 106–7.

10 Introduction

production, crafted flexibility into these books by introducing apparatus, such as titles, divisions, and even tables of content, to open these books out for use, including future uses that they may not have envisioned.[33] When making anthologies, publishers and printers, like other craftspeople, had 'repertoires of forms' in their heads and to hand from their experience of making other types of books and printed textual matter, such as ballads.[34] Such tacit knowledge meant that it was possible to improvise, to carry over techniques, apparatus, and other elements from other books resulting in hybrid forms. The hybrid malleability of the printed anthology is therefore, in part, a function of the craft of the printing house. The poetry anthology is best understood as a book in process, a dynamic crafted structure constituted by the activity of selecting, gathering, and organising verse for the purposes of transmission.

The Craft of Anthologies

The preliminaries at the front of the book are places where publishers and other compilers reflect on the idea of the anthology and its uses. Prefaces do not, of course, tell the whole story of production nor do they act as windows on to the work of compilation and the printing house in any straightforward sense. Instead, prefaces are rhetorical and performative spaces, putting into play multi-layered fictions of agency, production, transmission, and use. Prefaces before anthologies do not always tell the same story. Nonetheless discourses and tropes recur, such as the language of common profit, which sets out an ethos of publication, or the figure of the absent author or gentleman compiler, whose absence helpfully provides the occasion for the publisher to elaborate his own part in the book's production. The visibility of publishers in prefaces and the way they conceptualise their activity and the idea of the book demonstrates how the crafting of anthologies involved the creative, as well as manual, labour of its non-authorial agents. Anthologies are a special case in this respect because they so clearly disrupt the conventional subordination of the manual work of production to the intellectual work of composing.[35] Put together by compilers rather than authors, poetry anthologies productively

[33] Alexandra Gillespie, 'Poets, Printers, and Early English *Sammelbände*', *Huntingdon Library Quarterly*, 67 (2004), 210.
[34] Smith, 'In the Workshop', 13.
[35] On common profit, the hierarchy between production and composition, and 'book-making as a generative, creative act', see Kathleen Tonry, *Agency and Intention in English Print, 1476–1526* (Turnhout: Brepols, 2016), 3–12.

The Craft of Anthologies

blur the distinction between authorial and non-authorial agents. Moreover, by tracing the movement of poems in and out of these anthologies, both through manuscript and print channels, we can see how the bookshop and printing house were foundational cultural sites in the history of literary production and transmission. Publishers' stock, for example, could act as a type of library, providing a storehouse of texts on which to draw when compiling anthologies. Revised editions similarly alert us to the work of publishing, disclosing points of difference which require interpretation and bring different constellations of texts and actors into play. Anthologies, because they are compiled, reveal complex histories of textual transmission that bring the cultural domain of the bookshop and printing house into conversation with other sites for textual production and transmission – the court, universities, Inns of Court, and households in all their variety.

Poetry anthologies make visible the craft of editing – the processes of gathering and selecting verse from a variety of sources, planning the structure of a collection, and authoring elements of the paratext, from prefaces to tables of content. For Mary Thomas Crane, editing defines this class of books:

> Miscellanies . . . are collections of poems gathered by an editor who is not (necessarily) himself an author and who has great power over the texts that he gathers . . . Indeed, the string of popular miscellanies published in the middle of the [sixteenth] century seems to have gone some way toward establishing editorship – the judicious selection and rearrangement of poems – as equal, if not in some ways superior, to original authorship.[36]

While the practice of editing is visible in anthologies, it is less clear that there was a recognisable editor, in the modern sense of the word, who exercised authority over the collection in the way Crane describes. This proprietorial editor is said to emerge only in the eighteenth century: the first usage of the word in a recognisably modern sense is dated by the *OED* to 1712.[37] The poetry anthologies that are my subject often attribute responsibility to an individual compiler. *Paradyse of Daynty Devises* cites Richard Edwards, *Handefull of Pleasant Delites* names a Clement

---

[36] Crane, *Framing Authority*, 169.
[37] *OED*, 'editor, n.', 2: 'One who prepares the literary work of another person, or number of persons for publication, by selecting, revising, and arranging the material; also, one who prepares an edition of any literary work.' The example given is from Joseph Addison, Spectator, no. 470: 'When a different Reading gives us . . . a new Elegance in an Author, the Editor does very well in taking Notice of it.' John Jowett, 'Henry Chettle: "Your old Compositor"', *Text*, 15 (2003), 142; see also Sonya Massai, *Shakespeare and the Rise of the Editor* (Cambridge University Press, 2007), 1–2, 191–5.

12   Introduction

Robinson, *Gorgious Gallery*, a T. P., the initials of Thomas Proctor who authors sections of verse within the anthology, while *The Phoenix Nest* is assembled by R. S., and *A Poetical Rapsody* is claimed by Francis Davison in his preface. Yet, curiously, in each case, the agency attributed to these individuals is radically disrupted. Edwards dies ten years before *Paradyse* is printed and so is absent from the scene of publication; the identity of Robinson and R. S. is elusive and both make no further appearance in either *Handefull* or *The Phoenix Nest* beyond the title-page; the title-page to *Gorgious Gallery* acknowledges 'divers worthy workeman' alongside T. P., and moreover the entry in the Stationers' Register records 'R. Williams' as the compiler of an earlier iteration; and finally, Davison disavows responsibility for aspects of editing *A Poetical Rapsodie* and draws the figure of the 'Printer' into the frame.[38] The place we might want to allot to the proprietorial editor is therefore not fully available, but in a state of creative and productive flux.

If, in the sixteenth and seventeenth centuries, the editor as a proper name denoting the profession of an individual had not yet come into use, nonetheless editing can still be understood as a function of book production. The term 'publisher' was also not used in this period, and yet booksellers and printers did organise and finance the printing and distribution of books. As John Jowett points out, 'the absence of an appropriate vocabulary in the period reflects, not the absence of the equivalent activity, but the innovative fluidity of a state of emergence'.[39] Editing, like so many other aspects of book production, was not yet systematised as a set of practices and so makeshift, still in the process of being worked out. Here, the concept of craft is key because it signifies a mode of knowledge that is practised, tacit, improvised, and embodied, and so acquired through pragmatic modes of imitation. This does not mean that the methods employed were not 'carefully thought-out', rather that they were not codified and written down.[40] Methods for compiling commonplace books were taught in the humanist schoolroom, yet in practice compilers improvised.[41] In Nicholas Ling's prefaces before *Englands Helicon* and

---

[38] Edward Arber, ed., *Transcript of the Registers of the Company of Stationers, 1554–1640*, 5 vols. (London, 1875–7), II, 313.

[39] Jowett, 'Henry Chettle', 144; see also Massai, *Shakespeare*, 1–2. On the 'publisher', see the arguments put forward for the use of this term by Lesser, *Renaissance Drama* and Melnikoff, *Elizabethan Publishing*.

[40] Pamela H. Smith, *The Body of the Artisan: Art and Experience in the Scientific Revolution* (Chicago University Press, 2006), 7–8.

[41] Vine, *Miscellaneous Order*, 19–24.

The Craft of Anthologies 13

Politeuphuia, discussed in Chapter 4, methods of commonplacing meet the craft of the book trade. Instead of viewing editing as an individual occupation, we can see it as a collaborative process, a set of practices undertaken by various individuals across the different stages of book production. Writing of the textual editing of play-texts, Sonya Massai concludes that it was 'function- rather than agent-specific: several agents, in other words, including correcting authors and annotating readers, perfected the text as it was repeatedly committed to print'.[42] Poetry anthologies required different editorial methods to play-texts, given they are different types of books, and energies were concentrated on compilation – the selection, organisation, and framing of poems. Each anthology has its own complex history of compilation. Before reaching the press, an anthology may have gone through many different stages of compiling, each involving changing constellations of producers, some more active than others. Gathering and selecting verse, designing the book's structure, and preparing copy for the press, therefore, was work undertaken over an often lengthy period by an array of agents and within a range of locales, from scribal communities and performance cultures to the milieu of the printing house.[43]

Since they are the work of compilers, anthologies are therefore, in some sense, authorless. Yet, the situation of the author within their pages is more complicated than this suggests. Because these books collect the poems of so many authors, some living, some dead, they invite us to consider the place we might want to allot to the author as productively unfixed and in a state of play.[44] Anthologies are spaces in which the rich array of author functions that characterise early modern authorship are performed. Diverse print conventions are employed, from naming and initials to pseudonyms and anonymity, taking advantage of the early modern flexibility of designations of authorship.[45] Anthologies are gathered under authors' names, sometimes in their presence, other times in their absence. In the 1590s, publishers put out collections in the author's absence – Jones's *Brittons Bowre* and *Arbor of Amorous Devices* were gathered under the name of Nicholas Breton, and William Jaggard's *Passionate Pilgrim*, under Shakespeare, even though these are collections made up of the work of

---

[42] Massai, *Shakespeare*, 200.
[43] See Matt Cohen's account of publication as 'choral', in *The Networked Wilderness: Communicating in Early New England* (Minneapolis: University of Minnesota Press, 2010), 15.
[44] Wall, *Imprint of Gender*, 97–98.
[45] Marcy North, *The Anonymous Renaissance: Cultures of Discretion in Tudor–Stuart England* (University of Chicago Press, 2003), 71–85.

Introduction

other poets. Here, the author is a designation, a deliberately composite figure that advertises the re-creative affordances of the anthology. In other cases, authors advertise their presence at the scene of production, using the space of the anthology to reflect on the craft of poetic making through the practice of compilation – the tasks of gathering, framing, and organising textual matter into a collection.[46] Authors, acting as compilers, frequently employed *florilegium* terminology to figure their activities as compilers of their own and others' poetic labours. Hence, George Gascoigne styled his anthology as *A hundreth sundrie flowres bounde up in one Small poesie Gathered partely (by translation) in the fyne outlandish gardins of Euripides, Ovid, Petrarke, Ariosto, and others: and partly by invention, out of our owne fruitefull orchardes in Englande* (1573). Although the title-page is now lost, Isabella Whitney's anthology similarly employed *florilegia* tropes in the description of *A Sweet Nosgay, or pleasant Posye: contayning a hundred and ten Phylosophicall Flowers &c* (B2), which, as Andrew Gordon points out, 'suggests a playful game of literary one-upmanship with the title of Gascoigne's newly-published work'.[47] Whitney presents herself as working alongside her printer, Richard Jones, and her very distinctive response to other *florilegia* books illustrates the point where methods for compiling commonplace books and artisanal models of craft come into productive and creative contact.

Recreation: Poetry as Pastime

The term 'recreation' was used in two senses during this period. One, as we have seen, defined the activity of refreshing one's mind and body through pleasurable pastimes; the other, the action of making again.[48] Poems were re-created not only textually, but also through performance. Recognising the multimodal re-creative properties of poetry transforms our understanding of the cultural work of anthologies. The production and transmission of the poems collected in anthologies was enacted through and across a variety of media, both textual and extra-textual – manuscript, print, and performance cultures that included music, dance, and plays. The multimedia properties of anthologies return us to the embodiedness of

---

[46] On other single-author anthologies, see Megan Heffernan, 'Gathered by Invention: Additive Forms and Inference in Gascoigne's Poesy', *Modern Language Quarterly*, 76 (2015), 413–45; Knight, *Bound to Read*, chapter 3.

[47] Andrew Gordon, *Writing Early Modern London: Memory, Text and Community* (Basingstoke: Palgrave Macmillan, 2013), 91.

[48] *OED*, n.1, n.2.

Recreation: Poetry as Pastime 15

books and the *vocalité* of texts, a term Paul Zumthor has employed to account for the corporeal aspects of texts and hence 'their mode of existence as objects of sensory perception'.[49] The recreative conversation between musical cultures and poetry anthologies was especially pronounced and allows us to focus on what Scott Trudell has recently described as the 'multimodality' of early modern poetry:

> Musical, spoken, and written habits of poesis coexisted, combined, and overlapped so multifariously as to undermine conceptions of the early modern literary field defined exclusively in terms of script. In short, vocal music was poetry in early modern England, in the sense that verse, drama, and fiction were conceived as forms of poesy not limited to writing and speech.[50]

Anthologies advertise the multimodal uses of the poetry they collect. Jones's ballad before *A Handefull of Pleasant Delites* promises its buyers 'pleasaut [*sic*] songs to ech new tune' or 'fine Histories' to 'reade', as well as 'Songs to reade or heare'.[51] Other anthologies advertised the availability of poems for music-making and performance through titles and other framing devices. Or the acoustic properties of poems were crafted into the book in other ways, through the layout of poems on the page, as I will discuss in Chapter 4.

Recreation may have been viewed as a necessity in the early modern period, but attitudes towards leisure and pastimes varied considerably. Distinctions were made between honest and idle recreations, and pastimes were regulated according to age, gender, and social status.[52] These diverse recreational cultures are played out across the poems gathered in the anthologies studied in this book, from courtly pastimes to godly recreations, that which is profitable and that which is idle. Recreational literature therefore took a variety of forms, illustrating complex engagements with the Renaissance commonplace that the purpose of poetry is to profit and delight. When framed for both pleasure and instruction, poetry could be accommodated within the healthful properties attributed to recreation. Others condemned amorous poetry as an idle pastime, and instead proffered godly modes of recreation, as we shall see in Chapter 1. We need to

---

[49] Paul Zumthor, 'The Vocalization of the Text: The Medieval "Poetic Effect"', *Viator*, 19 (1988), 273–82; Shane Butler, *The Ancient Phonograph* (New York: Zone Books, 2015), 16.
[50] Scott Trudell, *Unwritten Poetry: Song, Performance, and Media in Early Modern England* (Oxford University Press, 2019), 9; see also Katherine Larson, *The Matter of Song in Early Modern England: Texts in and of the Air* (Oxford University Press, 2019), 110–19.
[51] *Handefull of Pleasant Delites* (c. 1566, 1584), A1v.
[52] Burke, 'Invention', 142–9; Arcangeli, *Recreation*, 11–21.

16   Introduction

keep in mind that recreational poetry was not the preserve of the elite. Throughout this study, I draw attention to the way ballads and a homely poetics shape demotic modes of recreation that operate alongside and often in dialogue with other, more courtly forms.

When anthologies attend to recreation, they characteristically locate the affordances of these books in the company of women to the extent that it becomes a trope in this period for addressing questions of poetic composition. It was a trope capable of diverse articulations, evident in the way it resonates across anthologies in varying forms. The mother's song, as we shall see in Chapter 1, was instrumental in defining domestic vernacular cultures, and operated alongside other figurations of the female household as an affective space for poetic recreation. I will argue that this trope does not necessarily codify restrictive gender identities, but rather provides conceptual spaces that generate possibilities for women's recreative performances. The trope of the company of women brings into view the household as a productive and transformative site for literary creativity and the role of women as consumers, performers, and producers.[53] This is most obviously the case with Isabella Whitney's compilations, which I will argue in Chapter 2 offer a complex reflection on poetic craft located in artisanal worlds and a domestic poetics that is alert to the texture of intrapersonal relations within the household and wider urban milieux of the middling sort. The 1590s see a variant of this trope, in which the company of women incorporates idle gentlemen. Recreational poetry in this company is characteristically defined as feminine and valued for its delightful ornamental properties. It is a type of poetry self-consciously characterised as 'minor' in that it has no interest in supporting dominant humanist literary values which maintain that poetry's pleasurable properties have their proper masculine end in virtuous action.[54] Instead it offers an alternative poetic, preferring female company to masculine occupations, and fitted for idle times and the exploration of states of pleasure. The

---

[53] On women's writing as an elite household pastime, see Martine van Elk, *Early Modern Women's Writing: Domesticity, Privacy, and the Public Sphere in England and Dutch Republic* (Basingstoke: Palgrave Macmillan, 2017), 8–9. On women's creativity within the household, see Susan Frye, *Pens and Needles: Women's Textualities in Renaissance England* (Philadelphia: University of Pennsylvania Press, 2013), chapter 3; on women's household performances, see Larson, *Matter of Song*, chapter 4.

[54] Juliet Fleming characterises 'minor' poetry that self-consciously neglects laureate ambitions in terms of 'ladies' text' that is directed 'specifically or "only" to women' by male authors. My use of the trope of the company of women differs from Fleming's ladies' text in that I read it as having generative potential and not always encoding restrictive gender ideologies; Fleming, 'The Ladies' Man and the Age of Elizabeth', in *Sexuality and Gender in Early Modern Europe: Institutions, Texts, Images*, edited by James Turner (Cambridge University Press, 1993), 158–81.

Recreation: Poetry as Pastime

models of poetic composition and reading it develops were available to women and men. *Crafting Poetry Anthologies in Renaissance England* explores the range of the trope of the company of women and uses the concept of a domestic Renaissance to open the history of vernacular poetry to so-called 'lesser' literary forms, like the ballad, and 'minor' cultural sites, such as the household, to reveal a thoroughly hybrid vernacular lyric tradition.

I begin with *Songes and Sonettes*, which I read alongside *Paradyse of Daynty Devises*, to establish the terms for understanding the craft of compilation used throughout this study. Richard Tottel and Henry Disle make use of the prefaces before *Songes and Sonettes* and *Paradyse*, respectively, to establish the credit of the publisher, fashioning complex models of agency that engage with humanist discourses. Both anthologies went into revised editions that make visible the processes of editing, and the organisational schema employed, which are designed to open these books to further uses. The representative genre of these anthologies, I will argue, is not so much the sonnet as the aphoristic poem; compiled out of proverbial matter, these 'commonplace' poems offer microcosms of the craft of anthology-making. The final section of this chapter traces the transmission of poems printed in *Songes and Sonettes* through the ballad trade, revealing the rich diversity of non-elite poetic cultures. This is the topic of Chapter 2, which focuses on the publisher, Richard Jones, a key figure in the production of poetry anthologies, who features across the first three chapters as the printer of *Paradyse* and publisher of anthologies from the 1560s to 1590s. Jones's collaboration with Isabella Whitney in anthology production is the basis of Chapter 2, which reads *A Handefull of Pleasant Delites* and *Gorgious Gallery, of Gallant Inventions* alongside Whitney's *Copy of a Letter* and *A Sweet Nosgay.* Jones and Whitney helped to shape and supply the market for domestic literature and to craft a poetics appealing to these socially diverse acoustic worlds. Whitney translates the classicism of humanist commonplace culture and its conceptual frameworks into consciously crafted forms that are made available to urban civic and artisanal cultures. In doing so, *The Copy of a Letter* and *A Sweet Nosgay* put into practice a version of the author as an artificer, a compiler and maker of texts in a very material and situated sense.

The 1590s are said to mark a turning point in vernacular literary culture brought about by the posthumous publication of Sidney's works. Across Chapters 3 to 5, I will argue that variant versions of Sidney are put into

18 Introduction

circulation from the 1590s, which, in turn, shape recreational poetic cultures into diverse forms. Poetry anthologies of the 1590s respond creatively to a poetics of leisure, giving new vitality to the trope of the company of women when fabricating recreational spaces within the form of the book. In *Englands Helicon* (1600), the very visible and audible dialogue with printed music books is designed to appeal to domestic recreative cultures. *A Poetical Rapsodie* (1602) locates the performative affordances of the anthology within a more exclusive, elite milieu and its private recreations, and is framed as a courtly production, the work of a gentleman compiler, Francis Davison. *Englands Helicon*, by comparison, is very much a trade book produced within a network dominated by publishers and printers, who reflect on the craft of editing. Yet, once we extend a model of craft to *A Poetical Rapsodie*, this anthology emerges as a far more collaborative venture. Davison's manuscripts, consisting of catalogues of poems and other textual material, demonstrate the manual crafts and systems of assembly practised in manuscript. Poetry anthologies have complex lives in manuscript and print. The concept of craft that informs this book means that it is possible to study the manual work, technologies, and skills shared across these media.

The anthologies studied in this group are often grouped together under the banner 'Elizabethan'. I have avoided this term throughout because the histories of these anthologies extend before and after Elizabeth's reign. *The Court of Venus* has been dated to the late 1530s and *Songes and Sonettes* is famously published in the last year of Mary's reign, and both build on preexisting traditions of lyric publication.[55] The ballads gathered in *A Handefull of Pleasant Delites* look back to late medieval carols and dance songs. The publishing history of *Paradyse of Daynty Devises*, *Englands Helicon*, and *A Poetical Rapsody* extends well beyond the end of Elizabeth's reign, with the latter two anthologies going into substantially revised editions in the early seventeenth century. The afterlife of these anthologies reminds us that books have complex histories well beyond the date of their first publication. If we shift attention from conventional models of periodisation to the careers of publishers and publishing networks, then what comes into view is how those in the business of making books shaped the form of the anthology. Exploring the transmission of the poems they gathered through other books, ballads, and other types of textual material

---

[55] See Julia Boffey, 'Early Printers and English Lyrics: Sources, Selections and Presentations of Texts', *Papers of the Bibliographical Society of America*, 85 (1991), 11–26.

alerts us to the vitality of performance cultures in which texts were dynamically re-created and transmitted in extra-textual forms, through the voice and body. The poetry anthology, because it is compiled, crafted, and embodied through re-creative performance, provides fertile ground for exploring how early modern cultures of recreation were shaped and re-shaped.

CHAPTER I

Books in Process
Songes and Sonettes *and* Paradyse of Daynty Devises

Songes and Sonettes and *Paradyse of Daynty Devises* are often characterised as illustrating the scribal origins of poetry anthologies, how 'the poetic exchanges of manuscript culture' were replicated in 'printed form' to produce simulacra of the gentleman's miscellany.[1] *Songes and Sonettes* is said to emerge out of elite scribal communities affiliated with Sir Thomas Wyatt and Henry Howard, Earl of Surrey, while *Paradyse of Daynty Devises* has its origins in the personal miscellany of Richard Edwards. Both, however, have much more complicated social and cultural lives than this suggests. Two of the most popular early poetry anthologies, they went through various stages of compilation, both in manuscript and in print, and had long shelf lives, spanning around three decades: *Songes and Sonettes* went into at least twelve editions from 1557 until 1587, and *Paradyse* at least ten, published from 1576 until 1606. Like many other anthologies, these were books in process, with poems added, removed, and reorganised across different iterations. As a result, the task of attributing the compilation and editing of these anthologies to any one set of agents, working within either scribal cultures or the milieu of the printing house, is fraught with difficulties. The aim of this chapter is therefore not to trace the origins of either *Songes and Sonettes* or *Paradyse* to Tudor networks, or to identify who was ultimately responsible for editing either anthology.[2] Instead, the first half of this chapter will examine how publishers and others working in the print trade intervened in these wider processes of production to articulate the corporate values of their craft and to shape the meanings of these anthologies. The publishers of *Songes and Sonettes* and *Paradyse*, Richard Tottel and Henry Disle, use the front of each book to set

---

[1] Wall, *Imprint of Gender*, 104–7.
[2] Jason Powell sets himself this task in order to locate the compilation of *Songes and Sonettes* in elite scribal culture and reclaim the anthology for manuscript studies in 'The Network Behind "*Tottel's' Miscellany*"', *English Literary Renaissance*, 46 (2016), 193–224.

20

Books in Process

out an ethos of publication that provides the framework for representing their own roles in bringing the poems gathered in these anthologies to a wider public. Both draw on civic humanist vocabularies to establish the credit that is due to the work of publication and to argue that it is the moral responsibility of stationers to facilitate textual transmission for the good of the commonwealth.[3] This task necessitated fashioning classes of readers of 'all estates', in the words of the title-page of the 1578 edition of *The Paradyse of Daynty Devises*, capable of profiting from the recreative properties of the books they produced. To this end, these anthologies were designed to be handy books, and various tools and schema were introduced to organise poetic matter and to make these anthologies available for future use and reuse. In this way, *Songes and Sonettes* and *Paradyse of Daynty Devises* participate in a civic Renaissance, in which humanism extends beyond the ambit of the court to fashion other communities and to incorporate the middling sort in the fashioning of an English vernacular poetics.[4]

The second half of this chapter focuses on the recreative and re-creative affordances of anthologies. These affordances are designed features that both make up the form of the anthology and are portable, and so can be acted upon in other locales and at other times. Anthologies and the poems they gathered had rich social lives. Tracing the uses of these poems takes us to early modern performance cultures in which the recreative properties of poetry were embodied through song. Compiled, in part, by Richard Edwards, the renowned music master of the Chapel Royal, *Paradyse of Daynty Devises* has long been associated with musical cultures.[5] By contrast, *Songes and Sonettes* is viewed as a different type of collection. Whereas Disle advertised the suitability of the 'ditties' gathered in *Paradyse* for music-making, it has been argued that decisions were made when editing *Songes and Sonettes*, including the removal of refrains from poems, in order to suppress song-like qualities.[6] Even if this was the case, such an intervention did not necessarily close down the performative properties of these poems or determine their uses. Many circulated as ballads and when John Hall read *Songes and Sonettes* alongside *Court of Venus* in his *Court of Vertue*, he recrafted these books of songs and sonnets into a songbook with

---

[3] On this vocabulary, see Tonry, *Agency and Intention*, 8–11.

[4] On a civic Renaissance, see Philip Withington, 'Two Renaissances: Urban Political Culture in Post-Reformation England Reconsidered', *Historical Journal*, 44 (2001), 239–67.

[5] Winifred Maynard, *Elizabethan Lyric Poetry and its Music* (Oxford: Clarendon Press, 1986), 12, 37.

[6] Amanda Holton, 'An Obscured Tradition: the Sonnet and its Fourteen-Line Predecessor', *Review of English Studies*, 62 (2001), 389–91; Maynard, *Elizabethan Lyric Poetry*, 12

22   Books in Process

musical settings. Both *Songes and Sonettes* and *Paradyse* take us to the multimodality of anthologies and their openness to the array of performance cultures in early modern England.[7] The re-creative properties of anthologies can also help us to understand how vernacular poetic traditions were shaped not only through practices of imitation established in male schoolrooms, but also within other cultural domains, including the mixed gender household. The final section of this chapter will focus on the ballad to illustrate how poems collected in these anthologies travelled to perhaps unexpected places. A focus on 'minor' poems and poets, alongside those with an established place in the literary canon, reveals how poems gathered in anthologies can tell different stories of the history of lyric poetry in England.

Common Profit: '…to publish, to the honor of the Englishe tong'

In his oft-cited preface, Tottel frames his collection of the verse of Surrey, Wyatt, and 'sondry good Englishe writers' in humanist terms. His act of publication is a necessary intervention in the wider process of cultural *translatio* that aims at the renovation of English poetry to rival that of the 'Latines' and 'Italians':

> It resteth nowe (gentle reder) that thou thinke it not evill don, to publish, to the honor of the Englishe tong, and for profit of the studious of Englishe eloquence, those workes which the ungentle horders up of such treasure have heretofore envied thee. And for this point (good reder) thine own profit and pleasure, in these presently, and in moe hereafter, shal answere for my defence.[8]

The story Tottel tells has proved compelling. By bringing the poetry of Wyatt and Surrey into the public domain and exhorting readers 'to learne to bee more skilfull', *Songes and Sonettes* is said to have challenged the next generation of poets to compose verse in new forms, including the sonnet and *ottava rima*, brought over from Italy.[9] The gathering of 'small parcelles' of verse of 'sondry' poets within its pages established a prototype for

---

[7] On poetry's multimodality, see Trudell, *Unwritten Poetry*, 4. See *Verse Miscellanies Online* for the 'Ballad Tunes', http://versemiscellaniesonline.bodleian.ox.ac.uk/glossaries-and-indexes/ballads/, and 'Musical Settings', http://versemiscellaniesonline.bodleian.ox.ac.uk/glossaries-and-indexes/musical-settings/.

[8] *Songes and Sonettes, written by the right honorable Lorde Henry Haward late Earle of Surrey, and other* (1557), Q1, A1v.

[9] See, for example, May, 'Popularizing Courtly Poetry', 418–31.

Common Profit 23

anthology-making. When Tottel stages a cultural confrontation between these 'ungentle horders' of scribal cultures and the 'good reder' of print, he is telling a story of technological change in the reproduction of texts, representing his book as a turning point that transforms a courtly and exclusive manuscript culture into the profitable marketplace of print.[10]

The persuasive fiction Tottel produces, however, is highly selective in its account, deliberately so, since his aim is to magnify the civic agency of the publisher.[11] Not all the 'treasure' had been kept from the press. Many of Wyatt's lyrics were circulating widely in manuscript, but they were also available in print in an earlier collection of lyric poetry, *The Court of Venus*, first put out by Thomas Gibson around 1538. Although the publishing history of *Court of Venus* is difficult to recover fully, since it survives only in a fragmentary state, it was in print until at least 1563, and so available for sale on the London bookstalls alongside *Songes and Sonettes*.[12] Richard Sherry, in his *A Treatise of Schemes and Tropes*, published seven years earlier in 1550, certainly assumed that readers were already familiar with Wyatt's poetry and reputation:

> What shuld I speake of that ornamente Syr Thomas Wyat? which beside most excellente gyftes bothe of fortune and bodye, so flouryshed in the eloquence of hys native tongue, that as he passed therin those wyth whome he lyved, so was he lykelye to have bene equal wyth anye other before hym, had not envious death to hastely berived us of thys jewel.[13]

By contrast, the lyric poetry of Surrey *was* new to print in 1557. A few years before *Songes and Sonettes*, the bookseller-publisher William Awen had published Surrey's *The Fourth Boke of Virgill* (1554); in the same year as his anthology, Tottel would put out Surrey's *Certaine Bokes of Virgiles Aenæis*. All three books were part of a concerted effort to get Surrey's works into print.[14] Awen, in his epistle dedicating his edition to Surrey's son, Thomas Howard, Earl of Norfolk, wrote of his difficulties in obtaining a copy of the work in remarkably similar terms to Tottel, complaining that 'I coulde understand of no man that had a copye thereof, but he was more

---

[10] For readings of this preface, see Wall, *Imprint of Gender*, 23–9; Marotti, *Manuscript, Print*, 212–17.
[11] Boffey demonstrates how *Songes and Sonettes* built on pre-existing traditions of lyric publication in 'Early Printers', 11–26.
[12] Warner, *Making and Marketing*, 195–6.
[13] Richard Sherry, *A Treatise of Schemes and Tropes (1550)*, ed. Herbert Hildebrant (Gainsville, FL: Scholars' Facsimiles and Reprints, 1961), 4.
[14] The second half of the 1540s sees other Surrey and Wyatt publications: Robert Toy published Surrey's *An excellent epitaffe of syr Thomas wyat with two other compendious dytties* (1545), reprinted in *Songes and Sonettes*; Wyatt's translation of Plutarch's *Quyete of Mynde* appeared in 1528 and his *Penitential Psalms* were published posthumously in 1549.

24 Books in Process

wyllyng the same should be kept as a private treasure in the handes of a fewe, then publyshed to the common profyt and delectacion of many.'[15] *Songes and Sonettes* represented a publishing coup, the first appearance of Surrey's lyric poems in print alongside a greatly expanded collection of Wyatt's verse. Not surprisingly, the reader encountered Surrey first in the anthology and his name dominates the title-page.

Tottel and Awen tell very similar stories of publication, grounded in the principles of civic humanism, from which they emerge as publicly minded Englishmen. These men were freemen, citizens of the City of London and active in the governance of the Stationers' Company, and as such could claim certain privileges and responsibilities. Pointing to the potential of *Songes and Sonettes* to transform vernacular poetry, Tottel insists that his intentions in publishing these poems were for 'the honor of the Englishe tong, and for the profit of the studious of Englishe eloquence', echoing Awen's justification of his act of publication for 'the common profyt'. Printer's epistles like other letters are agentive, they '"act for people" . . . in networks of agency extended across space and time'.[16] Prefaces are not, of course, straightforward expressions of intentions; rather the account of intentionality they provide is fabricated, mediated, refracted, and shaped through shared discourses and practices. Tottel's justification of his decision 'to publishe' is a humanist defence of his credibility, and by association that of the book trade. His recourse to this formula points to the early Tudor printing houses as important vectors in the transmission of humanist culture, including editing practices. Tottel had printed books with William Rastell, who, along with his father, John, established England's earliest humanist presses, and promoted continental humanist editing practices through the works they published.[17] Tottel's epistle is following a precedent set earlier in the century by these humanists, who defined the role of the printer through a concept of citizenship as an ethical agent motivated by a responsibility to publish for the benefit of the commonwealth.[18]

---

[15] *The fourth boke of Virgill, intreating of the love betweene Aeneas and Dido, translated into English, and drawne into a strauge metre by Henrye late Earle of Surrey* (1554), A2r. William Sessions describes Awen as an orator in Norfolk's household as he signs himself as 'hys most humble Oratour'; however, Awen was a stationer, with a shop in St Paul's Churchyard, and uses orator in the now obsolete sense of petitioner (*Henry Howard, the Poet Earl of Surrey: a Life* (Oxford University Press, 1999), 268).

[16] Warren Boutcher, 'Literary Art and Agency: Gell and the Magic of the Early Modern Book', in *Distributed Objects: Meaning and Mattering after Alfred Gell*, edited by Liana Chua and Mark Elliott (New York: Berghahn, 2013), p. 163.

[17] On the Rastells, see Massai, *Shakespeare*, chapter 2.   [18] See Tonry, *Agency and Intention*, 8–59.

Common Profit

The mechanical craft of his trade and humanist values combine in Tottel's promotion of the publisher as a 'lettered man', who is skilled in the matter of words and, like his prospective readers, 'studious of English eloquence'. The publisher's civic duty is to act in the public interest of these readers, to foster readerly behaviours. These 'good' readers are, in turn, called upon by Tottel to recognise their own part in this civic Renaissance; it is only through their use of the anthology for 'profit and pleasure' that the book will have meaning and purpose. Tottel 'exhort[s] the unlearned, by reading to learne to be more skilfull, and to purge that swinelike grossenesse, that maketh the sweet majerome not to smell to their delight'. In this variant on the *florilegium* motif, poems are equated with the properties of the sweetest smelling herbs in the garden; when read, their wholesome and restorative recreative qualities are activated. Reading these sweet poems acts as a purgative and their healthful properties will produce a class of discriminating active readers.[19] The language of purging and herbal remedies is shared with early modern recipe books, mixing humanist bibliophagic metaphors with more prosaic discourses. Tottel is advocating a model of healthful and morally improving reading that Isabella Whitney will return to in *A Sweet Nosgay* to open books to new classes of citizen readers.[20]

The profit to be gained from books is defined in terms of their circulation. Tottel follows Awen in criticising those who have restricted the transmission of Surrey's work. The problem is framed not so much in terms of manuscript as a medium, but rather the principle of exclusivity that keeps these texts, which are properly common cultural property, from the wider public – 'a private treasure in the handes of a fewe', in the words of Awen, as opposed to 'publyshed to the common profyt and delectacion of many'. Tottel's term 'ungentle horders' similarly figures the perversion of the proper civic use of texts, which is to circulate for the common profit. Behind the hoarder is the miser, the avaricious and covetous man, whose values were routinely opposed to those of the merchant, a figure who, in the idealising language of tracts promoting mercantile culture, trades in the circulation of goods for the profit of himself and others.[21] The language of commerce that runs across Awen's

---

[19] See Elizabeth Swann on the humoral properties of bibliophagic metaphors, '"To dream to eat Books": Bibliophagy, Bees and Literary Taste in Early Modern Commonplace Culture', in *Text, Food and the Early Modern Reader: Eating Words*, edited by Jason Scott-Warren and Andrew Zurcher (New York: Routledge, 2018), 69–88.

[20] See Chapter 2, 108.

[21] On the miser, see Ceri Sullivan, *The Rhetoric of Credit: Merchants in Early Modern Writing* (London: Associated University Presses, 2002), 84–6.

26 Books in Process

and Tottel's prefaces and mercantile literature speaks to the shared urban corporate culture of London in which stationers worked side by side with fellow members of guilds in London, exchanging skills and ideas.[22] The civic-minded publisher, like his fellow citizens and tradespeople, acts to ensure the health of the commonwealth by keeping these 'small parcelles' of verse in circulation.

A rhetoric of common profit similarly informs Henry Disle's epistle before *The Paradyse of Daynty Devises*. The fact that it is shared illustrates the ways in which these publishers were manufacturing credibility for the vernacular poetry anthology as a type of book and allaying readers' concerns about the quality of the poems gathered. Disle put out four editions of *Paradyse* up to 1580, each with substantial revisions, but he appears to have published very little else before his death around 1581.[23] The publishing commitment he made to *Paradyse* is therefore noteworthy. Disle dedicates *Paradyse* to Sir Henry Compton, who takes his place among the company of learned men addressed in the epistle.[24] The publication history Disle describes brings his bookshop into view as a cultural domain that, like the humanist study, is a meeting place for learned men. Disle, echoing Tottel, has rescued a manuscript book once '*collected togeather, through the travell of one* [Richard Edwards], *both of woorship and credite, for his private use*', and in danger of being lost. After careful reading, and '*not without the advise of sundry my freendes*', he '*set them in print*', persuaded by his friends' arguments that '*The wryters of them, were both of honor and worship: besides that, our owne countreymen, and such as for theyr learnyng and gravitie, might be accounted of among the wisest.*'[25] Disle describes how he intervened in a '*private*', in the sense of restricted, manuscript culture, in the wider public interest. Along with

---

[22] See Johns, *Nature of the Book*, 61–3; on artisanal exchanges, see Smith, 'In the Workshop', 9.

[23] Barnabe Rich, *A right exelent and pleasaunt dialogue between Mercury and an English Souldier* (1574, STC 20998), Richard Forster, *Ephemerides meteora graphicae* (1575, STC 443.13), Lodowick Lloyd, *An epitaph vpon the death of the honorable, syr Edward Saunders Knight, Lorde cheefe Baron of the Exchequer, who dyed the. 19. of November. 1576* (STC 16620), Jacques Bellot's French–English language book, *La maistre d'ecole anglais* (1580, STC 1855), and the last book which bears his colophon, a medical and culinary recipe book, John Partridge's *The Widowes Treasure* (1582, STC 19433.2), put out in the year his rights in *Paradyse* were assigned to Timothy Rider. The comparatively small number of entries in the Register may indicate that he concentrated on selling books published by others or imported books, or both.

[24] Compton was the ward of Sir William Herbert, first Earl of Pembroke, who acted as his patron until his death in 1570.

[25] *The Paradyse of Daynty Deuises* (1576), A2r–2v.

Common Profit 27

Tottel and Awen, he advertised his craft through the figure of the humanist publisher, who possesses both the financial means to bring the book to press and the critical judgement to assess its worthiness.

The errata list placed before the now-lost second edition of *Paradyse*, published a year later in 1577, similarly invites the reader to observe and to credit the work of the printing house and the publisher:

> The Printer to the Reader.
> Gentle Reader, through negligence of the woorkeman;
> There are certayn faultes escaped, which because I would
> Geve no occasion of offence to the Aucthours of the ditties
> (who for the most part are unknowen to me) I thought
> good to note them, whereby thy curious eye happening
> upon them, they may with more ease be corrected.[26]

Responsibility for ensuring the work is free of error is cast in moral terms, rather than primarily philological, since it is motivated by an ethical duty to the authors that goes beyond simple personal allegiance, given they 'for the most part are unknown to me'. Disle insists on his good intentions, that he can be trusted and is therefore creditable. To do so, he utilises a standard trope, that of the faulty 'woorkeman', who is characterised by his anonymity, which means this figure can readily absorb blame.[27] Richard Jones was the printer of *Paradyse* for Disle, but we should not necessarily assume the finger is being pointed at him. In any case, the task of printing required a range of workmen – the master printer, compositors, pressmen, and correctors. By mobilising this trope, Disle is able to give a nuanced account of agency, accepting responsibility for some aspects of production, while disavowing it for others. Through the act of compiling the errata list, Disle claims ethical responsibility for the work – a responsibility he willingly shares with the studious reader – another version of Tottel's 'good reder' – who is invited to correct the text and so participate in its production. In this way, both Disle and Tottel are modelling reading practices and classes of readers in order to establish the credibility of their own craft.

---

[26] Bodleian (Bod.) MS Douce e. 16, 3v. The 1577 edition was transcribed by the eighteenth-century antiquarian William Herbert from a copy that was later burnt in a house fire in 1785. See Steven May, 'William Hunnis and the 1577 *Paradyse of Dainty Devices*', *Studies in Bibliography*, 28 (1975), 72. On the errata list, see Smyth, *Material Texts*, 80–104.

[27] See Tonry, *Agency and Intention*, 31, 34.

28   Books in Process

The Craft of Anthology-Making

Pamela H. Smith's studies of artisanal craft and the workshop as a site for creative exchange and knowledge-making that is learnt on the job offers a productive approach for exploring the bookshop and printing house as cultural domains where the craft of anthology-making was practised and conceptualised.[28] Bringing these locales into view means that it is possible to glimpse the work of the diverse social body of actors engaged in the business of book production and in shaping literary culture in early modern England. Printing houses and bookshops, as historians of the book have long noted, were 'nodal points for the transfer of people, writings, and knowledge'.[29] J. Christopher Warner has illustrated how Tottel's specialism in law books meant that his shop was a meeting place for gentlemen of the Inns of Court, who not only provided a clientele for *Songes and Sonettes*, but also supplied him with poems for the 'Uncertain Authors' section.[30] The south-west door of Paul's Churchyard emerges as a key vector of transmission in the publication history of *Paradyse*, since it is here that Richard Edwards's manuscripts, Jones, and Disle converge. Disle worked in partnership with Jones on the four editions brought out in 1576, 1577, 1578, and 1580.[31] Jones, a printer-publisher, had been in the business of producing poetry anthologies and other types of vernacular compilations from the early 1570s. Jones and Disle appear to have had neighbouring shops at the south-west door of St Paul's Cathedral, since this is the place advertised in the colophons to Disle's books between 1574 and 1576 and those of Jones in 1570 and 1575.[32] Disle took over this shop from his master, William Jones, who may have been a kinsman of Richard.[33] Spatial proximity and kinship networks made up the

---

[28] Smith, 'In the Workshop', 4–31; Smith, *Body of the Artisan*.
[29] Johns, quoting Elizabeth Eisenstein, in *Nature of the Book*, 37; see also Helen Smith's *Grossly Material Things: Women and Book Production in Early Modern England* (Cambridge University Press, 2012).
[30] Warner, *Making and Marketing*, 4–5, 14–24.
[31] Only Disle is identified in the colophon, but he was a bookseller, not a printer. The editors of the *English Short-title Catalogue* identify the printer as Richard Jones
[32] I. P. [John Partridge?], *A meruaylous straunge deformed swyne* (1570, STC 19071) and Nicholas Breton, *A smale handfull of fragrant flowers* (1575, STC 3695).
[33] Disle was apprenticed to William Jones on 24 June 1563 for thirteen years until 1576 (Arber, *Transcript*, I, 198); William Jones's colophons in 1572 and 1574 advertise a shop at the south-west door. There is no record of Richard Jones's apprenticeship, except to mark its end in August 1564; he is unlikely to have been apprenticed to William, who only became a freeman in 1558, but there may have been a family connection. Soon after attaining his freedom, Richard is fined along with William Jones and others, sometime after 18 May 1565, for stitching books contrary to the order of the Company. Arber, *Transcript*, I, 71, 196, 277.

The Craft of Anthology-Making

everyday world of the book trade. These were knowable urban communities: people worked side by side within neighbourhoods, and shops and stock passed between family members, masters, and former apprentices.[34] Richard Jones emerges as a pivotal figure in the publication history of *Paradyse*. He had access to Edwards's manuscripts, publishing his only other printed work, *The excellent comedie of two the moste faithfullest freendes, Damon and Pithias* (1571). Jones entered this work in 1567/8, soon after Edwards's death. Disle claimed Edwards's manuscript book came into his possession '*not long since* [he] *departed this lyfe*', in other words, around the time of Jones's publication of *Damon and Pithias*. These conjunctions are suggestive of the means by which texts moved through the printing house and the bookseller's shop. In these cultural domains, manuscripts and printed material were bought, read, assessed, and made, activities that fostered interactions between authors, compilers, booksellers, printers, and readers.

When both Disle and Tottel assert the cultural role of the publisher and the book trade, they are participating in a wider civic Renaissance that was fashioning citizens and their cultural and political worlds in post-Reformation England.[35] Their accounts concentrate on their intellectual labours in bringing these books to the press, but within certain limits. Both make use of forms of discretion, withdrawing into the background in order to maintain fictions of compilation in which publishers make books public, but do not act as authors. Disle, for example, depicts himself working alongside unnamed others, to '*set them into print*'. Yet, what it is notable is how he turns attention away from his own labour, instead stepping into the background by asking the reader to '*credite*' the work of Edwards in compiling '*this small volume . . . being penned by divers learned Gentlemen, and collected togeather*' through his '*travell*' (A2r). Disle insists the anthology is all Edwards's work, glossing over the fact that ten years had passed between Edwards's death in 1566 and the publication of *Paradyse*. The passage of time is recorded in the contents of the anthology which includes 'A worthy dittie, song before the Queenes Maiestie at Bristowe', performed during her 1574 royal progress, and seven poems attributed to E. O, the initials of Edward de Vere, Earl of Oxford, which were probably composed between 1570 and 1576.[36] It is not clear how

---

[34] Johns, *Nature of the Book*, 76.   [35] Withington, 'Two Renaissances', 239–51.

[36] *Paradyse*, C4v, K1v–2r. A further poem, 'If care or skill, could conquere vaine desire', is attributed to M. B. in the 1576 edition, but then E. O. in all subsequent editions. For dating of Oxford's poetry, see Steven May, *The Elizabethan Courtier Poets: Their Poems and their Contexts* (first published Columbia: University of Missouri Press, 1991; Asheville, NC: Pegasus Press, 1999), 52–4, 269–70.

30 Books in Process

Oxford's verse came into the collection, but what its presence does tell us is that the copytext behind *Paradyse* was not the same manuscript book collected by Edwards, but a far more composite set of papers. Two factors are in play here. On the one hand, Disle's discrete presence in his preface is a deliberate strategy designed to advertise the integrity and credibility of *Paradyse* as a collection compiled not by Disle, its publisher, but by Richard Edwards, the well-known music master of the Chapel Royal.[37] On the other, it points to the nature of compiling and editing anthologies in this period. This was work undertaken over time, shared by many, who often have left little trace in the printed book and remain largely anonymous.[38]

Songes and Sonettes magnifies these issues. The question of who took part in editing this anthology continues to be debated. Tottel is most frequently cited as the principal editorial agent, but other candidates proposed include Nicholas Grimald, John Harington, and Thomas Norton. More recently, Jason Powell, in an impressive piece of forensic work, has identified 'a network of kin, admirers, and "frend*es* of olde S*ir* Thomas wiat" (Bodleian Rawl. D. 1087, fol. 16) that included one William Digges of Kent and his more famous cousin, Leonard Digges', and concluded that the copytext behind *Songes and Sonettes* was a now-lost manuscript compiled and edited by this 'Italianophile' network.[39] Yet, rather than searching for a single editorial agent or even a single network responsible for compiling and editing the anthology, the very profusion of potential candidates should alert us to the various constellations of actors involved during the long and uneven process of compiling the collections that make up an anthology and preparing it for the press. We can identify Disle's shop and Tottel's printing house as a nodal point where some of the various networks involved in the production of *Paradyse* and *Songes and Sonettes* momentarily converge, only if we keep in mind that these sites operated within a more extensive web of working relations operating over time and across locales in which textual material was produced and transmitted.

Editing did, nonetheless, necessarily take place. Attention to editorial practices discloses the designed features of anthologies, including the

---

[37] See Johns on publishers' discretion and credibility, *Nature of the Book*, 34.
[38] See North, *Anonymous Renaissance*, 56–7.
[39] Powell, 'Network', 195; the claim for Tottel's editorship of *Songes and Sonettes* was enshrined in J. Payne Collier's 1867 edition which gave it the title *Tottel's Miscellany*; H. J. Byrom, 'The Case for Nicholas Grimald as Editor of "Tottel's Miscellany"', *Modern Language Review*, 27 (1932), 125–42; *Tottel's Miscellany*, edited by Amanda Holton and Tom McFaul (London: Penguin, 2011), xv.

The Craft of Anthology-Making

organising principles and patterns at work. Since these forms of organisation are abstract, they are iterable, often coming from somewhere else and
then made available for use in other books and other contexts. Much has
been written about the editorial interventions in the life of the poems
gathered in *Songes and Sonettes*.[40] My focus here is on tools and the
organising schema employed when Tottel brought out a new edition
(Q2) at the end of July 1557, more than a month after the publication
of the first edition (Q1), because they foreground questions of design and
use. One tool that Tottel added to Q2 was a table of contents, introduced
at the end of the collection. The table was a feature of the humanist book,
especially large compilations, where it acted as a finding aid, training
readers in how to access and extract information and textual matter.[41]
Tables were designed for quick reference work, helping the reader to realise
the book's usefulness, advertising it as a 'handy' type of book.[42] Tottel had
worked with tables before, and it is this tool that links the law books he
printed with this verse anthology. When he took over the rights to Sir
Thomas Littleton's *Tenures*, he also inherited the alphabetical table from
the previous publisher, William Powell. The table was accompanied by a
set of instructions advising readers on how to use this tool to find cases in
the book and an explanation of the book's structure – its division into
units of text identified by letters of the alphabet.[43] The experience of
printing Littleton's *Tenures* similarly instructed Tottel in the table's
usefulness. Carried over to *Songes and Sonettes*, the table therefore exemplifies the point where the tacit knowledge of the skilled artisan, learnt
through setting the book, meets the tools of humanist pedagogy.[44] The
table at the end of *Songes and Sonettes* contributes to an idea of the

---

[40] See, for example, Rollins, in *Tottel's Miscellany*, ed. H. R. Rollins, 2 vols. (Cambridge, MA: Harvard
University Press, 1966), II, 95; May, 'Popularizing Courtly Poetry', 425; Holton, 'An Obscured
Traition', 389; Warner, *Making and Marketing*, chapter 2. Paul Marquis has provided a detailed
comparative study of the editorial design of Q1 and Q2 that tracks these changes. He does not single
out Tottel as the editor, instead arguing for an anthologising intelligence, given that the complex
task of gathering and organising poems from various sources necessarily involved 'what Sir Philip
Sidney calls an "idea or forconceit" of the whole'; see Marquis, 'Printing History and Editorial
Design in the Elizabethan Version of Tottel's *Songes and Sonettes*', in Hamrick, ed., *Tottel's Songes*,
15, 25–31.
[41] On tables of content, see Ann Blair, *Too Much to Know: Managing Scholarly Information before the
Modern Age* (New Haven: Yale University Press, 2010), 135–44.
[42] Parkes, *Scribes*, 62–4.
[43] *Lyttylton tenures newly revised and truly corrected with a table (after the alphabete to fynde out briefly
the cases desyred in the same) therto added very necessary to the readers* (1553), *2. See also Carol
Blosser, 'Making "English Eloquence": Tottel's Miscellany and the English Renaissance'
(unpublished PhD dissertation, University of Texas at Austin, 2005), 135–41.
[44] Smith, *Body of the Artisan*, 7–8.

32　　　　　　　　Books in Process

anthology, describing its function as a compilation of textual material that can be selected, gathered, rearranged, and reframed in different contexts. This tool bridges the instructional and the recreational, profit and pleasure, drawing attention to the conceptual and bibliographic structures of utility shared by these types of books.[45] It was also a device that helped readers to recognise and profit from the malleability of the anthology, allowing for different ways of reading, interpreting, and making use of the textual matter collected. Different anthologies employed different methods to make books easier to use. Rather than a table, numbering is used in *Paradyse of Daynty Devises* as a tool to organise and mark divisions between poems: '15. Promise is debt', '16. No wordes, but deedes', '17. He desireth exchaunge of life', '18. Of the instabilitie of youth' (1576, C1r–2v). Numbering both introduces seriality, resulting in a sequence that adds up to a larger whole, and marks out individual poems as units, capable of being extracted and recombined within other arrangements.

The flexible, handy design of the book is expressed through the way titles act as organisational structures, both marking up divisions and establishing points of comparison.[46] As a method of organisation, titles imply an understanding of order that appreciates the malleability of poetic material.[47] Within anthologies, titles act like the *topoi* used in common-place books and identify poems as textual units, in both a physical and intellectual sense, which are therefore suitable for excerpting and gathering. In this way, titles condense textual matter of the poem into a convenient, handy, and transferrable form.[48] Yet, while titles may promise to summarise a poem's meaning, they often seem to function as 'bad' readers. Later editors of *Songes and Sonettes* have noted with frustration how 'love' or 'lover' is often used in titles when this is not the poem's topic.[49] One reason for these seeming misreadings is that titles are appreciated for their iterability, not necessarily for their descriptive function. Titles frame poems through common cultural codes that are endlessly transferrable, and so do the work of conjoining within the anthology, while simultaneously identifying that the poem is reiterable and so

---

[45] See also Randall Ingram, 'Seventeenth-Century Didactic Readers, their Literature, and Ours', in *Didactic Literature in England, 1500–1800: Expertise Constructed*, edited by Sarah Pennell and Natasha Glaisyer (Aldershot: Ashgate, 2003), 72–3.

[46] On titles, see also Marotti, *Manuscript, Print*, 218–19; Wall, *Imprint*, 102–3.

[47] Kalas, *Frame, Glass, Verse*, 58–9.　　[48] Crane, *Framing Authority*, 17, 18, 38.

[49] See, for example, Holton and McFaul's notes to 2, 11, 50, 106, 112, 255.

The Craft of Anthology-Making

available for gathering in other forms.[50] Similarities between many of the titles of aphoristic or proverbial poems, for example, identify and read these poems relationally within broader categories, so that poems are interchangeable, either whole or in parts. The portability of proverbs is particularly noticeable in the case of mean estate poems, a subgenre within aphoristic poetry, which are clearly marked out by titles that recur across *Songes and Sonettes* and *Paradyse*.[51] Through this means, *sententiae* and more homely proverbial sayings circulate and resonate across the printed anthologies through an audible process of prosaic intertextuality.[52] In both *Songes and Sonettes* and *Paradyse*, proverbs or generic descriptors, 'Complaint', 'Description', or 'Dialogue', recur across the collection, setting up chains of association and variation.

Substantive changes between editions involve a series of manual and intellectual tasks that require time and labour and so make the craft of editing visible in the fabric of the anthology. Poetic material is read critically as part of this process; these readings are then put into practice, turned into work. When we attend to those points where poems have been introduced and the contents rearranged, the schema used to organise poems into a collection become legible and allow us to observe the material and conceptual methods for organising anthologies in action. Schema used in anthology-making characteristically operate at a local level, rather than enforcing a uniform design, and are very portable, providing handy tools for conjoining textual material that can be shared across compilations.[53]

---

[50] See Crane's point about the role of places or heads in commonplace books, *Framing Authority*, 38–43.

[51] For poems on the golden mean in *Songes and Sonettes*, see 'The meane estate is to be accompted the best' (163), 'Of the golden meane' (253); for those on the mean or low estate, see 'Of the mean and sure estate written to John Poins' (134), 'The meane estate is best' (160), 'The poor estate to be holden for best' (169), 'They of the mean estate are happiest' (140). For ease of reference, numbers from *Tottel*, ed. McFaul and Holton have been used. To follow the transmission of this topic across anthologies, see the relevant poems in *Verse Miscellanies Online*, http://versemiscellaniesonline .bodleian.ox.ac.uk/.

[52] The saying 'Time trieth truth' also circulates across anthologies: the poem given this proverbial title in *Songes and Sonettes*, 'Eche thing I see hath time, which time must try my truth' (*Tottel*, 176), is reprinted in variant form in *Gorgious Gallery*, 'Eche thing must have a time, and tyme doth try mens troth'(F4r); this proverb also closes 'For that a restles hed must somwhat have in ure' (*Tottel*, 174). The proverb that the highest trees are shaken or fall while low shrubs remain is frequently incorporated into gatherings of other sayings in aphoristic poems; see 'Who craftly castes to stere his boat' (*Tottel*, 163); in *Paradyse*, see Edwards, 'Prudence. The history of Damacles and Dionise' (1576, F4r–G1r), 'Of the meane estate' (1576, K4r–v); Jasper Heywood, 'Who waighteth on this wavering world, and veweth ech estate', (1578, A3vv). To follow the transmission of these proverbs across anthologies, see the relevant poems in *Verse Miscellanies Online*, http:// versemiscellaniesonline.bodleian.ox.ac.uk/.

[53] Vine, *Miscellaneous Order*, Introduction.

34   Books in Process

Like other crafted forms, schema are also often somewhat makeshift, recording the sometimes haphazard nature of bringing books to the press. The primary schema organising Q1 and Q2 of *Songes and Sonettes* is authorial. Q1 is made up of sections said to group together first the poems of Surrey, then Wyatt, Nicholas Grimald, and *'Uncertain auctours'*. The disposition of this first edition, however, is more makeshift than this suggests, since its structure appears to record a temporal glitch in production, with two additional sets of poems added at the end after the earlier sections: '*Other Songes and Sonettes written by the earle of Surrey*' (CC3v) and '*Other Songes and sonettes written by sir Thomas wiat the elder*' (Dd2). To an extent, the looseness of this framework registers the potential for further augmentation crafted into the form of the anthology. Tottel had alerted readers to the anthology's accumulative properties when he promised further additions, that there would be 'moe hereafter'. Q2 reorganises the anthology, with poems by Surrey and Wyatt now integrated into their respective authorial sections, followed by '*Songes and Sonettes of uncertain auctors*' (N2), then '¶ *Songes written by N. G.*' (Ff1).[54] Poems are also added to the 'uncertain authors' section. Here, answering poems are repeatedly used to aid in reorganising content at those points where new poems are introduced. Paired poems put in place flexible dialogic structures, audible patterns of response and counter-argument, in which various voices speak to each other across poems.[55] The resonant acoustic properties of these poems are complemented by titles which explicate their dialogic form.

Answering poems and dialogues often do the work of conjoining poems in anthologies. The dialogue is a highly portable form that was valued because it is so resonant, in the full acoustic sense of that term, and therefore capable of setting in play endlessly iterable and variable patterns of response and counter-response. In *Paradyse* (1576), the acoustic and visual properties of this form are foregrounded in a set of stylised and highly crafted stichomythic dialogues, between either male friends or male lovers and their mistresses, which are interspersed across ten pages (H3v–14r). Their artfully designed form is displayed typographically. Italicised capital letters have been selected by the compositor to denote alternating speakers at the start of lines and at mid-line breaks where they mark up

---

[54] All Grimald's occasional and love poems are removed, leaving only his public poems, translations, and epigrams. For detailed discussion of these changes, see Warner, *Making and Marketing*, 39; Marquis, 'Printing history', 30–2.

[55] On the conversational structure of other collections after *Songes and Sonettes*, see Cathy Shrank, '"Matters of Love as Discourse": the English Sonnet, 1560–1580', *Studies in Philology*, 105 (2008), 30–49.

The Craft of Anthology-Making 35

verse lines shared between speakers. Different initials are chosen to stand in for and to individuate the different speakers. The dialogue poem thus is taking generic shape on the page through the craft of the printing house and the work of the compositor as he translates the copytext into printed form.[56] The complaint '*He complaineth thus*' begins in the mode of the male-voiced complaint, turning into a *tenso*, a dialogue with his mistress in the second stanza:

L.   I yelde my self, what would you more of me,
A.   You yelde, but for to winne and conquer me,
L.   Saie and kill not madame,
A.   Forsake your sute for shame,
   No no no no, not so.

         (14r)

The female speaker takes over the final stanza to declare he 'hath this conquest gainde'. Typographic pointing animates the dialogue, embodying and distinguishing the speakers through the interplay of initials. At the same time, these typographic prompts set up contextual relationships between these dialogue poems across these pages by visually marking out their shared formal properties.

Answer poems are often organised into sequences in anthologies via counterpointing male and female voices through the epideictic structures of praise and blame. One effect of this patterning is to introduce variety, variations on a theme. Here, compilers are drawing on techniques for conjoining texts through *querelle des femmes* schema, which had provided English stationers with a ready-made formula for manufacturing books since the early days of print.[57] When new poems are added to the 'Uncertain Aucthors' section of Q2 (Bb1v-Cc2r), this is the schema employed to integrate poems, as the following list illustrates:

'The complaint of a hot woer delayed with doutfull cold answers', Q2
'The answer', Q2
'An epitaph made by W.G. lying on his death bed, to be set upon his owne tombe', Q1 (Bb4v)
'An answer', Q1 (Cc1r)
'An epitaph of maister Henry Williams', Q1 (Bb4r)

---

[56] For further discussion of the role of print in moulding genre, see Chapter 4, 163–5.

[57] Ann Coldiron, *English Printing, Verse Translation, and the Battle of the Sexes, 1476–1557* (Farnham: Ashgate, 2009); Lindsay Ann Reid, *Ovidian Bibliofictions and the Tudor Book: Metamorphosing Classical Heroines in Late Medieval and Renaissance England* (Farnham: Ashgate, 2014), 98–9, 104.

36 Books in Process

'Another of the same', Q2
'Against women, either good or bad', Q1 (CC1r)
'An answer', Q1 (CC1v)
'Against a gentilwoman by whom he was refused', Q1 (Bb4r)
'The answere', Q2.
'The lover dredding to move his sute for dout of deniall, accuseth all women of disdaine and ficklenesse', Q1 (R1v)
'An answere', Q1 (CC2v)

Aside from the paired funeral elegies for Henry Williams, all the other answer poems belong to a broader *querelle des femmes* tradition.[58] Such is the durability and utility of the answering poem that its organisational pull can override other methods of arrangement. Surrey's complaint against women's 'crafty wayes' (Q1, D1r) in Q2 is paired with 'An answer in the behalf of a woman of an uncertain aucthor', which had previously been printed in the 'uncertain author' section in Q1. The Q2 title registers that it is not Surrey's poem, 'An answer in the behalf of a woman of an uncertain author', and so is not in its proper authorial place. Instead, its new position in Q2 testifies to its formal integrity as an answering poem, in which the echoic textual *vocalité* of the two poems is very audible. The female complaint responds to the preceding male complaint correcting his faulty viewpoint:

Wrapt in my carelesse cloke, as I walkt to and fro:
I se, how love can shew, what force ther reigneth in his bow
 And how he shoteth eke, a hardy hart to wound:
 And where he glanceth by againe, that little hurt is found.
(Q1/Q2, D1r)

Girt in my giltles gowne as I sit here and sow,
I see that thinges are not in dede as to the outward show.
And who so list to looke and note thinges somewhat nere:
Shall finde wher plainesse semes to haunt nothing but craft appere.
(Q1, Aa3r; Q2, D1v)

The sartorial distinction between the 'carelesse cloke' and 'giltles gowne' carries with it contrasting moral stances. The pensive movement of the male speaker as he walks 'to and fro' in his 'carelesse cloke' physically embodies his reasoning process as he draws conclusions about women's character. The following response provides a critical reading that reveals his

---

[58] See Lindsay Ann Reid's discussion of the *querelle des femmes* schema in *Paradyse*, in *Ovidian Bibliofictions*, 97–8.

The Craft of Anthology-Making 37

rhetorical stance to be more ambiguous through a pattern of deictic reversal. In the female response, his 'Wrapt' implies dissimulation, 'outward show' rather than 'in dede', when compared with the ethical constraint of 'girt' that is carried across to the 'giltles gowne', claiming for its wearer the freedom from the sin of Eve that the male speaker attributes to all women. Her stasis during her household work, as she sits and sews, signifies an industrious moral stability that gives more credence to her plainness than that of the ethical restlessness of the male speaker. The reading provided by 'Girt in my giltles gowne' in its new position is so persuasive that it represents 'Wrapt in my carelesse cloke' as designed to invite the critique that is supplied in 'An answer'.

Editorial energies are frequently directed towards fashioning author functions in anthologies. The driver, however, is not singularity, but variety. *Songes and Sonettes* both attributed poems to authors – Surrey, Wyatt, and Grimald – and included a section of 'uncertain authors'. Gatherings of unattributed poems give the impression that the anthology collects a variety of authors. *Paradyse of Daynty Devises*, which makes much of the editorial and authorial presence of Richard Edwards, tends to attribute poems, using an array of conventions – names, initials, pseudonyms, and anonymity – that bear out the claims of its title-page that poems have been 'written for the most part, by M. Edwards ... the rest by sundry learned Gentlemen', whose names and initials are then listed below: S. Barnarde, Jasper Heywood, E. O., F. K., L. Vaux, M. Bevve, D. S., R. Hill, M. Yloop, 'with others'. Disle's preface claims that the presence of 'divers learned Gentlemen' resulted from Edwards's own work in compiling the collection. As we have seen, other hands were also at work gathering these poems, yet what I would emphasise is that Disle does not represent the anthology as emerging out of a milieu gathered around Edwards, but rather as the product of his work of compiling. Some of the poets gathered in *Paradyse* were engaged in textual exchanges, sharing and copying one another's poems. Francis Kinwelmarsh and Jasper Heywood, for example, were contemporaries at Gray's Inn.[59] Others, however, were out of this ambit: Lord Thomas Vaux died in 1556 and was part of the Surrey and Wyatt generation; the Earl of Oxford, the courtier poet, was from a much younger generation, and only sixteen when Edwards died; and the twelfth-century monk St Bernard heads the list because a translation of his popular devotional poem opens the anthology. The 'sundry learned

---

[59] On these networks, see Ros King, ed., *The Works of Richard Edwards: Politics, Poetry and Performance in Sixteenth-Century England* (Manchester University Press, 2001), 42.

38 Books in Process

Gentlemen' assembled in the anthology is advertised as a fabrication, the result of editorial work, 'the travell' of collecting and compiling.

The pseudonym, '*My lucke is losse*', illustrates how authorial markers are used flexibly in this anthology to perform the formal work of conjoining. The pseudonym acts as an author function, but with different signifying properties to a name. The opening two poems, the translation of St Bernard and 'Beware of had I wist', are attributed to '*My lucke is losse*', as well as a set of poems in the middle of the anthology (E1r–F1v). Attempts have been made to identify the author behind '*My lucke is losse*'.[60] This pseudonym, however, actively resists individuation. Instead, its character means that it takes on the function of a proverb and so is designated as a shared cultural property that is capable of reiteration and transference. All the poems attributed to this figure are complaints, both moral and amorous. Because of its aptness to the kind of poetry to which it is attached, '*My Lucke is losse*' signifies the author's character, not in an individualised but in a generic sense, as an iterable and portable author function appropriate to the mode of complaint gathered in *Paradyse*.

Each edition of an anthology constitutes a new publication event, distinct from, yet related to, past and future iterations. New editions bring changing sets of actors and local contexts of production into view.[61] In this way, they offer microhistories of publication that allow us to focus on questions of agency. Substantive changes made to content or paratext, or to both, draw attention to the actors involved, whether new collaborations have been formed, and how poems are recontextualised and new contexts brought into the frame. *Paradyse* was not only reprinted across almost three decades, it was also substantially revised across at least five editions, and changed hands in 1585 when Edward White took over the title and added new poems in further editions, finally removing Disle's preface in 1595. When Disle brought out a second edition in 1577, the list of 'sundry learned gentlemen' on the title-page was revised: gone are Bewe and Hill (their poems have also been removed from the collection or reassigned to other authors), and a new name is added – 'W. Hunis'. With the number of poems attributed to William Hunnis rising from seven to eighteen, he is now a dominant presence in the collection. Hunnis

---

[60] Steven May and William Ringler's *Elizabethan Poetry: a Bibliography and First-Line Index of English Verse, 1559–1603* (London: Thoemmes Continuum, 2004), follow Hazlitt's edition of *The Complete Poems of George Gascoigne* in identifying 'My luck is loss' with Gascoigne. Rollins disputes this identification, pointing out that the phrase is proverbial, *Paradise*, lvi. King identifies this figure with William Baldwin, in *Works of Richard Edwards*, 16.

[61] On the publication event, see Cohen, *Networked Wilderness*, 7, 15.

The Craft of Anthology-Making

was Edward's successor as Master of the Children of the Chapel Royal. Steven May has assembled very credible evidence 'to demonstrate', in his words, 'that William Hunnis was personally concerned with the make-up and printing of the 1577 edition' of *Paradyse*.[62] Editing leaves traces in the structure of anthologies that are visible when editions are compared – hot spots that point to activity. Changes cluster around the figure of Hunnis, with most of the editorial energy expended on his poems: he authors the majority of the new verse, care is taken with attribution of poems to Hunnis, and most of the substantive changes to this edition and all the corrections on the errata list are to his poems.[63] May cites this errata list as 'the most dramatic evidence of his personal involvement' in preparing the second edition, since its presence argues that 'Hunnis must have personally read the sheets and demanded certain corrections before the entire edition had been printed.'[64] The story the errata list tells, however, does not coalesce into a singular figure of the editor. Instead, the list necessarily brings Hunnis into conversation with others – with Disle, who pens the errata list and oversees the changes, and also with the anonymous 'printer', who stands in for the work of many and, in this sense, is representative of the thoroughly collaborative and often anonymous practices of anthology production.

Different kinds of agency are involved in anthology-making. When publishers become poets, their creative agency becomes very visible. For the fourth and final edition he published in 1580, Disle added a poem of his own composition, under his initials, on the death of his kinsman, 'His Especial Good Friend', John Barnabie of Southampton (K1r).[65] Epitaphs are added across editions, possibly because they were readily to hand, having been previously printed as broadsides, and possibly because their occasionality is useful, clearly signifying that they are new timely additions. Disle drew on his stock to augment the second 1577 edition, adding Lodowick Lloyd's 'An epitaph vpon the death of the honorable, syr

---

[62] May, 'William Hunnis', 64.

[63] In the 1577 edition, the attribution of 'When first mine eyes' to W. H. is removed, and five other poems reassigned to W. H.: 'Behold the blast' (D. S. in 1576), 'I would it were not', 'With painted speache' (M. B. in 1576), 'The higher that the Ceder tree' (L. V in 1576), 'In terrours trapp' (T. M. in 1576), 'Where sethyng sighes' (L.V. in 1576). 'What watche' is replaced by two Hunnis poems, 'Like as the dolefull Dove' and 'Alacke when I looke backe'; 'The lively Larke' (E. O.) and 'Lo heare the man' are replaced by two poems by Hunnis, 'In searche of thyngs' and 'In wealth we se'. May, 'William Hunnis', 69–73.

[64] Ibid., 73.

[65] This is possibly the same John Barnabie who held a civic office in Southampton in 1572, through the patronage of the Earl of Leicester, *Historical Manuscripts Commission, Corporations of Southampton and King's Lynn* (London, 1887), 20.

40 Books in Process

Edward Saunders Knight', which he had published as a broadside in 1576.[66] Added to the 1580 edition was Barnabe Rich's 'An Epitaph upon the death of syr William Drury, Knight, Lord Justice and Governor of Yreland, deceased at Waterford the third of October. An. Do. 1579' (M3r–4r). In the case of Disle's own epitaph for his kinsman, this figure of the publisher-as-poet productively blurs the distinction between authorial and non-authorial agents, and continues the impetus of the epistle in which the humanist publisher claims his place among the 'sundry learned gentlemen' gathered in the collection. Disle's funeral lament is incorporated within a set of love complaints: 'Finding no relief, he complaineth thus' (14v), and a set of four complaints attributed to the Earl of Oxford: 'If care or skill, could conquere vaine desire', 'A lover reiected, complaineth', 'Not attainyng to his desire, he complaineth', and 'His minde not quietly setled, he writeth thus' (K1v–2v). Placing a funerary elegy among love complaints might seem rather inappropriate. Yet, it is not quite so indecorous in formal terms, since they are of a kind within the broader category of lamentations.[67] The company that Disle's elegy keeps within the anthology serves to amplify his lament and, accordingly, it shares a plangent vocabulary with the surrounding complaints – 'The tricklyng teares, that fales along my cheeks' in 'A lover reiected' (K1v) have their counterpart in the 'trickling teares' of those lamenting the death of Barnabie, with assembled mourners 'enforce[d] ... to complaine', even though 'cruel death' 'derides my wofull words' (K1r).

Paradyse changed hands following Disle's own death soon after this 1580 edition, and the new publisher, Edward White, a bookseller-printer, brought out a further revised edition in 1585.[68] White was well connected; he had married Sara, the daughter of Sir Thomas Lodge, Lord Mayor of London, and his brother-in-law was the author Thomas Lodge. White

---

[66] See Herbert's transcription, Douce e.16, fols. 38–42. It is reprinted in all subsequent editions of *Paradyse*. Lloyd's only other printed work, *The Pilgrimage of Princes*, had been published in 1573 by Disle's master, William Jones. Lloyd's career, combining a career in print with a life at court, acting as a gentleman servant to Sir Christopher Hatton, resembles that of his associate, Thomas Churchyard, who provided a prefatory verse to *Pilgrimage*.

[67] George Puttenham, 'The Form of Poetical Lamentations', in *The Art of English Poesy: a Critical Edition*, edited by Frank Whigham and Wayne Rebhorn (Ithaca: Cornell University Press, 2007), 135–7.

[68] Some of Disle's copy after his death was obtained by Timothy Rider – *Paradyse* on 26 July 1582 and *The Widowes Treasorer* on 6 April 1584 – just before Rider's own death, when they transferred to White on 11 April (Arber, *Transcript*, II, 414, 430, 431). Disle may have died sometime after his last entry in the Register on 26 January 1580; the colophon to the 1582 edition of *The Widowes Treasure* (STC 19433.2) says it was printed by John Kingston for Disle, but it may have been for Rider (Arber, *Transcript*, II, 430).

The Craft of Anthology-Making 41

published Lodge's epitaph on his mother, Lady Anne Lodge, in 1579.[69] Among the new poems added to this edition was a set of poems by Jasper Heywood at the end of the anthology. All of Heywood's known verse was published in *Paradyse*: four in the first 1576 edition, another added in 1578, and then three in 1585. This is perhaps not surprising since Heywood's poems are moralising and religious and so very representative of this anthology. Yet, the inclusion of three previously unpublished Heywood poems in 1585 raises many questions, not the least since he was by now a controversial figure. Returning to England from Rome in 1581 on a Jesuit mission, he had set about converting the earls of Arundel and Northumberland to Catholicism; in late 1583, he was imprisoned in the Tower, put on trial for treason the following year, and in January 1585 deported to France, along with other priests. Why, then, did White publish Heywood's poems in 1585? White may have been capitalising on Heywood's notoriety as part of a wider publishing strategy. Between 1581 and 1587, White was publishing ballads and pamphlets celebrating the execution of Heywood's associate, Edmund Campion, and exposing ongoing Catholic 'heresies': he entered a ballad in August 1581 entitled 'Nowe we goe, of the papistes newe overthrowe', and in 1582 he published three pamphlets by Anthony Munday on the trials and executions of Campion and his accomplices.[70]

The question of how White accessed Heywood's poems in the mid-1580s, particularly given there is no surviving evidence for their circulation, brings others into the frame. When Heywood returned to England in the early 1580s, it is likely his poetry was popular in recusant communities; this is also the period when the Catholicism of Thomas Lodge, White's brother-in-law, appears to be coming to the attention of the authorities.[71] It is therefore possible that Lodge was White's point of contact. Heywood's poems in 1585 were open to a topical reading even if they are not explicitly framed in these terms in *Paradyse*. Two of the newly added Heywood poems are penitential complaints, in which the speaker acknowledges his sins. The first, given the title *The complaint of a sorowfull Soule*, employs the conceit of an arraignment, at which 'So many Judges

---

[69] Arber, *Transcript*, II, 363; *Prosopopeia: The teares of the holy, blessed, and sanctified Marie, the Mother of God* (1596, STC 16662a, 16662b) and *A Treatise of the Plague* (1603, STC 16676).

[70] Arber, *Transcript*, II, 400.

[71] Alexandra Halascz, 'Thomas Lodge', *Oxford Dictionary of National Biography* (hereafter *ODNB*). One of the later works of his brother-in-law that White published is Lodge's Marian and overtly Catholic text, *Prosopopeia: The teares of the holy, blessed, and sanctified Marie, the Mother of God* (1596).

42 Books in Process

shall against me sentence give', calls on God to 'Behold my faults most foule, which follie first did frame, / In loving them I should have loathed, whens breedeth all my bane', and looks for repentance through God's grace (M3v–4r). The second, '*Alluding his state to the prodigall child*', similarly acknowledges that the speaker has betrayed himself through false beliefs:

> He traveld farre, in many forraigne landes,
> My restlesse minde, would never raging leave.
> False queanes did him, of all his coine bereave,
> Fonde fancies stuft my braine with such abuse.
>
> (M4r)

This poem closes with a plea for pardon. In 1585, with Heywood once again in exile for his 'life misled' in the service of the Pope and the Jesuits, these poems could be read in confessional mode, and so are available for an anti-Catholic reading that was in tune with other ballads and pamphlets White was publishing. Recusant readers, on the other hand, like White's brother-in-law, Thomas Lodge, would have read these poems rather differently. The form of the anthology leaves these poems open to interpretation and to diverse readers, both present and future.

The work of compiling and editing an anthology is an embodied practice, a craft that necessarily takes us to the work of people at different historical moments.[72] The changing contents and organisation of editions momentarily make visible the various associations of poets, compilers, publishers, printers, some known, many unknown, with one another, with books, ballads, and an array of textual material. Attending to those moments of editorial intervention allows access to these microhistories of production, embodied in the fabric of anthologies, that can tell us about the working practices of those in the book trade, the situation of poets whose verse they collect, and the transmission history of certain poems. In this way, anthologies are made up of complex social and textual interactions that generate compelling and diverse stories about agency, design, and transmission.

Books for Use: '… thine own profit and pleasure'

Poetry anthologies are compiled through methods of organisation that were integral to humanist cultures and had long served as practices for

---

[72] See Knight, *Bound to Read*, 8.

Books for Use 43

making books within scriptoria and the print trade. These technical skills, as we have seen, are visible in the material form of anthologies, from the organisation of the *mise-en-page* to the inclusion of apparatus, such as titles, rubrics, and indexes. Methods of organisation and the type of tools used varied across poetry anthologies according to the practices of publishers and the printing houses. Even so, all introduce tools designed to help readers to find their way around compilations, making them easier to use.[73] These macrotechnologies find expression at the microlevel in the poems gathered in anthologies, specifically those proverbial or aphoristic poems that populate the pages of these books. Proverbial or aphoristic poems were ubiquitous in the poetry anthologies published in the mid-sixteenth century and continue to make up the contents of collections in the early seventeenth century. Composed from proverbs, the form of these poems embodies the craft of anthology-making in miniature. Indeed, they encapsulate a culture of compilation to such an extent that they can be called commonplace poems. Proverbial poems are said to belong to a minor, alternative Tudor strand of poetry, the 'drab' cousin to the Petrarchan sonnet, the culturally dominant Renaissance lyric form of Puttenham's Italianate 'courtly makers'.[74] Once we give credit to the compiled form of these poems, then it is possible to see how their crafted properties fashion subjectivities and modes of poetic making built around the exercise of *techne* that then becomes accessible to a wider social range of participants. Proverbial poems are characterised by their social mobility; the craft they encapsulate is available to those of 'all estates', as Disle advertised on the title-page of *Paradyse*.[75] These are handy poems, which promote cultural models of imitation that do not simply enable the readers invoked by Tottel and Disle to imitate their social betters, those 'courtly makers', but have their own uses. The pragmatic modes of imitation they put into practice take us once more to a model of an English Renaissance that is heteroglot and incorporative, engaging a wide social range of participants.[76] These socially mobile proverbial poems travelled widely in Renaissance culture, disclosing points of interconnection between the humanist schoolroom and the household, the court and the road.

---

[73] Parkes, *Scribes*, 52–8.   [74] Puttenham, *Art of English Poesy*, 148.
[75] Crane, *Framing Authority*, 137, 168.
[76] Jeffrey Todd Knight discusses pragmatic imitation in *Bound to Read*, 88.

44   Books in Process

Commonplace poems are assembled from proverbial sayings and *sententiae*. These 'small parcelles', to use Tottel's phrase, put into practice the methods of compilation used when making an anthology. Tottel's 'parcelles' is an apt term. Its older meanings are a 'component part of a whole' and, more specifically when referring to a physical object, 'a number of things put together wrapped in a single package'.[77] Commonplace poems gather and reassemble bits of textual matter and wrap and reframe them to craft a new work. Their compiled form means that they both illustrate anthology-making in miniature and provide lessons in pragmatic modes of imitation. Their form expresses an understanding of poetry as made up of textual and linguistic matter that can be broken up into parts, prosodic units, and reworked into new compositions. Commonplace poems thus apply the methods used to teach prosody in grammar schools. Students were instructed to note down 'Poeticall phrases' in their commonplace books, and to compile a 'store of Epithetes', poetic figures, and words measured according to 'the quantities of syllables'.[78] When composing their own poems, students should then draw on this stock, and use this textual matter to build verse lines, carefully weighing syllables, while ornamenting their compositions with poetic figures. Since commonplace poems are so consciously compiled and crafted, they foreground these technologies of poetic making and put into practice a model of *techne* that brings together skilful fabrication with creative design and invention.[79]

This method of poetic composition is very evident in an anonymous poem in the 'Uncertain Author' section of *Songes and Sonettes*, which crafts a series of commonplace images of Hades into a love sonnet:

> The restlesse rage of depe devouryng hell,
> The blasing brandes, that never do consume,
> The roryng route, in Plutoes den that dwell:
> The fiery breath, that from those ymps doth fume:
> The dropsy dryeth, that Tantale in the flood
> Endureth aye, all hopelesse of relief:
> He hongersterven, where frute is ready food:
> So wretchedly his soule doth suffer grief:
> The liver gnawne of gylefull Promethus,
> Which Vultures fell with strayned talant tyre:
> The labour lost of wearyed Sisiphus:

---

[77] 'Parcel', *OED*, 2a, 10a.
[78] John Brinsley, *Ludus Literarius* (1612), 193–96; O. B. Hardison, *Prosody and Purpose in the English Renaissance* (Baltimore: The Johns Hopkins University Press, 1989), 101–7.
[79] Kalas, *Frame, Glass, Verse*, 54–6.

Books for Use   45

These hellish houndes, with paines of quenchlesse fyre,
Can not so sore the silly soules torment,
As her untruth my hart hath alltorent.

(Q1, R2r)

The accumulation of commonplace images carries weight, a hellish load of hopelessness and grief that finally finds its referent in the torment the lover experiences knowing his mistress lies. The opening set of five lines draws attention to the craft of assembling lines of verse through the material and rhetorical features of language. *Exargasia*, the repetition of ideas of hell in different figures, is coupled with the heavy alliteration of a native lyric tradition, compounded by the use of isocolon, which involves repeating phrases with the same grammatical structure and with the same number of syllables at the start of each of the first five lines. This sonnet has weight and matter not only because it is proverbial, but also because of these resounding vocal properties. The way proverbs can be assembled to make up a poem illustrates their availability 'as compositional tools' that could be put to a variety of uses, from crafting a love sonnet to setting out 'memorable moral lessons'.[80] The value of these rhetorical and proverbial figures lies not so much in their novelty, although they could be put to surprising uses, but in the fact that they are so commonplace and therefore capable of iteration, for gathering and repurposing within new compositions.

One early reader of the songs and sonnets of Wyatt and Surrey, Thomas Whythorne, gave an account of his composition of aphoristic, commonplace poetry in his autobiography. I will be returning to Whythorne, and some of his companions, throughout this chapter because they provide evidence for how modes of composition were practised in this period within certain locales – in Whythorne's case, across different households. The title he gave to his life story, 'A book of songs and sonnets, with long discourses set with them, of the child's life, together with a young man's life, and entering into an old man's life', not only echoes *Songes and Sonettes*, but also illustrates how poetic composition was understood to be an embodied practice, a method of character formation.[81] When a boy, in 1545, Whythorne was placed in John Heywood's household 'to be both his servant and scholar' for three years, learning music alongside poetic composition. Part of his instruction was to 'write out for him divers songs

---

[80] James McBain, 'John Heywood's Use of Proverbs' (unpublished MPhil. thesis, Oxford, 2002), 43.
[81] *The Autobiography of Thomas Whythorne: A Modern Spelling Edition*, edited by James M. Osborn (Oxford University Press, 1962). I am quoting from the modernised edition, owing to the difficulties of reproducing Whythorne's invented orthography.

46 Books in Process

and sonnets that were made by the Earl of Surrey, sir Thomas Wyatt the elder', and others, many years before their publication by Tottel. He then moved on 'to imitate and follow their trades and devices in writing' by composing his own verse. His model for one composition was a letter written to him by his uncle offering the youth wise counsel: 'There is a philosopher named Plato who giveth counsel to choose the best way in living, or to live by, the which use and custom shall make easy and pleasant.' Whythorne reconstructs his uncle's letter in verse form, rearranging, substituting, and adding words to build lines of verse and compose a poem:

> The wise Plato, as thus doth counsel give
> Choose thou the ways the best thou canst to live
> The which custome, and use therof shall make
> Pleasant, if not, too much therof thou take.[82]

Just as his uncle had gathered adages from his reading of classical philosophers, so too Whythorne digests and reconstitutes his uncle's letter, recycling its moral matter in his poem. He engages in a process of edification, from the Latin *aedificare*, 'to build', whereby these portable forms of wisdom, taken together, are meant to impart moral stability and strength, resulting in a material sense of a self that is gathered, composed. Whitney will employ a similar model of edification in her *A Sweet Nosgay* when she puts together a figure of the author as artificer.[83]

Whythorne's apprenticeship to Heywood brings the humanist household into view as a space for poetic making. An English homeliness, which is constitutive of a domestic, vernacular Renaissance, often enters the vocabulary of aphoristic poems through proverbs. Surrey's measured ode, 'Of thy life, Thomas, this compasse wel mark', is a reading of Horace's *Ode* 2.10, that ends with a homely proverb: 'And so wisely, when lucky gale of winde / All thy puft sailes shall fil, loke well about: / Take in a ryft: hast is wast, profe doth finde' (Q1, D1v). 'Ryft' is an Old English word for sail, that by the early sixteenth century was rarely found in poetry.[84] Alongside the very prosaic 'hast is wast', 'ryft' works to assert the cultural value of the 'English tong'. E. K., in his epistle before Edmund Spenser's *The Shepheardes Calender*, will later write of the need 'to restore, as to theyr rightfull heritage such good and natural English words'.[85] Wyatt's satire, entitled 'Of the meane and sure estate written to John

---

[82] Whythorne, *Autobiography*, 5–7, 12. I have retained the punctuation of the original.
[83] See Chapter 2, 106–8.   [84] *OED*, 'rift', n. 1.
[85] Edmund Spenser, *The Shorter Poems*, edited By Richard McCabe (London: Penguin, 1999), 27.

Books for Use 47

Poins', similarly begins in the household, among women at work and in the mother tongue: 'My mothers maides when they do sowe and spinne: / They sing a song made of the feldishe mouse' (QI, LIV). The Aesopian fable of the country and the town mouse was available from a variety of sources and in different forms and moved freely between vernacular cultures and the male schoolroom, where translating Aesop's fables formed part of the curriculum.[86] Wyatt's simultaneously humanist and homely satire sets in play a complex dialogue between these locales that characterises proverbial poetry more broadly. The opening frame to Wyatt's satire locates the fable within a domestic space occupied by female servants. Here, the household is imagined as a place in which the matter of poetry originates and circulates, becoming available for imaginative recrafting and recreation. The singing of the 'song made of the feldishe mouse' keeps time with the work of his 'mothers maides when they do sowe and spinne' (QI, LIV); it sets in motion the metaphoric and material association between weaving and needlework and poetic making that incorporates the latter into the fabric of the household. The home, here, becomes an alternative space, set off from court life and identified with the virtues and safety of the mean estate. It must be said, Wyatt complicates this situation, as is so often the case in his satires, and the harsh life the country mouse must endure reveals that the truth of the proverb finally cannot be maintained.[87]

The type of proverbial poems collected in *Songes and Sonettes* and *Paradyse* made their way into the everyday world of households, where they were valued for their applicability as well as their portability. John Leche, the owner of a manuscript anthology of devotional poems, carefully copied a set of poems from *Paradyse* into a ruled paperbook. The book was part of his household – on the blank leaf at the front of the paperbook, he records his marriage to his wife, Frances.[88] Poems are transcribed from *Paradyse* in a fair, neat italic hand, on the whole, seriatim, selecting the devotional and proverbial poems, and skipping those poems on the theme of love. Care was taken to transcribe the moralising titles of the poems extracted from *Paradyse*, so that they are carried across as an integral part of the poem. This degree of attention did not extend to author attributions,

---

[86] Thomas Wyatt, *The Complete Poems*, edited by R. A. Rebholz (Harmondsworth: Penguin, 1978), 445–6; on Aesop in the schoolroom, see William P. Weaver, 'Marlowe's Fable: "Hero and Leander" and the Rudiments of Eloquence', *Studies in Philology*, 105 (2008), 388–408.
[87] See Chris Stamatakis on Wyatt's verse epistles, in *Sir Thomas Wyatt and the Rhetoric of Rewriting: 'Turning the Word'* (Oxford University Press, 2012), 135–48.
[88] Folger MS v.a.149, fol. 1.

48   Books in Process

which are not copied from the source text; instead this reading concentrated on the moral, making it available for household use.[89] Versified proverbs both offered memorable moral lessons and were part of the ornamental fabric of the godly household, painted on to walls, inscribed on to plates, or embroidered into fabric. The 1570 edition of Thomas Tusser's *A Hundreth Good Pointes of Husbandry* includes four sets of posies – for the hall, the parlour, the guest's room, and 'thine owne bed chamber' – that are composed of portable couplets of proverbial lore designed for painting on the wall. Part of the crafted fabric of the household, proverbial poetry marks out the space of the household, giving it material, moral, and emotional definition. Tusser's book, which offers practical instruction for householders, both men and women, was put out by Tottel in the same year as *Songes and Sonettes*.[90] These two publications address and give shape to a 'vernacular community' of Englishness, peopled by the studious, a constituency of readers of printed books who desire 'by reading to learne to bee more skilfull'.[91] Tusser's book showcases a variety of verse forms, if not to the extent or sophistication of *Songes and Sonettes*, as he admits, advising readers, in a poem added to the 1570 edition, that if 'lookest thou here' for 'Trim verses' 'Of Surry (so famous)', then they will find 'nothing but rudenesse in these' (A2r). What both books do share are models of poetic craft and technologies of book production that mark up poems for further use. Tusser's 'hundreth good poyntes' take the form of numbered quatrains that, like the titles in *Songes and Sonettes* and *Paradyse*, belong to practices of *compilatio* in which the disposition of textual matter in the form of the printed book becomes a craft.[92] By attending to these household uses, other locales for poetic making emerge. As we will see, Surrey's poems, those elegantly made 'Trim verses', were re-created as homely proverbial ballads for the trade in broadsides. The poems of Wyatt, Surrey, and 'others' prompted subsequent generations of poets to be more skilful; yet, given the variety of the vernacular poetry in this period, there were alternative communities of

---

[89] The poems from *Paradyse* are copied across fols. 12–28.
[90] The date given in the colophon at the end of STC 1012 is 'the third day of February .An. 1557', which could be old style and 3 February 1558 in the new calendar. Thomas Tusser, *A Hundreth Good Pointes of Husbandry* (1570), 39v–40v; see also Hamling and Richardson, *A Day at Home*, 47.
[91] Wall, *Staging Domesticity*, 36.
[92] For detailed discussion of the conceptual and material status of these 'points' in Tusser, see Jessica Rosenberg, 'The Point of the Couplet: Shakespeare's *Sonnets* and Tusser's *A Hundreth Good Pointes of Husbandrie*', *English Literary History*, 53 (2016), 1–21.

Household Recreations 49

practice available that take us to the ballad trade and household recreations.

Household Recreations: '… ditties both pithy and pleasant'

Tusser, like Whythorne, was trained and employed as a musician.[93] The composition of music and poetry went hand in hand as they learnt their craft, illustrating how closely these modes were interlaced in practice. Not all poems were composed with musical settings in mind, but all had the capacity for performance in some form. Song was the dominant vehicle through which most people in the sixteenth century experienced poetry, whether in the form of sophisticated musical settings, metrical psalms sung at church services, or through the performance of ballads. Levels of musical literacy varied in this period, from those trained musicians, like Tusser and Whythorne, and others who could read music, to those who learnt tunes by ear.[94] As this suggests, the multimedia properties of music and poetry in this period were variously articulated across different performance sites. The ways in which songs were performed and heard are context sensitive, bringing into play a range of social, cultural, physical, and literary codes. Music-making enabled interactions between people, often through musical instruments and books, shaped experience, affective states, and identities, establishing intimacies and distance, and marked out times of leisure and recreation within the day. One of the primary sites for amateur music-making was the early modern household, a locale that took diverse social forms and hence made possible variant performance cultures within its domain. The early modern household was complexly gendered, bringing together women and men in relationships of co-residence and authority that were differentially articulated according to social status. Middling and elite households, for example, were multi-status entities and incorporated servants and apprentices as well as kin.[95] The recreational household is therefore a productive site for exploring the protean and multimodal forms of vernacular poetry in this period and for elaborating alternative literary histories that can take account of non-elite forms, such as the ballad, so often elided in accounts of lyric poetry.

---

[93] Trained as a chorister, Tusser was then employed in the household of William, Baron Paget, before becoming a farmer; see Andrew McRae, 'Thomas Tusser', *ODNB*.

[94] See Christopher Marsh, *Music and Society in Early Modern England* (Cambridge University Press, 2010), 6–7; Trudell, *Unwritten Poetry*, 4–10; Larson, *Matter of Song*, Chapter 3.

[95] See Hamling and Richardson, *A Day at Home*, chapter 5, on recreation in households of the middling sort.

50   Books in Process

Poems collected in anthologies capture the multivalence of performance cultures in this period. A poem, like Thomas Vaux's 'I lothe that I did love', might be sung to a ballad tune that travelled widely as well as set to sophisticated settings in songbooks within households. *Paradyse of Daynty Devises* advertised its origins in the manuscript book kept by Richard Edwards, music master of the Children of the Chapel Royal. His songs circulated widely through amateur music-making within the household. Claudius Hollyband's *The Frenche Schoolemaister*, published three years earlier in 1573, incorporates just such a scene of domestic music-making at which Edwards's songs take centre stage. This homely vignette is in keeping with the overarching frame of Hollyband's book which advertises on its title-page that it is designed for those learning French 'privatly in their owne study or houses'. The household recreation Hollyband imagines illustrates how songs gathered in anthologies were transmitted and remade within domestic acoustic fields of the gentry and middling classes. The household Hollyband describes in *The Frenche Schoolmaister* is part of a wider urban soundscape that resounds with music-making, coming into the home from the streets. Family members are kept awake by the music accompanying May festivities and a wedding; leaving home for church, they are enraptured and spiritually elevated by the psalms, presumably those of Sternhold, sung at prayers.[96] Edwards's songs are performed at the end of a meal bringing together the wider household – master, mistress, sons and a daughter, and servants – who are joined by gentlemen and gentlewomen friends. Music-making creates micro-socialities, bringing various participants into social and affective relationships with one another and with their environment.[97] The manuscript music books are kept carefully locked in a chest; the book chosen is described as 'the best corrected',[98] implying that there are others in different states and testifying to the sophisticated amateur music-making within the household. Family members have their allotted roles in this entertainment: Katherine, the daughter, is entrusted with the key to collect the book from the closet; it is her brothers who sing this song in four parts. We should not conclude, however, that women were excluded from musical cultures. In fact, music teaching within the household was typically for women and girls of Katherine's class, since they were usually taught at home, while brothers

---

[96] Claudius Hollyband, *The Frenche Schoolemaister* (1573), 68–76.
[97] Georgina Burn, 'Music: Ontology, Agency, Creativity', in *Distributed Objects*, ed. Chua and Elliott, 130–51.
[98] Hollyband, *The Frenche Schoolemaister*, 126.

Household Recreations

51

went to school.[99] The acoustic world imagined through this performance is that of the prosperous urban middling and gentry classes in which music-making establishes the credit of the household within the community, along with the wine and cheese served to guests.

Disle addressed this market for household music in the preface to *Paradyse*, advertising that its '*ditties both pithy and pleasant, aswell for the invention as meter ... wyll yeelde a farre greater delight, being as they are so aptly made to be set to any song in .5. partes, or song to instrument*' (A2v). 'Ditty' defined any composition in verse, be it a poem or a song.[100] Its use here advertises that the verse collected in the anthology can be taken away and set to music, whether sophisticated settings '*in .5. partes*', or any other song performed on an instrument, or even to simpler ballad tunes. Beside the title, 'The complaint of a Sinner, and sung by the Earle of Essex vpon his death bed in *Ireland*', in the 1596 edition of *The Paradice of Dainty Devises*, a reader has written that it is to be sung 'To the Tune of Rogero'.[101] Very few printed songbooks were available in the period, which is why Whythorne decided to put out his own music book, published in 1571, five years before *Paradyse*. It too was aimed at the amateur household, advertising that it catered for different degrees of musical literacy – 'some hard, some easie to be songe, and some betweene both'.[102] Families, like those imagined by Hollyband, kept their own manuscript music books. Thomas Mulliner, a chorister at Magdalen College, Oxford, like Whythorne before him, was apprenticed to John Heywood, albeit several years later between 1559 and 1563. He compiled his music book in Heywood's household, including settings for poems printed in *Songes and Sonettes* and seven poems later printed in *Paradyse*.[103] The Heywood household, where boys were trained in penmanship and humanist methodologies, including practices of imitation and song and poetic making, emerges as one of the vectors in the re-creative history of the poems gathered in *Songes and Sonettes* and *Paradyse*.

---

[99] Katie Nelson, 'Love in the Music Room: Thomas Whythorne and the Private Affairs of Tudor Music Tutors', *Early Music*, 40 (2012), 20.

[100] Disle defines the musicality of the ditty in terms of its 'meter', which is suitable for setting to music; see Lindley on lyric, musicality, and metre, '"Words for Music, Perhaps": Early Modern Song and Lyric', in *The Lyric Poem: Formations and Transformations*, edited by Marion Thain (Cambridge University Press, 2013), 10–29.

[101] Edwards, *The Paradice of Dainty Deuises*, Folger STC 7521, L2r.

[102] Thomas Whythorne, *Triplex, Of Songs, for three, fower, and five voyces* (1571), title-page.

[103] Thomas Mulliner, *The Mulliner Book*, ed. John Caldwell (London: Stainer and Bell, 2011), xxix. For these settings, see *Verse Miscellanies Online*: http://versemiscellaniesonline.bodleian.ox.ac.uk/glossaries-and-indexes/musical-settings/.

52 Books in Process

Proverbial poems as well as love lyrics were sung and, through their performance, helped to establish the cultural value of the household within vernacular poetic cultures. This is the topic of Edwards's 'In goyng to my naked bedde, as one that would have slept', which was set as a part song to the lute and copied by Mulliner into his music book. One of Edwards's most popular songs, it provides a complex reflection on the affective properties of poetry-as-song as it activates and shapes sites of performance.[104] 'In goyng to my naked bedde' is a domestic fable that locates the origins of the type of moralising commonplace poetry that fills the pages of *Paradyse* in the mother tongue – songs heard in the company of women at the mother's knee or among Wyatt's 'mothers maides'. The space of the song's composition and performance is the maternal household. The male narrator is kept awake by a mother singing to her fretful infant, so he takes up 'paper, penne and ynke, this proverbe for to write'; since her song carries such moral 'waight' it therefore must be recorded for posterity (1576, F IV). Edwards's song activates the resonant cultural trope of the breastfeeding mother nursing her infant, a son, who imbibes eloquence and ethos from his mother's milk. It is a distinctively maternal paradigm, encompassed in the concept of the mother tongue, and used to figure cultural reproduction and the nurturing of vernacular traditions. This trope extended to poetic making. Poetry was equated with breast milk to signify its fecundity, its capacity for creativity and invention.[105] Through this maternal domestic scene, Edwards's song sets in motion a myth of poetic origins, telling a story of a vernacular culture founded in an English homeliness.

Edwards's poem is an example of *prosopopoeia* that brings the question of who is speaking into critical focus. The poem's frame establishes an acoustic setting in which the male speaker in his bedchamber overhears 'a wife', who is located in a distinct, yet related place, where she can be heard singing 'unto her little bratte' (F Iv) – 'wife' and 'bratte' are lowly terms that bring into play a social and cultural distinction between the male speaker and female singer. This frame would seem to encourage a reading of 'In goyng to my naked bedde' as an act of male ventriloquy, in the well-rehearsed terms of Elizabeth Harvey, 'an appropriation of the

---

[104] It can be found set to music in British Library (BL) Add. MS 36526A, fols. 1, 6; London, RCM 722, fol. 62v; London, RCM 2111, fol. 4v. On music and transmission, see Trudell, *Unwritten Poetry*, 4.

[105] Jacqueline T. Miller, 'Mother Tongues: Language and Lactation in Early Modern Literature', *English Literary Renaissance*, 27 (1997), 177–96.

Household Recreations

female voice' that speaks 'to a larger cultural silencing of women'.[106] The mother's song is therefore scripted in the interests of a male humanist culture that confines female creativity to orality and the household. The Latin title given to the poem, '*Amantium iræ amoris redinti gratio est*', which is translated in the proverbial refrain to the song, 'The fallying out of faithfull frends, is the renuyng of love', derives from Terence, a staple author in the Tudor schoolroom, and excerpted in printed commonplace books in this period.[107] Attached to the mother and child in this poem, it reads rather oddly since it replaces the maternal relationship with male friendship and takes us to the many moralising poems on this theme gathered in *Paradyse*. Read from this vantage point, the poem sets in place a hierarchy in which women's song is subordinate to the male writing subject, who possesses the educational capital to preserve her voice for posterity.

There is, however, something more to the mother's song that resists any easy appropriation. The nursing mother stands out as a figure for female creative – and ethical – agency. This is noticeable when contrasting the maternal model of poetic making behind the concept of the mother tongue with Aristotelian tropes of poetic making in terms of childbirth. In the former, the nursing woman re-creates the child in her own image; in the latter, the woman provides the generative matter that the male then fashions and gives form.[108] In the humanist cultural fable set out in Edwards's poem, the maternal household is the privileged civic space in which the cultural and ethical foundations of the commonwealth are laid out. The household was, of course, the 'first school' and the primary site for socialisation, hence the moral and spiritual authority of women was valued in this space.[109] The proverbial lore the mother sings to her infant son instructs him in the proper acquisition of manhood: 'She saied that neither kyng ne prince, ne lorde could live a right, / Untill their puissance thei did prove, their manhode & their might' (F iv). Yet, the mother's song moves beyond generating ethical subjects, since it also speaks to affective communities open to other experiences. There is a spatial and temporal slippage in the poem that discloses this interpretive openness. The male speaker hears the woman at a distance, from another room, but he locates

---

[106] Elizabeth Harvey, *Ventriloquized Voices: Feminist Theory and English Renaissance Texts* (London: Routledge, 1992), 12.
[107] Terence, *The Woman of Andros*, III.iii.23; Ian Green, *Humanism and Protestantism in Early Modern English Education* (Farnham: Ashgate, 2009), pp. 46, 243.
[108] Miller, 'Mother Tongues', 189–93; see Chapter 3 for further discussion of these tropes, 129–30.
[109] Hamling and Richardson, *A Day at Home*, 8.

54   Books in Process

himself imaginatively in the moment when he narrates something he could not see:

> She sighed sore and sang full sore, to bryng the babe to rest,
> That would not rest but cried still, in suckyng at her brest.
> She was full wearie of her watche, and greued with her child,
> She rocked it and rated it, untill on her it smilde.
>
> (F1v)

The attention given to the prosaic affective interactions between mother and infant relies on and activates primal memories located in sensory experiences and emotions that are heightened by the liminal state of the speaker, who is on the threshold between sleeping and waking. The act of watching here flickers between mother, the baby boy, and the adult male's mind's eye. This openness is amplified in performance. Capable of being sung by men, women, and children, when performed its meanings and the affective communities it fashions are contingent upon local sites of music-making not necessarily anticipated by Edwards or the compilers of *Paradyse*.[110]

The early modern household was capable of being differently inhabited and variously imagined. Whereas the maternal household in Edwards's proverbial poem is figured largely in didactic terms, in the female-voiced complaints 'O Happy dames, that may embrace' (Q1, B4r) and 'Good Ladies, ye that have your pleasures in exile' (Q1, C1v), attributed to Surrey in *Songes and Sonettes*, it is a place for courtly pastimes. These poems are coupled in *Songes and Sonettes* through their title, 'Complaint of the absence of her lover being upon the sea', which heads both poems, inviting a contextual and intertextual reading. I am focusing on these complaints because, like dialogue and answering poems, their acoustic properties are iterative and resonate across poems gathered in anthologies beyond *Songes and Sonettes*, raising broader questions about transmission. The authorship of 'O Happy dames' is not quite settled. One story told about their composition, which derives from Surrey's editor, George Nott, is that Surrey wrote these complaints in the voice of his wife, Frances de Vere, and they are a counterpart to his petitions to Henry VIII to allow his wife and family to join him on his military campaigns in France. This is not the only story that has been told since the copy of 'O Happy dames' in the Devonshire manuscript is in the hand of Surrey's sister, Mary Howard,

---

[110] See Trudell on evanescence and local sites of performance, *Unwritten Poetry*, 21.

Household Recreations 55

Duchess of Richmond.[111] Agencies multiply at every turn. The Devonshire manuscript was a household book, shared between those associated with Anne Boleyn's court. To address these particular issues of composition, Elizabeth Heale puts forward a model of *prosopopoeia* as an alternative to that of authorship, arguing that 'Whether composed by men or by women, in a system of manuscript copying, appropriation and adaptation, the question is less one of the name or gender of an originating author than of the kinds of voices and gestures the available discourses make possible to copiers and readers of both genders.'[112] The 'kinds of voices and gestures' these two female-voiced complaints make available are distinctive, since these are the first complaints in English in which the primary audience is other women, thus re-creating and privileging a female homosociality. One of the effects of these complaints is to give voice and gesture to a desiring female subjectivity that reverberates not just in manuscript but in print and performance cultures because of its distinctive rhetorical and acoustic properties. The speakers of these complaints seek not so much redress as company, bringing the companionate, resonating voice and its affective capacities to the fore.

These complaints achieve this effect through the apostrophe, the rhetorical figure of address, and a near neighbour of *prosopopoeia*, in that it too is a mode of bodying forth in which it is the speaker who gives life to the addressee. The *vocalité* of the figure of apostrophe, in other words its corporeal, sensory aspects, allows us to hear the embodied voice in the text.[113] The opening address to 'Happy dames' and 'Good Ladies' across these complaints embodies their speakers in the company of women. The apostrophe uses the vocative case, from *vocare*, 'to call', which Shane Butler notes 'is remarkable for being a linguistic form that embodies a kind of extra-linguistic performance'.[114] The dialogue between the speaking subject and addressee is carried across from internal to external auditors, who are thus transformed into potential interlocutors. In these complaints, apostrophe dramatises performative communities and opens out their

---

[111] Jonathan Goldberg identifies the hand as that of Mary Shelton (*Desiring Women Writing: English Renaissance Examples* [Stanford University Press, 1997], 153); however, the consensus is that it is that of Mary Howard; see Helen Baron, 'Mary (Howard) Fitzroy's Hand in the Devonshire Manuscript', *RES*, 45 (1994), 318–35.

[112] Elizabeth Heale, *Wyatt, Surrey, and Early Tudor Poetry* (London: Longman, 1998), 45.

[113] Gavin Alexander, '*Prosopopoeia*', in *Renaissance Figures of Speech*, edited by Sylvia Adamson, Gavin Alexander, and Katrin Ettenhuber (Cambridge University Press, 2007), 107–9; Mark Robson, *The Sense of Early Modern Writing: Rhetoric, Poetics, Aesthetics* (Manchester University Press, 2006), 137; Butler, *Ancient Phonograph*, 16.

[114] Butler, *Ancient Phonograph*, 68.

56   Books in Process

authorship and acoustics to other participants. As such, they perform the
conditions of their own re-creative imitation. By recognising the work of
this rhetorical figure, we can see how the Ovidianism of these complaints is
translated within performance cultures. One of the models for 'O Happy
dames' and 'Good Ladies' is certainly Ovidian: their speakers bring
together the figures of Penelope awaiting the return of her Ulysses from
across the seas and Dido watching Aeneas' departing sails. Ovid's heroines
are 'bookish' and tell stories of writing and reading.[115] Yet, this is not the
only situation of the speakers of 'O Happy dames' and 'Good Ladies' since
they are not so much writing girls, as singing and dancing ladies, equally at
home in late medieval dance songs, and whose pastimes are key to the
figurations of voice and gesture in these complaints.

The frames to both 'O Happy dames' and 'Good Ladies' are remarkably
similar in their deictic modes of address, which create an embodied
spatiality:[116]

> O Happy dames, that may embrace
> The frute of your delight,
> Help to bewaile the wofull case,
> And eke the heavy plight
> Of me, that wonted to rejoice
> The fortune of my pleasant choyce:
> Good Ladies, help to fill my moorning voice.
>
> (Q1, B4r)

> Good Ladies, ye that have your pleasures in exile,
>   Step in your fote, come take a place, & moorne with me a while
>   And such as by their lordes do set but little price,
>   Let them sit still: it skilles them not what chance come on ye dice.
>   But ye whom love hath bound by ordre of desire
>   To love your lords, whose good deserts none other wold require:
>   Come ye yet ones again, and set your foote by mine.
>
> (Q1, C1v)

These lamenting women sing in company, inviting other like-minded
ladies to join them in the song and in the dance. The space of these
performances is the elite household, a courtly, feminised space, defined by
pastimes – singing, dancing, and games, playing at dice. The opening

---

[115] Reid, *Ovidian Bibliofictions*, 3.
[116] See Heather Dubrow's study, *Deixis in the Early Modern Lyric* (Basingstoke: Palgrave
Macmillan, 2015).

Household Recreations 57

invitation re-creates a performative community, bringing the 'Happy dames' and 'Good Ladies' into physical, temporal, and affective proximity with the speaker. Their emotional states may differ in 'O Happy dames', given their 'delight' contrasts with her 'heavy plight', yet she gathers them to 'me', through the remembrance of her 'pleasant choyce', and asks them to add their voice to hers to give succour, 'help to fill my moorning voice'. 'Good Ladies' specifically imagines its performance as a dance song. Auditors are divided into those who are physically and emotionally aligned to the singer and invited to follow her steps in the dance, and those others, outside this affective community, who are instructed to sit out the dance. 'Good Ladies' is all about the motion and emotion: 'Come ye yet ones again, and set your foote by mine'.

The songs these ladies and dames sing in consort is domestic and erotic, describing a variant acoustic field to the maternal household imagined in 'In goyng to my naked bedde'. Their speakers are figured as actively desiring subjects. In 'O Happy dames', the speaker fantasises about others' sexual embraces at night: 'When other lovers in armes acrosse, / Rejoyce their chiefe delight' (B4r). Both songs use temporal and spatial displacements, playing with memory by featuring dream sequences of erotic and domestic longing that flicker between presence and consummation, and absence and lack. One dream in 'Good Ladies' is a domestic scene, full of pathos, in which the speaker finds her beloved 'playeng ... with his faire little sonne'; when he expresses concern for her welfare, 'my dere, how is it now, that you have all thys paine?' (C2r), she wakes crying with relief that quickly turns to anguish. The domestic realm of the companionate marriage depicted in these complaints is eroticised, dependent on the mutuality of desire, and invested with an emotional intensity and intimacy. This state is fragile and rendered highly provisional through the disjunctive shifts between past and present, here and there, proximity and distance, encapsulated in the closing line of 'O Happy dames' given over to desire and doubt: 'Now he comes, will he come? alas, no no' (B4v).

'O Happy dames' was set to the keyboards by John Shepherd; this setting was copied by Mulliner into his songbook, which we may remember also included Edwards's household song, 'In goyng to my naked bedde'. These different household songs shared the same performance spaces where they were open to acts of re-creation. The Shepherd setting is polyphonic, in four parts; as is characteristic for this type of music, it allows for 'more verbal material than' the written poem, which means that the verse is amplified and re-created through performance, with 'single words, whole lines, or phrases' repeated, as Ivy Mumford explained, some

58   Books in Process

'more than once, when the poem is sung'.[117] Singers understood their performance in terms of improvisation and re-creation, rather than straightforward interpretation. Both composers and singers were advised, in the words of Giovanni del Lago, to 'consider carefully ... which affections of the soul they should move with that song'. In order to move the affections of auditors and to 'imprint a passion in another', vocalists must fully inhabit this state themselves, embodied in voice, eyes, and gesture.[118] Not surprisingly, songs were considered a mode of *prosopopoeia* in this period. The 'singer feigns' the emotions of the character imagined in the lyrics, employing techniques of delivery to move the audience to the emotional state figured in the lyrics.[119]

Both 'O Happy dames' and 'Good Ladies' are engaged in complex reflections on these re-creative properties of performance. These songs are explicitly pastimes, lyrics about passing the time while awaiting the return of the beloved; the speaker frames her song in relation to other women, not simply as passive auditors but as co-performers, who sympathise with her state and will be moved by her words to accompany her in song and the dance. Female auditors are invited to become co-creators of the song, to incorporate their own affective experience into the act of performing the lyric, to 'help to fill my moorning voyce' and, in the case of the dance-song 'Good Ladies', to 'Step in your foote, come take a place, & moorne with me a while', figuring forth an embodied space in which voices resonate and bodies are in motion. The company of women addressed and brought into being by the speaker and her song are drawn together by affective bonds, sharing and moved by the same passions. Of course, the vocal properties of complaint do not rely solely on its delivery as song, since both singing and reading aloud shared the same rhetorical methods of delivery.[120] That said, arguably music does enhance pathos, even when it functions at a figurative level in complaint. By this, I mean those instances in which complaints deploy a vocabulary of song that then functions as a generic marker, inflecting the operation of pathos in the song and supercharging *prosopopoeia*, amplifying its re-creative and emotional properties. The vividness with which these complaints invited and dramatised performative communities opened out their re-creative properties to other performance cultures outside the elite household. Ballads in

---

[117] Ivy Lilian Mumford, 'Musical Settings to the Poems of Henry Howard, Earl of Surrey', *English Miscellany*, 8 (1957), 16–17.
[118] Cited in Robert Toft, *With Passionate Voice: Re-creative Singing in 16th-Century England and Italy* (Oxford University Press, 2014), 10.
[119] Ibid., 201.   [120] Ibid., 6.

Household Recreations 59

the mid-sixteenth century respond to and re-create the invitation to 'good ladies', including 'The complaint of a woman Lover' published in *A Handefull of Pleasant Delites* (*c.* 1566), which, as we shall see in the following chapter, was answered by Whitney's 'Admonition' in *Copy of a Letter*.[121]

The use of song to facilitate intrapersonal affective relationships can be more complicated than the model of *prosopopoeia* set out in manuals suggests. Whythorne writes of using songs to broker his relationships with women in the households where he was employed, both fellow servants and employers. Whythorne insisted that his education and gentle status distinguished him from other employees, claiming that music teachers within the household 'may esteem so much of themselves as to be free and not bound, much less to be made slave-like'.[122] His elevated under-standing of his status encouraged Whythorne to court one of his employers, a well-to-do widow. The performance of love songs, the medium through which Whythorne sought to test the affections of his employer, rather than a straightforward performance of desire, offered a sophisticated medium of negotiation. He writes of music as a form of communication that has the capacity to 'draw the mind of the hearer to be more attentive to the song', creating an affective proximity and intimacy. Yet, since the lyrics are re-created, they are not quite his own, 'for singing of such songs and ditties was a thing common in those days'; the emotion expressed, since conventional and generic, therefore can be disavowed and set off from his own desires.[123] An internal distance is established that renders their meaning and performance uncertain, illustrating how perfor-mances are always negotiable, contingent upon local encounters.

Other responses to the recreative properties of the poems gathered in *Songes and Sonettes* were not so receptive to these uses of amorous songs. When John Hall read *Songes and Sonettes* alongside the *Court of Venus* in his own anthology, *Courte of Vertue* (1565), he objected precisely to such courtly songs. His *Courte of Vertue* is a godly response to the burgeoning trade in ballads and vernacular books of poetry, especially those anthologies of songs and sonnets currently available on the London bookstalls:

> Suche as in carnall love rejoyce,
> Trim songes of love they wyll compile,
> And synfully with tune and voyce
> They syng their songes in pleasant stile,

---

[121] See Chapter 2, 83–6. [122] Whythorne, *Autobiography*, 46.
[123] Ibid., 40; Nelson, 'Love in the Music Room', 18–22.

60   Books in Process

To Venus that same strompet vyle:
And make of hir a goddes dere,
In lecherie that had no pere.

A booke also of songes they have,
And Venus court they doe it name.
No fylthy mynde a songe can crave,
But therin he may finde the same:
And in such songes is all there game.
Whereof ryght dyuers bookes be made,
To nuryshe that moste fylthy trade.[124]

Hall's use of the verb 'compile' initially refers not so much to the activity of gathering verse from various sources into a book – anthology-making – but to practices of composition and re-creation, especially the making of songs to be set to tunes and sung in mixed company when at leisure. This activity then carries across to the next stanza where Hall does address compilations, the 'booke also of songes they have'. The specific reference seems to be to *The Court of Venus*, but it can incorporate that other book, *Songes and Sonettes*. In these volumes, compilers can find material, 'such songes', that are intended solely for pleasure and diversion, in other words, for ungodly recreation. Hall's *The Courte of Vertue* was published in 1565, the same year that a further edition of *Songes and Sonettes* appeared – the last known edition of *Court of Venus* had been printed a few years earlier, in 1563. In fact, both Hall's songbook and *The Court of Venus* were put out by the same publisher, Thomas Marsh, and so both were available in his stock. Publishing both *Courte of Vertue* and *Court of Venus* allowed Marsh to capitalise on these books of songs, offering buyers alternatives, and piquing their interest in those other 'Trim songes of love' Hall writes of at the front of his book. Hall's avowed aim was to reform this growing market for songs performed during leisure hours by providing more godly versions for household recreation. Before *The Courte of Vertue*, Hall had been penning moralising ballads in the early 1560s which similarly condemned the 'filthy toyes' produced by fellow ballad writers.[125] The ongoing response and counter-response helped to shape and stimulate this market for recreational poetry.

Hall set out to compile a songbook. *The Courte of Vertue* prints simple strophic settings to many of the poems; for those without settings, instructions are included that point the reader to the music to which it should be

---

[124] John Hall, *The Courte of Vertue* (1565), B5v-6r.
[125] John Hall, *The Court of Virtue* (1565), ed. Russell A. Fraser (London: Routledge and Kegan Paul, 1961), xiii.

Household Recreations 61

sung, for example, in the case of 'A song of the lute in prayse of God', the performer is directed to 'Syng this as, My pen obey. &c.' (M3r). Others do not point the reader to settings, but still have the capacity to be sung. Hall was fully immersed in the reformed musical tradition represented by Thomas Sternhold's metrical version of the psalms; his own versions of the psalms were printed alongside those of Sternhold, Wyatt, and Hunnis in 1551.[126] The settings provided in *Courte of Vertue*, with their simple 'restricted rhythmical formulae', are in keeping with the musicality of metrical psalms and produce a reformed soundscape that is open to those without any formal music training.[127] The songs provide matter for the godly household, generating and marking out its acoustic field. Hall includes a set of songs versifying Juan Lodovicus Vives's *Introduction to Wisdom*, designed to regulate behaviour, dress, and manners.[128] Even a humble household object, the birch broom or besom, is given its own song in which the disciplinary uses of its various components – the twigs, the haft – are related in detail, from whipping the 'buttockes of boyes' (S3r) to hanging thieves 'by the necke': 'Besides that for which most men do them kepe, / Namely theyr kitchens or houses to swepe', these brooms dispense punishments that 'Either good or dead they wyll hym sure make' (S3v).

When Hall turns to reforming and re-creating Wyatt's lyrics, he does so in similarly homely godly fashion. He composes moralising sacred parodies of Wyatt's 'Blame not my lute', 'My lute awake', and 'My pen take pain'. It is unclear whether 'Blame not my lute' was available in *The Court of Venus*, given we are left with only fragments of this anthology – there is a contemporary lute setting – the other two appear in this collection, with 'My lute awake' also printed in *Songes and Sonettes*.[129] Hall admired Wyatt. One of Hall's songs was printed alongside Surrey's epitaph for Wyatt in a commemorative pamphlet published in 1545.[130] When Hall recrafts Wyatt's verse, he either keeps the first line, for example, 'Blame not my lute though it doe sounde', or retains the opening phrase, in the case of 'My lute awake', then echoing the rest of Wyatt's line alliteratively, so that 'perform the last' becomes 'praise the lord', or he simply keeps just the

---

[126] *Psalmes of Dauid drawen into English metre by Tomas Sterneholde* (1551).
[127] John Stevens, *Music and Poetry in the Early Tudor Court* (Cambridge University Press, 1961), 125–6.
[128] *An Introduction to Wysedom, made by Ludovicus Vives. Wherein is plentiful matter for al estates to governe the[m]selues by ... Translated into Englyshe, by Richard Moryson* (c. 1540).
[129] Ivy L. Mumford, 'Musical Settings to the Poems of Sir Thomas Wyatt', *Music and Letters*, 37 (1956), 315–22.
[130] *An excellent epitaffe of syr Thomas wyat* (1545). Warner, *Making and Marketing*, 194–6, 204–5.

62 Books in Process

opening words 'My pen'. All act as audible prompts that alert the performer and auditor to the source poem. The Wyatt poems chosen by Hall
address the physical instruments of expression and creativity – lutes and
pens – the twinned instruments of the musician's and the poet's craft. In
Hall's *Courte of Vertue*, pens and lutes take their place alongside brooms
and other prosaic objects within a godly household. When Hall sets about
purging Wyatt's poems of amorous desire, he is a more responsive reader
than this might suggest. His reformed lyrics consistently cast courtly love
as sinful, warning in 'Blame not my lute' that 'some also abuse the lute /
With sinfull songes of lechery' (M2r), and in 'My lute awake' that 'This
plesant song shall not song be, / To the goddesse of lechery' (M2v). What
he takes over from Wyatt and re-creates is the lute as an instrument of
plain-speaking, truth-telling, and admonition and the antagonism the male
lover expresses towards his mistress. Wyatt's speaker in 'Blame not my
lute' angrily indicts his mistress for her petulance:

> Blame but thyself that has misdone
> And well deserved to have blame,
> Change thou thy way so evil begun
> And then my lute shall sound the same.[131]

His love complaint relies on a mistress who deserves blame and requires
reformation. The anger directed at the mistress does violence to the
language of courtly love, refuting its idealising rhetoric, and turning
instead to invective. Hall takes over and redirects this hostility to admonish
a fallen public in urgent need of reform:

> Blame not my lute, nor blame not me,
> Although it sound against your sinne:
> But rather seeke for to be free,
> From suche abuse as ye are in.
>
> (M2v)

Wyatt's lute is borrowed in service of the Protestant cause. It is still a
disciplinary instrument, but in Hall's hands its song is one of religious
chastisement that can be accommodated within and give strict guidance to
the household devotions of the middling sort.

Hall recognised the efficacy of poetry-as-song in forging religious and
affective communities that make up a wider reformed public. Music-
making within the household brought its participants together into col-
lectivities and animated communities. The songs performed within those

---

[131] Wyatt, *Poems*, 130: XCIV.

Songes and Sonettes *and the Ballad Trade* 63

households imagined in *Songes and Sonettes* and *Paradyse* took various forms, from amorous complaints to proverbial and reformist songs. The female-voiced complaints 'O Happy dames' and 'Good Ladies' imagine a courtly and leisured household space in which affective intrapersonal bonds are prioritised, whereas Edwards's proverbial lyric, 'In goyng to my naked bedde', is more homely and prosaic, and its household the locus of moral instruction. When Wyatt's courtly songs are recrafted by Hall, their acoustics are similarly re-created to speak to and bring into being a godly community that is markedly more demotic. The multimodality of anthologies, like *Songes and Sonettes* and *Paradyse*, meant that the poems gathered in their pages moved freely between elite and non-elite performance cultures, thus opening these books to socially diverse communities. When we attend to poetry's re-creative properties, then evidence emerges for an English vernacular poetic tradition that is socially varied and thoroughly protean.

Songes and Sonettes **and the Ballad Trade: 'When Ragyng Love' and 'I lothe that I did love'**

The history of the broadside ballad is bound up with that of the poetry anthology within the wider market for vernacular poetry in the mid-sixteenth century.[132] Poems moved in and out of *Songes and Sonettes* and *Paradyse of Daynty Devises* through the broadside ballad trade. Two of John Canand's ballads, 'By fortune as I lay in bed' and 'O evill tounges, which clap at everie wynd', which had been printed in *Songes and Sonettes*, later appeared in a little compilation of ballads published as a broadside by Andrew Lacy in 1566. Here, they are placed alongside Bernard Garter's 'Who trusts before he tries' to make up a little garland of moralising ballads, a different, yet related compilation to the poetry anthology in which they had appeared almost a decade earlier and was still available on the bookstalls.[133] Surrey's 'When ragyng love' and Lord Thomas Vaux's 'I lothe that I did love' have other lives as ballads that illustrate the hybridity of vernacular lyric poetry in this period. Both proved very mobile, travelling across various locales in ways which illuminate the

---

[132] See also Eric Nebeker, 'Broadside Ballads, Miscellanies, and the Lyric in Print', *English Literary History*, 76 (2009), 989–1013.

[133] Carole Rose Livingston, *British Broadside Ballads of the Sixteenth Century: a Catalogue of the Extant Sheets and an Essay* (New York: Garland, 1991), 289. Lacy had previously paid for separate licences for the two longer ballads, Canand's 'By Fortune as I lay in bed' and Bernard Garter's 'When that Apelles lived in Greece', and therefore may have also issued them as separate broadsides.

64   Books in Process

richness and diversity of non-elite vernacular performance cultures in this period.[134]

The case of 'When ragyng love' is especially intriguing since it circulates in various parodies that are akin to Hall's recrafting of Wyatt's lyrics in the *Courte of Vertue*. Why did Surrey's 'When ragyng love' attract this degree of re-creation across successive ballads? One answer takes us to those practices of composition that are attentive to extra-linguistic prosodic properties and hence to a poetic materiality that is embodied in sound and through the voice.[135] The musical features of 'When ragyng love' are manifold. Composed in the form of the sextilla, a traditional Spanish ballad stanza made up of octosyllabic lines rhyming ababcc, it was set to music, shared its opening phrase with a ballad tune, and was admired by Puttenham for the musicality of its metre.[136] He drew attention to its opening line in his *Art of English Poesy* more than any other poem from *Songes and Sonettes*. The first four lines are cited as an example of how to build metres out of mono-, bi-, and polysyllables, and is 'passing sweet and harmonical', and pleasing to the ear, because of the skilful breaking of bisyllables:

> When raging love, with extreme pain,
> Most cruelly doth strain my heart,
> And that the tears like floods of rain
> Bear witness of my woeful smart.[137]

The acoustics of Surrey's ballad move fluidly between European and native vernacular forms. The form is continental, but the distinctive vocal patterning of the four-stress line, the mid-line caesura on alternate lines, and alliteration and assonance, all derive from native traditions.[138] Parodies of 'When ragyng love' always retain the verse form, the sextilla, and much of the vocal patterning, even as the words and general meaning are radically changed. What this tells us is that this poem had a distinctive sound that was part of its performative appeal.

---

[134] Stephen Hamrick, '"Their Gods in Verses": the Popular Reception of *Songes and Sonettes*, 1557–1674', in *Tottel's Songes and Sonettes in Context*, ed. Hamrick (Farnham: Ashgate, 2013), 163. Other poems published in *Songes and Sonettes* were registered as broadsides in the late 1550s and early 1560s: Surrey's 'In winter's just return' and 'When youth had led me', John Heywood's 'Give place you Ladies', Lord Thomas Vaux's 'When Cupid scaled first the fort', and the anonymous ballads, 'Phyllida was a fair maid' and 'Who loves to live in peace'.
[135] On the musical quality of metre, see Butler, *Ancient Phonograph*, 105–7.
[136] A musical setting is included in the Braye lute book, compiled around 1570, Yale Osborn Music MS 13. Sessions describes the poem as an 'extended *frottola*', an Italian song form, in *Henry Howard*, 178. Surrey's poem was not sung to the tune 'Raging Love'; see Chapter 2, 83–4.
[137] Puttenham, *Art of English Poesy*, 208, 216.   [138] Sessions, *Henry Howard*, 180.

Songes and Sonettes *and the Ballad Trade*   65

At least three ballads parodying 'When ragyng love' were produced in the sixteenth century. The most sophisticated of these is the 'newe balade', which claims in its title to have been 'made by Nicholas Balthorpe which suffered in Calys the xv. daie of marche M.D.L.' Balthorpe appears to have been a soldier serving in the garrison at Calais, and it is possible that this ballad was first composed around 15 March 1550, in response to the surrender of Boulogne, in the Pays de Calais, to the French in that year, which would mean that Surrey's 'When ragyng love' was circulating widely in the late 1540s.[139] However, it is also possible that this ballad was prompted both by the publication of *Songes and Sonettes* in 1557 and, more particularly, by the siege and catastrophic fall of Calais in January 1558.[140] The Balthorpe ballad translates 'When ragyng love' into the language of Protestantism. Its reading of Surrey's complaint concentrates on the trauma of the Trojan war, the 'longe time warre of valiant men'. The ballad responds to the question posed by 'When ragyng love' about a 'life well spent... / Servying a worthier wight' (Q1, B3v) by confirming the value of service to a reformed God. In doing so, the Balthorpe ballad writes women out of Surrey's lyric and its mode of complaint. This is a poem of spiritual comfort composed on the eve of battle as the speaker reconciles himself to death in the *ars moriendi* tradition. The emphasis on *sola fide*, salvation only though faith in God's grace, is that of the reformer. There is no call to pray for his soul when dead, although his audience can 'praie for me whiles I do live'; instead, the speaker calls on others to bear witness to his death, turning himself into an exemplum for the reformed faith. He has no need for the intercession of the saints, only God's mercy:

> Beare record now ye Christians al
> That seethe the ende of this mi life
> For helpe to none of you I cal
> But vnto God for mercie rife
> But this to you I calle and crye
> Witnes a christian do I die.[141]

Surrey's complaint is remade into a ballad of religious martyrdom with a strident reformist emphasis on the steadfastness of the speaker's faith in God's grace in the face of death.

---

[139] The licensing of broadsides only began to be recorded in the Stationers' Register in 1557; the ballad was entered in the first year of registration.
[140] C. S. L. Davies, 'England and the French War, 1557–59', in *The Mid-Tudor Polity, c. 1540–1560*, edited by Jennifer Loach and Robert Tittler (London: Macmillan, 1980), 159, 179.
[141] Nicolas Balthorpe, *A Newe Balade made by Nicholas Balthorp which suffered in Calys the .xv. daie of marche* (1557).

66   Books in Process

When re-creating 'When ragyng love', the Balthorpe ballad clearly echoes its musicality. The sextilla is retained, and a further seven stanzas added. The first stanza, especially the first line, is key to setting the acoustics of the ballad since it establishes the shared soundscape with Surrey's poem:

> When raging death with extreme paine
> Most cruelly assaultes my herte
> And when my fleshe although in vaine
> Doth feare the felinge of that smarte
> For when the swerde will stop mi brethe
> Then am I at the poynt of deathe.

John Stevens notes how 'moralized versions of courtly and of popular song' use 'the first words in an unmistakable way both to point to a moral and to point out a tune'.[142] The Balthorpe ballad carries over the four-stress line, the alliteration, the alternate mid-caesura breaks, and rhyme words from Surrey's poem, both in the first stanzas and in the A rhyme of the second stanza, whereby Surrey's great/beate becomes greate/sweat. By changing the key phrase 'ragyng love' to 'raging death', the ballad begins the process of reforming and thereby silencing the hyperbolic Petrarchanism of Surrey's poem through a moralising plainness that locates the speaker's experience in the concrete. 'Most cruelly distrains my hart' (B3v) is converted to 'Most cruelly assaultes my herte', making physical sense of the violence of the following lines which describe the speaker's fears of having his flesh pierced and his breath stopped by 'the swerde', not through the pains of love. The Balthorpe ballad echoes the soundscape of Surrey's poem, including its affective properties, but radically recasts its meaning and redirects its pathos to godly ends.

The reformist reworking of Surrey's 'When ragyng love' in the Balthorpe ballad is akin to Hall's parodies of Wyatt's love poems and illustrates how amatory verse could be reworked to provide a repertoire of Protestant poetry suitable for performance in godly households and other reformed locales. The Balthorpe ballad was followed by other moralisations of Surrey's 'When ragyng love' that are similarly attentive to its musicality and introduce a tone of godly admonition. A ballad beginning 'When Ragyng dethe doth drawe his darte', and attributed to 'sponer', survives in a manuscript book (Bodleian MS Ashmole 48) compiled entirely of ballads. Attributions to ballad composers and performers are

---

[142] Stevens, *Music and Poetry*, 125

Songes and Sonettes *and the Ballad Trade* 67

often recorded – 'expliceth quoth Rychard Sheale' or 'q^{u}od lord Vawes' or just 'Sponer'. Anonymity was not necessarily a characteristic feature of ballads and non-elite literary cultures. Certain ballad writers, like Sheale, Spooner, and William Elderton, gained fame as either performers or composers or both. This manuscript book is a rare example of a collection composed entirely of ballads, often recording names of composer-performers, which raises questions about the circumstances of its composition. One possibility is that it belonged to a minstrel, probably more than one, given the different hands in which the ballads are copied, and was used in performance; another is that its compilers were collecting ballads for printing as broadsides; or it could have begun as the former, and ended as the latter. In any case, the collection records the movement of ballads along trade routes as they made their way in and out of London and across the country, as well as those points of intersection between travelling minstrels and the London broadside ballad trade. Richard Sheale, whose name is recorded at the end of ballads in the collection, was a minstrel attached to the Stanley family as well as travelling the country as a pedlar and ballad-singer and supplying ballads for the London market.[143] One of his ballads copied into Ashmole 48, 'O god what a world ys this now to se', uses an event from his own life to provide the subject of a moralising song that laments a wider social fragmentation. His song relates how he was robbed on the road, when travelling as a ballad-singer and pedlar with his wife, a silk woman. Particular attention is given to conveying the devastating emotional impact of this event, when 'I colde neathar syng nor talke my wyttes wer so dismayde'.[144] It is a striking example of a mode of versifying that weaves the texture of non-elite life into song that is then re-created in different locales as Sheale travels the country performing his ballad.

Henry Spooner was probably also a minstrel, like Sheale, who travelled the country, performing in noble houses as well as inns and other local, communal spaces. His ballads feature prominently in Ashmole 48 – twelve are attributed to Spooner, one of the few authors named in the collection. Most of his ballads are moral and religious. Three use the Spanish ballad

---

[143] On Sheale and Ashmole 48, see Andrew Taylor, *The Songs and Travels of a Tudor Minstrel: Richard Sheale of Tamworth* (York: York Medieval Press, 2012); Michael Chesnutt, 'Minstrel Poetry in an English Manuscript of the Sixteenth Century: Richard Sheale and MS Ashmole 48', in *The Entertainer in Medieval and Traditional Culture: a Symposium*, edited by Flemming G. Anderson, Thomas Pettitt, and Reinhold Schröde (Odense University Press, 1997), 73–100; H. E. Rollins, 'Concerning Bodleian MS Ashmole 48', *MLN*, 34 (1919), 340–51.

[144] Bod. MS Ashmole 48, 95v.

68   Books in Process

form, the sextilla – the Surrey parody, 'When Ragyng dethe doth drawe his
darte', 'I wyll not paynt to purchase prayse', a song in praise of music that
also advocates the education of girls, and 'A songe Exortinge to the laude of
God' (Ashmole 48, 64–6r, 5–6v, 66–7v). Spooner's 'When Ragyng dethe'
shares with the Balthorpe ballad the *ars moriendi* theme of 'raging death',
suggesting that it, rather than Surrey's ballad, is Spooner's model. The
Spooner ballad swells the twelve stanzas of the Balthorpe ballad to sixteen
which proffer a litany of examples of how death comes to all regardless
(Ashmole 48, 65v).

     There is one further known ballad that riffs on Surrey's 'When ragyng
love', and that is William Fulwood's 'A New Ballad against unthrifts',
entered in the Stationers' Register in 1561/2 by John Allde along with
Fulwood's monstrous birth ballad advertising 'straunge monstrous sightes'
as God's warning to the godly to keep them on their toes, and, lastly, an
entry in the ballad war with William Elderton, 'A supplication to
Eldertonne', that calls on him to leave his 'filthy rymes' and 'wicked
toyes'.[145] Fulwood, a member of the Merchant Taylors' Company,
belonged to an urban mercantile community and his reforming ballads
speak to this civic culture. Like Hall's *Courte of Vertue* and the parodies of
Surrey, Fulwood's 'New Ballad against unthrifts' is directed to a readership
for godly admonitory verse, turning Surrey's poem into a mundane
complaint against excessive spending: 'When raging louts with feble
braines / moste wilfully wyl spend awaye'. Compared with Balthorpe's
ballad, its response to Surrey's ballad seems perfunctory. And yet, like
Balthorpe, Fulwood responds to Surrey's ballad at the level of form,
re-creating the rhetorical and prosodic frame of 'When ragyng love'.
Surrey's poem is an example of persuasive writing, what Puttenham
termed '*etiologia* or the Reason-renderer', which enables the speaker to
'fortify allegations by rendering reasons to everyone' and is often used in
amorous verse.[146] The confirmatives that open each stanza – 'when', 'I call
to minde', 'And how', ' Then thinke', and the concluding 'Therefore' – are
recast in Fulwood's ballad – 'When' opens the first six stanzas setting out
examples of moral turpitude, 'Then' opens the next six stanzas relating the
consequences of such prodigality, and finally the 'Wherefore' of the last
stanza sets out the moral. Fulwood is remaking Surrey's ballad through a
pragmatic mode of imitation, responding to it as a model for composing

---

[145] William Fulwood, *A Supplication to Eldertonne* (1562); H. R. Rollins, 'William Elderton:
     Elizabethan Actor and Ballad-Writer', *Studies in Philology*, 17, 2 (1920), 213.
[146] Puttenham, *Art of English Poesy*, 313.

Songes and Sonettes *and the Ballad Trade* 69

and building verse through units of sound and sense.[147] Early modern culture sustained a variety of modes of imitation that were not confined to the written word, but operated across different media and through an array of performance cultures. The result was a rich and mobile body of vernacular literature.

The poems of Lord Thomas Vaux in *Songes and Sonettes*, 'When Cupid first scaled the fort' and 'I lothe that I did love', like Surrey's 'When ragyng love', travelled easily between various performance cultures. 'I lothe that I did love' was set to the lute, can be found amongst a minstrel's repertoire in Ashmole 48, was printed as a broadside, lent its first line to the name of a ballad tune, and was sung on stage during Shakespeare's *Hamlet*.[148] Puttenham listed Vaux alongside the 'courtly makers', Surrey and Wyatt, albeit mistaking him for his father, Nicholas, and praised him for his 'facility in vulgar makings'. He particularly commended 'When Cupid first scaled the fort'. While Puttenham makes no mention of Vaux's 'I lothe that I did love', it too exemplifies the metrical skills of Vaux that he admired. Composed in iambs, it is a very good example of the interlacing of monosyllables and bisyllables that Puttenham praised so effusively in Surrey's 'When ragyng love' for its musicality.[149] While its musicality may account for its popularity as song, its topic also speaks to a taste for moralising poetry. 'I lothe that I did love' balances anacreontic mourning for passing youth, for the 'lusty life' that 'away she leapes, / As there had bene none such' (x3r), with the rejection of earthly pleasure as the speaker moves towards death in the *ars moriendi* tradition. In Ashmole 48, where the verse is attributed to 'lord Vawes', it is followed by a similarly sombre ballad from *Songes and Sonettes*, 'The lyf ys longe y^t lothesomlye dothe last' (37v). Both ballads concentrate on fleeting, ephemeral wordly pleasures and the inevitability of death. Alongside Spooner's parody, 'When Ragyng dethe', the acoustics of these ballads give shape to a sober, devotional culture.

'I lothe that I did love' was performed by professional minstrels who travelled the country and in households able to afford musical instruments and lessons, where it was copied into manuscript songbooks. At the end of a carefully crafted manuscript book (British Library Additional MS 4900) is a compilation of songs copied either by a skilled amateur or by a

---

[147] Knight, *Bound to Read*, 94–5.
[148] Claude M. Simpson, *The British Broadside Ballad and its Music* (New Brunswick: Rutgers University Press, 1966), 340–1.
[149] Puttenham, *Art of English Poesy*, 150, 325, 216.

70 Books in Process

professional musician working in the household, like Whythorne or Mulliner. This is a highly crafted household book, an object of value like the 'best corrected' songbook Katherine retrieved from the chest in Hollybande's *French Schoolemaster*. Great care is taken with copying, and the book has been embellished through the addition of decorative features such as small woodcuts cut out from printed books and used to ornament the page. The layout of the book is intended for performance in the household. On the verso of the preceding page, the musical setting and lyrics of 'I lothe that I did love' are written upside down and then right way up on the facing page. This layout means that two or more performers could use the book at the same time, facing each other across the open pages. The music book thus brings singers into physical proximity during the performance, helping to create affective bonds between performers.[150] 'I lothe that I did love' is one of three songs copied in a set: the first is a love song, 'My lytell prety one / my pretie boni one / she is a joylie one', the second a love complaint, 'What cause have I for to rejoyce' that ends 'Destroie me not', and the third is 'I lothe that I did love' (62v–63).[151] These are the type of 'Trim songes of love' that drew Hall's reforming zeal. However, there is a further complexity to the performance context of these lyrics. The woodcut pasted on to the bottom corner of the page is an ornamental figure – an attractive female grotesque, naked to the waist (see Figure 2). The sensory interplay between the visual ornament and the *vocalité* of the songs both is a reminder of the moral dangers of desire – the corruption lurking behind beauty – and carries its own erotic charge.

Like many other ballads, Vaux's song made its way on to the stage, where it was sung by the Gravedigger as he digs Ophelia's grave in Act 5, scene 1 of Shakespeare's *Hamlet*. Ballads made up the demotic soundscape of the early modern playhouse and the wider urban environment. Sung on stage by actors and sold and performed by ballad-sellers on the streets outside the theatres, ballads may have also made their way into the playhouse in the packs of hawkers among the other ware on sale to assembled playgoers.[152] The performance of Vaux's song in the

---

[150] Scott Trudell, 'Performing Women in English Books of Ayres', in *Gender and Song in Early Modern England*, edited by Leslie C. Dunn and Katherine R. Larson (Farnham: Ashgate, 2014), 18–19.

[151] The Vaux poem is also found with a lute setting in a songbook that was similarly copied by either a skilled amateur or a professional, and given the title 'Certaine pretie Songes hereafter following Drawn together by Richard Shawe. 16ii', BL Add. MS 38599, fol. 133v.

[152] On the pamphlets and other textual material on sale at playhouses, see Tiffany Stern, 'Watching as Reading: the Written Text in Shakespeare's Playhouse', in *How to Do Things with Shakespeare*, edited Laurie Maguire (Oxford: Blackwell, 2008), 139–40.

Songes and Sonettes *and the Ballad Trade* 71

Figure 2   British Library, Add. MS 4900, Banks Collection, fol. 62v.

72   Books in Process

Gravedigger scene offers a reflection on the textual and social malleability of ballads as they travel across various acoustic fields. The variants introduced in the Gravedigger's song result from a process of re-creation that is responsive to the rhythms and objects of a working life:

> But age with his stealing steps
> Hath clawed me in his clutch
> And hath shipped me into the land
> As if I had never been such.
> (*Hamlet* 5.1.67–70)

The Gravedigger combines two stanzas from Vaux's song, singing a variant of the first two lines, 'For age with stelyng steppes, / Hath clawed me with his cowche', then substituting a line from elsewhere, 'And shipped me into the land', before returning to the fourth line 'As there had been none such' (*Songes and Sonettes*, Q1, x3r). Shakespeare is not so much presenting the audience with a 'corrupt' text, resulting from a chaotic and unreliable popular memory; instead this is a lyric that has been carefully re-crafted through the tools and rhythms of the working life. The Gravedigger's 'clutch' draws attention to his manual work, the physical action of digging the earth or 'land' for the body that will be 'shipped . . . into the land', and makes a neat verbal and visual segue to the next snatch of song, which begins with the Gravedigger invoking the tools of his labour – 'A pickaxe and a spade, a spade', which echoes Vaux's stanza beginning 'A pickax and a spade' (x3v).

Vaux's 'I lothe that I did love' was able to move in very different social company – from the sober devotional ballads performed by minstrels to the intimacies of songs sung during household performances and into the demotic worlds of the playhouse. It was a mobility shared with other poems gathered in anthologies and reveals how the re-creative affordances of ballads were activated and recalibrated locally and variously across the diverse social worlds of early modern England. The Gravedigger's song in *Hamlet* returns us to Sheale's ballad in which he sings of the travails of his working life and looks forward to Isabella Whitney's mode of poetic making discussed in Chapter 2, which similarly turns to the everyday world of work for its poetic matter. Tracing the way that poems in anthologies are recrafted and re-created as they move through diverse acoustic worlds opens these books to other rich histories of poetic making.

CHAPTER 2

Household Books
Richard Jones, Isabella Whitney, and Anthology-Making

Richard Jones is the most significant publisher of poetry anthologies in sixteenth-century England, one who actively engaged, throughout his career, with the possibilities afforded by the form. Jones specialised in the type of vernacular literature that appealed to the recreational cultures emerging in Elizabethan England, publishing poetry anthologies alongside ballads, plays, and prose romances.[1] This chapter will concentrate on the anthologies Jones produced in the 1560s and 1570s. Despite notable work, these decades continue to be neglected, perceived to be the lean, drab years before the arrival of Spenser, Marlowe, Sidney, and Shakespeare in print.[2] If we turn to non-elite literatures, however, these years were far from lean; instead the production of books of verse designed 'to recreate ones minde', in the words of the title-page to *Gorgious Gallery*, flourished. Jones was very active in this period, publishing a variety of poetry compilations – *A Handefull of Pleasant Delites* (*c.* 1566), Isabella Whitney's *The Copy of a Letter* (*c.* 1567) and *A Sweet Nosgay, or Pleasant Posye* (*c.* 1573), Nicholas Breton's *A Smale Handfull of Fragrant Flowers* (1575) and *A Floorish upon Fancie* (1577), and *A Gorgious Gallery, of Gallant Inventions* (1578). *A Handefull* was a collection of those 'Trim songes of love' that John Hall had complained of in *The Courte of Vertue* (1565) because they were used by young men and women purely for pleasure and amorous entertainments.[3] The poetry anthologies Jones produced in the 1560s and 1570s open much-needed windows on to the diversification of literary cultures across these decades, which allow us to see how those in the business of

---

[1] On Jones, see Massai, *Shakespeare*, 82; Kirk Melnikoff, 'Richard Jones (fl. 1564–1613): Elizabethan Printer, Bookseller and Publisher', *Analytical and Enumerative Bibliography*, 12 (2001), 153–84; Melnikoff, 'Jones's Pen and Marlowe's Socks: Richard Jones, Print Culture, and the Beginnings of English Dramatic Literature', *Studies in Philology*, 102 (2005), 184–209.
[2] For key essays on these decades, see Part III of *The Oxford Handbook of Tudor Literature*, edited by Pincombe and Shrank.
[3] See Chapter 1, 59–60.

73

74 Household Books

making books responded to and shaped the interests of the various constituencies making up the middling sort, from prosperous artisans and merchants to those aspiring to gentry status.[4]

One of Jones's most productive partnerships in the 1560s and 1570s was that with Isabella Whitney. Whitney's status as the first English professional woman writer has secured her place in literary history. This chapter considers the part she played in anthology production, how she responded to a humanist culture of commonplacing, and crafted a distinctive vernacular poetics. Jones's collaborations with Whitney were his earliest and longest standing. He entered, printed, and sold all of Whitney's known works – *The Copy of a Letter* (*c.* 1567), *A Sweet Nosgay, or Pleasant Posye* (*c.* 1573), while 'The lamentacion of a Gentilwoman upon the death of her late deceased frend, William Gruffith Gent.' has been attributed to Whitney and was printed by Jones both as a broadside and at the end of *A Gorgious Gallery*.[5] Through their various collaborations, Jones and Whitney helped to shape and supply the market for domestic literature made up of those recreational and practical books aimed at the early modern household that were discussed in the previous chapter. The anthologies produced in the 1560s and 1570s craft a poetics that would appeal to these socially diverse acoustic worlds. On offer are proverbial, commonplace poems and songs of love and courtship that map the complex and shifting gender relations within the early modern household. Miscellanies replete with recipes and herbals have long been recognised for their household uses. The *florilegium* trope of *A Sweet Nosgay* resonates in this domestic setting, figuring a range of household crafts from making herbals to ward off sickness and gifts for use in courtship, to patterns for needlework.[6] The collections produced by Jones and Whitney translate humanist practices of compilation, which we have seen at work in *Songes and Sonettes* and *Paradyse of Daynty Devises*, into household and artisanal forms, their nosegays and buildings turning the craft of making anthologies into an everyday skill.

---

[4] On mid-Tudor literary culture and the middling sort, see Crane, *Framing Authority*, chapter 7.
[5] See the attribution made by R. J. Fehrenbach, 'Isabella Whitney (fl. 1565–75) and the Popular Miscellanies of Richard Jones', *Cahiers Elisabethains*, 19 (1981), 85–7, and Randall Martin, 'Isabella Whitney's "Lamentation upon the death of William Gruffith"', *EMLS*, 31.1 (1997), 2.1–16, https://extra.shu.ac.uk/emls/03–1/martwhit.html#.
[6] See Wendy Wall, *Recipes for Thought: Knowledge and Taste in the Early Modern Kitchen* (Philadelphia: University of Pennsylvania Press, 2016); Whitney Trettien on *florilegia* and needlework in 'Isabella Whitney's Slips: Textile Labor, Gendered Authorship, and the Early Modern Miscellany', *Journal of Medieval and Early Modern Studies*, 45 (2015), 505–21.

'What lack you maister mine': *A Handefull of Pleasant Delites* and Isabella Whitney's *The Copy of a Letter* and *A Sweet Nosgay*

A Handefull of Pleasant Delites and *The Copy of a Letter* emerged from Jones's printing house around the same time, between *c.* 1565 and 1567. They contributed to the growing stock of small and medium-sized books of vernacular poetry produced for the rapidly expanding and diversifying markets of the mid-sixteenth century. The first printed works of secular poetry authored by a woman, the importance of *The Copy of a Letter* and *A Sweet Nosgay* in forging a popular classicism and an urban poetics is now well-recognised.[7] In the case of *Copy of a Letter*, attention has tended to focus on her revisionary dialogue with Ovid's *Heroides*.[8] The place of her poetry within non-elite vernacular poetic cultures remains shadowy, largely because this minor field of literature is so often overlooked in favour of more canonical literary traditions.[9] Yet, as I have argued, these minor traditions can alter our field of vision, bringing voices into play that often go unheard. This is especially the case with a ballad anthology like *A Handefull of Pleasant Delites*. The part it plays in the history of vernacular poetry has not been fully appreciated. The earliest known ballad anthology, a genre that remained popular throughout the early modern period, it collects early and very rare examples of amorous ballads that were circulating as broadsides and within performance cultures more broadly.[10] It therefore is a crucial resource when studying the wide variety of secular non-elite vernacular poetry available in mid-sixteenth-century England.

The framing of both *A Handefull* and *The Copy of a Letter* differs markedly from the epistles Tottel and Disle placed before *Songes and Sonettes* and *Paradyse*. In these, the publisher was fashioned as a lettered man, motivated to publish by the common profit to be gained from the

---

[7] For early seminal studies, see Ann Rosalind Jones, *The Currency of Eros: Women's Love Lyric in Europe, 1540–1620* (Bloomington: Indiana University Press, 1990), chapter 2; Danielle Clarke, *The Politics of Early Modern Women's Writing* (London: Longman, 2001).

[8] Important examples are Danielle Clarke, '"Formd into words by your divided lips": Women, Rhetoric and the Ovidian Tradition', in *'This Double Voice': Gendered Writing in Early Modern England*, edited by Danielle Clarke and Elizabeth Clarke (Basingstoke: Macmillan, 2000) 61–87; Reid, *Ovidian Bibliofictions*, 136–43.

[9] Exceptions include Rosalind Smith, 'A "goodly sample": Exemplarity, Female Complaint and Early Modern Women's Poetry', in *Early Modern Women and the Poem*, edited by Susan Wiseman (Manchester University Press, 2016), 181–200.

[10] For other ballad anthologies, see the discussion of Anthony Munday's *Banquet of Daintie Conceits* (1588) in Chapter 4, 187–8. Richard Johnson's ballad anthologies, *The Crowne Garland of Golden Roses* (1612–92) and *The Golden Garland of Princely Pleasures and Delights* (1620–90), were popular throughout the seventeenth century.

76 Household Books

anthology and the verse it collects. Jones puts forward a very different persona in the ballads he places at the front of these compilations; the common profit he describes owes less to humanism and more to a prosaic language of trade and commerce. The ballads before *A Handefull* and *Copy of a Letter* are so similar they turn these collections into companion books in Jones's stock. Both put into circulation readers who are conceptualised as book buyers, and so defined by their acquisitive relationship with the print trade. Through the trope of the anthology as the bookseller's stall, these ballads skilfully employ deixis to imagine vividly a scenario in which readers are buyers who browse Jones's bookstall, perusing the title-pages and leafing through his stock, before deciding on their purchases. Opening with a lively prosaic mode of address, Jones asks those browsing at his stall to pick up *A Handefull* and examine its contents:

> You that in Musicke do delight
>   your minds for to solace:
> This little booke of Sonets m[*ight*]
>   wel like you in that case,
> Peruse it wel ere you passe by,
>   here may you wish and have,
> Such pleasaut [*sic*] songs to ech new tune,
>   as lightly you can crave.
> Or if fine Histories you would reade,
>   you need not far to seek:
> Within this booke such may you have,
>   as Ladies may wel like.
> Here may you have such pretie thinges,
>   as women much desire:
>   (*Handefull*, A IV)

The Copy of a Letter similarly opens with the cry of the bookseller at his stall, 'What lack you Maister mine?', who then assists his customers in their choices, offering them both novelty and variety: perhaps 'some trifle that is trew',

> Or yf you minde to reade,
>   some Fables that be fained:
> Buy this same Booke, and ye shall finde,
>   such in the same contained.
>   (*Copy*, A IV)

Both books of ballads, *A Handefull* and *Copy of a Letter*, are merchandise, one of the many commodities in the shops of Elizabethan London on sale to the discerning customer. Kirk Melnikoff argues that this type of

'What lack you maister mine' 77

publisher's epistle markets a 'spatial, material sense of reading as browsing' that is particularly suitable to the type of 'browsable book' on offer – a miscellaneous collection of a variety of literary genres.[11] What interests me is the way in which the act of browsing is remarkably peopled and experiential in Jones's ballads. These little books can be used for all kinds of social engagements and are open to various modes of performance and transmission – reading, silently or aloud and in company, singing, and gift-giving. Within the pages of *A Handefull* are 'Songs to reade or heare' when at leisure, which can be used in acts of courtship and other exchanges between men and women, either given as gifts or read or performed in company. The acoustic field of these ballads is an urban recreational world in which people have the leisure time to browse, shop, read, sing, and court. Women occupy a central place in the stories these ballads tell about the production and transmission of Jones's browsable books. They are consumers of books in *A Handefull*, and makers of texts in the case of the 'young gentilwoman' author of *The Copy of a Letter*, who speaks to other '*yong gentilwomen, and to all other mayds*', as the title-page announces. In the *Handefull* ballad, the book buyer addressed is ostensibly male, since he will buy 'such pretie thinges, / as women much desire', activating a trope in which the body of the book is equated with desiring and desirable women. Yet, we should not be too quick to argue that Jones's feminised and eroticised fiction of the pleasures of this 'little booke of Sonets' (AIV) closes off the book to women; instead, it situates its ballads of love and courtship in the company of women. When read alongside *Copy of a Letter*, these ballads tell a story of exchange in which women are not simply objectified as passive consumers, but actively engage in producing and reproducing the cultural meaning and social uses of these texts.

The opening ballad framing the 1584 edition of *A Handefull* advertises the anthology's multimodal uses: 'A Nosegaie alwaies sweet, for Lovers to send for Tokens, of love, at Newyeres tide, or for fairings, as they in their minds shall be disposed to write' (A2). The 'Nosegaie' is a prosaic, meta-anthologistic trope typically used to figure *florilegia* and their affordances, functioning self-referentially to make visible the interplay between the crafted object, made by many hands, the concept of the compilation, and its literary and material uses.[12] Whitney will later use this *florilegium* motif to figure her own compilation, *A Sweet Nosgay*. Posies, which

---

[11] Melnikoff, *Elizabethan Publishing*, 115.
[12] See Seth Lerer on meta-anthologistic figures, in 'Medieval English Literature and the Idea of the Anthology', *PMLA*, 118 (2003), 1255.

78 Household Books

Puttenham described as 'things to be carried away', are portable, mobile properties, put to different uses in different locales.[13] The reader is invited to use this text as a pattern for crafting their own posies or 'Tokens, of love' to be given as New Year's gifts or presents bought at fairs. Ballads, like other lyrics collected in anthologies, are dynamic objects that incorporate the mechanisms for their own recirculation. Posies or love tokens demand the agency of readers, here figured as both consumers and makers, who are instructed to recraft the verse to suit their own purposes. Each of these flowers and herbs in 'A Nosegaie' – lavender, rosemary, sage, violets, rose, thyme, and so forth – heads an octet, which can itself be broken up and so made portable, carried away, and copied on to paper or into a miscellany, or on a ring, plate, or other object, or stitched into fabric. The nosegay, in this sense, is ornamental household matter comparable to those quatrains that Tusser designed to be painted on the walls of various rooms in the home.[14] At the same time, the interweaving of flowers within a nosegay is a meta-anthologistic figure for the dynamic interplay between the part and the whole within an anthology. While poetic matter can be broken up, this is also a ballad in which stanzas can be read sequentially, building upon one another to make up a profession of love. It therefore is a highly flexible poetic property, encoding within itself a variety of reading experiences and textual, material, and social uses.

The form of the compilation, as we have seen, is accretive and adaptable, always open to further interventions. With *A Handefull* and *The Copy of a Letter*, Jones capitalised on this adaptable form to repurpose textual material in his stock. Their publication history, like that of so many other books in this period, is difficult to recover fully since both survive only in unique copies. Fragmentary and missing books leave traces in the records that provide evidence for histories of production that may be difficult to pin down, yet are nonetheless suggestive. Like the earlier *Court of Venus*, *A Handefull* survives in fragments that sketch out a long publishing history. Only one copy of the 1584 edition of *A Handefull* has been found, yet even this is incomplete, missing a leaf; a fragment of a quire of an edition possibly printed in 1575, and a leaf from an edition that has been dated to around 1595 have also been recovered.[15] Similarly, there is only one known copy of *Copy of a Letter*, which can be found in a *Sammelband*

---

[13] Juliet Fleming, *Graffiti and the Writing Arts of Early Modern England* (Cambridge: Reaktion Books, 2001), 19.
[14] See Chapter 1, 48.
[15] See STC 21104.5 (*c.* 1575, sig. D2,3,6,7, only), STC 21105 (1584, lacks B6), 21105.5 (*c.* 1595, D2 only). Arber, ed., *Transcript*, I, 141.

'What lack you maister mine'

in the Bodleian Library. As I have argued elsewhere, bibliographic evidence argues that this copy is from a second or possibly later edition.[16] The title-page, in any case, wants to give the impression that it is a compilation that has gone through different iterations:

> *The copy of a letter, lately written in meeter, by a yonge gentilwoman: to her unconstant Lover. With an admonitio[n] to al yong gentilwomen, and to all other Mayds in general to beware of mennes flattery. By Is. W. Newly joyned to a Loveletter sent by a Bacheler, (a most faithfull Lover) to an unconstant and faithles Mayden.*

This is not simply a description of the pamphlet's contents, but an account of its history of compilation. A publishing scenario is presented in which a single-authored pamphlet authored by a 'yonge gentilwoman' has been 'Newly joyned' to another text, of similar type – a love letter addressed by a man to an unconstant maiden. The conjoined texts make up a new product, a little anthology of female and male complaints in the tried and tested *querelle des femmes* structure for compiling poetic matter within anthologies. The affordances of the compilation, its capacity for further addition, are illustrated by what happened next to *The Copy of a Letter* when bound in the *Sammelband*. At some point before the mid-seventeenth century, a fragment of another pamphlet, a verse epistle, *R. W. Against the wilfull Inconstancie of his deare foe E. T.*, also published by Jones, was added after *The Copy* and bound together in this *Sammelband*, which also collects similar types of texts – translations of classical tragedies, romances, and Italian *novella*, by 'gentlemen' authors, printed in the 1560s and 1570s.[17] Compilations like *The Copy of a Letter*, because of their form, encouraged further addition and gathering, resulting in this case in a composite volume of books and pamphlets.

A Handefull of Pleasant Delites went through many iterations, with new ballads added to subsequent editions. Much of Jones's business from the mid-1560s into the early 1570s was in broadsides, and so he had a ready store of verse to hand on which he could draw.[18] By repackaging ballads in the form of anthologies, Jones created new copy out of old, capitalising effectively on his stock, and offering consumers a different type of product

---

[16] O'Callaghan, '"my Printer must, haue somwhat to his share": Isabella Whitney, Richard Jones, and Crafting Books', *Women's Writing*, 26 (2009), 18–20.

[17] Bodleian 8° H. 44. Art. Selden. For fuller discussion of the status of *A Copy of a Letter*, see my 'my Printer', 21–2.

[18] Rollins traced many of the ballads to printed broadsides; see *A Handful of Pleasant Delights by Clement Robinson and Divers Others*, edited by Hyder E. Rollins (Boston: Harvard University Press, 1924), pp. viii–x. On the trade in broadside ballads, see Marsh, *Music and Society*, 225–32.

80 Household Books

to the broadside. The ballad trade was lucrative. Broadsides are examples of a 'little job', consisting of a text that fitted on one sheet and so could be printed quickly and cheaply; staple work for bookseller-printers like Jones.[19] Their capacity for repurposing meant they were endlessly reiterative, spawning imitations, especially in the form of moralisations and responses, as we have seen in the case of 'When ragyng love'. Publishers appear to have protected their investment in broadsides in a manner that offers an instructive contrast to that of the poetry excerpted in anthologies. The latter occasioned little complaint from fellow stationers, probably given there was no direct competition, since overall the anthology and the book from which the poem or poems were sourced remained very different products.[20] The reprinting of broadsides owned by others in any form was a different matter. Since these were typically single ballads on a single sheet, their format meant their commercial value was easily compromised if reprinted by another. In 1578, Henry Carr was fined for 'printinge in a ballad of his [three] staves out of another ballad of Edward Whytes'.[21] A ballad anthology, therefore, raised many red flags. It is not clear whether Jones owned the copy to all the ballads previously printed as broadsides.[22] In 1576, concerns were raised and on 13 August, Jones surrendered 225 copies of a book 'intituled A handful of Delightes' to the Stationers' Court; almost a year later on 10 June 1577, the copies were returned to Jones, with no indication any action had been taken.[23] A plausible explanation for why this book was impounded is that other stationers believed Jones was reprinting ballads that he did not own and called for the collection to be examined.

A Handefull proved popular because it was innovative. Jones put out at least four editions until 1595, if not later, with new ballads added. He claimed on the 1584 title-page that it was now printed '*With new additions of certain songs, to verie late devised notes, not commonly knowen, nor used heretofore*'.[24] What made *A Handefull* very new in 1565 was Jones's careful

---

[19] Peter Stallybrass, '"Little Jobs": Broadsides and the Printing Revolution', in *Agents of Change: Print Culture Studies After Elizabeth L. Eisenstein*, edited by Sabrina Alcorn Baron, Eric Lindquist, and Eleanor Shevlin (Amherst: University of Massachusetts Press, 2007), 315–41.

[20] See Chapter 4, 157–8.   [21] Arber, *Transcript*, II, 848.

[22] A ballad, 'the goddess Diana &c', was entered by Lacy between 1565 and 1566, and may have been the same ballad that Jones printed under the title 'The History of Diana and Actaeon' (B6–7); see *A Handful*, ed. Rollins, 91; Arber, *Transcript*, I, 313.

[23] W. W. Greg and E. Boswell, eds., *Records of the Stationers' Company, 1576 to 1602 from Register B* (London: Bibliographical Society, 1930), lvii, 86.

[24] Rollins gives provisional dates for the ballads in the contents list of his edition, *A Handful*, xvii–xix; see his notes to individual ballads.

'What lack you maister mine'

recording of the tunes to which the ballads could be sung. This would become a conventional part of the machinery of the broadside ballad from the 1580s onwards, but in the 1560s it was a novel practice.[25] Through its ballads and their tunes, *A Handefull* reveals a popular domestic lyric *translatio* that operated through the ballad and alongside the more familiar Petrarchanism, which conventionally defines the English Renaissance. The collection makes available a diversity of metrical forms that rivals *Songes and Sonettes*, although here there is no drive to regularise metres into iambs; instead this is stress verse in keeping with the performance cultures in which it circulated. Whereas in *Songes and Sonettes* French forms were altered to follow Italian models, in *A Handefull* the older French verse forms dominate. *A Handefull* is culturally heteroglot, mixing the English vernacular with the French inheritance of late medieval poetry and song.[26] This cosmopolitan musical soundscape is evident in the sheer variety of verse forms represented in this anthology: there are ballads composed in fourteeners and poulter's measure alongside the sextilla, the Spanish ballad form used by Surrey, carols, and variants of the French *formes fixes*. The prosodic variety of these poems is displayed in their layout on the page. Lineation follows the interplay of long and short lines, the use of triple rhymes, and to identify the refrains. These graphic features point out the vocal properties of the verse, enabling readers to recognise and so respond to the rhythmic structures of these ballads in their own performances.[27] The layout of the ballads on the page thus works in tandem with the tune identified in the title to mark out the multimodal properties of these ballads – in the words of Jones's ballad, 'songs to ech new tune' as well as to 'reade' (A1v).

A Handefull of Pleasant Delites captures a decisive point of transition in the history of the ballad in England. The anthology both looks back to an early Tudor ballad culture that was still very dependent on European musical traditions and integrates these 'cross-Channel influences' into a domestic recreational culture where, as John Ward points out, they were 'fast acquiring an English character'.[28] Many of the tunes recorded in

---

[25] The first known ballad printed with a tune under the title is 'A Proper New balad of the Bryber Gehesie', 'To the tune of Kynge Salomon', printed by Thomas Colwell (1566, STC 17802); Livingston, *British Broadside Ballads*, 299–300. For the tunes in *A Handefull*, see *Verse Miscellanies Online*: http://versemiscellaniesonline.bodleian.ox.ac.uk/glossaries-and-indexes/ballads/.
[26] See Stevens, *Music and Poetry*, 137–8.
[27] On lineation and the prosodic structures of poetry on the page, see M. B. Parkes, *Pause and Effect: an Introduction to the History of Punctuation in the West* (Aldershot: Scolar, 1992), chapter 8.
[28] John Ward, 'Music for "A Handefull of pleasant delites"', *Journal of the American Musicological Society*, 10 (1957), 180.

82 Household Books

A Handefull take their titles from European dances, such as the quarter branles ('The Historie of Diana and Actaeon', B5r), Kypascie or Qui passa ('A Sonet of two faithfull Louers', D3r), Labandala Shot ('A sorrowfull Sonet, made by M. George Mannington, at Cambridge Castle', E1r), and the new Almain ('The Louer complaineth the absence of his Ladie', E3r).[29] Dances continued to be performed to these tunes in Elizabethan England. As we shall see, their choreography was copied into household miscellanies. Dancing was part of the fabric of recreational life across social classes in this period, from the courtly dance imagined in 'Good Ladies: ye that have your pleasures in exile' in *Songes and Sonettes*, to the more demotic *carole* or round-dances.

The ballads collected in *A Handefull* travelled through diverse locales in mid-sixteenth-century England, moving freely across elite and non-elite spaces. 'The scoffe of a Ladie', 'Attend thee, go play thee', was copied into a household miscellany compiled by the aristocratic Harington family and shared its tune and verse form with a song performed in Francis Marbury's university play, *The Marriage of Wit and Wisdom*, 'Lye still & heare nest the'.[30] 'An excellent Song of an outcast Lover', to be sung to the tune 'All in a Garden green' (C7v), can be found in the minstrel book associated with Richard Sheale and Henry Spooner, and so followed the itinerant movement of ballads from London along trade routes, in the packs of ballad-selling and singing pedlars.[31] The discourse of love as it is expressed in these ballads is not Petrarchan or courtly, but rather draws on a rich vocabulary shared with early Tudor carols and other vernacular modes. Its protagonists are socially hybrid; they are deemed 'gentle' and termed as 'Ladies', but they are not courtly and instead share the prosaic concerns of the middling sort. The social range represented by the ballads collected in *A Handefull* is that of this diverse social grouping, and takes us to the multi-status household, which included servants alongside ladies and gentlemen. Here, books and other textual material, as Tara Hamling and Catherine Richardson have shown, did not have a 'fixed place' or a clearly identified reader; instead a book or a ballad might be read by a master or

---

[29] Ibid. These ballads illustrate the metrical variety of *A Handefull*; the sigla and schema is taken from May and Ringler, *Elizabethan Poetry*: 'The Historie', EV5310, aaa6b4ccc6b8d10e2anap.d10e2anap. f10fff6, irreg.; 'A Sonet', EV22398, abab8c6ci8d4d8; 'A sorrowfull Sonet', EV10409, aa8; 'The Louer', EV20267, aa14, poulter's measure.

[30] *The Arundel Harington Manuscript of Tudor Poetry*, edited by Ruth Hughey, 2 vols. (Columbus: Ohio State University Press, 1960), II. On 'The scoffe of a Ladie', see my '"Good Ladies be Working": Singing at Work in Tudor Women's Song', *Huntingdon Library Quarterly*, 82 (2019), 107–26.

[31] Bod. Ashmole 48, fol. 110v. See the discussion of this minstrel book in Chapter 1, 66–8.

'*What lack you maister mine*' 83

mistress and then picked up and read by another member of the family or even an apprentice or servant in the household.[32] One of the ballads collected in *A Handefull*, 'A proper new Song made by a Studient in Cambridge, To the tune of I wish to see those happie daies', ascribed to Thomas Richardson, is a male complaint written in the *querelle des femmes* form and is specifically addressed to the homosocial worlds of the universities:

> Here Cambridge now I bid farewell,
> adue to Students all:
> Adue unto the Colledges,
> and unto Gunvil Hall:
> And you my fellowes once,
> pray unto Jove that I
> May have releef, for this my grief,
> And speedie remedie.
>
> (A6r)

It is followed in the 1584 edition by the ballad, 'Attend thee, go play thee', the locale of which is the working household in which a maidservant is busy at her spinning and needlework for her mistress, among other 'Good Ladies' who 'be working' (A7r). Here, she is importuned by a young man, given the homely name 'Peter Picks' (A8r), in the following 'An answer as pretie to the scof of his Lady'. His name punning on 'pick' in the sense of a weapon (it was a word for the pike) is in keeping with the stab of the flout, and is a tool for manual labour, signifying his status as a working man. Jones marketed *The Copy of a Letter* and *A Handefull* as complementary books because both ballad collections give voice to household spaces in which women and men across the social scale conversed and contracted espousals. Reading ballads from *A Handefull* alongside *The Copy of a Letter* helps to fill out the acoustic field of Whitney's very distinctive mode of female-voiced complaint and locates her domestication of a Heroidean tradition within the rich vernacular poetics of the 1560s and 1570s.

'The complaint of a woman Lover', sung to 'the tune of Raging love', is a very audible example of the dialogism of early modern ballads. This tune may share its title with the opening phrase of Surrey's 'When ragyng love', but these ballads were not sung to the same tune. Surrey's ballad was probably sung to a popular tune that at some point was given the alternate names 'Troy Town' or 'Queen Dido' – the phrase 'Troye towne' (Q1, B3v), of course, is shared with the second stanza of Surrey's poem. Ballads sung to this tune are sextillas and so also share the same metrical

---

[32] Hamling and Richardson, *A Day at Home*, 195.

84   Household Books

soundscape as Surrey's 'When ragyng love'. 'The complaint of a woman Lover', by contrast, is composed in quatrains and so could not be sung to the same tune as Surrey's sextilla.[33] Moreover, unlike the other ballads riffing on 'When ragyng love', which notably echo its soundscape, 'The complaint' is not obviously a parody of Surrey's poem.[34] Instead, this *Handefull* ballad looks beyond 'When ragyng love' to the female-voiced complaints 'O Happy dames' and 'Good Ladies' in *Songes and Sonettes*, taking over and responding to their sophisticated use of the rhetorical figure of address, the apostrophe. The dialogue between these ballads is an illustration of how effectively 'O Happy dames' and 'Good Ladies' put into circulation an embodied re-creative space in which female auditors were invited to become co-performers in the song, brought together by affective bonds, moved by the same passions, and therefore capable of sympathy. The answering complaint in *A Handefull* stages its own performance as one that is framed in response to the offer of female companionship in 'Good Ladies':

> Good Ladies yet my inward paine,
> So pricketh me I have no holde:
> But that I must my griefe bewray,
> Bedewed in teares with doleful tunes,
> That you may heare, and after say,
> Loe, this is she whom love consumes.

And again, at the close of the complaint: 'Good Ladyes helpe my dolefull tunes, / That you may here and after say: / Loe this is she whom love consumes' (D 1v–2r). This 'woman Lover' mimics the vocative address of the earlier complaint, inviting other 'Good Ladies' to add their voices to her 'dolefull tunes' and to act as sympathetic witnesses who will testify to her fate for all posterity. The *vocalité* of apostrophe is realised through this embodied recreative exchange. Performative subject positions are purposely fashioned so that they can be inhabited by others. Echoing so many earlier complainants, the female lover turns herself into an example of misplaced trust in the male beloved, 'Whose fained teares I did beleeve, / And wept to

---

[33] I am grateful to Una McIlvenna and Jenni Hyde for information about the tune 'Troy Town'/ 'Queen Dido' and the ballads sung to it. For a recording of this tune, go to *English Broadside Ballad Archive*: http://ebba.english.ucsb.edu/ballad/35243/recording.

[34] This lost tune of 'Raging love' raises the question of whether Surrey was parodying an earlier popular ballad that also used this phrase, perhaps in its opening line. John Stevens points out that, in the early sixteenth century, 'dozens of popular songs were known within the court circle and formed a staple of both literary and musical composition. As a result, the connection between words and *tune* was ever present in people's minds; "metrical" words were still naturally connected with melody'; *Music and Poetry*, 54.

'*What lack you maister mine*' 85

heare his wailing voice' (D IV), and now warns, 'You comly Dams, beware by me, / To rue sweete words of fickle trust' (D 2r). Like the speaker of 'O Happy dames' and 'Good Ladies', this woman lover is a desiring subject, full of erotic longing, who 'haunts the place where he hath beene', to 'kisse the Bed whereon we laye' (D 2r). What is notable is the way this complaint uses the language of witnessing to invite sympathy; in this, 'The complaint of a woman Lover' differs from later moralisations in which this abandoned woman lover is to be blamed as much as pitied.

'The admonition by the Auctor, to all yong Gentilwomen: And to al other Maids being in Love' is Whitney's companion ballad to her epistle 'To her unconstant Lover' in *The Copy of a Letter*, which castigates her lover for disdaining her to marry another. It also answers 'The complaint of a woman Lover' by picking up the conversation this complaint began with 'Good Ladies' to address those women lovers 'Whose hartes as yet w*ith* ragingelove / most paynfully do boyle', and to reiterate this ballad's warning to 'Beware of fayre and painted talke, / beware of flattering tonges' (A6r). In the chain of conversation, from 'Good Ladies' to 'The complaint of a woman Lover' and to Whitney's 'The admonition', fictional women speak directly to each other across poems, time, and space. This reiterative mode of address generates stories of poetic transmission and literary imitation that are crucially dependent on the company of women. While the address to 'Good Ladies' certainly can be deployed by male writers, the fictions it puts into circulation are especially sympathetic to female authors, readers, and performers. Whitney brings to this conversation an emphasis on reading, specifically the dangers and value of Ovidian reading matter. Those treacherous male lovers, responsible for the downfall of many a female lover, were acting by the book, since 'Ovid, within his Arte of love, / doth teach them this same knacke' (A6r). Female readers, on the other hand, may learn by the example of the fate of women in Ovid's other book, his *Heroides*, not necessarily in order to govern their desires, but to put its lessons into practice and to learn how to become a better reader of others. When reading the *Heroides* in this 'Admonition', and in her other Ovidian complaints, Whitney uses the methods of commonplacing, gathering apt examples – Scylla, Oenone, Phyllis, Hero – under headings that take the form of proverbial sayings that are to be stored for future use:

> Trust not a man at the fyrst sight,
> but trye him well before:
> I wish al Maids within their brests
> to kepe this thing in store.
>
> (A6v)

86 Household Books

'Store', a favourite word of Whitney's, signifies this process of collecting necessary matter, moral lessons, for present and future uses. This is a very pragmatic version of humanist commonplacing that involves reading for action, grounded in a feminised realm of civic behaviour, which involves managing oneself and negotiating espousals. Whitney responds to the *Handefull* ballad, intervening in a wider conversation with other 'Good Ladies', by recrafting this complaint into an admonition that proves an argument and is oriented towards future action.

Whitney's admonition prompted a further response to 'The complaint of a woman Lover' penned by George Whetstone. His 'The complaint of a gentlewoman being with child, falsely forsaken' forms part of the 'Garden of unthriftinesse: wherein are many sweete flowers, . . . of honest love', in his *The Rocke of Regard* (1576). Whetstone's complaint is in direct dialogue with the *Handefull* ballad, clearly echoing the woman lover's complaint at numerous points:

> Good Ladies yet, my pinching paine,
> Injoynes mee here, the truth to say,
> Whose wretched plight, and pensive state,
> Surmounteth farre, Queene *Didoes* fate.

Again the speaker warns, 'Yet Ladies all beware by mee, / To rue sweete wordes, of fickle trust'.[35] The Ovidian lens through which Whetstone reads this ballad, however, is shared with Whitney. The lying and thieving men chosen are also found in Whitney's 'To her unconstant lover': 'Thou *Jason* false by perjurde flight, / Thou *Theseus* thefte, decypherest plaine, / I *Dido* wretch (thou *Troyan* knight)'. The difference is that Whetstone's reading is a moralisation that, unlike Whitney's admonition, casts the gentlewoman as blameworthy, closing with the warning that women must 'rule your love by reasons lore, / Least future plagues, you do deplore' (90). Whetstone's contrasting response to the *Handefull* complaint highlights what is distinctive about Whitney's poetry, particularly her style of admonition, which credits women's capacity for self-governance and their ability to profit from their reading.

The idiom of love and desire and its various transactions in these ballads is non-courtly. Lovers in *Songes and Sonettes* write of kisses stolen, gifts given, letters torn, and a lady's finger pricked while at her needlework, although she is listening to her lover's 'piteous song', not at work for her

---

[35] George Whetstone, *The Rocke of Regard* (1576), 89–90. Intriguingly, Whetstone's ballad, like 'When ragyng love', is a sextilla and so could be sung to the tune of 'Queen Dido' or 'Troy Town'.

'What lack you maister mine'

mistress like the lady in the *Handefull* ballad 'Attend thee, go play thee', who scolds her suitor for interrupting her at her spinning and sewing.[36] The business of courtship and marriage, its negotiations and contracts, are the subject of two complaints in *A Handefull*: 'A proper wooing Song, intituled: Maide wil ye love me: ye or no?' (D6–7) and 'A proper Sonet, Intituled, Maid, wil you marrie' (C4–5v). 'Maid, wil you marrie' takes the late medieval form of a *tenso*, a type of debate poem voiced by male and female speakers.[37] Here, a maid and a man discuss the nature of promises to marry made in courtship. The male and female voices are not divided between stanzas, but interlaced, which means that it is often difficult to distinguish who is speaking. These uncertainties of voice may have been resolved in performance, but could just as easily have been enhanced, and register the creative instability of this ballad's acoustic field and its speakers' situation. This ballad is to be sung to the black almaine, a dance tune which puts into motion patterns in which the bodies of the dancers come together and move apart: couples step towards each other and away, and take and drop hands. The dance is an appropriate form for the *tenso*, embodying the to and fro of the voices in debate. The ballad's opening gambit is to do with courtship, and the terms in which it is negotiated belong to social transactions familiar to those new readerships emerging in the sixteenth century. The maid does not invoke courtly feudal obligations; she is not bound by her father or other male members of her family, but rather by a marriage contract. The male suitor petitions the young woman, 'Maid, wil you marie?', and she offers her excuses, 'I pray sir tarie / I am not disposed to wed', advising him to 'go seeke some other wight, / That better may your heart delight' (C4–4v). This opening dialogue is a prelude to a male complaint condemning woman's fickleness. Yet unlike other versions of these male complaints that fill the pages of anthologies, when the young woman presents her case, she is not the conventional cruel, disdainful mistress. Instead, she counsels that 'if I could, be sure I would, / consent to your desire'; the problem is that she is contracted to marry another:

> But promise now is made,
> Which cannot be staide;
> It is a womans honestie,
> To keep her promise faithfully.

---

[36] See Wyatt's erotic lyric 'She sat, and sowed', in *Songs and Sonettes*, G1v–2r; on 'Attend thee', see my 'Good Ladies', 121–4.
[37] Doris Earnshaw, *The Female Voice in Medieval Romance Lyric* (New York: Peter Lang, 1988), 45–7.

88 Household Books

And so I do meane til death to do,
Consider and gather, that this is true:
Choose it, and use it, the honester you.

(c4v)

The account of 'womans honestie' is cast in the form of proverbial wisdom: it is a truth that can be gathered, collected, committed to memory, and used for edification. 'Honestie' in this passage is not simply operating as a synonym for chastity – women's sexual honesty. It also describes the ability to keep a promise within a contract. The maid voices her credibility in a proverbial, socio-economic, and sexual sense; she can be trusted to honour promises and, on this basis, is accorded a degree of autonomy in negotiating her own exchange value.

The ballad, however, is not this straightforward. Instead, 'Maid, wil you marie' is tonally unsettled and unsettling. In part, this results from the *querelle*-like structure of the *tenso*: the female-voiced sections assert women's honesty in the manner of defences of female virtue; however, they are then countered by the longer male-voiced sections, which offer conventional complaints against women's pride and fickleness. The maid's response to her would-be suitor is seemingly honest, since the grounds for the rejection are credible and are delivered without a scoff attacking her suitor's character. She is not, for example, the maid of 'A proper wooing Song', who is accused of not telling 'the trothe' and so causing a lover to 'linger' without hope (D 5r). When the male speaker then rejects the maid's assertion of her 'honestie', he delivers a series of homely misogynist proverbs that ascribe to women a treacherous changeability that are characteristic of this type of rejected lover's complaint. And yet, his response sounds like a misapprehension of the mode in which the maid speaks. This dissonance between the two voices suggests a cultural moment in which socio-literary languages are in a state of creative flux and the resulting tensions and contradictions are made audible. 'Maid, wil you marie' alerts us to the other socio-literary scripts alongside the Petrarchan, Ovidian, and chivalric that were available for constructing subject positions and addressing gender relations in matters of love. This ballad, like others of its kind, turns the circumstances of everyday life into poetic matter that is then made available for recreational purposes and sung to tunes, like the black almaine, with their own history of performance. The ballads gathered in *A Handefull* help us to understand the distinctive strands of vernacular poetry that animate Whitney's ballads, and which coalesce in a female subject capable of articulating her desires, while insisting on her credit.

'What lack you maister mine'   89

'Certain familier Epistles and friendly Letters by the Author: with Replies' in Whitney's *Sweet Nosgay* is a little anthology of domestic verse epistles addressed to her sisters, brothers, friends, kinsmen, and male friends. These epistles do more than mimic verse exchange within scribal cultures.[38] Instead, they illustrate how Whitney experiments with the forms of household poetry, going beyond Tusser and others to provide readers with a body of vernacular poetry suitable for imitation. In doing so, Whitney models a domestic poetics that emerges out of and speaks to the middling sort in all its diversity, including literate domestic workers. Whitney's family illustrates the complexity of this social group, encapsulating its plasticity. Isabella is thought to be the daughter of Geoffrey Whitney, of Combermere, Cheshire, and sister of Geoffrey, the author of *A Choice of Emblems and Other Devices* (1586). Descended from the minor gentry, Geoffrey Senior was a tenant farmer in the early sixteenth century and his eldest son attended university and a minor Inn, either Thavies or Furnivall, from 1570 to 1574, when *A Sweet Nosgay* was published.[39] Much of Isabella Whitney's life story has been constructed from the details provided in these verse epistles. Social placing is built into the form of the verse epistle and its modes of address which are designed to give the impression that interlocutors talk to each other in defined situations. Her sisters are said to work as maidservants, once also her occupation; her brother, Brooke, is apprenticed to a master, and her older brother, G. W., probably Geoffrey, is in London during the law year. Younger sons and daughters in families from lesser gentry and the middling sort were often apprenticed or went into service.[40] The kinship group emerging from these conversations is simultaneously fabricated and grounded in a recognisable milieu that is very different from the social worlds conventionally evoked in the verse epistle. Anthologies are full of such poems exchanged between male friends whose conversations are located in the homosocial environments of the Inns of Court or universities or cognate worlds.[41] Whitney's 'Certain familier Epistles' are distinctive amongst others of this type because of the vividness with which they give life to a

---

[38] Clarke follows Wall's reading of these poems as pseudomorphs of manuscript exchanges, which 'replicate private textual circulation' (Wall, *Imprint of Gender*, 297), in her *Politics of Early Modern Women's Writing*, 195, 202.

[39] Betty Travitsky, 'Isabella Whitney', *ODNB*.

[40] Christopher Brooks, 'Apprenticeship, Social Mobility and the Middling Sort, 1500–1800', in *The Middling Sort of People: Culture, Society and Politics in England, 1500–1800*, edited by Jonathan Barry (Basingstoke: Palgrave, 1994), 53–4.

[41] See Shrank, 'Matters of Love', 30–49.

90   Household Books

milieu made up of men and women with such diverse occupations, who
exist on the threshold between the non-elite and the elite. Maidservants,
sisters, a university-educated brother, another working for a master, and
friends are brought together in a dynamic that characterises the
middling sort.

'Certain familier Epistles' incorporates poems of advice and complaint.
'An order prescribed by IS. W. to two of her yonger Sisters servinge in
London' is a versified guide to service akin to Tusser's 'A hundreth good
pointes of huswiferye', first published in his *A Hundreth Good Pointes of
Husbandrie*; an expanded edition, *Five Hundreth Good Pointes*, was pub-
lished in the same year as *Sweet Nosgay*. Both are structured as points to be
read, taken away, committed to memory, and turned into action, part of
the proverbial wisdom that fashions subjectivities within the household.[42]
'An order' is marked for special consideration within the 'Certain familier
Epistles'. It is given its own running title, 'A Modest meane for Maides'
(C7v, C8v, D1), which advertises this poem as a feminised form of the
mean, thereby inviting comparison with those other proverbial poems on
the mean that make up poetry anthologies. The difference is that in 'An
order' the typically masculine civic principles of self-government work to
fashion working female subjectivities and to establish the literate domestic
worker as a class of transactive readers. Like Tusser's points of housewifery,
these orders turn the experience of domestic work into the proper matter
for poetry and enhance the role of women in this domain, in this case, the
maidservant. A series of analogies are set in place in which good govern-
ment of the self is equated with that of the household and, by analogy, the
wider commonwealth. The cultural efficacy of this mode of poetry operates not through the court or its satellites, but through households, the
representative figures of which are working women and men, who participate in a wider civic Renaissance.[43] Whitney's following epistle addressed
'To her Sister Misteris A. B.' similarly valorises the household, especially
'huswyfery', in civic terms – her sister's 'prety Boyes' will go 'strong' in
'learning' through her guidance, contributing to the health of the commonwealth (D2r).

Whitney's household poetry is of a different order to that of Tusser in
that it is much more alert to the texture of intrapersonal relationships. Her

---

[42] Michelle M. Dowd, *Women's Work in Early Modern English Literature* (Basingstoke: Palgrave
Macmillan, 2009), 30–8; Laurie Ellinghausen, *Labor and Writing in Early Modern England,
1567–1667* (Aldershot: Ashgate, 2008), 20–8.
[43] Patrick Cheney, *Reading Sixteenth-Century Poetry* (Oxford: Wiley Blackwell, 2011), 144.

'What lack you maister mine' 91

verse epistles to close kin – her sisters and brothers – make sophisticated use of spatial and temporal deixis that introduces an anxious poetics of loss even into 'An order'. The verse imagines the time 'when I / shal further from you dwell' (c7v); it is this absence that drives the need to remember her, both as a moral exemplar and as a sister full of care: 'let me remembred be: / So wyll I you, and thus I cease, / tyll I your selves do see' (d2v). There is a generic complexity to these familial complaints that results from the hybridity of this domestic poetics. The absence of the beloved that drives the desire for physical and emotional proximity in the Heroidean tradition of complaint can be heard in the epistles that Whitney addresses to her brothers, resulting in a rich affective poetic language of kinship attuned to the circumstances of familial relations. These epistles set out situations in which the family bonds, on which individual members rely, have become dangerously attenuated through the geographical distance which separates sister and brothers.[44] When her brother, G. W., is absent from London at 'vacant time' (c6r), he is lost to her, leaving the city's communication networks for the country, where he is difficult to contact. The 'fertyl feelds' in which he abides contrast with her dearth, since 'No yeldyng yeare' Fortune 'me allowes, nor goodes hath me assind'; the juxtaposition gives moral weight to the claim she has on her brother: 'You are, and must be chiefest staffe / that I shal stay on heare' (c6r–v). The loss that generates this complaint is twofold: her brother's distance, her main moral and financial support, and the loss of employment, of 'service' to her 'vertuous Ladye' (c6v), a prosaic version of the courtly mistress. The absence of her brother, Brooke, who is working at some distance from the family for a 'Maister', is a source of 'dread' and 'deepe dispaire'. Writing, 'within this Paper weake', is only an approximate; the letter attempts to summon his presence, but it only serves as a reminder of his absence. Familial bonds, reputation within the wider community, and the various ties of obligation provide the matter of these familiar epistles precisely because they are all very much at risk through the mobility and economic uncertainty that characterised early modern society.[45] These epistles give poetic voice to a household made up of complex emotional and economic dependencies, beset by risks and anxieties, its contours shaped and reshaped through fortune and distance.

One household in which the ballads gathered in *A Handefull* were performed was that of the Gunter family. Two ballads, shared with this

---

[44] Clarke, *Politics*, 200–2; on the wider urban dislocations in *Sweet Nosgay*, see Gordon, *Writing Early Modern London*, 84–109.
[45] Fumerton, *Unsettled*, 3–32.

92   Household Books

anthology, were copied into a miscellany that once belonged to Edward
Gunter and his sister, Elinor: 'A faithful vow of two constant Louers' (D8–
E1) and 'Fain would I haue a pretie thing' (D5–6).[46] The Gunter family,
like that of Whitney, were of the middling sort. Edward and Elinor were
the same generation as Isabella, coming of age in the 1560s. Edward was
admitted to Lincoln's Inn in February 1563. His was not a gentry family;
instead, attendance at the Inns of Court would entitle him to call himself a
gentleman, and he entered the legal profession, called to the bar in
February 1574.[47] Elinor practises her signature in a fair italic hand on
the end papers of the book.[48] Their household miscellany includes recipes,
poetry, and choreography for fifteen dances. These were the measures for
the basic dances taught at Tudor dancing schools and were performed on a
wide social range of occasions.[49] The presence of choreography in the
Gunter household book reminds us how dance was central to early
modern performance cultures and, in turn, shaped the recreative poetics
of anthologies. A number of these dances share names with the tunes to
which ballads are to be sung in A Handefull, for example, the Cecilia Pavin
('The Lover co[m]plaineth the losse of his Ladie', B8r) and the black
almaine, as we have seen, was the tune to 'Maid, wil you marie?' (C4r).[50]
When Edward, Elinor, and others performed or heard ballads sung to
these dance tunes, they would also have in mind the bodily experience of
the choreography of the dance.[51] Attending to dance tunes enhances our
understanding of the embodied and affective properties of recreative poetry
like ballads.

    'Fain wold I have a pretie thing / to give unto my Ladie' is one of the
ballads shared between the Gunter household book and A Handefull. It
was sung 'To the tune of the lusty gallaunt' (fol. 44), a popular dance song.
Nicholas Breton, in The Workes of a Young Wyt, Trust up with a Fardell of

---

[46] Bod. MS Rawl. poet. 108, fols. 43–3v, 44.
[47] Records of the Honourable Society of Lincoln's Inn: Admissions Register, vol. 1 (1896), 70; Records of the
    Honourable Society of Lincoln's Inn, Black Books, vol. 1 (1897), 389.
[48] Bod. MS Rawl. poet. 108, fol. 18.
[49] James Cunningham, Dancing in the Inns of Court (London: Jordan and Sons, 1965), 16–20; D. R.
    Wilson, 'Dancing in the Inns of Court', Historical Dance, 2.5 (1986–87), 3, 14; John Ward,
    'Apropos "The Olde Measures"', REED: Newsletter, 18 (1993), 2–21. On the performative
    properties of early modern dances, see Emily F. Winerock, '"Mixt" and Matched: Dance Games
    in Late Sixteenth- and Early Seventeenth-Century Europe', in Playthings in Early Modernity: Party
    Games, Word Games, Mind Games, edited by Allison Levy (Kalamazoo: Medieval Institute
    Publications, 2017), 29–48.
[50] Bod. MS Rawl. poet. 108, fols. 10r–11r.
[51] Butler's point that readers heard texts with 'the memories of sung words and singing voices' in mind
    can be extended to the movement of the body in dance, Ancient Phonograph, 96–9.

'What lack you maister mine'   93

Pretie Fancies, described the movement of dancers to 'first Galiardes, then Larous, and Heidegy', then 'Did lustie gallant, all floures of the broome':

> And to it then, with set and turne about,
> chaunge sides, and crosse, and minse it like a hauke:
> Backeward and forward, take handes then, in and out,
> and now and then, a litle holsome talke:
> That none could heare, close rounded in the eare:
> well I say nought, but much good sport was there.[52]

These are incorporative dances of courtship, permitting intimacy between couples, with bodies brought close together and endearments whispered. Dances offered women a degree of agency, since women alternated with men to lead the dance.[53] In keeping with its tune, 'Fain wold I have a pretie thing' is a ballad of courtship; its popularity meant that it was parodied in numerous moralisations – 'fayne wolde I have a godly thynge to shewe unto my ladye' and 'fayne would I have a vertuous wyfe', all registered around 1566/7 – designed to counter the amorous encounters 'Fain would I have a pretie thing' permitted.[54] The tenor of this ballad can be heard in the fantasy of consumption offered by Jones at the front of *A Handefull*, when advertising its recreative delights: 'Here may you have such pretie thinges, / as women much desire' (a1v).

This ballad was made and remade through performance; it exists in so many variant states because its structure is so open and accumulative, and couplets can be easily added or left out. The version copied into the Gunter commonplace book is shorter than the *Handefull* version because the speaker's shopping trip is truncated and so, for example, he misses 'The Gravers of the golden showes' and 'The Shemsters in the shoppes that sowes' (d5v–6r). To prove that the 'pretie thing' the speaker would buy for his lady is beyond value, he goes shopping: 'I walke the towne, and tread the streete, / in every corner seeking' (d5v), which takes him by mercers, silk wives, down Cheap Street, and past engravers. The structure is peripatetic and embodied; the speaker and audience move within an urban landscape made up of places to buy things. Like Jones's ballad framing the anthology, it is about browsing, searching through the shops of London to find something that embodies the value of his lady, which, of course,

---

[52] Nicholas Breton, *The Workes of a Young Wyt, Trust up with a Fardell of Pretie Fancies* (1577), fol. 36.
[53] Winerock, '"Mixt" and Matched', 45.
[54] These ballads were entered in the Stationers' Register; however, no copy survives: Arber, *Transcript*, I, 340, 342. 'Fain would I have a virtuous wife' was copied into Folger v.a.339, fol. 150.

94 Household Books

cannot be found since her worth is beyond material value. The unattainability of the mistress does not proceed in Petrarchan and courtly fashion, but through shopping. The result is that the conventional objectification of the lady within love poetry is here demystified and instead rematerialised in the processes of commodification and consumption that make up the social and economic transactions of the city. It is this self-consciously manufactured urban text that, in turn, provides the matter for poetry.

'Fain wold I have a pretie thing' shares its peripatetic and accumulative structure with Whitney's ballad 'Wyll and Testament', which closes *A Sweet Nosgay*. Both map London, sharing a view of the city, in the words of Whitney's 'Wyll and Testament', in which 'fayre streats there bee, / and people goodly store' (E3v). 'Store', meaning both 'a body of persons' and an abundant supply of goods, food, and money, functions in both ballads as a material and mercantile form of the rhetorical figure of *copia*.[55] The peripatetic narrative structure of both ballads proceeds through the form of lists that accumulate people and goods. 'Fain wold I have a pretie thing' constructs consumers as desiring subjects, playfully figured in terms of a paradox, wanting both something and nothing, reiterated throughout the ballad in the refrain '*I name no thing, nor I meane no thing, / But as pretie a thing as may bee*' (D5v). The well-known joke of Whitney's mock-testament is that she leaves to London what it already has and what she lacks, putting into motion a shuttling between material dispossession and poetic possession.[56] The city in both these ballads is walked on the ground, rather than viewed from a single vantage point, and it is populous and practised, made up of people going about their business. Because of the way it is traversed, the city is known through selected places, rather than fully comprehended, and the relations between places are variable, rather than fixed, dependent on the travels, and travails, of the speaker. Intriguingly, Jones also entered a ballad, now lost, in August 1576 under the title 'a walkynge Ladyes now goo we somme pleasant thinges to view and see'.[57] The figure of the walking lady is shared with 'Wyll and Testament', a ballad in which Whitney defines her authorship in terms of walking the city. We cannot know if Whitney was its author, but the title of the ballad does seem to recall deliberately the peripatetic form of 'Wyll and Testament' and to advertise this connection.

In both 'Wyll and Testament' and 'Fain wold I have a pretie thing', the peripatetic movement through the cityscape provides a model for poetic compilation. Both ballads put into practice a flexible, material mode of

---

[55] *OED*, 1a, 3, 4.   [56] See, Clarke, *Politics*, 212–13.   [57] Arber, *Transcript*, II, 302.

Artisanal Poetics: A Gorgious Gallery, A Sweet Nosgay   95

copia that enables stanzas and couplets to be added and joined together via the movement of the speaker from one place and set of goods and services to the next. 'Store', as we have seen, is a very apt figure for a mercantile literary culture that Whitney both addresses and criticises for its lack of charity in 'Wyll and Testament'. 'Store' also denotes a method of compilation that opens humanist practices of commonplacing to a wider social range of readers who might be interested in gathering textual material to make their own compilations. It is to this feature that this chapter will now turn.

Artisanal Poetics: *A Gorgious Gallery, of Gallant Inventions* and *A Sweet Nosgay*

A Gorgious Gallery, of Gallant Inventions and *A Sweet Nosgay* are exercises in anthology-making in which the humanist craft of *compilatio* is expressed through discourses and practices that belong to artisanal worlds. The art of poetic making thus is given a productive place in the artisan's workshop as well as the humanist schoolroom. *A Gorgious Gallery*, like *Songes and Sonettes* and *A Paradyse*, is part of a wider civic Renaissance. It can be also be distinguished from these earlier anthologies because the way it is framed draws attention to the processes of making through these distinctively artisanal motifs. As we have seen, the paratext to *Gorgious Gallery* sets out an architectural trope that marks out the embodied spatiality of the anthology, which, in turn, is ascribed to the craft of those engaged in its assembly, its 'worthy workemen'. The grounding for this architectural metaphor is the urban artisanal worlds of workshops and printing houses which are thus established as loci for cultural production. Here, poetic making still retains its medieval association with manual labour and the craft of the artisan, an affiliation that becomes increasingly attenuated in accounts of poetic composition and compilation in the latter half of the sixteenth century.[58] *A Sweet Nosgay* similarly gives expression to an artisanal craft of compilation. Prompted by Hugh Plat's *The Floures of Philosophie* (1572), Whitney eschews his classicism; instead, in her hands, a *florilegium* lexicon is grounded in manual work and embodied action and integrated into the urban fabric of everyday life.[59]

---

[58] See Henry Turner, 'Plotting Early Modernity', in *The Cultures of Capital: Properties, Cities, and Knowledge in Early Modern England*, ed. Turner (London: Routledge, 2002), 85–127.
[59] See Vine on Whitney's reading of Plat, *Miscellaneous Order*, 170.

96   Household Books

The entry for *Gorgious Gallery* in the Stationers' Register is curious and suggests that the anthology, or at least its title, was in a state of flux for some time until the artisanal architectural frame was set in place. The various permutations take us to the other anthologies Jones worked on in the late 1570s – *Paradyse of Daynty Devises*, which he was printing for Disle, and *A Handefull of Pleasant Delites*, copies of which had recently been confiscated by the wardens, and were released just five days after he first entered *A Gorgious Gallery* on 5 June 1577. The initial entry was a title that amalgamated *A Handefull* and *Paradyse of Daynty Devises*, with a suggestion of Tottel's 'small parcelles' plucked out of the confines of elite manuscript cultures: '*a handefull of hidden Secretes conteigninge therein certaine Sonetes and other pleasante Devises pickt out of the Closet of sundrie worthie writers and collected together by* R Williams'. Then in the margin a different title was recorded, 'Delicate Dainties to sweten lovers lips with-all', which identifies the anthology as a recreational collection of amorous verse. This was later crossed out, and the eventual title 'a gorgious gallery of gallant invencons' written below.[60] These variations on a theme point to a process of deliberation during which different ways of conceptualising an anthology were in a state of play. 'R. Williams', identified as the compiler of *a handefull of hidden Secretes*, does not appear on the 1578 title-page of *A Gorgious Gallery*, nor anywhere else in the volume.[61] Instead, his place is taken on the title-page by 'T. P.', the initials of Thomas Proctor, who provides much of the verse in the last section of the anthology that follows 'Proctors Precepts' (K4). These different iterations disclose changing, dynamic scenes of production that bring different sets of agents and networks of association into play.

The framing of *A Gorgious Gallery* is very different to Jones's earlier compilations, *A Handefull* and *The Copy of a Letter*. Whereas these earlier anthologies had been prefaced by Jones's ballads addressed to new book-buying publics, he is absent from the front of *A Gorgious Gallery* – there is no printer's ballad or epistle. Instead, T. P., Thomas Proctor, is a domi-nant presence in the anthology, while A. M., Anthony Munday, writes

---

[60] Arber, *Transcript*, II, 313.
[61] None of the known R. Williams are likely candidates. Richard Williams, a ballad writer, is from a later generation – his 'The Poore Mans Pittance' was dedicated to James I and consists of ballads on the Babington Plot, the fall of Essex, and the Gunpowder Plot; see *Ballads from Manuscripts*, vol. II, part 1: *A Poore Mans Pittance, by Richard Williams*, edited by F. J. Furnivall (London: Ballad Society, 1873). Sir Roger Williams (1539/40–1595), a soldier-author, unlike his associates, Thomas Churchyard and Lodowick Lloyd, whose ballad Disle published in *Paradyse*, did not publish poetry (*ODNB*).

Artisanal Poetics: A Gorgious Gallery, A Sweet Nosgay   97

'Unto all yong Gentilmen, in commendacion of this Gallery and worke-men thereof', and Owen Roydon defends the book against 'the curious company of Sycophantes', thus appealing to a more discriminating reader; his initials are also subscribed to the opening ballad, 'To a Gentilwoman that sayd: All men be false, *they thinke not what they say*' (A3–3v).[62] *A Gorgious Gallery* is said to mark a step-change in Jones's publishing strategy. From the late 1570s, he addresses books to the gentleman reader, suggesting he is targeting a narrower, but more affluent consumer group.[63] The verses of Munday and Roydon certainly do fashion a more discrim-inating 'gentleman' reader. However, this figure is more socially hybrid and inclusive than this formulation implies. For one thing, this 'gentleman reader' is asked to admire the 'workemanship' of *A Gorgious Gallery*, 'by worthy workeman wrought', and so invited into the artisanal and cultural domain of the printing house.

Proctor and Munday's modelling of craft emerged from their work in the book trade and so looks forward to *Englands Helicon* with its network of publishers, printers, compilers, and authors, including, once again, Munday. Both were 'brothers' in the Stationers' Company, fellow appren-tices in John Allde's printing house. Munday, the son of a draper, was apprenticed for eight years on 24 August 1576, and Proctor was made free of the Stationers' Company on 17 August 1584, which means that it is likely both were apprenticed at the same time if Proctor's term was also eight years.[64] Proctor is thought to have been the son of John Proctor, the master of Tunbridge Grammar School in the 1550s. Other Proctors can be found in the book trade: William and John Proctor were apprenticed in the 1580s.[65] It is not improbable that the son of a schoolmaster was a stationer's apprentice, since sons of the lesser gentry were regularly appren-ticed in the trades and crafts.[66] Some of Munday's early publications were printed by Allde, who employed his apprentice in producing copy for the press. Three extant ballads penned by Munday emerged from this part-nership: 'Mundaies Dreame', 'Balet against Playes', and 'Encouragement of an Englishe Soldier'; in August 1578, Allde was fined for printing

---

[62] Rollins suggests Owen was a relative of the poet Matthew Roydon, whose verse would later be published in *The Phoenix Nest*; *A Gorgeous Gallery of Gallant Inventions (1578)*, ed. Hyder Rollins (Cambridge, MA: Harvard University Press, 1926), xx–xxi.
[63] Melnikoff, 'Richard Jones', 160–2.   [64] Arber, *Transcript*, II, 69, 692.
[65] Rollins, *Gorgeous*, xviii–xix; Arber, *Transcript*, II, 41, 54.
[66] Brooks, 'Apprenticeship', 53–4, 60–1.

98   Household Books

'Mundaies dreame for hyme selfe without a licence'.[67] Working with
Richard Ballard, a draper-bookseller, Allde printed Munday's *The Mirour
of Mutabilitie* (1579), prefaced by a commendatory verse from Proctor. In
the same year, Munday and Proctor would appear in print together again
in the prefatory material before T. F.'s *Newes from the North*, also printed
by John Allde; these are said to be the initials of Francis Thynne, a pupil of
John Proctor at Tunbridge School. Thomas Proctor's *Triumph of of Trueth*
(1585?, STC 20404) was entered by the draper-bookseller Yareth James in
1582. The only extant copy of this work is a fragment that was bound
together with *Gorgious Gallery* by Edward Malone.[68] Like 'Proctors Precepts' and his other verse in *Gorgious Gallery*, this is moralising poetry in
the *Mirror for Magistrates* tradition – a style also used by Munday for
Mirrour of Mutabilitie – and like *Gorgious Gallery*, advertised as '*Set down
with sundry Inventions for modest Recreation*'.[69]

The paratext to *Gorgious Gallery* evokes this learned and literary artisanal
world of the printing house and its 'worthy workemen'. The title establishes
an overarching architectural metaphor in which the embodied, spatialised
form of the anthology is equated with a gallery 'joined together and builded
up' through the labour and craft of its compilers, those 'divers worthy workeman' who 'First framed and fashioned' the poems it collects 'in sundrie
formes'. Both compiler and poet are akin to the craftsman because both
use *techne*, craft-based knowledge that fuses intellectual and manual skill. The
poet-as-artisan is a trope that dates back to the medieval period, in which
the manual work of the craftsman was valued and aligned with God as the
divine architect.[70] 'Frame' and 'fashion' on the title-page are equivalent terms,
meaning to mould or shape, to give matter a form. The spelling of the word
'formes' may incorporate a pun on forme, the body of type made fast in a
chase used to print the sheets that make up the book. Munday's commendatory verse reiterates the overarching architectural and artisanal metaphor: 'this
Gallery of delightes' is made up of 'buyldings brave, imbost of variant hue: /
With daynties deckt, devisde by worthy wights' (A2r). Imagining a book as a
building was not uncommon in the Renaissance.[71] What is distinctive here

---

[67] Arber, *Transcript*, ii, 847; Celeste Turner, *Anthony Mundy: an Elizabethan Man of Letters* (Berkeley:
    University of California Press, 1928), 8.
[68] Thomas Proctor, *The Triumph of Trueth* (1585?), Bod. Malone 464b.
[69] The title-page to *Gorgious Gallery* states that it has been compiled 'to recreate eche modest mine
    withall'.
[70] Cooper, *Artisans*, 8–10.
[71] See William Sherman, 'On the Threshold: Architecture, Paratext and Early Print Culture', in *Agent
    of Change: Print Culture after Elizabeth L. Eisenstein*, edited by Baron et al., 67–81.

Artisanal Poetics: A Gorgious Gallery, A Sweet Nosgay   99

is how the emphasis is not simply on a *textual* edifice, a containing space or architectural threshold, but on embodied practice, how it has been crafted through the agency of 'worthy wights'. Craft governs the way that the various poems that make up the anthology are imagined in a material sense as painted architectural ornaments; 'devisde' is used not only to define a mental process, but in its older, now archaic sense of a manual, mechanical task of constructing, framing, and fashioning.[72] When intellectual labour is accounted for in the processes of composition – these 'worthy workemen' with 'studies toyle' – such 'learning' cannot be disaggregated from technical, manual skill. Munday calls on his 'gentleman' readers 'To yeelde them prayse, so well a worke to wright' (A2r). The closing homophonic pun on 'write' and 'wright', to build, reinforces the fact that writing, penmanship, is a manual craft, even for gentlemen, and insists on the embodied materiality of intellectual work, that it is labour dependent on and akin to that of the craftsman. It is a very different model of poetic craft to that maintained by Sidney. When Sidney writes that 'For any understanding knoweth the skill of each artificer standeth in that idea or fore-conceit of the work, and not in the work itself,' making or craft is understood to be an intellectual and generative activity. While it may offer a material and embodied concept of poetic making, it has lost its medieval grounding in the *techne*, the productive manual labour of the artificer.[73]

The architectural trope carries through from the title-page and Munday's verse to the *mise-en-page*. The language of joinery that underpins the overarching architectural conceit possessed a metaphorical utility in early modern England. One of its primary meanings was secured, as Patricia Parker has shown, in the 'artisanal craft of the joiner who fits parts together into a material object', hence its architectural use to describe the material structure of this anthology as a 'gallery'.[74] It could therefore be mobilised to express the physical and conceptual form of the book crafted by compositors who join together and build up type and formes to make up sheets that are then joined together to make a book. The *mise-en-page* is very similar to that of *Paradyse of Daintie Devises*: use of white space is

---

[72] OED, 5a: something material, as a work of art or a mechanical contrivance. (Formerly including the notion 'to construct, frame, fashion'; now expressing only the mental process of inventing or contriving.) Cooper, *Artisans*, 12.

[73] Todd Knight argues for a level of materiality to Sidney's notion of the poet as artificer who brings a work into being, so that it is embodied in the idea of generation; Knight, *Bound to Read*, 116. I would argue that Sidney removes the 'taint' of manual labour from the figure of the artificer.

[74] Patricia Parker, '"Rude Mechanicals": *A Midsummer Night's Dream* and Shakespearean Joinery', in *Shakespeare from the Margins: Language, Culture, Context* (University of Chicago Press, 1996), 89.

100 Household Books

generous compared with that in *A Handefull* and *A Sweet Nosgay*, titles are centred and set in contrasting type, as are attribution markers – roman in *Gorgious*, italic in *Paradyse*. When setting *Gorgious Gallery*, Jones made more use of ornamental devices which give physical, typographic expression to the workmanship celebrated by Munday in his commendation. Decorative capital letters are used throughout, with a few exceptions. Poems are also set in double columns. This has a practical function in that all poems composed in shorter lines, typically trimeters, are set in double columns, thereby saving space.[75] Yet, this work would have been time-consuming, requiring additional labour and expense. Care would need to be taken when preparing copy and casting off for printing to ensure both columns were equal, particularly when a poem set in double columns is on the same page as a poem set in a single block of type. The resulting visual effect displays the variety of stanza forms on offer in the anthology, or, in Munday's words, 'this Gallery' made up of 'buyldings brave, imbost of various hue'.

The sheer variety, the 'various hue', of metrical forms represented in *A Gorgious Gallery* rivals that of *Songes and Sonettes* and *Paradyse*. The anthology includes examples of sextilla, rhyme royal, ottava rima, variants on sonnet form, and, of course, ballads. *Gorgious Gallery* is an amalgam of other previously published anthologies in so many ways. It opens with a series of verse epistles in which speakers with names drawn from popular romances – Ruphilus, who writes to his Elriza, Narsetus to his Rosana – and other generic lovers declare their fidelity or complain of infidelity, drawing on classical exemplars familiar from the stock figures of the complaints gathered in anthologies. For some ballads, the convention established in *A Handefull* is followed and the tune given in the title: 'A propper Dittie. To the tune of lusty Gallant' (D1v), and 'The Lover exhorteth his Lady to bee constant. To the Tune of Attend thee go play thee' (E3v), which shares the distinctive verse metrical form and sound patterning with the ballad in *A Handefull*, the first line of which lends its name to this tune. All the poems in this section of the miscellany are unattributed, even those borrowed from *Paradyse*, where they are attributed to authors. Initials come into play in the collection of poems gathered within the anthology under the name of Thomas Proctor, marked by the heading 'Pretie pamphlets, by T. Proctor' (L4r) and ending, appropriately, with 'T. P. his Farewell unto his faythfull and approved freend. F. S.' (N3v). Yet, even here, it is not clear whether all the poems in this section

[75] See D1r, D2r–2v, E2r–3r, F2v–3r.

Artisanal Poetics: A Gorgious Gallery, A Sweet Nosgay   101

are Proctor's, since many are unattributed. 'A short Epistle written in behalf of N. B. to M. H.' (L4v), included in this section, deliberately plays with authorial identities, foregrounding the process of authorial fabrication. The initials N. B. were beginning to be standardised as those of Nicholas Breton, in large part through the work of Jones.[76] What is unusual about this epistle, an otherwise conventional invitation to love that offers the mistress the role of Penelope to his Ulysses, is that the title identifies it as a *prosopopoeia* in which the anonymous author writes 'in behalf' of a known author and literary property, N. B. Through this pretence, it playfully appropriates Breton's voice and deliberately confuses the issue of authorship. The experimentation with authorial signatures in this poem and others looks forward to the self-referentiality of 'Gentilwoman' author of 'The Lamentacion … upon the death of her late deceased frend William Griffuth' at the end of the anthology.

A Gorgious Gallery is an amalgam of other anthologies in a more particular sense. A set of composite ballads in this anthology have been 'joyned together and builded up' out of other previously printed ballads from Thomas Howell's *Arbor of Amitie* (1568), *A Handefull*, and *Songes and Sonettes*. They demonstrate, in a very mechanical sense, how the work of compilation extends from anthology-making to the composition of poems. The proverbial or commonplace poems familiar from *Songes and Sonettes* and *Paradyse* are one example of verse that is made through creative and material acts of composition and these composite ballads are another. Their form illustrates how pragmatic practices of imitation travelled between humanist cultures of compilation and those of the print trade.[77] The language of joinery is especially apt in the case of the composition of these ballads. Puttenham, when considering the task faced by 'our maker or Poet', made a comparison with the technical skill of this 'craftsman': 'For in that he useth his metrical proportions by appointed and harmonical measures and distances, he is like the carpenter or joiner, for borrowing their timber and stuff of nature, they appoint and order it by art otherwise then nature would do.'[78] The poet-as-craftsman joins words and sentences together, building lines of metrical feet and units of sound and sense.[79] The *techne* displayed in these composite, conjoined poems takes us once more to the work of the printing house when compiling textual material. Late fifteenth- and early sixteenth-century printed books

---

[76] North, *Anonymous Renaissance*, 73–4.   [77] Knight, *Bound to Read*, 93.
[78] Puttenham, *Art of English Poesy*, 385.
[79] Kalas, *Frame, Glass, Verse*, 44–5; Parker, 'Rude Mechanicals', 90–1.

102   Household Books

of vernacular poetry often incorporated composite poems and these were
often crafted for a very pragmatic purpose – to fill up the blank leaves and
spaces in books.[80] Composite poems were therefore a creative poetic
product of the material practices of making books in the printing house
and continued to be a feature of anthology production well into the
eighteenth century.[81]

The fact that the three composite poems in *Gorgious Gallery* are ballads,
as are the source texts they take apart and reassemble, is significant and
reveals the affordances of this form in action. Composite ballads encapsulate the creative mechanical craft of the ballad trade, which fostered its own
set of compilation practices. Broadside ballads have a complex machinery
and are made of 'moveable parts' – the ballad text, tunes, woodcuts, and
other ornaments – all of which were 'rearrangeable' in different combinations by printers.[82] The ballad text could also be broken up into stanzas
and other bits of textual matter by printers and ballad writers, and
recombined to make up new composite ballads. The mode of poetic
making embodied in the form of these ballads puts into practice 'a material
and technical process of joining' those 'metrical proportions' or units
Puttenham describes, which, in turn, are made up of blocks of type.[83]
The first composite ballad in *Gorgious Gallery*, 'The lamentable lover
abiding in the bitter bale of direfull doubts towards his Ladyes loyalty,
writeth unto her as followeth' (A4r–v), is built out of two ballads from
Howell's *Arbor of Amitie* (1568) – 'The languishing Lover to his Ladie'
(E2r–v) and 'The Lover almost in dispaire, showeth his great greefe and
craves redresse' (F5r–6v). These ballads have been repurposed to fit the
opening section of *Gorgious Gallery* since they are remade into an epistle,
which can now take its place alongside those other ballads in this section in
which lovers 'writeth' to their mistresses. At first glance, the rebuilding of
two ballads into one seems to be a simple case of intersplicing: the first
twelve lines of the new ballad are taken from 'Languishing Lover' followed
by a larger section of thirty-four lines added from 'Lover almost in
dispaire', then alternating couplets from each. There is, however, a craft
to this process of conjoining units of verse. For one thing, the places where
the verse lines join are smoothed over in 'The lamentable lover'. If one

---

[80] Boffey, 'Early Printers', 18–21.   [81] Smyth, *Profit*, 84–5.
[82] Patricia Fumerton, 'Remembering by Dismembering: Databases, Archiving, and the Recollection of
Seventeenth-Century Broadside Ballads', in *Ballads and Broadsides in Britain, 1500–1800*, edited by
Fumerton, Anita Guerrini, and Kris McAbee (Farnham: Ashgate, 2010), 17.
[83] Kalas, *Frame, Glass, Verse*, 55.

Artisanal Poetics: A Gorgious Gallery, A Sweet Nosgay   103

looks to the first transition, then the compiler-poet smooths over the join by selecting sections from the source ballads with similar sound patterning: 'Save only thou, the salve and sore, of this my captive hart, / Thou art the branch yt sweetly springs, whose hart is sound & true' (A4). No changes are made to the originals, yet the alliteration across the join – 'save', 'salve', 'sore', 'sweetly springs' – as well as the repetition of 'hart', harmonises the composite lines. The same practice can be seen at work again in the second section of interspliced couplets from the two source ballads: 'Thou canst and art, the only helpe, to heale the same agayne. / Then heale the hart, that loves thee well, untill the day hee dye' (A4v). Other rhetorical techniques are used for the purpose of integration, evident in the iteration of 'heale' across the lines, an example of *ploche*, meaning 'weaving', that Puttenham also calls 'the Doubler'. The value of this type of rhetorical figure resided in its 'auricular' properties, its sound patterning in which the well-tuning of words is designed to please the ear of the hearer.[84] The effect in the composite ballad, 'The lamentable lover', is to bring the different sections of the ballad into tune. Lines have been selected for points of transition with their meaning in mind, but also with an ear to their physical, sensory properties – their status as units of sound with the capacity for recrafting and re-creating.

The other composite ballad in *Gorgious Gallery*, 'The Lover complayneth of his Ladies unconstancy' (E2r–3r), is a looser construction built around stanzas of three ballads taken from *A Handefull*. The tools employed here include metre and rhyme, which are used to rebuild the quatrains. The first of the ballads taken from *Handefull*, 'Dame Beauties replie to the Lover late at libertie' (A8r–B2), is in poulter's measure; its couplets were broken into quatrains when printed in *A Handefull*, which means that only the second and third lines rhyme. Couplets are sometimes broken in this way by compositors for practical purposes because they are too long for the page width. Hence, in *A Handefull*, a little octavo volume, all ballads written in fourteeners or poulter's measure have their couplets broken at the caesura, resulting in unrhymed lines:

> Her beautie thee bewitcht,
>   thy minde that erst was free:
> Her corps so comely framd, thou saiest,
>   did force thee to agree:
>   (B1r)

---

[84] Puttenham, *Art of English Poesy*, 285–6.

104   Household Books

When this quatrain, with its broken couplets, is recast in 'The Lover complayneth' in *Gorgious Gallery* efforts are made to regularise by making the lines rhyme:

> For when bewitch shee had
> My minde that erst was free,
> And that her cumly beauty bad
> My wounded hart agree.
>
> (E2v)

These alterations mean that the verse line and the typographic line are now brought into alignment. A similar procedure is at work in the case of the second quatrain borrowed by 'The Lover complayneth' from 'The complaint of a woman Lover' in *A Handefull* (D1v). The *Handefull* ballad is composed of four-stress lines which are then recast and shortened to three stresses to fit the metrical pattern of the *Gorgious Gallery* ballad. One of the drivers for the recasting of sense in the quatrains borrowed from the *Handefull* ballads in 'The Lover complayneth' is a material, sensory understanding of the verse line as a unit of sound and sense. Rhyme and rhythm are manipulated to knit together the various bits and pieces of verse taken from other ballads, with their diverse metrical and rhyme schemes. Regularising the rhyme and metre works to ensure a harmonious soundscape. The crafting of these compiled ballads in *Gorgious Gallery* illustrates how composition is both typographic and prosodic. The verse line is simultaneously understood to be both a unit set in type on the physical space of the page and a unit of sound and sense. To appreciate how these composite ballads were composed and read requires an enriched model of materiality that brings together the visual, graphic aspects of the printed page with the extra-textual embodied properties of voice.

When the two ballads taken from *A Handefull* – 'The complaint of a woman Lover' and 'Dame Beauties replie' – were recrafted into 'The Lover complayneth of his Ladies unconstancy', they also underwent a process of re-gendering. Lines originally voiced by a woman are recast as the lament of a male lover within a misogynist warning to 'gallant youths' to 'Take heed of wome*n*s subtil lore' (E3r). For Elizabeth Heale, these revisions epitomise the patriarchal strategies put in place by anthologies that began to close down spaces of female agency present in manuscript culture in the drive to gender the author in print as male, 'humanist-educated and socially aspiring.'[85] One certainly could read this as an example of male

---

[85] Heale, 'Misogyny', 233.

Artisanal Poetics: A Gorgious Gallery, A Sweet Nosgay 105

craft, a method of poetic making that expresses patriarchal control over the female voice and its creative powers. This is certainly part of the ideological work undertaken by anthologies, yet it is only ever partial, and the 'codification of restrictive (gender and other) identities' operates in tension with more generative practices.[86] The polyphonic texture of this type of book means that they are also always open to other voices and alternative perspectives. Not all the recrafted ballads in *Gorgious Gallery* systematically shut down female voices: 'The Lady beloved exclaymeth of the great untruth of her lover' (D2v–3) reworks lines from a male complaint in *A Handefull* – 'The painefull plight of a Lover oppressed with the beautifull looks of his Lady' (D7–8) – into a female-voiced complaint. Moreover, *Gorgious Gallery* ends with 'The lamentacion of a Gentilwoman upon the death of her late deceased frend William Gruffith Gent' (P2v–4v) that markets the 'gentlewoman author' as a writer of complaint and trades off the success of Whitney's *The Copy of a Letter* and *A Sweet Nosgay.*

Whitney's anthologies published by Jones illustrate this complex mediation of women's craft within the early modern book trade. Helen Smith's work has shown how the trade was open to women, who frequently took over their husbands' business, acting as both booksellers and printers.[87] John Allde's widow, Margaret, for example, took over his bookselling business after his death in 1584. Women who sought to publish their writings had some purchase when negotiating its structures. Across *Copy of a Letter* and *A Sweet Nosgay*, Jones worked with Whitney to craft an authorial identity and to establish the initials 'Is. W.' as recognisable as other marketable sets of initials, like N. B., in his stock. *A Sweet Nosgay* is a more ambitious project than Whitney's earlier work. One of its primary models is Hugh Plat's *The Floures of Philosophie, with Pleasures of Poetrie annexed to them* (1572), which, as its title indicates, combines a set of 883 aphorisms with a poetry anthology. Whitney announces her dependence on Plat, closely imitating his work, turning his sententious sentences into verse 'in one hundred and ten Phylosophicall Flowers' (B2r). *A Sweet Nosgay* is engaged in conversations with an array of other contemporary compilations. Gascoigne's *A Hundreth Sundrie Flowres Bounde Up in One Small Poesie* was published in the same year as *A Sweet Nosgay*. These two compilations are framed as *florilegia* in similar terms, and, more than this, both explore the possibilities made available when the author becomes the

---

[86] Wall is writing of the gendering of domestic making through repressive hypotheses, *Recipes for Thought*, 4.
[87] Smith, *Grossly Material Things*, chapter 3.

106   Household Books

compiler of their own and others' texts.[88] Like Gascoigne, Whitney is depicted in *A Sweet Nosgay* as the gatherer of her own work, the one who gives it shape, transforming it into a corpus of work. It is, of course, always a composite work, compiled from textual matter gathered from other compilations and requiring the labour of an array of fellow craftspeople.

Unlike *The Copy of a Letter,* Whitney is very present in the preliminaries of *A Sweet Nosgay*. That said, since the first three leaves (A1–3), including the title-page, are missing from the only surviving copy now held in the British Library, it is impossible to recover its paratext fully.[89] We do not know, for example, if Jones placed his own texts before Whitney's dedicatory epistle to George Mainwaring, as he had done with *The Copy of a Letter*, since these are precisely the pages that are now lost. What is apparent is the way that Whitney's editorial authority over the anthology is established through the dedication and the verse 'Auctor to Reader' in which she claims responsibility for gathering and assembling the texts in the collection. Like many of the university-educated gentleman authors Jones published, in the dedicatory letter to Mainwaring, Whitney's authorship is framed through classical citations – Demades of Athens, Diogenes – references that may have derived from a commonplace book. Advertising her access to this storehouse of accumulated textual matter locates her identity as a learned gentlewoman author within a wider humanist textual economy. Authorship, here, is quite clearly defined in terms of compilation, not because Whitney is a woman author and therefore secondary and always supplementary, but because she shares a pragmatic mode of imitation with other writers in this period. Hence her elaboration of the *florilegium* metaphor to account for her poetic practice: 'though they be of anothers growing, . . . they be of my owne gathering and making up' (A4v). What is described here is a model of authorship and poetic making that is practised, put into action, through the craft of compilation.

Whitney's ballad, 'The Auctor to the Reader', frames the collection, providing an interpretive guide to the verse that follows and narrating an authorial identity through a story that charts the transformation of a working woman into a working author who compiles her own and others' work. It is a remarkable poem for the way it recasts the *florilegia*

---

[88] Gordon, *Writing Early Modern London*, 91–3.

[89] British Library, c.39.b.45. There is no record of its entry in the Stationers' Register because the records from 1571 to 1576 are lost. However, Jones can be identified as the printer-publisher since the printer's emblem following 'Wyll and Testament' was also used by him for Thomas Twyne's commonplace book, *The Schoolemaster, or Teacher of Table Philosophie* (1576, STC 24411, sig. U2v).

Artisanal Poetics: A Gorgious Gallery, A Sweet Nosgay   107

formula, revising its classical associations to give it practical application to a working life:

> This Harvest tyme, I Harvestlesse,
>   and servicelesse also:
> And subject unto sicknesse, that
>   abrode I could not go.
> Had leasure good, (though learning lackt)
>   some study to apply:
> To reade such Bookes, wherby I thought
>   myselfe to edyfye.
>
>   (A5v)

'Harvest tyme' is an appropriate trope for a writer working in a *florilegium* tradition, carrying with it the action of harvesting and gathering choice textual matter, here, materialised in the working life that provides the narrative frame of the ballad. One of the influences behind this emphasis on the practical application of knowledge is Tusser's *A Hundredth Goode Pointes of Husbandrie*, newly expanded in 1573. Points, like philosophical flowers, are forms of portable wisdom, with the capacity for reinscription and recirculation, and put together to guide men and women in the management of the self and relations with others. Yet, characteristically, Whitney approaches this practical literature aslant. Its availability to this author is put into question, since she is 'Harvestlesse, / and serviceless also', seemingly excluded from its terms of employment and engagement. This move alerts us to the way that Whitney so often incorporates the mode of complaint into her fabrication of a poetic identity. The gentlewoman author is turned into an unsettled identity, subject to the economic instability and mobility that characterises those dependent on paid employment.[90] That said, rather than closing off opportunities, the state of being 'servicelesse' enables another occupation – authorship. Out of work, she has 'leasure good', and what she applies herself to is learning, setting out a humanist fiction in which the author is made through reading those authoritative works 'wherby I thought / myselfe to edyfye'. Edify, as we have seen in Whythorne's case, signifies character-building achieved through reading ethically and spiritually improving works.[91]

Rather than located in the schoolroom, authorial self-fashioning is situated in the household. Or, more properly, the household is the schoolroom. When the speaker applies herself to her learning within this space, however, it is not through the feminine motifs of *chanson de toile*, in

---

[90] Fumerton, *Unsettled*, 12–21.   [91] See Chapter 1, 46.

108   Household Books

which weaving and sewing figure specifically female modes of textuality and performativity.[92] Instead, this woman author goes to work in the garden, drawing on the civic rhetoric of household management prevalent in a *florilegium* tradition. The activity of compiling, of gathering textual matter from Plat's *Floures of Philosophie*, propels the author on to the streets to the gardens of urban householders, where she stops to harvest wholesome medicinal flowers for her own nosegay at Hugh Plat's garden, 'his Plot' (A5v–6r).[93] The reader is counselled to go themselves 'to Master *Plat* his ground', to gather their own herbs, taking care 'that / thou lettest in no Swine: / No Dog to scrape, nor beast that doth / to ravin styll inclyne' (A7v–8r). The allusion is to Matthew 7:6: 'Give not that which is holy unto dogs, neither cast ye your pearls before swine, lest they trample them under feet, and turn again and rend you.' This scriptural passage lies behind Tottel's reference to 'swinelike grossenesse' when he challenges the 'unlearned' to reform themselves through profitable, healthful reading.[94] In Whitney's hands, the biblical citation is rendered through such quotidian physical actions – dogs digging in the garden – that the intellectual, spiritual, and textual activities of compilation are translated into the idiom of everyday life, the work of harvesting medicinal herbs for the household. In Whitney's verse, the *florilegium* motif is so thoroughly grounded in recognisable manual activity that it starts to become metonymic, realised in the here and now, and set towards its context in the lives of working people in sixteenth-century London. Humanist commonplacing is thereby made accessible to the working commonality as a practical method and conceptual framework for understanding their intellectual activity when reading and crafting their own texts.

Whitney and Jones were in the business of making books that promoted the figure of the gentlewoman author. *A Sweet Nosgay* is replete with authorial signatures. The subscriptions and titles framing verse within the 'Famylier and friendly Epistles' put this author function into circulation. The 'servicelesse' female epistoler of complaint, who appeared alongside the practical humanist author in 'The Auctor to the Reader', now dominates: 'Your lovyng (though lucklesse) sister, IS. W.' (c4v), 'Your poore Kinsewoman, IS. W.' (D2v), 'A carefull complaynt by the

---

[92] E. Jane Burns, 'Sewing like a Girl: Working Women in the *chanson de toile*', in *Medieval Women's Song: Cross-Cultural Approaches*, edited by Ann Klinck and Ann Marie Rasmussen (Philadelphia: University of Pennsylvania Press, 2002), 98–124.
[93] On the social range of gardens, see Jill Francis, 'Order and Disorder in the Early Modern Garden, 1558–*c*. 1630', *Garden History*, 36 (2008), 22–35.
[94] See Chapter 1, 25.

Artisanal Poetics: A Gorgious Gallery, A Sweet Nosgay   109

unfortunate Auctor' (D3), 'IS. W. to C. B. in bewaylinge her mishappes' (D5v), signed 'Your unfortunate Friend. IS. W.' (D6v), 'An other Letter sent to IS. W. by one: to whom shee had written her infortunate state' (D8v), and finally, 'IS. W. beyng wery of writyng, sendeth this for Answere' (E1v). The effect is accumulative and composite, and it positions the 'Aucthour' of the following 'Wyll and Testament' in the role of the female author of complaint. The female complainant in Whitney's hands is a peripatetic, unsettled figure, possessing a mobility, if nothing else, that enables her to put herself into circulation. Repetition defines this author function as endlessly iterable, and capable of taking on a life of her own beyond the text. A similar degree of stylisation was evident in the use of the pseudonymous complaint signature, 'My lucke is losse', in *Paradyse of Daynty Devises*.[95] The figure of *prosopopoeia*, so integral to complaint, foregrounds the arts of impersonation, of bodying forth, and encouraged such self-conscious play with a composite and malleable authorial identity.

'The lamentacion of a Gentilwoman upon the death of her late deceased frend William Gruffith Gent.', chosen by Jones and his fellow compilers to close *Gorgious Gallery*, makes much of its gentlewoman author of complaint.[96] Fehrenbach claims a number of the female-voiced complaints in *Gorgious Gallery* and *A Handefull* for Whitney, largely on the basis of her collaboration with Jones. Marcy North, quite rightly, is sceptical, concluding that because so many female-voiced complaints are unattributed, 'Anonymity tends to illuminate similarities between voices that might not be visible if poems were attributed.'[97] The lamenting woman was generic in this period. And yet, this is precisely the point. What is notable when reading across *Copy of a Letter*, *Sweet Nosgay*, and 'The lamentacion' is the commodification of female-voiced complaint and its complex gentlewoman author. 'The lamentacion' is a deliberate intervention in this process, since its gentlewoman author is very aware of her fame and insistently returns to the question of how to publish an impassioned, erotic complaint as a woman author. Jones published 'The lamentacion' both as a broadside ballad, now lost, and in *Gorgious Gallery*.[98] When printed in *Gorgious Gallery*, 'The lamentacion' seemingly is set from the broadside since it departs from the style established throughout the rest of the anthology. The variation in the *mise-en-page* thus gives the impression that

---

[95] See Chapter 1, 38.
[96] The poem was first attributed to Whitney in Fehrenbach, 'Isabella Whitney', 85–7.
[97] North, *Anonymous Renaissance*, 226.
[98] The broadside was entered on 20 December and *Gorgious Gallery* on 5 June 1577; Arber, *Transcript*, II, 313, 322.

110 Household Books

it has come from somewhere else, momentarily captured in the pages of the anthology before heading off elsewhere – a scenario that, as we shall see, is fictionalised in the ballad's account of its transmission. There is no definitive evidence that the author of 'The lamentacion' is Whitney. What we can say is that the ballad wants to trade on the fame of its gentlewoman author, a very distinctive author function that had been fashioned and put into circulation in earlier Whitney–Jones productions. The opening envoi advertises its author alliteratively and reiteratively as a 'A doutfull, dying, dolefull, Dame', who 'Here doth she mourne and write her will'. But since this is an elegy not a will, the envoi insistently takes the reader to the doleful, dying gentlewoman author of 'Wyll and Testament'. While its subject, William Gruffith, is named, the gentlewoman author is not. However, as she explains to the reader, her anonymity is deliberate, a precondition of her lamentation:

> Yet hurtfull eyes, doo bid mee cast away,
> In open show, this carefull blacke attyre:
> Because it would, my secret love bewray,
> And pay my pate, with hatred for my hyre:
>   Though outwardly, I dare not weare the same,
>   Yet in my hart, a web of blacke I frame.
>
> (P3r)

'The lamentacion' is very conscious of the gender politics of anonymity. Since she is neither Gruffith's wife nor kinswoman, but a 'Mayde', she is not entitled to take part in official mourning rituals, and so the strictures of female modesty demand her silence. The only forms available to her to publish her grief are therefore those of anonymity. Through this highly self-conscious publishing scenario, the female-voiced complaint is advertised as a form that specialises in anonymity, teasing its readers with modes of self-disclosure that make public secret female passions that are properly kept hidden.

'The lamentacion' is replete with references to the mechanics of writing and publishing. The opening line, 'With Poets pen, I do not preace to write' (P2v), puns on press, meaning both to thrust oneself forward and to commit her writings to the printing press. Later, 'The lamentacion' introduces the generic marker of Ovidian epistolers, 'to blot this scratched scroule' (P3v), which both describes the compulsion to write and materialises feminine writing in the liminal space between cultural legibility and erasure, figuring its marginality within master narratives. The style of 'The lamentacion' is defined in Ovidian terms, evident in the use of the very

Artisanal Poetics: A Gorgious Gallery, A Sweet Nosgay   111

rare phrase 'tristive tunes' (p4r).[99] Since the poem's language is otherwise
not Latinate, this is part of a very bookish pattern of Ovidian intertextuality that responds to Thomas Churchyard's translation of the first three
books of Ovid's *Tristia*, first published in 1572, with a second edition
appearing in 1578. Most strikingly, this gentlewoman author is fashioned
in competition with another, rival poet. There may well have been a rival
poet, a friend of Gruffith, whose initials were I. H., who wrote an epitaph
that was either sold as a rival broadside in St Paul's Churchyard, hence
posted outside a bookseller's stall, or even posted on one of the doors or
pillars of the cathedral itself.[100] More importantly, the rival poet functions
as trope for locating this gentlewoman author within a wider literary field
given material form in the London booksellers' stalls. 'The lamentacion'
vividly fictionalises the conditions of its own production and reception:
just as I. H.'s epitaph 'hangs at Pawles as every man goes by' (p3r), so too
'The lamentacion' was published as a broadside ballad that was sold in
Paul's Churchyard. The rival poet's epitaph is reputed in public opinion
'Rime Ruffe... [as] the common sentence goes' (p3r). In place of its
hackneyed terms, the gentlewoman author offers readers a more 'authentic'
Ovidian female script of her private impassioned self, her 'scratched
scroule' set forth by 'Virgins fist' (p3v). The deliberate play on initials
'I. and H. his name did show no more' (p3r), alongside the anonymity of
the gentlewoman author, turns the author's name into a tantalising thing
that might be possessed – in other words, a very desirable commodity.
Withholding information may defer to social decorum, but it is also
tactical and productive, offering these secret names to the reader as
potentially valuable ware.

The gentlewoman author of 'The lamentacion' continually trades on
her fame, repeatedly addressing this issue of her marketability. The reading
public imagined in the ballad is populated by 'bad' rival poets and 'bad'
critical readers – 'Some Zoylus sot', 'Some Momus match'(p3v), or 'byting
bugs' (p4v) – figures which both represent the transmission of books
through the forces of cultural constraint and advertise their desirability.
This may well be writing under erasure, but it is a very deliberate,
purposeful tactic. Taken together, these tropes work to establish the place
of the female-voiced complaint and the gentlewoman author within print
culture as a highly desirable commodity. This author may be party to her

---

[99] The *OED* lists this as the only usage.
[100] Martin has suggested that the initials I. H are those of Jasper Heywood; 'Isabella Whitney's
"Lamentation"', 2.8 n. 15.

112 Household Books

own objectification, but in a manner that is also highly opportunistic. The closing lines, 'Therefore farewell, and ask no more of mee, / For (as I am) a lover will I dye' (p4v), affirms complaint as the signature style of the author, recalling the recent 'Wyll and Testament', and returning this figure to circulation in order to trade off her success.

The modes of textual exchange figured in 'The lamentacion' establish a pattern in which this gentlewoman author is in conversation with other iterations across the pages of *Gorgious Gallery*. 'A Letter written by a yonge gentilwoman and sent to her husband unawares (by a freend of hers) into Italy' (k1v–2v) is part of a sequence of complaints distinguished by their epistolary form and the dialogue between female and male 'authors'. This young gentlewoman author similarly characterises herself as an Ovidian epistoler, a faithful Penelope whose 'blurred lines' are 'scribled out of frame' (k1v). By identifying such similarities, I do not intend to claim this complaint for Whitney, but rather to illustrate how shared rhetorical postures and tropes function within the intertextual and contextual fabric of the anthology to create these echo effects and to fashion authorial characters through a process of reiteration and augmentation. This poem 'by a yonge gentilwoman' and its pair are formulaic. The title recalls 'Good Ladies' and 'O Happy dames' from *Songes and Sonettes*, in which the wife laments her separation from her beloved across the seas of Europe. These resonant complaints, as we have seen, prompted imitations, including 'The lady prayeth the return of her lover abiding on the sea' in the 'Uncertain Authors' section of *Songes and Sonettes*.[101] The set of loving letters in *Gorgious Gallery* are framed by descriptive titles that point to their location within a wider narrative fiction: the woman's complaint is answered by 'A Letter sent from beyond the Seaes to his Lover, perswading her to continew her love towardes him' and 'An other loving Letter'. Just as their gentlewoman author is a marketable literary property, so too the status of these poems as collectable objects is advertised: at the end of each of the epistles are stanzas set off from the rest of the poem in italics, and so styled as gifts or tokens that can be taken away and reinscribed in other formats, from handkerchiefs to rings.

The anthologies Jones and Whitney produced in the 1560s and 1570s give substance to a domestic Renaissance. These collections establish an alternative vernacular lyric tradition transmitted through the ballad; its *loci* are those diverse early modern households that make up an urban landscape. *A Sweet Nosgay* and, to a lesser extent, *Gorgious Gallery*, adapt

---

[101] *Songes and Sonettes* (Q2, 1557), Q2v–3.

Artisanal Poetics: A Gorgious Gallery, A Sweet Nosgay   113

humanist methods for compiling commonplace books, translating humanism's classicism and conceptual framework into consciously crafted forms that are made available to artisanal cultures. Whitney's authorship is an organising principle in the anthologies she published with Jones, which drives the compilation of textual matter. Whitney, in turn, puts into practice a version of the author as an artificer and a maker of texts in a very material and situated sense. The writing life constructed in *A Sweet Nosgay* depends on the act of compiling her own textual matter and that of others. The result is a type of authorship that is made and remade through compilation, a process that we will again see in action in the early 1590s when versions of Sidney and Breton are compiled and put into circulation through the form of the anthology.

CHAPTER 3

'To the Gentleman Reader'
Re-creating Sidney in the 1590s

The 1580s were comparatively lean years for the publication of new multi-authored poetry anthologies, even though book buyers were well supplied by further, often revised editions of those collections first compiled in the preceding decades.[1] The 1590s saw the production of new titles: *Brittons Bowre of Delights* (1591, 1597), *The Phoenix Nest* (1593), *Arbor of Amorous Devices* (c. 1593, 1597), and *The Passionate Pilgrime* (1599). The event that stimulated new production and commanded the attention of so many writers and publishers was the posthumous publication of the works of Sir Philip Sidney: his *Countess of Pembroke's Arcadia* in 1590, *Astrophil and Stella* in 1591, and *An Apology for Poetry* in 1595. Not since Surrey and Wyatt had there been a poet who combined the prestige of court service with humanist dedication to literary experimentation across the major genres. Early funeral elegies mourning his death commemorate Sidney primarily as a Protestant knight, a pattern of chivalry and courtliness, making only brief reference to his writings, if at all, even though many of his works, especially his songs, had been circulating in manuscript throughout the 1580s. What transformed Sidney's reputation is print. In Gavin Alexander's words, Sidney's 'life as a published author was posthumous'.[2] The sheer range of his works, from pastoral romance, songs and sonnets, and religious poetry to translations and a treatise on poetry, transformed the field of literary production. The Sidney remembered in the 1590s was now newly embodied through his literary corpus. Elegies for Sidney frame *Brittons Bowre* and *The Phoenix Nest*, turning the anthology into a space for determining Sidney's literary legacy and its implications for vernacular poetry. The Sidney who emerges from this process, however, is less uniform than is often assumed. Instead, variant versions of Sidney were put into circulation that then become the basis for alternative histories of vernacular poetry.

---

[1] See Bibliography for further editions of anthologies first published before 1580.
[2] Gavin Alexander, *Writing after Sidney: the Literary Response to Sir Philip Sidney, 1586–1640* (Oxford University Press, 2006), xix; see also Marotti, *Manuscript, Print*, 228–38.

Remembering Sidney: the Craft of Compilation 115

One version of Sidney that emerges from these anthologies is not so much the active masculine Protestant poet-soldier as the idle feminine courtier poet-lover. The latter is the literary progenitor for a recreational poetics that is characteristically located in the company of women. An appreciation of the recreational properties of poetry, as we have seen, was a feature of the pre-1590s anthologies. In the 1590s, the vocabulary of recreation becomes increasingly prominent in the framing of anthologies. These collections put into circulation models of recreation that are less interested in the moral profit to be gained from reading and composing delightful poetry, than in the sweet delights of the poems they collect in and of themselves. Leisure is depicted as idle time when one can benefit from the delightful properties of poetry, which may be restorative, but not necessarily lead to edification. The figures that preside over these recreational cultures in the 1590s anthologies are leisured gentlemen and gentlewomen who have the time and the capital 'to recreate them selves', in the words of Jones's preface before *Arbor of Amorous Devices*. New types of verse are collected in anthologies alongside sonnets and songs. These novel poems consciously engage with the ornamental properties of poetry to explore its capacity to delight in sensory terms and have little interest in the moral imperative to be profitable.

Remembering Sidney: the Craft of Compilation

Remembering Sidney in the 1590s is undertaken through the form of the anthology. This is fitting, since the practice of selecting, gathering, and organising poems into a collection lends itself to memorialising the dead. Funerary anthologies are the most obvious examples of how the activity of compilation can give textual and spatial embodiment to a community of mourners, its organisation designed to mirror the funeral procession attending the hearse.[3] The year after Sidney's death in 1586, four university funerary anthologies were published, two affiliated with Oxford, one with Cambridge, and another with Leiden.[4] When the dead are poets, then compiling provides a mechanism for setting out poetic lineages and modes of literary affiliation. Once the first of his corpus began to appear in print in 1590, the anthology was put into service to recover Sidney as a

---

[3] Andrea Brady, *English Funerary Elegy in the Seventeenth Century* (Basingstoke: Palgrave Macmillan, 2006), 20.

[4] John Lloyd, ed., *Peplus. Illustrissimi viri D. Philippi Sidnaei*; William Gager, *Exequiae illustrissimi equitis, D. Philippi Sidnaei*; Alexander Neville, ed.. *Academiae cantabrigiensis lacrymae*. See Dennis Kay, *Melodious Tears: the Funeral Elegy from Spenser to Milton* (Oxford: Clarendon Press, 1990), 67–78.

116   'To the Gentleman Reader'

point of origin for an English lyric tradition. Newman's first 1591 edition of *Syr P. S. His Astrophel and Stella*, as Arthur Marotti explains, was 'an "augmented" one', which added a collection of poems by '*sundry other rare Sonnets of divers Noblemen and Gentlemen*' to Sidney's sonnets.[5] Thomas Newman's edition demonstrated to others how the act of placing poems alongside each other could set in motion patterns of literary affiliation. The posthumous publication of Sidney's work therefore prompted renewed attention to the affordances of the anthology, resulting in innovations in the form. Both *Brittons Bowre* and *The Phoenix Nest* turn the front of the anthology into a space for remembering Sidney, which then frames the collection, providing an interpretive pathway through the following poems and authorising the form that the anthology takes. When Spenser experiments with the form of the elegiac anthology in *Astrophel*, he is responding to this earlier work of anthologising, even borrowing whole sections of verse from *The Phoenix Nest*. As a result, Spenser's self-consciously compiled and composite book disrupts its own fictions of authorship.

Songes and Sonettes offered a precedent for crafting spaces within the anthology to memorialise dead poets and to consider their poetic legacy.[6] In its pages, two of Surrey's elegies for Wyatt – 'Dyvers thy death doe diversly bemone' and 'W. resteth here, that quick could never rest' (D2r–v) – are incorporated into a sequence of poems he either addressed to Wyatt or are framed as such in titles. By placing verses in relation to each other in this way, distinct spaces are marked out within the anthology. It is worth spending some time on Surrey's elegies for Wyatt in *Songes and Sonettes* both because they draw attention to the role compilation plays in memorialising the dead and because echoes can be heard in those poems composed for Sidney, reminding us that, as a courtier-poet who died before his time, Wyatt was an important precedent for those memorialising Sidney. Wyatt is not only the first English poet whose death was commemorated in print, but also the first to be styled as a literary progenitor at his moment of passing.[7] John Leland's *Naeniae in mortem Thomæ Viat equitis incomparabilis* and the pamphlet, *An excellent Epitaffe of syr Thomas Wyat*, which included Surrey's elegy, 'Wyat resteth here', were printed shortly after his death in October 1542. Leland's *Naeniae* uses the phoenix to imagine Wyatt's singular pre-eminence, putting in place a

---

[5] Marotti, *Manuscript, Print*, 231.
[6] Seth Lerer, *Courtly Letters in the Age of Henry VIII: Literary Culture and the Arts of Deceit* (Cambridge University Press, 1997), 165.
[7] See Cathy Shrank, '"But I, that knew what harbred in that hed": Sir Thomas Wyatt and his Posthumous "Interpreters"', *Proceedings of the British Academy*, 154 (2008), 375–9.

Remembering Sidney: the Craft of Compilation   117

myth of literary origins, defined by the phoenix's mystical capacity for rebirth, akin to Christ's resurrection, that traces a line of poetic succession from Wyatt to Surrey:

> The world a single Phoenix can contain.
> And when one dies, another one is born.
> When Wyatt, that rare bird, was taken away
> By death, he gave us Howard as his heir.[8]

Surrey is the consolation for Wyatt's death and reparation is made through poetry. Surrey, in turn, fulfils his filial duty by turning Wyatt into an exemplar worthy of succession in his long elegy, 'W. resteth here', composed in heroic quatrains. Wyatt is anatomised by Surrey, his body remembered through a blazon – his head, face, hand, tongue, eye, heart, that make up 'A valiant corps, where force, and beawty met'. Surrey's Wyatt forcibly takes command of English poetry: 'A hand, that taught, what might be sayd in ryme: / That reft Chaucer the glory of his wit' (D2v). Through his anatomy, Surrey, in turn, takes possession of Wyatt, artfully dismembering and remembering his body; he is the true custodian of his memory because only he knows Wyatt perfectly, inside out.

It is the act of placing Surrey's Wyatt poems alongside each other in *Songes and Sonettes* that sets in play these complex literary conversations. Although the ode 'Of thy lyfe, Thomas, this compasse well mark' (D1v) was probably addressed to either Wyatt's son or Surrey's son or brother, at least one sixteenth-century reader, encouraged by the ode's place at the start of the sequence of poems Surrey addresses to Wyatt, assumed it was Wyatt the elder, writing 'Sir Tho. Wiatt' against the line in the 1587 edition.[9] In this location, it becomes part of an expression of manly and loving friendship running across these poems, epitomised by Surrey's funerary sonnet, 'Dyvers thy death doe diversly bemone':

> But I, that knew what harbred in that hed:
> What vertues rare were temperd in that brest:
> Honour the place, that such a jewell bred,
> And kisse the ground, whereas thy corse doth rest,
> With vapord eyes: from whence such streames avayl,
> As Pyramus dyd on Thisbes brest bewail.
>
> (D2r)

---

[8] Translation from the Latin by Kenneth Muir, *Life and Letters of Sir Thomas Wyatt* (Liverpool University Press, 1963), 265.
[9] Bod. Selden 80 H.43.Art, fol. 15v.

118   'To the Gentleman Reader'

Once again, readers are asked to witness how intimately Surrey knew Wyatt, except here the body is not so much the 'valiant corps' of his heroic elegy, but that of the beloved. In the closing sestet, the lament is thoroughly personalised, and the eroticism of male friendship is given full expression in tears and kisses as Surrey transfigures their friendship into that of legendary tragic lovers.

Brittons Bowre of Delights *(1591)*

Brittons Bowre of Delights, published by Richard Jones in 1591, is the earliest anthology to use an elegy for Sidney to frame the collection. It is a pivotal anthology in many ways: it confirms the shift in Jones's publishing strategy towards fixing on the gentleman reader as the target audience, and it is one of the books that marks Breton's return to print after an absence of more than a decade. Sidney is key to both. An affiliation with Sidney distinguishes the anthology, acting as the guarantor of its cultural value. Jones was the main publisher of Breton's texts in the 1570s and was instrumental in defining his authorial identity in print. The publishing relationship between Breton and Jones was akin to that he enjoyed with Whitney. Both Breton and Jones were in the business of producing compilations, those medium-sized books of vernacular verse to be read at leisure. Jones published Breton's *A Smale Handfull of Fragrant Flowers Selected and Gathered out of the lovely Garden of Sacred Scriptures* (1575) and *Floorish upon Fancie . . . To which are annexed manie pretie pamphlets, for pleasant heads to passe away idle time withal* (1577), with two further editions put out by Jones in 1582 and 1585. The 'Breton' of this period is a very different literary property to the author who re-emerges in the 1590s. His books are addressed to gentlewomen and gentlemen, but these are socially hybrid compilations, as we have seen in the case of Jones's other publications in the 1560s and 1570s.[10] The voice of these prefaces is colloquial, rather than learned, and the properties of these books are defined in relation to other, rather more prosaic commodities. Breton playfully compares books and cheeses in his preface before *The Workes of a Young Wyt, Trust vp with a Fardell of Pretie Fancies* (1577) to imagine a marketplace of print characterised by voracious and indiscriminate consumers: books and cheese are alike because both 'come out of the presse', on to the market, where they are sold, and 'tasted of many, before [they] be bought' (A2r).

[10] See Chapter 2, 82, 97.

Remembering Sidney: the Craft of Compilation 119

Breton returns to print with *The Historie of the Life and Fortune of Don Frederigo*, published in 1590, once again by Jones; then in the following year, Jones publishes *Brittons Bowre*. Jones cultivated working relationships with writers, but the way these operated and were conceptualised in print varied. Both Jones and Breton tell publishing stories in their prefaces to *Brittons Bowre* and *The Pilgrimage to Paradise* of absence and distance that deliberately complicate events. As a result, the precise nature of their relationship is difficult to pin down. What these prefaces do reveal are the ways in which authorial identities are put together through an array of print conventions. Breton owns *Historie of . . . Don Frederigo* as his work: his name is on the title-page, newly accompanied by a motto, 'Coelum virtutis Patria', one of his authorial markers on subsequent publications. He also authors the prefatory material – the dedication to Richard Blount and the epistle to the reader – print conventions which act to locate the author at the scene of publication. With *Brittons Bowre of Delights*, the author's name is incorporated in the title, he is the body of the book, but he is otherwise absent from the front of the book. Instead Jones owns the preface: 'I present you here, in the Authours absence, with sundrie fine Devices, and rare conceytes, in English verse' (¶2r). The absent author is a print convention that allows the publisher to fashion his role in making the work public. Compared with Disle or Tottel, however, Jones is remarkably circumspect, even deferential when writing of his part in the book's production. The preface to *Brittons Bowre* submits the book not to his own critical judgement, but to that of 'Gentlemen Readers', placing himself entirely at their 'service': he is '(onely) the Printer of them', who has undertaken this work, 'chiefly to pleasure you, and partly to profit my selfe'(¶2r). Jones expresses a very limited, largely economic sense of profit compared with the language of common profit mobilised by Tottel and Disle to articulate the agency of the humanist publisher.[11] This 'poore Printer' defers to the 'good Gentlemen' and to the author, advising that 'any fault' should be attributed to 'the Printers negligence, then (otherwise) by any ignorance in the Author', thus decorously distancing the author from the scene of printing. The language of craft so prominent in the paratext of *A Gorgious Gallery* (1578), which located its 'worthy workemen' within the creative milieu of the printing house, is here largely absent; instead the cultural value attributed to vernacular poetry at this Sidneian moment correlates with a reconfiguration of the fictions of

---

[11] See Chapter 1, 22–7.

120   'To the Gentleman Reader'

anthology production around gentlemen authors, readers, and their
'poore Printer'.

Breton denies any involvement in *Brittons Bowre* in his epistle placed
before *The Pilgrimage to Paradise, Joyned with the Countesse of Penbrookes
love, compiled in verse by Nicholas Breton Gentleman* (1592). Breton cor-
roborates Jones's story, but he does so in order to take control over what
his name signifies at the front of a book. His address 'To the Gentlemen
studients and Scholers of Oxforde' makes much of the credibility invested
in an author's name, precisely because its ownership is contested. Breton,
like so many others in this period, is able to hold seemingly contradictory
concepts of the authorship simultaneously: on the one hand, he appreciates that the author's name is detachable from personhood, and so manip-
ulable; and, on the other, he insists that it acts for the author to his credit,
and is therefore his rightful property. Breton complains that Jones has
appropriated his name:

> Gentlemen there hath beene of late printed in london by one Richarde
> Ioanes, a printer, a booke of english verses, entituled *Bretons bower of
> delights*: I protest it was donne altogether without my consent or knowl-
> edge, & many thinges of other mens mingled with few of mine, for except
> *Amoris Lachrimae* an epitaphe upon Sir Phillip Sydney, and one or two
> other toies, which I know not how he unhappily came by, I have no part
> with any of the[m]: and so I beseech yee assuredly beleeve.

Breton's account of how his lyrics came into print seems straightforward:
Jones somehow got hold of his poems, either in the form of a manuscript
miscellany, in which they were already copied alongside 'many thinges of
other mens', or this mingling was undertaken by Jones himself. Of course,
Breton's account is partial and, for one thing, omits his prior publishing
relationship with Jones. It is also noticeable how the persona Breton is
fashioning here is very different to the Breton who embraced commodification in 1577 and compared books to cheeses. This 1592 Breton claims a
more discriminating relationship to print, and his credibility is invested
not only in his name, but in his ability to associate his name with the
elite – Mary Sidney, Countess of Pembroke, to whom *Pilgrimage to
Paradise* is addressed and his patron in the 1590s, and the University of
Oxford, whose printer, Joseph Barnes, publishes the book.[12] Tellingly,
even as he distances himself from *Brittons Bowre*, he does want to own part
of it, namely, his elegy for Sidney, putting in place affiliations that establish

---

[12] On Breton and Pembroke, see Mary Ellen Lamb, *Gender and Authorship in the Sidney Circle*
(Madison: University of Wisconsin Press, 1990), 47–52.

Remembering Sidney: the Craft of Compilation 121

the value of a Breton anthology in the wider market for 'booke[s] of english verses'. The markedly Sidneian Breton promoted in *The Pilgrimage of Paradise* is thus not an entirely different literary property to the author put into circulation by Jones, but instead is dependent on the alliances that make up *Brittons Bowre*.

Brittons Bowre is an early experiment in how to manufacture a Sidneian anthology. The volume revives the armorial crest of the Dudley family, that of a bear with a ragged staff, belonging to Sidney's uncle, Robert Dudley, Earl of Leicester, which replaces the printer's emblem on the title-page.[13] The incorporation of Leicester's crest styles Jones's book as a companion volume to *The Countesse of Pembrokes Arcadia*, printed the previous year by William Ponsonby, with Sidney's crest and its distinctive porcupine on the title-page. There is a question of who authorised Jones to use Dudley's arms, and the answer is probably no one. Leicester had died in September 1588, followed in January 1590 by his brother, Ambrose Dudley, third Earl of Warwick, who also used this device, which meant the earldoms of Leicester and Warwick were now extinct. A Dudley crest on the title-page in 1591 was a memorial to a dead knight and an extinct noble line and so casts an elegiac pall over the anthology. The confluence of Leicester's arms, the address to gentlemen readers, and the elegy for Sidney marks out a different spatiality for the verse anthology to that of Jones's earlier collections. Gone is the trope of the bookseller's stall that framed *A Handefull of Pleasant Delites* and *The Copy of a Letter*. In its place is an alliance with a noble house, now a tomb, and with gentlemen readers. That said, this new location is not all that distant from the earlier scene given that it is an unsecured alliance, without any basis, made up by a 'poore printer', who can make no claims on the dead Leicester or Sidney family.

Breton's long elegy for Sidney, 'Amoris Lachrimae. A most singular and sweete Discourse of the life and death of S. P. S. Knight', frames the collection. Breton owns this verse, which had another life in manuscript channels where it circulated alongside the poems of Sidney, Sir Edward Dyer, and other courtier-poets. It was copied into a manuscript anthology (Bod. MS Rawl. poet. 85), compiled by a student at St John's College, Cambridge, possibly John Finett, a courtier, who was at the college in the

---

[13] This crest was used for publications dedicated to Leicester between 1565 and 1578: STC 4558, 5686, 24777, 1534, 22229, 11488, 5962, 12464, 17520, 825, 4738, 11096. A more elaborate coat-of-arms was also used between 1578 and 1581 (STC 13974, 6848, 23333) and finally in 1588 (STC 23689).

122   'To the Gentleman Reader'

1580s at the same time as Robert Sidney, which Henry Woudhuysen suggests might explain the number of Sidney poems and the anthology's other Sidneian connections.[14] The collection illustrates how Breton's poetic reputation was taking shape in relation to Sidney in the 1580s and 1590s through the types of literary associations put in place when a collection is compiled. The St John's manuscript anthology is carefully crafted: it is a pre-bound paperbook, paginated, with margins ruled in red ink, and catchwords used throughout. Poems are copied carefully in a fair hand, typically begin on new pages, end with a finis and decorative marks, and, more often than not, are subscribed with authors' names or initials or markers of anonymity. The level of design evident in this volume demonstrates scribal craft practices – how manuscript anthologies could be transcribed and compiled with skill and care. The way certain poems are placed alongside each other and in groups is purposeful and generates meaning. Organisational schema, based on authorship, genre, and other types of affiliation, familiar from printed anthologies, are employed to bring poems together in 'miscellaneous order'.[15]

Authors whose names or initials are recorded in this anthology include Breton, Sidney, Dyer, Henry Noel (a courtier), George Peele, and the Earl of Oxford. After Sidney and Dyer, Breton's name is recorded most frequently. The manuscript does not passively reflect a scribal community, but rather brings it into being through the way it sets in play poetic conversations and locates poems and their authors in identifiable contexts. The poems the St John's compiler chooses to copy, and their order, locate Breton close to the court. The first poem is a song, 'When I was fayre and younge', attributed to Queen Elizabeth in a headnote, which is immediately followed by two Breton songs, one of which was performed before the queen on progress at Elvetham in September 1591. The company that Breton keeps through this process of compilation helps to make sense of why Puttenham and others placed Breton among a new generation of 'courtly makers, noblemen and gentleman', alongside Sidney, Raleigh, Edward Dyer, and Fulke Greville in the 1580s.[16] Breton's poems are copied alternating with those of Sidney across a sequence that culminates

---

[14] Henry Woudhuysen, *Sir Philip Sidney and the Circulation of Manuscripts, 1558–1640* (Oxford: Clarendon Press, 1996), 259–60.
[15] The phrase is Angus Vine's, *Miscellaneous Order*. See the discussion of the compilation of this manuscript anthology and its practices of contextualising and recontextualising in Joshua Eckhardt, *Manuscript Verse Collectors and the Politics of Anti-Courtly Love Poetry* (Oxford University Press, 2009), 1–4, 15–17.
[16] Puttenham, *Art of English Poesy*, 149.

Remembering Sidney: the Craft of Compilation 123

in his two elegies for Sidney, 'Deepe lamenting loss of tresure' and 'Amoris Lichrimae <*sic*> on the deathe of Sr P. Sidneye' (26v–34v). Breton's elegies are then immediately followed by Song 8 from *Astrophil and Stella*, 'In a grove most riche of shade' (34v–36v). The compiler places Breton and Sidney in close conversation, even misattributing Song 10 from *Astrophil and Stella*, 'Oh dear love when shall it be', to Breton (107v– 8r).[17] The mistaking of a Sidney song for Breton's points to the ways in which poems and poets can become interchangeable as poems are shared, exchanged, copied, placed alongside each other, and imitated. Voices blend through shared tropes, verse forms, and other literary devices. This echo effect is very pronounced in the Rawlinson manuscript. A poem by James Resholude, 'An Echo made in imitatione of S^r P Sidneys echo going before page :5:' (85r), as Woudhuysen notes, is probably responding to Sidney's echo poem in *Old Arcadia*; yet the Sidney poem is not to be found on page 5 of this manuscript and so was either never copied or pages have been removed or the title is copied from elsewhere. What is copied on page 5, in the original numbering, is Breton's song sung before Elizabeth, 'Sweet Phillis is the shepherds queene' (2r). Preceding Reshoulde's echo poem is another 'Sweet Phillis' song, also another imitation, this time in response to Thomas Watson's Latin poem, *Amyntas* – 'Verses made in manner of an argument upon 11: lamentationes of Amintas' (84v).[18] Connections may be lost and broken, but others are continually brought into play. Echoes and imitations loosely affiliate poems and poets and cluster around the figure of Sidney – as a poet, a subject of poetry, and a literary exemplar to be followed.[19] Through the process of anthologising, the Rawlinson manuscript is fashioning a Sidneian poetic that is composite, made up of the work of other poets through acts of poetic affiliation and imitation.

The Sidneian Breton who emerges from the Rawlinson manuscript presides over *Brittons Bowre*. Breton's long elegy for Sidney, 'Amoris Lachrimae', is given pride of place through the ornate styling of the *mise-en-page* reserved only for this poem: it begins with a very large ornate drop capital, a border of printers' flowers encloses the elegy, and it has its own running title. Breton's elegy features the usual encomiastic elements through which Sidney's singularity as the ideal courtier is brought to the fore – the man who combines learning, courtesy, chivalry, and martial

---

[17] Spenser's Sonnet 8 from his *Amoretti* is attributed to 'Mr Dier', fol. 7v.
[18] See Woudhuysen's discussion of these poems, *Sir Philip Sidney*, 260.
[19] On dialogue and Sidney, see Alexander, *Writing after Sidney*, chapter 1.

124   'To the Gentleman Reader'

valour. What is distinctive about Breton's elegy is its eroticising of literary affiliation. 'Amoris Lachrimae', love's tears, echoes a powerful precedent, Surrey's elegy for Wyatt, 'Dyvers thy death', in which he weeps lover's tears over Wyatt's body. Breton similarly combines the funeral lamentation and lover's complaint to produce a devotional poem in which Sidney is the object of desire. His beloved body can never be fully recovered, thus compelling the elegist to speak to and for the dead. Breton's elegist distinguishes himself amongst other mourning voices by claiming an extraordinary intimacy with the dead Sidney: 'Oh heavenly powers take pitie of my crie, / Let me not live, and see my Lover die', and then again at the start of the following stanza, 'Oh my love, ah my love, all my love gone' (A4v). This line is mocked in the preface to Newman's *Syr P. S. His Astrophel and Stella* by Thomas Nashe, who recognised the breach of decorum, even as he was prompted to respond with his own eroticising of Sidney's corpus. Another, later reader similarly recognised the intimate, loving friendship to which Breton lay claim, and made sense of its homoeroticism by attributing 'Amoris Lachrimae' to Sidney's close friend, Sir Edward Dyer.[20]

The Sidney who is fashioned alongside Breton in *Brittons Bowre* is a writer of amorous, recreational poetry, both the love poet of *Astrophil and Stella* and the Arcadian shepherd-poet mourned in Breton's elegy by 'Corridon poor sillie wretched swaine' (B1v) – the very type of verse Jones advertises to his 'Gentleman readers' in his preface, 'some of worthines, some of wantonnes, yet … wittie, pleasant, & commendable' (¶2r). The eroticised body of Sidney laid out in Breton's elegy is thus remembered through the gathering of sundry types of courtly love poetry in *Brittons Bowre*. The moralising, aphoristic verse that had filled the pages of earlier poetry anthologies is now muted; instead titles emphasise the mellifluous and pleasing properties of the verse: 'A Pleasant Poem', 'A Sweete Pastorall', 'A prettie Fancie', and 'A pleasant sweet song'. 'Sweet' is a quality that carries across all the senses – taste, smell, sound – designating something as pleasing and wholesome.[21] What is emphasised in these titles are the recreative properties of that which is sweet, here specifically associated with song, and so pleasing to the ear and mind. For Puttenham, sweetness was a particular quality of the harmonious aurality of poetry, in terms of both its metre and certain rhetorical figures that are

---

[20] A variant of this elegy is given the title 'An Epitaph composed by Sr Edward Dyer of Sr Philip Sidney', in *The Dr Farmer Chetham Ms*, ed. A. B. Grosart II (1873), pp. 166–77.

[21] *OED*, 'Sweet', 3a.

Remembering Sidney: the Craft of Compilation

constructed in such a way 'as the ear may receive a certain recreation, although the mind for any novelty of sense be little or nothing affected', in other words, their meaning will 'reach no further than the ear'.[22] Sweetness may be wholesome, but not necessarily have a clear moral direction. A mellifluous soundscape is on show in 'A Sweete Pastorall'. Composed in poulter's measure, the heavy alliterative beat of earlier poetry is modulated through internal rhyme and assonance to create a 'sweet harmonie' typified by its polysyllabic rhymes:

> Good Muse rocke me asleepe with some sweet harmonie,
> This weary eie is not to keepe, thy warie companie,
> Sweet Love be gone a while, thou knowst my heavines,
> Bewtie is borne but to beguile my heart of happines.
>
> (B3v)

These sweet and pleasant pastorals, songs, and sonnets gathered in *Brittons Bowre* equate Sidney with a type of poetry that is characterised as sweet, mellifluous, valued for its sensory capacity to delight, and a mode of poetic making that is so often framed in terms of courtship – prompted by his mistress's love, beauty, disdain, and fickleness – and hence defined by the company of women. Associated with this poetic is an alternative lyric model of masculinity that makes no claims to moral seriousness and instead takes pleasure in female company, as well as the exquisite pains of love, and in the homoeroticism of loving male friendship.[23] It is this eroticised version of Sidney as the sweet-singing love poet of *Astrophil and Stella* that *Brittons Bowre* puts into circulation and to which Thomas Nashe will respond.

Syr P. S. His Astrophel and Stella *(1591)*

Thomas Nashe's epistle, 'Somewhat to reade for them that list', placed before Newman's *Syr P. S. His Astrophel and Stella* (1591), picks a fight with *Brittons Bowre* and, in doing so, provides an early reading of the version of Sidney compiled in this anthology. Newman had turned *Syr P. S. His Astrophel and Stella* into a compilation by adding 'sundry other rare Sonnets of divers Noble men and Gentlemen'. Both Jones's and Newman's collections were therefore competing over a share in the market

---

[22] Puttenham, *Art of English Poesy*, 246–7; also see Trudell on these auricular figures, *Unwritten Poetry*, 32.

[23] See Catherine Bates, *Masculinity, Gender and Identity in the English Renaissance Lyric* (Cambridge University Press, 2007), 1–3.

126   'To the Gentleman Reader'

for books of vernacular lyric poetry stimulated by the publication of *The Countesse of Pembrokes Arcadia*: it too can be viewed as compilation of sorts, since it incorporated inset sections of eclogues, sonnets, and songs and provided lyric material for later anthologies, especially *Englands Helicon*. Nashe, as others have noted, uses the architectural metaphor of the theatre to introduce Newman's edition of Sidney's sonnet sequence to his readers, a framing device which both dramatises the passage of Sidney's lyric poetry from manuscript circulation on to the public stage of print, and acts as the interpretive threshold to collection, putting in place tropes for comprehending the following sonnet sequence.[24] Yet, I would want to argue that the 'paratextual performativity' of the theatre-as-book in Nashe's hands proves less a fixed architectural frame, than a dynamic, jostling, and contested space.

Nashe asks his 'Gentlemen' readers to witness a contest for the right to represent Sidney. The metaphoric ground for this battle is the experiential multimodal world of the theatre-as-book – a space for reading, performance, and consumption that is open and differently inhabited by an array of performers and consumers. Precisely because the space of theatre is demotic, it can be used to set in place socio-cultural distinctions between different classes of books. The reader is asked 'to turn aside' from the lowly cheap 'puppet play' that is *Brittons Bowre*, in which they 'have seene *Pan* sitting in his bower of delights', with 'a number of *Midasses* to admire his miserable hornepipes', and instead enter Newman's edition, 'this Theater of pleasure, for here you shal find a paper stage streud with pearle, an artificial heav'n to overshadow the faire frame, & christal wals to encounter your curious eyes, whiles the tragicommody of love is performed by starlight' (A3r).The starriness of this theatre plays on the two star-crossed lovers of *Astrophil and Stella*, and their apotheosis in Sidney's work. By contrast, the metaphor used for *Brittons Bowre* is that of common stuff: it is a 'Gravesend barge', 'fraught of spangled feathers, golden Peebles, Straw, Reedes, Bulrushes, or any thing' (A4r). The barge anthology is a commercial container and the poetry it promiscuously gathers is without value or profit, possessing only a superficial appeal to the undiscriminating consumer. And yet, as we will see, it is not all that distant from the attractions of Nashe's 'Theater of pleasure', with its superficial play of light on glittering surfaces.

In this preface, Nashe is trying to wrest control over the Sidney that *Brittons Bowre* had put into print and circulation – the recreational and

---

[24] See Sherman's discussion, 'Architecture, Paratext', 75.

Remembering Sidney: the Craft of Compilation   127

amorous love poet embodied in his *Astrophil and Stella*. The Sidney who emerges in the 1590s is not only the exemplary masculine Protestant soldier-poet, but a far more internally divided figure.[25] Thomas Newman was uncertain how to place *Astrophil and Stella* in the wider literary field, both apologising that its amorous subject 'perhaps may seem too light', while promoting 'the worthiness of the Author' (A2–2v). And there is a wilful impropriety to the way Nashe brings Sidney into public view, not as a rarefied Petrarchan love poet, but as an Ovidian poet of erotic and illicit verse. His preface elaborates a model of reading for pleasure that has its expression in the voyeuristic delights of the glittering theatre of consumption that is *Astrophil and Stella*. If, as William Sherman argues, Nashe's readers 'would have recognized' the sources of the Latin quotes woven into his preface and how they 'depict Sidney and his alter ego, Astrophel, as the true revivers of Ovidian arts of love', then they would have also recognised that these are illicit seductive arts.[26] The Latin tags all derive from Ovid's erotic works, his *Amores* and *Ars Amatoria*. The preface opens with '*Tempus adest plausus aurea pompa venit*' from Ovid's *Amores* ('Now is the time for applause, the golden procession is coming', 3.2.44), which Nashe cites to dismiss *Brittons Bowre*, 'the Sceane of Idiots', and to announce the arrival of Newman's edition: 'enter *Astrophel* in pompe' (A3r).[27] The context of this quote in Ovid's elegy is one of seduction: the lover, a devotee of Venus, uses the cover of a day at the races to pursue his adulterous affair. Nashe then introduces another metaphor for the publication of *Astrophil and Stella*: 'Which although it be oftentimes imprisoned in Ladyes casks, & the president bookes of such as cannot see without another mans spectacles, yet at length it breakes foorth in spight of his keepers, and useth some private penne (in steed of a picklock) to procure his violent enlargement' (A3r). The lady's casket is a particularly rich spatialising metaphor for figuring verse transmission and the form of the compiled book. Poems are copied on to loose sheets that come to rest momentarily in a gathered state, whether in a casket or a precedent book,

---

[25] Bates argues for a polarisation between Sidney and Astrophil, that is 'frequently ... mapped onto those of the active Protestant hero, on the one hand, and the idle courtier, on the other – two positions, furthermore, that are implicitly if not explicitly gendered. Where Astrophil is identified with the effeminate and trifling courtier ... Sidney, by contrast is identified with the masculine hero' (*Masculinity, Gender and Identity*, 35). I am arguing that these divisions, and their variants, are constitutive of the figure of Sidney fashioned across an range of books.

[26] Sherman, 'Architecture, Paratext', 75.

[27] Ovid, *Amores*, trans. Grant Showerman, rev. G. P. Goold (Cambridge, MA: Harvard University Press, 1977), 452–3. All subsequent references are to this edition.

128   'To the Gentleman Reader'

presumably a commonplace book, and then released again through copying.[28]

There is, however, something disturbing about this extended metaphor of ladies' caskets. Not only is Nashe's meaning slippery and difficult to pin down, the hoped for 'violent enlargement' secured through the agency of 'some private penne' seems to define textual transmission as something aggressively sexually illicit. We can see Nashe's 'ladies casket' as a variant on the 'ladies' text' described by Juliet Fleming: those texts addressed by male authors to women readers, which function within 'the register of the erotic', and enable male writers both to claim mastery over poetic making and publication, and yet disavow laureate ambitions, instead preferring the company of women.[29] The passage from *Ars Amatoria*, which frames Nashe's introduction of the metaphor of the ladies' caskets – '*Quide petitur sacris nisi tantum fama poetis*' ('What is sought by the sacred bards but fame alone', 3.403) – within its Ovidian context, means that fame is achieved through the visibility afforded by publication. When Nashe conflates this tag with ladies' caskets, it mirrors the way in which publication is sexualised in this passage from *Ars Amatoria*. Ovid equates the fame attendant on publication with the voyeuristic exposure of women's bodies to the male viewer through the logic that 'What is hidden is unknown' and 'No one desires what is unknown' (3.397). Opening ladies' caskets, when read through Ovid, means revealing the woman's body to a desiring male gaze. It is thus a multivalent metaphor for transmission, reception, and the sonnet sequence itself that equates Sidney's *Astrophil and Stella* with the desirable woman's body; its publication, making that which is hidden known, turns reading into a voyeuristic act. The accumulative effect of the quotes from Ovid, alongside the introduction of ladies' caskets, eroticises processes of textual production and exchange, writing and reading, imagining the mistress's body, or more particularly her genitalia, in the form of the book made flesh.[30] With Sidney's *Astrophil and Stella* transformed into a 'ladies' text' at the very front of the book, Nashe asserts his masculine ability to unlock its secrets to a reading public. Nashe's Sidney is a different literary property to the poet fashioned in Breton's 'Amoris Lachrimae', suggesting that the figure of Sidney as the idle love poet, who prefers female company, was itself available for variant readings.

Even within the pages of Newman's edition, very different versions of Sidney are put into circulation. Variety is facilitated by the format of a

---

[28] See Woudhuysen's reading of 'precedent book', *Sir Philip Sidney*, 367.
[29] Fleming, 'The ladies' man', 159–64.   [30] Wall, *Imprint of Gender*, 45–6.

Remembering Sidney: the Craft of Compilation 129

compilation, which can be divided into distinct sections, each with different sets of participants. Nashe's illicit Ovidian Sidney at the front of the book contrasts markedly with the rarified Petrarchan poet fashioned at its end. The 'Poems and Sonets of sundrie other Noble men and Gentlemen' added after *Astrophil and Stella* and his 'Other Sonnets of variable verse' (46) are framed by and so read through Sidney. The collection is made up of Daniel's sonnet sequence, published the following year under the title *Delia*, a set of five songs by Thomas Campion, here unattributed, a Greville poem ('Faction that ever dwelles'), given the title '*Megliora spero*', assigned to E[arl]. O[xford]., and an anonymous song, 'If flouds of teares could clense my follies past' (79–80).[31] Since the running title 'Syr P. S. his Astrophel and Stella' is retained across the volume, Sidney's work becomes the mould which determines the form of this collection and establishes his presence as the impetus for such poetic gatherings. Hence, Daniel's opening sonnet, the envoy, is in close conversation with the first sonnet of *Astrophil and Stella*, imagining the sonnet sequence as his child parthenogenically issuing from his love-sick mind:

> Go wayling verse the infant of my love,
> *Minerva* like, brought foorth without a mother:
> That beares the image of the cares I prove;
> Witnesse your fathers griefe exceeds all other.
>
> (62)

This trope, in which poetic making is imagined in terms of human reproduction, imitates Sidney's opening sonnet in which Astrophil had proclaimed himself 'great with child to speak'. Once these two sonnet sequences are placed alongside each other in this volume, a reading emerges that styles Daniel as the heir to Sidney's legacy. To follow Sidney is to engage in an act of Sidneian poetic procreation.[32]

Daniel's parthenogenic trope follows Aristotle in locating the origins of physical and poetic creation in the male mind.[33] Male poets often represented themselves as pregnant with or giving birth to 'wayling verse', appropriating the language of female reproduction. Daniel takes this further by explicitly arguing that parthenogenesis does not require women's bodies, making it clear that no mothers are involved in his act

---

[31] Marotti, *Manuscript, Print*, 231. Campion's *Canto Secundo*, 'What faire pompe', follows Sidney's experiments in quantitative measure; see Trudell, *Unwritten Poetry*, 67, n. 125.
[32] Zarnowiecki, *Fair Copies*, 108–28.
[33] Elizabeth A. Spiller, *Science, Reading, and Renaissance Literature: the Art of Making Knowledge, 1580–1670* (Cambridge University Press, 2004), 62–74.

130 'To the Gentleman Reader'

of poetic making. In this way, his act of poetic re-creation contrasts instructively with Edwards's 'In goyng to my naked bedde', which relies on the figure of the nursing mother to define the nourishing properties of the mother tongue.[34] Such an all-male model of literary imitation can avoid the associations set in play in Nashe's preface between ladies' caskets, women's bodies, and Sidney's corpus. If Daniel is offering an embodied model of poetic reproduction, then he is very particular about the gender and class of this body. The model of poetic making embodied in Aristotelian parthenogenesis is also far removed from that embodied in the labouring body of the poet-as-craftsman. The anthologies of the 1570s, like *Gorgious Gallery* and Whitney's *A Sweet Nosgay*, as we have seen, deploy very different tropes for conceptualising poetic craft to these Sidneian anthologies of the 1590s.

When Newman brought out a second edition of *Astrophil and Stella* in the same year, this collection of 'Poems and Sonets' was removed along with the prefaces of Newman and Nashe. It is not clear why this material was excised, nor why the 'Poems and Sonets' were reprinted again by Matthew Lownes when he brought out an edition of *Syr P. S. His Astrophel and Stella*, at some time after 1597; Newman had died in 1593, the plague year Jones would write of in his preface to *Arbor of Amorous Devices*, which caused so much hardship for the London trades.[35] Nor, indeed, is it clear why Newman's edition was called in in the first place: there is no substantive evidence that it was called in after Mary Sidney, Countess of Pembroke, intervened, as is often assumed. Woudhuysen concludes: 'There was clearly something offensive about Newman's publication which led to its "taking in", but the Stationers' Register gives no hint of why it was undertaken or who initiated it.'[36] We might be tempted to argue that it caused offence because of the way Nashe framed Sidney's *Astrophil and Stella* through the erotic figure of the 'ladies casket'. But then, the Sidney that Mary Sidney would fashion through the 1598/9 edition of *The Countess of Pembroke's Arcadia*, as Patricia Pender points out, is also at home in ladies' caskets and looks like a prodigal poet, a writer of secular amorous poetry.[37] What we can say is that the early 1590s witness the emergence of variant Sidneys that often jostle together in the same spaces, even at the front and back of the same book. These variant Sidneys carry

---

[34] For a discussion of this trope of the mother tongue, see Milller, 'Mother Tongues', 192; Chapter 1, 52–3.

[35] STC 22538; the title-page is undated.   [36] Woudhuysen, *Sir Philip Sidney*, 367–9.

[37] Patricia Pender, *Early Modern Women's Writing and the Rhetoric of Modesty* (Basingstoke: Palgrave Macmillan, 2012), 119–20.

Remembering Sidney: the Craft of Compilation 131

with them alternative models of literary production and transmission, whether in ladies' caskets and spectacular theatres of consumption or among the 'shepheards nation' of Spenser's funeral anthology for Sidney, *Astrophel*.

The Phoenix Nest *(1593) and* Colin Clouts/Astrophel *(1595)*

The Phoenix Nest is reputed to be one of the finest Elizabethan poetry anthologies alongside *Englands Helicon*. The quality of its copy is taken as evidence that this anthology captures the work of a gentleman compiler, who had unique access to poems only circulating in exclusive manuscript channels. Rollins argued that *The Phoenix Nest* can be clearly distinguished from earlier anthologies, which 'were strictly commercial publications, arranged for and carried through by booksellers': 'In striking contrast, *The Phoenix Nest* was a purely literary work, supervised and probably initiated by a gentleman of the Inner Temple, who discloses only his initials, R. S.', and who 'included poems only from those authors whom he knew personally'.[38] The implication is that this anthology has literary merit, unlike those 'strictly commercial publications', because it is closer to manuscript culture than it is to print. As we shall see, such a distinction between *The Phoenix Nest* and earlier 'commercial' anthologies put out by publishers is difficult to maintain. Those authors whose poems are gathered in *The Phoenix Nest* were popular in print and many had appeared in earlier 'commercial' anthologies. Moreover, not all poems printed in *The Phoenix Nest* derive from manuscript, since a number had been previously printed in *Brittons Bowre*. *The Phoenix Nest* is in close dialogue with Jones's anthology, a dialogue that Jones would resume in *Arbor of Amorous Devices*. In fact, what brings the anthologies discussed in this chapter together is not only Sidney, but relatedly how they engage in conversation with each other, borrowing poems, typographic features, tropes, and print conventions, and so learning from each other the craft of anthology-making.

The elite literary gathering so often admired in *The Phoenix Nest*, to a large extent, is a fabrication consciously manufactured through sophisticated uses of print conventions and the machinery of the book. *The Phoenix Nest* was published by a consortium, the Eliot's Court printing house established in 1584 – a partnership between Arnold Hatfield,

---

[38] R. S., *The Phoenix Nest*, ed. H. E. Rollins (1931; Cambridge, MA: Harvard University Press, 1969), ix, xxxii. See also North, *Anonymous Renaissance*, 72.

132 'To the Gentleman Reader'

Edmund Bollyfant, Ninian Newton, and John Jackson, whose name appears on the title-page, that specialised in printing classical Latin works.[39] Whereas Jones and Newman had made their presence known at the front of their books by supplying prefaces, the 'printer' is notably absent from *The Phoenix Nest*, apart from the colophon. This may be a consequence of publication by a consortium who held stock in common, rather than an individual publisher, like Tottel, Disle, or Jones, who owned the title and publicised their agency at the front of the book. Or it may be an example of the discreet distance kept by publishers to downplay their role in the book's production, insisting as it states on the tite-page that it has been 'Set foorth by R. S. of the Inner Temple *Gentleman*', and so entirely his work.[40] Whatever the reason, the absence of the printer's epistle leaves an editorial space at the front of the volume that is open to others to fill. It is surprising, then, that R. S. does not occupy this space, nor does he surface anywhere else in the collection, and his identity remains elusive.[41] Instead, the front of the book is given over to the Sidney family. Allegiance is declared with the opening defence of Leicester, 'A Preface to the Reader upon the dead mans Right'. The names of Sidney and Queen Elizabeth grace many of the headnotes to the poems, and appear alongside authors who are identified by initials that are routinely accompanied by status markers – G. P. Master of Arts, N. B. Gent., T. L. Gent., E. O., Sir W. H., W. S. Gent., and T. W. Gent. Those responsible for this aspect of the production of *The Phoenix Nest* carefully and consistently utilised initials, a well-established print convention for signifying the social discretion claimed by the elite, turning it into standard practice for this type of gentlemanly publication.[42] Because initials coincide with status markers, literary and class ambitions are interlinked to give the impression of an elite literary milieu, emerging out of the environs of the court, universities, and Inns of Court, thus giving credence to the claim on the title-page that the anthology has been 'Built up with the most rare and refined workes of Noble men, woorthy Knights, gallant Gentlemen, Masters of Arts, and brave Schollers' – a far cry

---

[39] Ninian Newton left the partnership in 1586; Jackson was a member of the Grocer's Company and so foreign to the Stationers, which may be why he entered into this partnership. He died some time before 1596, but no one else in the consortium brought out a further edition of *The Phoenix Nest*. See H. R. Plomer, 'Eliot's Court Printing House, 1584–1674', *The Library*, 2 (1921), 175–8.

[40] Johns, *Nature of the Book*, 34.

[41] Rollins (*Phoenix Nest*, xxv–xxix) favoured Richard Stapleton, a friend of George Chapman; however, he is not listed in the admission books of the Inner Temple.

[42] See, on initials, North, *Anonymous Renaissance*, 72.

Remembering Sidney: the Craft of Compilation 133

from the 'worthy workeman' who 'joyned together and builded up' *A Gorgious Gallery*.

The compilers of both *Brittons Bowre* and *The Phoenix Nest* recognised the value of framing the anthology through the funerary elegy. Earlier anthologies included elegies, which, when placed in relation to other poems, could put in play models of literary affiliation, as we have seen in the case of Surrey and Wyatt in *Songes and Sonettes*. When placed at the front of the volume, elegies act as the frame through which the following poems are apprehended and as a threshold offering privileged access to a textual community gathered to honour and memorialise Sidney. The act of compiling an elegiac collection gives textual and material embodiment to the communal impulse of the funerary elegy to assemble and give voice to those who hold in trust the memory of the dead. Placing an elegy for a dead poet like Sidney in the opening pages locates the author and his corpus at the centre of the task of compiling an anthology. *The Phoenix Nest* takes this equation between compilation and commemoration a step further by naming the anthology after Sidney in his transfigured state, the phoenix. Since Leland's elegy for Wyatt, the phoenix had been available to canonise English poets. The phoenix's nest is a metaphor for the anthology that defines its purpose in terms of cultural renewal and canonising poetic lineages. The bird's nest was a humanist metaphor for the generative properties of compilation that drew on 'the Platonic metaphor of the memory as an aviary or dovecote'.[43] The memory nest is transformed into the phoenix's miraculous and sacred funeral pyre, from which Sidney-as-phoenix will rise from the ashes, regenerated and remembered through the work of the poets gathered in the volume. Three elegies are gathered at the front of *The Phoenix Nest*, all unattributed, and follow on from one another without page breaks, emphasising their close affiliation with each other and with Sidney. First is Matthew Roydon's elegy, given the title 'An Elegie, or friends passion, for his Astrophill', then Raleigh's 'An Epitaph upon the right Honorable sir Philip Sidney knight: Lord governor of Flushing', and 'Another of the same. Excellently written by a most woorthy Gentleman.', possibly by Fulke Greville. The phoenix, which presides over the anthology, is fired in Roydon's opening elegy, 'Hir ashes flying with the winde', establishing Sidney as the poetic progenitor, whose literary legacy is re-created in the works of those select authors gathered in the collection: 'Haply the cinders driven about, / May breede an offspring neere that kinde' (7). The Sidney remembered in these elegies is an

---

[43] Vine, *Miscellaneous Order*, 39.

134 'To the Gentleman Reader'

amalgam of the manly soldier-poet and the love poet of *Astrophil and Stella*. The 'Astrophill' fashioned in Roydon's elegy is transfigured, his love confers immortality and is conceived in neo-Platonic terms: Stella is now 'Most rare and rich of heavenly blis' (5). Sidney is apostrophised by Raleigh as the virtuous soldier whose learning is put into practice through military endeavour, the 'Scipio, Cicero, and Petrarch of our time' (10), while in Fulke Greville's elegy, he is removed from female company and mourned as the ideal male friend and this poet's better self: 'Sidney is dead, dead is my friend, dead is the worlds delight' (10).

Spenser's *Astrophel* learnt its lessons in how to craft an elegiac anthology from these earlier Sidneian compilations. *Astrophel* was published alongside his *Colin Clouts Come Home Againe* (1595), two years after *Phoenix Nest*. Rather than a single-authored volume, it is a compilation made up, in large part, of poems by other authors already in print: Lodowick Bryskett's 'The mourning muse of Thestylis' was entered in the Stationers' Register on 22 August 1587, and the final section reprints the opening set of three elegies from *Phoenix Nest*. The layout of *Astrophel* does not disguise its borrowing from other books. Instead its dependence on earlier acts of publication is signalled by marking out those poems taken, or said to be taken, from elsewhere with printers' ornaments. The layout of the *mis-en-page* gives the impression that its author, Spenser, working in collaboration with William Ponsonby, has assembled these texts into one collection. Ponsonby was not only Spenser's preferred publisher in the 1590s, he was also the Sidney family publisher, putting out editions of Sidney's works, including *The Countesse of Pembrokes Arcadia* 'authorised' by Mary Sidney.[44] *Astrophel* is dedicated to Frances Walsingham, Sidney's widow, now Countess of Essex. What emerges from this act of anthologising is a distinctly composite author, a Spenserian Sidney. 'With the *Astrophel* volume', as Dennis Kay wrote, 'Spenser invented Spenserian poetry'.[45] An unusual feature of the *Colin Clouts* volume is that it gives no notice on its title-page that it includes *Astrophel*, which has its own title-page within the volume. Since the running title across both sections is 'Colin Clouts come home againe', *Astrophel* is folded into the preceding work. Patrick Cheney has described the two parts as 'creating a diptych', a particularly apt metaphor since it describes an object folded to create two leaves that,

---

[44] Woudhuysen, *Sir Philip Sidney*, 232–5; on Ponsonby and the Sidney family, see Steven Mentz, 'Selling Sidney: William Ponsonby, Thomas Nashe, and the Boundaries of Elizabethan Print and Manuscript Cultures', *Text*, 13 (2000), 151–74.
[45] Kay, *Melodious Tears*, 65.

Remembering Sidney: the Craft of Compilation   135

while distinct, only function in relation to each other, so it is neither one nor the other.[46] The hinge that provides the point of intersection is Colin Clout, the shepherd-poet through whom Spenser and others dramatise his career in the style of the English national poet.[47] Yet, since in *Astrophel* the poet has become an anthologiser of his own and others' works, this compilation puts into circulation a collaborative, co-creative mode of authorship that does not fully cohere into a unified author. The 'shepheards nation' that is formed in *Colin Clouts* will provide the next generation of Spenserian poets with a model for collaborative authorship and compiled books.[48]

Astrophel is consciously compiled. The interplay between the physical organisation of the contents – through the disposition of white space, page breaks, printers' ornaments, and other devices – and its governing pastoral fiction redefine the anthology, turning it into a pastoral drama. Much attention has been given to a section, now given the title 'The Dolefull Lay of Clorinda', and how the *mise-en-page* and the way it is framed within the narrative both pose and confound questions of authorship – whether the author is Spenser or 'Clorinda', Mary Sidney, Countess of Pembroke – or offer a more fluid, co-creative, and collaborative mode of authorship.[49] These questions of authorship have meant that 'The Dolefull Lay' has been excerpted from *Astrophel* and reprinted in other anthologies where it is attributed to Mary Sidney, while editions of Spenser normally excise those elegies attributed to other poets.[50] The precedence given to Mary Sidney in this processional funeral anthology articulates the ways in which she is the motivating presence in generating a composite Sidneian poetics, in which Philip is always dependent on Mary's agency.[51] The ways in which *Astrophel* has been broken up and reassembled in other forms by modern editors tells us something about its deliberately composite

---

[46] Patrick Cheney, '*Colin Clouts come home againe, Astrophel*, and 'The doleful lay of Clorinda', in *The Oxford Handbook of Edmund Spenser*, edited by Richard McCabe (Oxford University Press, 2010), 237–55.

[47] See Bart Van Es, 'Spenserian Pastoral', in *Early Modern English Poetry: a Critical Companion*, edited by Patrick Cheney, Andrew Hadfield, and Garrett A. Sullivan (Oxford University Press, 2007), 86–7.

[48] Michelle O'Callaghan, *The 'Shepheards Nation': Jacobean Spenserians and Early Stuart Political Culture, 1612–1625* (Oxford: Clarendon Press, 2000), chapter 1.

[49] Danielle Clarke, '"In sort as she sung it": the Doleful Lay of Clorinda and the Construction of Female Authorship', *Criticism*, 42 (2001), 451–68.

[50] See, for example, Danielle Clarke, *Isabella Whitney, Mary Sidney, and Aemilia Lanyer: Renaissance Women Poets* (London: Penguin, 2000); Spenser, *Shorter Poems*, edited by Richard McCabe (London: Penguin, 1999) – this edition includes the 'Doleful Lay', but not the other elegies.

[51] Pender, *Early Modern Women's Writing*, 110–21.

136 'To the Gentleman Reader'

structure. *Astrophel* opens with a pastoral narrative frame set off in italics, in which the shepherd-poet addresses and so assembles the community that is given expression in the following collection: '*Hearken ye gentle shepheards to my song / And place my dolefull plaint your plaints emong*' (E4r). Here, apostrophe, as we have seen in other uses of this figure, brings to the fore the dramatic vocal properties of this compilation. Song, both performed and heard, becomes the means of establishing relationships between interlocutors, and figures forth a shared embodied, re-creative, and co-creative space. At the same time, the spatialising language of placing and conjoining – '*place my dolefull plaint your plaints emong* ' – marks out the physical properties of the compiled book. Spenser's elegy is placed among and alongside elegies by other poets, which, in turn, make up his song. This pastoral scene thus fictionalises the process of compiling a funerary anthology.

The complex oscillation between embodied voice and the material form of the book continues throughout much of the collection, giving a distinctive shape to this anthology.[52] Colin's opening elegy for Astrophel closes by returning to the gathering of shepherd-poets assembled to hear his lament, who are busy devising their own plaints. Precedence is given to Clorinda's 'dolefull lay': 'Which least I marre the sweetnesse of the vearse, / In sort as she it sung, I will rehearse' (F4v). Her song is appropriately set off from the preceding text by a sizeable amount of white space so that it begins on a new page. The duration of Clorinda's lay across four full pages is framed by borders of printers' flowers, which identify it as a distinct subsection within the compilation. At the end of her song, Colin returns to introduce the following set of elegies, first Thestylis, who 'made the *Muses* in his song to mourne', and then the others, 'The which I here in order will rehearse, / As fittest flowres to deck his mournfull hearse' (G3r). The two elegies attributed to Bryskett follow as a pair – 'The mourning muse of Thestylis' and 'A pastorall Aeglogue upon the death of Sir Phillip Sidney Knight' – ending with the Latin motto '*Virtute summa: catera fortuna*', the initials L. B., and a printer's ornament; and finally the set of elegies taken from *The Phoenix Nest* start on a new page, each page framed by a border of printers' flowers, mirroring that of 'Clorinda's lay', and so, once again, marked up as a spatially distinct and portable section, which indeed has been taken from elsewhere. Colin, however, does not return between these sets of elegies, nor does he appear at the end; instead, his task is completed at the point when he introduced this compilation as an anthology, the

---

[52] See Trudell's definition of intermediation in *Unwritten Poetry*, 7 n. 24.

Remembering Sidney: the Craft of Compilation

constituent parts of which will be rehearsed 'in order', in a sequence governed by the overarching conceit of the funerary anthology, flowers decking the hearse, and his place will thus be taken by other poets.

Spenser's collaborative pastoral fiction of compilation differs markedly from the *florilegia* motifs used by other poets, most notably Whitney, to figure the editorial agency of the author in gathering textual material into a collection, and instead puts in play a model of poetic making far removed from field of work. The gathering involved in this pastoral funerary anthology is not that of Whitney's husbandman or urban gardener, but of recreative shepherd-poets, whose gentle life of *otium* is defined by the absence of agrarian manual labour.[53] The flowers or posies that deck the hearse are elegies written on paper and gathered in this anthology memorialising Sidney. Flowers and posies are also consistently referred to as songs and so imagined as transmitted through texts, bodies, and voices, a process of intermediation that is integral to the way that the activity of compilation is imagined in the collection and captured in Spenser's very slippery use of the term 'rehearse'. 'Rehearse' referred primarily to the act of reciting. When Spenser uses this term, it is specifically in relation to that which is already in circulation – published – both as song and as text. The rhetorical figure to which 'rehearse' is attached in *Astrophel* is *prosopopoeia*, in the words of Abraham Fraunce, the 'fayning of any person, when in our speech, we represent the person of anie, and make it speake as though he were there present'.[54] In doing so, *Astrophel* deliberately confounds questions of authorship, offering instead a fluid, composite, and finally indeterminate and pluralised figure of author-performer-compiler. Spenser employs *prosopopoeia* alongside apostrophe. Shepherds are invited by the poet to hearken and to respond. The combined rhetorical effect of these figures animates the pastoral drama structuring this compilation, in which a community is summoned and then gathers to speak and to sing to one another. By this means, textual transmission is located within bodies, and made present through acts of compilation that are choral, operating through texts, songs, and performance. The posthumous publication of Sidney's works prompted renewed attention to the craft of anthology-making. Volumes published in the early 1590s experiment with the form of the anthology and the spaces it is possible to conceptualise and make within the pages of the book, from bowers and nests to the pastoral

---

[53] Louis Montrose, 'Of Gentlemen and Shepherds: the Politics of Elizabethan Pastoral Form', *English Literary History*, 50 (1983), 431–2.
[54] Quoted in Alexander, '*Prosopopoeia*', 103.

138 'To the Gentleman Reader'

gathering of *Astrophel*. The anthologies considered in this chapter utilise different models of compilation to earlier collections. What we are witnessing here, however, is less a decisive sea-change, than diversification. *Englands Helicon* published at the end of the century in 1600, as we will see in the following chapter, returns to the topic of the travail, the labour, and craft involved in compiling an anthology within the milieu of the printing house.

'Any pleasing pamphlet to recreate your mind': Recreational Poetry and the Company of Women

Poetry anthologies of the 1590s respond creatively to a poetics of leisure, fabricating recreational spaces within the form of the book. Sidney's own writings are profoundly and productively ambivalent on this subject. *An Apologie for Poetrie* (1595), published alongside Sidney's other works, gave English poetry a credibility as a serious art form, arguing for its instructive, moralising capacity to delight and so persuade its readers to virtuous action. At the same time, Sidney famously characterised his own poetry as a pastime, the 'toyes' of youth, uncoupling delight from instruction, and jesting that 'in these my not old yeres & idelest times', he had 'slipt into the title of a Poet', his 'unelected vocation'.[55] To slip suggests both moral fallenness and the pleasurable lightness and ease attributed to a lack of forethought. The tension, here, between *officium* and *otium*, poetry as a vocation, worthy of study, and as pastime, a form of recreation that occupies idle times, shapes how recreational literature is framed in anthologies in the 1590s.

When poetry is framed in terms of recreation, it is typically located in environments in which women play an active role alongside men as readers, auditors, performers, and co-creators of lyrics. Sidney's letter to his sister, Mary, printed the previous year before *The Countesse of Pembrokes Arcadia*, evokes an elite recreational space that is defined by the active presence of women, who preside over this domain. The scene Sidney imagines is a domestic setting, replete with familial metaphors, and he willingly locates his work within this space: his work is a child, which he is 'loath to father', and in need of a midwife to be delivered, and will enter the service of his sister within her household, 'bearing the liverye of your name'.[56] Unlike Daniel's parthenogenetic trope, this recreational model of poetic making is crucially dependent on the agency of women to bring it to

---

[55] *An Apologie for Poetrie* (1595), B1v. [56] *Countesse of Pembrokes Arcadia* (1590), A3r-3v, A4r.

Recreational Poetry and the Company of Women 139

fruition. The relationship between brother and sister within this space is re-creative and co-creative, and particularly intimate in its expression of consanguinity of both blood and mind; the production of his romance is crucially dependent on Mary Sidney, 'being done in loose sheetes of paper, most of it in your presence, the rest, by sheetes, sent unto you, as fast as they were done'. She acts as the compiler – his 'midwife' – who gathers his work together, and more than this gives it life, form, and meaning. The analogy Sidney uses to describe his 'idle worke' is that of a 'Spiders webbe'; yet while an Arachnean meaning might lurk behind this allusion, its apparent meaning is more mundane and to do with housewifery, since this it 'will be thought fitter to be swept away, then worn to any other purpose' (A3r). Within this domestic space, Sidney's romance is construed primarily in terms of the pastime: 'this idle worke of mine' is but 'a trifle' and 'triflinglie handled', and so to be read 'at your idle tymes' (A3r–4r). Sidney, of course, is being playful and skilfully deploying the rhetoric of modesty to invite the reader not to take him too seriously.[57] Yet, this is precisely the point. Sidney, in performatively idle fashion, offers his sister a different kind of literature that is productively non-productive, designed for ornament and consumption, rather than moral improvement, and made to be enjoyed at times of leisure. The value Sidney asks his sister to find in recreational literature, which is also made through her agency, discloses other lighter, minor histories of the lyric that are taking shape alongside those national, laureate stories of literary generation set out in Spenser's 'shepheards nation'.

Recreational poetry is typically termed idle, yet it was also understood to require skill and instruction, for both its composition and appreciation. Puttenham described the 'chief purpose' of the third book of *The Art of English Poesy* on the topic 'of Ornament' in terms that bring together the recreational and the instructional, and women and men:

> And because our chief purpose herein is for the learning of ladies and young gentlewomen, or idle courtiers, desirous to become skilful in their own mother tongue, and for their own private recreation to make now and then ditties of pleasure – thinking for our part none other science so fit for them and the place as that which teacheth *beau semblant*, the chief profession as well of courting as of poesy – since to such manner of minds nothing is more cumbersome than tedious doctrines and scholarly methods of discipline, we have in our own conceit devised a new and strange model of this art, fitter to please the court than the school, and yet not unnecessary for all

---

[57] See Pender, *Early Modern Women's Writing*, 98–100,

140 'To the Gentleman Reader'

such as be will themselves to become good makers in the vulgar, or to be able to judge other men's makings.[58]

The equation between gentlewomen and 'idle courtiers' may seem pejorative, since 'idle', in the sense of lack of proper occupation, can be moralised as indolent. Yet Puttenham is clearly offering a positive alternative to a regulatory model of learning that combines pleasurable activity with skill and judgement. Puttenham's 'ladies and young gentlewomen, or idle courtiers' are interchangeable, which means that either subject position is open to the other, disclosing the gender fluidity within the trope of the company of women. Private recreation is a feminised occupation for Puttenham and others, distinct from the world of masculine public service, and comparable to Sidney's 'idlest times', when he was not occupied in public duties of office. There is an art to such pastimes. The humanist language of common profit can be heard in Puttenham's appeal to those gentlewomen and men who want 'to become more skilful in their own mother tongue', and so gain training in poetic composition in the vernacular as well as cultivating their literary judgement. Poetry therefore becomes a proper 'vocation' for gentlewomen, given their exclusion from direct engagement in civic affairs. Puttenham offers his book as an alternative schoolroom, 'because we are to teach ladies and gentlewomen to know their school points and terms appertaining to the art', a place for study within the privacy of the household.[59] We might recall the feminised household-as-schoolroom imagined in Edwards's 'In goyng to my naked bedde'. The difference is that Edwards is promoting proverbial, moralising poetry through the mother's song. Here, recreational poetry is located in a milieu in which 'courting' and 'poesy' are interchangeable and identified by Puttenham with *beau semblant*, those poetic and rhetorical forms that are ornamental, all surface, and so designed to give pleasure through their sensory appeal.[60]

There is a class dimension to this account of the poetry of recreation as a suitable occupation for gentlewomen. Whitney, in *A Sweet Nosgay*, had also framed poetry as an alternative vocation for women. But, when Whitney gave an account of poetic making at times of leisure, it was defined in relation to work – she only has leisure to write because she is

---

[58] Puttenham, *Art of English Poesy*, 243. See also the discussion of this passage in Sasha Roberts, 'Women's Literary Capital in Early Modern England: Formal Composition and Rhetorical Display in Manuscript and Print', *Women's Writing*, 14 (2007), 248–51.

[59] Puttenham, *Art of English Poesy*, 252.

[60] On pleasurable rhetorical figures, see Robson, *Sense of Early Modern Writing*, 78; see also Craik, *Reading Sensations*, 37–47.

Recreational Poetry and the Company of Women 141

'servicelesse' (A5v), and so subject to the economic instability of those dependent on paid employment. If, as Sasha Roberts argues, Puttenham is promoting 'women's literary capital', then he describes a skill, taste, and poetic style the acquisition of which signals membership of the gentle social classes. This particular language of poetic making is attuned to an elite class of 'ladies and young gentlewomen, or idle courtiers' who have no duty to work and are far removed from the necessity of physical labour. When Jones addresses *Brittons Bowre* and *Arbor of Amorous Devices* to the 'gentleman reader', he too is invoking this class-based model of 'private recreation' that is dependent on leisured time and country estates. His preface to *Arbor*, first published in 1594, opens by noting that the 'absence' of his gentleman readers 'this long time of vacation hindered my poore Presse from publishing any pleasing Pamphlet, to recreate your minds', and hopes for their 'speedy return to London . . . to the comfort of all poore men of Trades' (A2r–v). Jones's plea was especially urgent since the vacation had been extended in 1593 owing to plague, resulting in economic hardship for London tradespeople.[61] Newman, the early publisher of *Astrophil and Stella*, died in that year. The *otium* of the country estate that Jones invokes in his epistle is hedged around by another narrative of economic necessity and the dependency of London tradespeople on the business of their clientele. The 'pleasant Arbor for Gentleman' he has produced is a simulacrum of 'your pleasant Arbors of the countrie' manufactured by a poor man of trade dependent on the vagaries of work.

Whereas Jones's ballads before *A Handefull* and *The Copy of a Letter* placed him among his customers at his bookstall, here cultures of consumption are carefully socially stratified and demarcated, defined through a distinction between men of leisure and men of trade. Jones still offers his customers a poetry of recreation to be bought and sung, in the words of *Arbor*'s title-page, 'to court the love of faire Ladies and Gentlewomen', but there is a discernible idiom of social distinction at work in his modelling of a book-buying public compared with his earlier anthologies that invited readers to buy into a culture of recreation belonging to the leisured classes. Jones's 1590s anthologies nonetheless continued to remain open to a broader readership, just as his earlier anthologies moved between different classes of readers. The composite gentleman reader should be seen less as a descriptor of actual readers than as a container that can be inhabited by others not necessarily belonging to this social class or, indeed, gender, especially since this figure is characteristically located in female company.

---

[61] Rollins, ed., *Arbor*, xii.

142 'To the Gentleman Reader'

The openness of this figure is evident in the variety of reading experiences gathered under its designation. The gentleman reader has his counterpart in the gentleman author, in the case of Jones's anthologies, N. B. gent., a designation that is similarly open and composite, and a product of anthology-making. Not all the poems gathered in *Brittons Bowre* were authored by Breton – the Earl of Oxford's initials are subscribed to one poem in the collection – while Jones openly admits that *Arbor* gathers '*many mens workes . . ., most, not the meanest in estate and degree*'. Instead, like the gentleman reader, N. B. gent. signifies certain literary and cultural properties, given that his name in the 1590s was associated with the category of courtly makers. *The Passionate Pilgrime*, published in two editions by William Jaggard in 1599, similarly traded off the name of '*W. Shakespeare*' who, like N. B. gent. earlier in the decade, is a composite figure compiled out of the work of many poets.[62]

The recreational properties of these anthologies meant that like earlier collections they invited multimodal uses. Gathered in *Bowre* and *Arbor* are poems for which contemporary musical settings survive either in manuscript or in printed music books, and ballads with tunes given in the title. Of course, this does not mean that others were not sung as well as read. The title of a ballad, a doleful lover's complaint, in *Bowre* specifies the tune to which it is to be sung, 'A Sonet to the tune of a hone a hone' – 'a hone' or 'o hone' is an Irish or Scots word of lamentation.[63] The opening ballad of *Arbor*, given the title 'A Lovers Farwel to his Love and Joy', which does not specify a tune, sounds like others in *A Handefull*. Composed in fourteeners, this *Arbor* ballad makes extensive use of interlaced anaphora:

> Adue mine onely joy whose absence breedes my smart,
> whose parting did amaze my minde & damped much my hart,
> Adue mine onely love, whose love is life to me,
> whose love once lost, no life can tast within my corps to be.
>
> (A3r)

Called by Puttenham 'the dancing figure', because it 'lead[s] the dance to many verses in suit', anaphora draws attention to the aural musical property of words and their movement. One set of notes and steps

---

[62] On *Passionate Pilgrime*, see Henry Woudhuysen, 'The Foundations of Shakespeare's Text', *Proceedings of the British Academy*, 125 (2004), 79–80; James Bednarz, 'Canonizing Shakespeare: The Passionate Pilgrim, England's Helicon, and the Question of Authenticity', *Shakespeare Survey*, 60 (2007), 252–67; Francis X. Connor, 'Shakespeare, Poetic Collaboration, and *The Passionate Pilgrim*', *Shakespeare Survey*, 67 (2014), 119–30.

[63] On this tune, see Simpson, *British Broadside*, 235. This tune seems to have had many variants, given the different verse forms of the ballads to which is it attached.

Recreational Poetry and the Company of Women 143

responds to and repeats another, leading the performer bodily through the verse as in a dance. Information that would tell us the tune to which this ballad was sung is now lost, just as so much information about musical and textual transmission is fragmentary.[64] Ballads are themselves prone to fragmentation, since they have the inbuilt capacity to be broken up and rearranged, as we have seen in the case of the composite ballads in *Gorgious Gallery*, and could be sung in fragments, or snatches. A different iteration of a song published in *Bowre*, under the title 'A Pastorall', 'Sweet birds that sit and sing amid the shadie vallies' (F3v), was performed on stage in Thomas Heywood's *Fair Maid of the Exchange* (1607). Frank Golding enters in Scene I singing first a snatch, a stanza from William Elderton's ballad 'Ye gods of Love, that sit above', before singing a version of this song, 'Ye little birds that sit and sing'.[65] Whereas the *Bowre* song is in poulter's measure, the song Golding performs takes over the 8/6 ballad form of 'Ye gods of Love': what it shares with 'Sweet birds that sit and sing amid the shadie vallies' are the falling cadences of the feminine endings. Lyrics, such as these, were constantly recrafted in other forms, read in anthologies, copied, sung to tunes or settings already in circulation, performed on stage and in other sites of performance, at leisure times when men and women came together for recreation.

Recreational poetry typified Puttenham's *beau semblant*, its highly crafted poetic surface appealing to sight, as well as sound, in keeping with its ornamental properties. A distinctive feature of both *Bowre* and *Arbor* is the number of acrostics addressed to Elizabeth's ladies-in-waiting filling its pages. Intended as gifts, acrostics are occasional and encomiastic verses; akin to heraldic devices, they blaze the virtues of the person signified by the name and so are purpose-made, fabricated for the recipient. Acrostics are very tangible material textual objects that rely on the ocular and ornamental properties of poetry for their effects and so are designed to delight when apprehended. The material and literary form is governed by the name of the addressee: the first letter of the name starts each line, so that the poem is read both horizontally and vertically. Acrostics exemplify the type of verse advertised on the title-page of *Arbor* intended 'to court the love of faire Ladies and Gentlewomen' and so locate the anthology and its

---

[64] On the importance of incorporating 'embodied experience of song into interpretative analysis' and the problems posed by the 'gaps and absences' in historical evidence, see Larson, *Matter of Song*, 5–11.
[65] Thomas Heywood, *The Dramatic Works*, 6 vols. (London: J. Pearson, 1874), II, 32–3. On Elderton's ballad, see Bruce Smith, *The Acoustic Worlds of Early Modern England: Attending to the O-Factor* (University of Chicago Press, 1999), 196–8.

144 'To the Gentleman Reader'

gentleman readers in women's company. The set of acrostics that grace the page immediately following Breton's elegy for Sidney, 'Amoris Lachrimae', in *Brittons Bowre* curiously appear to attribute authorship to the women who are recipients of the verse: the acrostic for Anne Parker ends 'Finis. A. P.', that for Elizabeth Trentham, 'Finis. Trentame', and Elizabeth Garret, 'Finis. Garet.' (B3r). The material properties of acrostics turn women into objects of exchange. And yet, this oscillation between author and recipient, subject and object, aptly illustrates how acrostics are agentive forms of verse, in that they act for the people whose names are inscribed in the verse, claiming to make them materially present and their memory durable. In both anthologies, acrostics are often gathered in sets. *Arbor* prints six acrostics on Elizabeth's ladies-in-waiting: Elizabeth Throckmorton, Elizabeth Mackwilliams, Sarah Hastings, Katharine Ratcliff, Anne or Elizabeth Cavendish, and Elizabeth Southwell (C1v–2r). In doing so, it makes the company of women present in the anthology and, in this sense, can be said to act for these court ladies within the exchanges that make up the anthology.

When Jones considered the content of *Arbor of Amorous Devices*, he employed spatialising metaphors in which the physical form of the anthology and the affective properties of the poems it gathered are associated with the garden and its recreative qualities: '*had not the Phenix prevented me of some of the best stuffe she furnisht her nest with of late: this* Arbor *had bin somewhat the mote* [sic] *handsomer trimmed vp, beside a larger scope for gentleman to recreate them selves*' (A2r). *Florilegia* metaphors, often used to frame anthologies, tend to concentrate on the labour of gathering choice flowers and herbs for their healthful properties. Here we have a variant on this motif. Jones compares the anthology as a book to the garden as a whole, in which readers have the scope, the room, to move in and, more particularly, to take exercise, 'to recreate them selves'. The book becomes an embodied, sensory, and conceptual space endowed with performative and expressive capacities. The qualities Jones ascribes to these garden-books belong to an early modern discourse of recreation that emphasised its healthful properties.[66] The anthology provides its readers with scope for refreshing and enlivening themselves through pastimes. Recreational reading, in this context, is promoted as having healthy sensory and affective effects that are not necessarily framed in terms of the moralising function of poetry. This is not so much about refining tastes through embodied, sensory reading practices, as we have seen in Tottel's use of the qualities of

[66] Arcangeli, *Recreation*, chapter 3.

Recreational Poetry and the Company of Women   145

'swete majorome' to figure cultivating healthy readerly discrimination.[67] Instead, Jones concentrates on the physical benefits of healthy recreative reading, not its moral properties. The book Jones was reading when he formulated this metaphor of the anthology-as-a-garden and its recreational properties was, of course, *The Phoenix Nest*. What particularly drew his attention was its publication of a set of Breton poems, which had deprived him '*of some of the best stuffe*'. His interest in this rival anthology was not simply to do with competition over Breton's poems, but rather with how they are framed in *The Phoenix Nest*, handsomely 'trimmed up' with 'a large scope' for readers 'to recreate them selves', in other words, how the garden metaphor was realised in spatial, typographic form within its pages.

Those printing *The Phoenix Nest* made innovative use of ornaments to fabricate the type of recreational garden spaces within the anthology Jones describes. Large decorative capital letters begin prose sections, with borders of printers' flowers framing pages within the anthology. Printers' flowers are stylised foliated blocks of type. Unlike decorative letters which form part of words, printers' flowers are abstract patterns and so are purely ornamental, having no denotative meaning.[68] Their usefulness derives from their visual sensory properties. As we have seen in the case of *Astrophel*, printers' flowers were used to signal different spaces within the compilation, and this is how they function in *The Phoenix Nest*. Borders of printers' flowers make up the headers to the prefatory material, and are not used again until they frame or mould the section of Breton poems: flower borders are placed above the 'The Preamble to N. B. his Garden plot', again frame the following 'An excellent Dreame of Ladies and their Riddles: by N. B. Gent' (23), and then close off the section after the envoy (30). This is the type of arbour created in material and conceptual form that Jones described in his preface. Because the border of printers' flowers is adjacent to Bretons' 'Garden plot' and 'An excellent Dreame', which occurs 'In Orchard grounds, where store of fruit trees grew' (23), it sets in play resemblances between the visual form of the page and the poetic content. This ornamental garden plot exemplifies how the book like an arbour can give 'scope' for readers 'to recreate them selves' and allows for a mode of reading that is not given over to edification, but is primarily recreational, appealing to the intellectual delights attendant on sensory pleasures and refreshing the mind through such delightful activity. The

---

[67] See Chapter 1, 25; on readerly discrimination and bibliophagy, see Swann, 'To dream', 76–8.
[68] Juliet Fleming, 'How to Look at a Printed Flower', *Word and Image*, 22 (2006), 165–87.

146 'To the Gentleman Reader'

resulting garden fabricates a very different space within the anthology to the opening set of elegies dedicated to Sidney's memory. The poet who lingers in this garden is not the manly poet committed to the pursuit of virtuous action, but self-consciously idle, preferring female company.

This type of pleasurable and recreative ornamental poetry is styled as a feminine mode. The set of Breton poems are dream visions, 'fancies', forms of *beau semblant*. The first part of the garden plot, which includes a preamble and a 'strange description', is a bad dream that troubles the solitary sleeper: his mind is oppressed by sorrow, so that his garden is a 'ground of griefe: where selfe wils seeds are sowne, / Whereof comes up the weedes of wo, that joies have overgrown'(21). The cares of this garden plot are dispelled in the second part, 'An excellent Dreame of Ladies and their Riddles'. In this orchard, the speaker is joined by 'a Saint', a second Eve, who plucks an apple from the tree because it 'doth like my fancie best'; the male speaker interjects with a conventional moralising definition of sapience and the spiritual dangers of indulging tastes for their experiential pleasures:

> Such fruit (quoth I) shall fancie chiefly feede:
> Indeede tis faire, God grant it proove as good,
> But take good heede, least all to late it breede
> Ill humors such as may infect your blood.
>
> (23)

Yet, his very orthodox view, which is highly critical of fancy as a fallen faculty, is given no quarter and met with curt dismissal, 'Peace foole, quoth she, and so waked mee' (23). The speaker is left in a state of moral confusion and repeatedly questions the meaning of the dream. One might expect this to lead into another dream vision providing lessons in proper discrimination, taste, and judgement, but instead subsequent dreams engage the speaker in states of play that are certainly more pleasurable and restorative of his spirits than his earlier depressing moralising and solitary dream.

These pleasurable and idle dreams will become more erotic in Robert Greene's long dream poem, 'A most rare, and excellent Dreame', which follows this set of Breton's poems. Slumber brings him 'a Ladie faire' (33), whose body is a 'garden plot' (34) laid out for the delight of the dreamer. She comes to him because he has been sick, 'falne into a sudden fever' (36), and the charity she wants to bestow on her neighbour is to restore him to erotic health. The physic she offers takes the form of eroticised household remedies, part of the craft of housewifery. Sitting beside him she asks, 'Is't

Recreational Poetry and the Company of Women 147

in my garden that may doe thee good? / . . . or in my closet of conserves' (36). Finally, when he is at the point of death, it is her vigorous laying on of hands ending 'with a kisse' that 'drew up my life againe' (42); at this climax 'I through the surfeit of the joy awooke' (43). Medical regimens are translated into an eroticised language of love and sexual arousal. The healthful properties of recreative poetry, its capacity to restore the spirit, are defined in the sensual terms of erotic pleasure. Breton's 'garden plot' is less erotic, but nonetheless one of primarily sensory pleasures, full of 'sundrie flowres so super sweete of smell, / As there me thought it was a heaven to dwell' (24), where he finds himself in the company of 'Sweete pretie soules', gathered to 'Devise' and play 'ridling sports' (25), which then make up the following set of riddles. A song follows that is a hymn to the recreative properties of such games that delight the senses and wit, the mind: 'For we with sweetes doe feede our fancies so, / With sweetes of sight, and sweetness of conceit' (27). It is difficult to square this paean to fancy and pastimes with the earlier criticism of fancy. We might argue that the repetition of sweet, while it brings together the sense and intellect, is also potentially a little cloying, with a hint of fallen appetite conveyed in how it 'doe feede our fancies'. The poem, however, does not seek a moral resolution, promising only more 'ridling toies' for 'perhaps another night' (27): the next set of poems are also a game, 'The Chesse Play. Very aptly devised by N. B. Gent'. What emerges across Breton's various garden plots is a poetry of pastimes which is valued for its healthful, restorative, and pleasurable properties, even as it is also vaguely troubled by its lack of moral direction.

Breton's riddles and 'The Chesse Play' that follow his 'Garden Plot' exemplify the symbiosis between pastimes and poetry within cultures of leisure of this period. *The Phoenix Nest* includes one of the most popular early modern poems – a trick poem – reprinted in anthologies across the late sixteenth and seventeenth century, including *Brittons Bowre*:

Hir face,	Hir tong,	Hir wit,
So faire,	So sweete,	So sharpe,
First bent,	Then drew,	Then hit,
Mine eie,	Mine eare,	My hart.
		(71)

Trick poems are related to pattern poems in that they are contrived; in other words, they are a self-referential literary composition, an example of *beau semblant*, in which their material design and ornamental properties make up their meaning. The trick is that the poem can be read from left to

148 'To the Gentleman Reader'

right and vertically down each column. The visual and spatial layout of the poem on the page is designed to encourage non-linear, errant readings that are recreative, playful, articulating the maze-like twists and turns of courtship. This trick poem is idle – Rollins called it 'the most worthless poem' in *The Phoenix Nest* – a witty toy, one of Puttenham's 'ditties of pleasure', suitable for gift-giving and composition by gentlewomen and men 'for their private recreation'. The visual properties of this poem would argue that it was intended to be seen and read. Yet, this trick poem had other pleasing, recreative qualities that were realised through musical performance. Its inclusion in *A New Booke of Tabliture* (1596), where it is to be sung to the musical settings provided by William Barley, neatly demonstrates the choral, multimodal visual and musical affordances of early modern poetry.[69] Barley addressed his music primer to Bridget Radcliffe, Countess of Sussex, since music is 'a fitting companion of Princely personages'. The dedication did not preclude users much lower down the social scale: 'for that every one cannot have a Tutor, this booke will sufficiently serve to be Schoolmaster unto such that will but spare some of their idle howers, to observe what this booke expresseth unto them'.[70] This is a book designed for amateur household performance, and therefore is carefully calibrated to different degrees of musical literacy so that 'thou maiest accord or tune these Instrumentes by Arte or by eare ... by observing of which rules thou maiest in a short time learne by thy selfe with very small help of a teacher' (A3v). The ease with which lyrics move between poetry anthologies and music books points to the processes of intermediation integral to cultures of recreation – those 'idle howers', when women and men learnt to be skilful in composing, writing, performing, and sharing lyrics in company within the household.

The anthologies discussed in this chapter are in close conversation, sharing poems, poets, methods of compilation, and design features. The 1590s are often characterised as a watershed, but how different are the poetry anthologies first produced before and after this period? I would argue that what does develop across the 1590s, albeit unevenly, is a language of recreation that places more emphasis on its leisured aspects and a model of poetic making that is attentive to poetry's delightful ornamental properties, which are not necessarily framed in relation to moral improvement. The poetry gathered in earlier anthologies did not suddenly go out of fashion in the 1590s. *A Handefull of Pleasant Delights* was reprinted until at least 1595, and *Paradyse* until 1605. Other

[69] Trudell, *Unwritten Poetry*, 9.   [70] William Barley, *A New Booke of Tabliture* (1596), A2v.

Recreational Poetry and the Company of Women 149

anthologies did not simply disappear from cultural consciousness: *Songes and Sonettes*, last printed in 1587, is called for onstage by Slender in Shakespeare's *Merry Wives of Windsor*, first performed in 1597 and his most domestic play, set in the urban world of the prosperous middling sort. Slender cries out that 'I had rather than forty shillings I had my book of *Songs and Sonnets* here', and a moment later he asks his servant, Peter Simple, if he has 'the *Book of Riddles* about you'.[71] Slender needs these books to court Anne Page over dinner at her house; songs, sonnets, and riddles are interchangeable because of their domestic, recreative properties. The 'book of *Songs and Sonnets*' is both a particular book and a type – any of those books of songs and sonnets made 'to court the love of faire Ladies and Gentlewomen' in the words of the title-page to *Arbor of Amorous Devices*. The movement of books between master and servant reminds us that books had no fixed place or readership, especially in multi-status households.[72] The anthology addressed to the gentleman reader may well be picked up and read by his servant or wife, sister, or daughter. Social and material processes of circulation and recirculation are built into the form of anthologies. *Arbor of Amorous Devices* looks back to the stuff of earlier anthologies, including versions of ballads from *Songes and Sonettes*.[73] Jones was recycling material, including broadside ballads, to capitalise on his stock, especially in this lean plague year: the last set of eight poems were simply taken from *Brittons Bowre* to make up the rest of this anthology. Anthology production so often relied on using materials that were to hand in the booksellers' stock. As we shall see in the following chapter, *Englands Helicon*, published at the end of the century, similarly reprints poems from earlier anthologies – *Brittons Bowre*, *Arbor of Amorous Devices*, *The Phoenix Nest*, *The Passionate Pilgrim*, and *Songes and Sonettes*. These borrowed poems illustrate how compilers and publishers were studying earlier anthologies, alongside other types of books, and learning their craft on the job.

---

[71] Shakespeare, *Merry Wives of Windsor*, ed. David Crane (Cambridge University Press, 2010), 1.1.158–59, 161.
[72] Hamling and Richardson, *A Day at Home*, 195.
[73] *Bowre* had similarly included a reworking of Surrey's 'Laid in my quiet bed' (G2r–2v).

CHAPTER 4

'Impos'd designe'
Englands Helicon *and Re-creative Craft*

Englands Helicon (1600) has been described by Rollins as the 'most beautiful of the Elizabethan poetical miscellanies'.[1] The quality of its production is down to the work of a highly effective network of compilers, publishers, printers, and writers specialising in compilations in the late 1590s, often known as the 'Bodenham circle', after its patron and fellow compiler, John Bodenham, a wealthy gentleman Grocer.[2] *Englands Helicon* is a highly crafted book in a number of interrelated senses. The anthology is embedded in the social and cultural world of those guilds active in the book trade in the late sixteenth century that were, in turn, incorporated within the wider civic community of early modern London. Not surprisingly, when accounts are given of the craft of compilation in the prefatory material, an earlier humanist language, now familiar from the epistles of Tottel and Disle, is called upon to set out the ethical foundations of the book trade and its service to the commonwealth. The collaborative working practices fostered through these company structures inform the craft of editing displayed in *Englands Helicon*, from the anthology's design to the account given of editing in its prefatory material. *Englands Helicon* provides this study with an opportunity to explore how specialisation in the production of certain classes of books, in this case, the compilation, shaped the form and meaning of the anthology. *Englands Helicon* was part of a wider publishing project. Those engaged in its production compiled and edited a series of compilations in quick succession – *Politeuphuia, Wits Common wealth* (1597), *Wits Theater of the Little*

---

[1] John Bodenham, *England's Helicon*, ed. H. R. Rollins, 2 vols. (Cambridge, MA: Harvard University Press, 1935), II, 3.

[2] On the 'Bodenham circle', see Franklin B. Williams, 'John Bodenham, "Art's Lover, Learning's Friend"', *Studies in Philology*, 31 (1934), 198–214; Celeste Turner Wright, 'Anthony Mundy and the Bodenham Miscellanies', *Philological Quarterly*, 40 (1961), 449–61; Zachary Lesser and Peter Stallybrass, 'The First Literary *Hamlet* and the Commonplacing of Professional Plays', *Shakespeare Quarterly*, 59 (2008), 371–420.

150

Englands Helicon 151

World (1599), *Bel-vedére or the Garden of the Muses* (1600), and *Englands Helicon* (1600). Specialisation by publishers, as Zachary Lesser has shown, was a commercial imperative providing a means of managing resources and protecting investments.[3] In this chapter, my interest is in the craft aspects of specialisation: how the hands-on experience of making compilations was shared among those engaged in their production, enabling reflection on the craft of editing that is then given material expression in the design of *Englands Helicon.*

The decision to publish an anthology devoted to pastoral lyric certainly made commercial sense given the popularity of this genre in the late 1590s. Pastoral also has formal properties that lend themselves to anthology-making. It is an extraordinarily capacious mode which means that compilers can readily incorporate variety and miscellaneity within its overarching schema. *Englands Helicon* capitalises on the generic diversity of the pastoral mode. Poems are excerpted from sonnet sequences, pastoral romances, plays, songbooks, and other anthologies. Not all poems gathered in *Englands Helicon*, however, began life as pastoral lyrics; their reframing and recasting to bring them into line with the organising principle of this anthology illustrates how genres are crafted not only by authors, but through the work of the printing house. Those engaged in its production were making, reading, and responding to earlier anthologies and other types of books, especially romances and songbooks, tacitly learning the craft of compilation through their example. *Englands Helicon* offers readers a choice selection of the most collectable authors of lyric poetry – Sir Philip Sidney, Edmund Spenser, Thomas Lodge, Nicholas Breton, and Sir Edward Dyer – and experiments with the recreative affordances of the anthology, capitalising on the success of printed music books. Numerous lyrics are excerpted from the songbooks of William Byrd, Nicholas Yonge, Thomas Morley, and John Dowland. Lyrics had been moving freely between these types of books during the 1590s, when printed music books entered the market in increasing numbers alongside verse anthologies. Publishers of both poetry and music anthologies were establishing a domestic market for books designed for recreation within the household. If it is difficult to draw clear distinctions between these types of books in this period, it is because publishers exploited this porousness to open the book to performance cultures and so allow customers to use them for diverse recreational purposes.

---

[3] Lesser, *Renaissance Drama*, 26–45.

152   *Englands Helicon*

The Networked Book

Englands Helicon is advertised not as a stand-alone book, but as part of a carefully designed series that brings a collaborative publishing project to completion to the 'wondrous profit' of the commonwealth. A. B.'s address, 'To his Loving Kinde Friend, Maister *John Bodenham*', presents *Englands Helicon* as the final instalment in a series of compilations, named in order of publication, said to be the brainchild of Bodenham, and produced through his '*paines*', his labour, alongside that of others, including A. B.:

> Wits Common-wealth, *the first fruites of thy paines,*
> *Drew on* Wits Theater, *thy second Sonne:*
> *By both of which, I cannot count the gaines,*
> *And wondrous profit that the world hath wonne.*
> *Next, in the* Muses Garden, *gathering flowres,*
> *Thou mad'st a Nosegay, as was never sweeter:*
> *Whose sent will savour to Times latest howres,*
> *And for the greatest Prince no Poesie meeter.*
> *Now comes thy* Helicon, *to make compleate,*
> *And furnish up thy last impos'd designe:*
> *My paines heerein, I cannot term it great,*
> *But what-so-ere, my love (and all) is thine.*
> > *Take love, take paines, take all remaines in me:*
> > *And where thou art, my hart still lives with thee.*
> > > (A3)

Combining the language of *florilegia* with that of intellectual patrimony, A. B. magnifies the agency of Bodenham, who is all – patron, progenitor, and compiler. Others, writing of 'the Bodenham circle', have tended to follow this view.[4] Yet, the idea of a circle constellating around Bodenham has distinct limits. For one thing, it is only one of many stories of book production narrated in the prefatory material. In the following epistle, addressed to Bodenham's kinsmen Nicholas Wanton and George Faucet, it is A. B. who claims responsibility for seeing *Englands Helicon* through the press, after just downplaying his role: 'Helicon, *though not as I could wish, yet in such good sort as time would permit, having past the pikes of the Presse, comes now to* Yorke *to salute her rightfull Patrone first, and next (as his deere friends and kindsmen) to offer you her kinde service*' (A3v). H. H. Child concluded that A. B. was therefore responsible for the 'editorial work', and

---

[4] See Williams, 'John Bodenham', 198–214; Lesser and Stallybrass, 'First Literary Hamlet', 371–420.

The Networked Book

153

Bodenham's role was limited to that of patron.[5] This is not the end of the matter, since L. N. in his epistle presents himself as responsible for much of the editorial work, outlining his role in gathering and selecting the verse, deciding on the organisation of the collection, and assigning authorship. Editorial agents thus begin to proliferate. An open-ended process of collaboration emerges that turns the 'Bodenham circle' into a more porous and dynamic network. Those involved do not necessarily have fixed roles, but instead share various tasks within the production process. What links those within this network are the intrapersonal corporate affiliations of civic communities and, above all, the books they produced.

The identity of A. B., like R. S. of *The Phoenix Nest*, and that of so many others involved in producing anthologies, is a mystery. He occupies the front of the book, a space often reserved for addressing questions of compilation, and where publishers typically give an account of their own labours in bringing these books to press. The preface provided by L. N., the reversed initials of Nicholas Ling, a bookseller-publisher, is an example of this type of epistle.[6] A. B., by contrast, resists identification, serving to highlight the difficulties involved in establishing the identity of those who prepared compilations for the press given the makeshift, collaborative, and often anonymous practices of editing.[7] There is something more purposeful, however, to the use of these initials, and others, at the front of the book. A. B. is a print convention; as the first two letters of the alphabet they were often used non-referentially, a type of empty signifier, rather than as initials denoting an individual's name.[8] Anyone, or indeed more than one person, can inhabit the space they provide. These non-initials had appeared in another book in the series, *Bel-vedére*, whose commendatory verse, 'Of this Garden of the Muses', is attributed to A. B. Strikingly, initials recur alongside names across the prefatory material before these compilations – Bodenham, A. B., A. M., N. L., L. N., N. Ling, R. A., Robert Allott. In *The Phoenix Nest*, as we have seen, initials were a class marker employed to signify the social discretion accorded to the authors gathered in the collection. Here, the initials are those of non-authorial agents and they summon up a community of the book in which individuals are brought together through a shared publishing project.

---

[5] H. H. Child, 'The Song Books and Miscellanies', in *The Cambridge History of English Literature*, edited by A. W. Ward and A. R. Waller, 15 vols. (New York: G. P. Putnam's Sons, 1907–17), IV, 136.

[6] Bodenham, *Englands Helicon*, II, 41–63; Pomeroy, *Elizabethan Miscellanies*, 94–5.

[7] Massai, *Shakespeare*, 30.   [8] Bodenham, *Englands Helicon*, II, 68.

154 *Englands Helicon*

Politeuphuia, Wits Theater of the Little World, Bel-vedére, and *Englands Helicon* were published over three years from 1597 to 1600. As Lesser and Peter Stallybrass caution, the 'exact contribution of any member . . . to any specific volume remains unclear'; nonetheless, it is possible to identify some of those individuals whose names are associated with certain compilations. *Politeuphuia* was published by Nicholas Ling and printed by James Roberts; *Wits Theater* was printed by Roberts for Ling; *Bel-vedére* was printed by Felix Kingston for Hugh Astley, a draper-bookseller; and finally *Englands Helicon* was printed by Roberts for John Flasket, another draper-bookseller.[9] It is likely Bodenham initiated the project: prefaces suggest he had a keen interest in compiling commonplace books since his youth, and worked with others to bring these volumes to fruition. Ling, Robert Allot, and Anthony Munday wrote of their own editorial work in prefaces before *Politeuphuia* and *Englands Helicon, Wits Theatre,* and *Bel-vedére,* respectively, and it is likely that Ling, Munday, and others had a hand in other volumes. Even so, the list provided by A. B. does not include all the compilations associated with this milieu. If we track collaborations, then other works come into focus. *Englands Parnassus,* also published in 1600, for example, was compiled by Allot, among others, and published by Ling, Cuthbert Burby, and Thomas Hayes, while Ling was also publishing other compilations in this period.[10] If we follow Ling, he takes us to other collaborative publishing ventures, such as the partnership, made up of Ling, John Busby, Thomas Gubbins, and John Smethwicke, that specialised in prose romances, publishing five editions of Lodge's *Rosalynde* between 1590 and 1604; Ling was also publishing Robert Greene's *Menaphon* at this time (1599, 1605).[11] Ling's career is characterised by such collaborative publishing ventures. He entered comparatively little copy in his own name, instead preferring partnerships in which he concentrated on financing the printing, organising the sale of the books, and undertaking editing work.[12] The connections that make up networks always open on to to other sets of affiliations. The aim in bringing this network into focus in not to use *Englands Helicon* simply to uncover the

---

[9] Lesser and Stallybrass, 'First Literary *Hamlet*', 384 n. 34.

[10] *The Harmonie of the Holy Scriptures. With the seuerall sentences of sundry learned writers* (STC 1891.5), printed by Roberts, and Leonard Wright's *A Display of Dutie, dect with sage sayings, pythie sentences, and proper similies* (1602, STC 26026); see Gerard Johnson, 'Nicholas Ling, Publisher 1580–1607', *Studies in Bibliography,* 38 (1985), 203–14.

[11] Steve Mentz, *Romance for Sale in Early Modern England: the Rise of Prose Fiction* (Aldershot: Ashgate, 2006), 114–15, 155.

[12] Johnson, 'Nicholas Ling', 203; Melnikoff, *Elizabethan Publishing,* 158.

The Networked Book 155

various actors involved in its production, not the least because such an approach implies that their work somehow goes on behind the book. Instead, when the work of form is conceptualised in terms of embodied practices – craft – rather than as immanent in the text, then it brings into focus the communities in which these books were made.

The way *Englands Helicon* is framed represents this anthology as the high point of a civic Renaissance brought about through the work of learned citizens. Clear echoes can be heard of the rhetoric of common profit employed by Tottel and Disle to give credibility to the publisher and his trade.[13] Title-pages to these compilations exhibit a uniformity of design that asks their readers to consider these different books in terms of a civic humanist publishing venture. All include a Latin tag above or below the printers' device, which visually dominates the page: Ling's device is prominently displayed at the front of *Wits Theater* and *Politeuphuia*, Kingston's before *Bel-vedére*, and Roberts's before *Englands Helicon*.[14] The dialogue between the Latin tag and the printer's device locates these books within traditions of humanist book-making. On the title-page of *Englands Helicon* is the following tag from Tibullus's *Elegies*, 1.2: 'Casta placent superis, / pura cum veste venite, / Et manibus puris / sumite fontis aquam' ('The powers above ask purity. Clean be the raiment that ye come in, and clean the hands to take the waters from the spring').[15] The classical meeting place of poets and the muses has now been translated on to English soil and into a native English lyric tradition through the publication of this anthology. Below is Roberts's device. Read relationally, they describe the space of the anthology in terms of a cultural *translatio* that is crucially dependent on the book trade and its partnership with learned men.

A civic culture of incorporation underpinned the production of these books. The working relationships of those responsible for *Englands Helicon*, and the other 'Bodenham' compilations, depended on membership of the early modern guilds. If universities and Inns of Court were cultural domains that fostered habits of collaboration, then so too did these urban companies.[16] The milieu of the bookshop and printing house was an

---

[13] See Chapter 1, 22–7; Lesser and Stallybrass, 'First Literary *Hamlet*', 420; Vine, *Miscellaneous Order*, 130.

[14] See R. B. McKerrow, *Printers' and Publishers' Devices in England and Scotland, 1485–1640* (London: Bibliographical Society, 1913), 118 (no. 301), 40 (no. 112), 128, (no. 328): the device for *Belvedere* was designed for this volume and later used by Kingston.

[15] Tibullus, *Elegies*, Book I, 1, ed. J. P. Postgate, in *Catullus. Tibullus. Pervigilium veneris*, rev. G. P. Goold, 2nd ed. (Cambridge, MA: Loeb, 1988), 253.

[16] On collaboration in the publishing world, see Melnikoff, *Elizabethan Publishing*, 12–16.

156   *Englands Helicon*

environment in which ideas of the book were shared; its literary exchanges are characterised by pragmatic practices of imitation, in which knowledge of forms and methods of compilation, in part, are acquired tacitly through sharing experience, imitating practices, and the study of books for how they are made. The incorporated world of London consisted of working households, made up of masters, mistresses, kin, apprentices, and servants.[17] Those engaged in this publishing venture were contemporaries, affiliated through guilds, sometimes apprenticed at the same time, even to the same master, and often connected through marriage and kinship.[18] Their careers are characterised by partnerships that were sustained over periods of time. Flasket, the publisher of *Englands Helicon*, for example, regularly sent work to Roberts in the late 1590s and early 1600s, as well as to Kingston, the printer of *Bel-vedére*. The fact that many were foreign to the Stationers' Company helped to establish and to reinforce working relationships. Grocers and drapers, such as Kingston, Astley, and Flasket, were permitted to work in the book trade according to the custom of the City which allowed for any freeman to practise the trade of any other company.[19] However, from the 1570s, the Stationers' Company moved to strengthen its monopoly by restricting the ability of those non-members to enter copy and to practise as printers. Many drapers had successfully circumvented these restrictions by entering into partnerships with stationers, like the draper-friendly printer John Charlewood, himself an ex-grocer, and his successor, Roberts, who married Charlewood's widow, or Paul Linley, the partner of the draper-bookseller Flasket.[20] The Stationers' Company eventually proved successful in squeezing out non-members. Kingston, a grocer-printer, transferred to the Stationers in the early 1590s. On 22 May 1600, all remaining draper-printers and booksellers were made over to the Stationers' Company.[21] A few months later, in August 1600, *Englands Helicon* was entered by Flasket, who had just transferred to the Stationers, and he continued to work with Roberts, his draper-friendly printer.[22] Echoes of this dispute, which had at its heart

---

[17] Phillip Withington, *The Politics of Commonwealth: Citizens and Freemen in Early Modern England* (Cambridge University Press, 2005), 10; Brooks, 'Apprenticeship', 53–4.

[18] On the fraternity of the book trade, see Johns, *Nature of the Book*, 76.

[19] Ian Gadd, '"Being like a field": Corporate identity in the Stationers' Company, 1557–1684', unpublished DPhil. thesis, Oxford University, 1999, 175.

[20] Gerald Johnson, "The Stationers versus the Drapers: Control of the Press in the Late Sixteenth Century", *The Library*, 10, 1 (1988), 1–16.

[21] Ibid., 1–3.   [22] Arber, *Transcript*, III, 168.

The Networked Book 157

monopolistic practices, can be heard in Ling's epistle when he addresses the vexed question of literary property.

One of the distinctive features of *Englands Helicon* is that, in comparison with other anthologies, it is made up of a high proportion of previously printed material. This anthology therefore provides valuable evidence for how ownership of copy was negotiated within the book trade. Poetry made its way into anthologies via manuscript channels and from other printed books. *Englands Helicon* is a special case because many of the authors represented in its pages had previously been published by those within the network, most commonly through the partnership of Ling and Roberts.[23] Trade relationships thus can help to explain how poems made their way into this anthology. Ling, working mostly with Roberts and sometimes Flasket, published Drayton's *Englands Heroicall Epistles* (1597–1603), *Ideas Mirrour* (1594), *The Owle* (1604), and *Poems* (1605–6); after 1600, Roberts took over from John Charlewood as one of Munday's preferred printers.[24] Well over three-quarters of the lyrics in this anthology were excerpted from previously printed books; in the case of new, unpublished verse many were penned by those connected with this network, including Munday, in the guise of Sheepheard Tonie, and Drayton. Tracing ownership of the copy of those books from which poems were excerpted in *Englands Helicon* frequently takes us to titles owned by these men or to copyrights that were open to negotiation. Copyright, the primary form of property regulation within the book trade, is often characterised negatively as a primarily restrictive practice, epitomising the monopolistic drive of the Stationers' Company. William St Clair has even gone so far as to argue, erroneously as we shall see, that the Company's protection of copyright had a regressive cultural effect, resulting in the 'clamp-down on the publishing of printed anthologies which drew on previously printed sources' after 1600.[25] However, if we trace the means by which copy changed hands in relation to *Englands Helicon*, then a picture emerges in which copyright was open to negotiation and generative, in that it operated as a vector for textual transmission.

A good proportion of the copy reprinted in *Englands Helicon* was already owned by those within the network or their partners; for example, eleven poems were taken from Lodge's romances and seven from books by

---

[23] See also William J. Hebel, 'Nicholas Ling and *Englands Helicon*', *The Library*, 5 (1924), 158–9.
[24] See STC 5326–7, 18163, 19165.
[25] William St Clair, *The Reading Nation in the Romantic Period* (Cambridge University Press, 2004), 66.

158   *Englands Helicon*

Greene that either Ling or his partners published, sometimes with Roberts as the printer.[26] Other cases involved a calculation of risk given that this 'property' was in the hands of others.[27] For example, fourteen Sidney poems are shared with *The Countesse of Pembrokes Arcadia*, a valuable work that William Ponsonby published three times between 1588 and 1598. There is no record that Ponsonby objected to the reprinting of Sidney's poems in *Englands Helicon*. He did, however, object to the reprinting of the whole book, which did compete commercially with his edition. A few months after he entered *Englands Helicon*, Flasket was one of the book-sellers prosecuted for selling cheaper copies of the *Arcadia*, printed by Robert Waldegrave in Edinburgh, in direct competition with Ponsonby's edition.[28] When only a small proportion of the whole book is excerpted, as Ling explained in his epistle to the reader, it does not impinge upon a stationer's commercial interest in the volume as a whole, since the circulation of such 'small parcelles', in Tottel's words, is part of a wider cultural commerce that profits the commonwealth.

The epistles before the compilations this network produced provide a space for those involved to reflect on their craft and to formulate a language for describing editing. Because this network specialised in producing compilations, skills and ideas could be shared, and technical knowledge reproduced and refined through the imitation of others' practices.[29] As a result, Ling's epistles before *Politeuphuia* and *Englands Helicon* develop a language of editing that is informed by the wider network's production of commonplace books. A reliance on the idiom of commonplacing in these epistles to describe the work undertaken is hardly surprising since it was the established *praxis* for compiling books of extracts and so readily available to describe the specialised technical skills of the publisher who undertakes editorial work. The cultural value attributed to

---

[26] Poems taken from Lodge's *Rosalynde* (1596, 1598, Ling and Gubbins), *Englands Helicon*, G2–v, H2v–3, H3v–4, P1v–2, S1–iv, S2–2v, X2–2v; Lodge's *Phillis* (1593, Roberts for Busbie), *Englands Helicon*, G3–3v, M3, X2v–3v; Lodge, *Margarite of America* (1596, Busbie), *Englands Helicon*, L4; Greene, *Menaphon* (1599, Ling), *Englands Helicon*, C4v–D, E2–2v, E4v, G3v–4, I1v; *Greene's neuer too late* (1600, Roberts and Ling), *Englands Helicon*, N1v–2v, P3–4.

[27] The owners of the titles from which the poems of George Peele and Henry Chettle were excerpted were dead, and copy had not been reassigned: Peele, *Araygnement of Paris* (1584, Henry Marsh, died in 1589), *Englands Helicon*, Bb4, Bb4–4v; Chettle, *Piers Plainnes* (1595, Thomas Gosson died in 1599), *Englands Helicon*, L3–3v. Nine poems were taken from *The Phoenix Nest* (see *Englands Helicon*, L1v–2, L2–2v, L2v–3, N3v–4, N4–4v, O3v–4, Q4–4v, T1–1v, X2v–3v), which had not been reissued; John Jackson died in 1596. *Songes and Sonettes*, from which two verses were taken (F1v–3, G2v–3), had not been reissued since its last edition, published by Robinson, in 1587.

[28] Greg and Boswell, *Records of the Stationers' Company*, 80.

[29] See Smith's discussion of artisanal knowledge, 'In the Workshop', 4–7.

The Networked Book 159

craft in Ling's epistles before *Politeuphuia* and *Englands Helicon* is shared with Munday's verse before *A Gorgious Gallery*, which, as we have seen in Chapter 2, similarly translates humanist practices of *compilatio* into artisanal terms. The first 1597 edition of *Politeuphuia* is advertised as 'a methodicall collection of the most choice and select admonitions and sentences, compendiously drawne from infinite varietie, divine, historicall, poeticall, politique, morrall, and humane'.[30] The preface uses a favourite *florilegium* trope – that of the bee gathering pollen and making honey from flowers – to describe the process of selecting texts: 'I give thee the best gleanings, leaving the honny to thy eare, the travaile to my pen' (A3). While thoroughly conventional, the way in which Ling employs this trope directs the reader's attention to the publisher's ability to utilise a system for gathering and storing intellectual matter – a task that requires judgement, discrimination, learning, and 'travaile'. Ling repeatedly asks readers to value his editorial labour, his 'travailes, which I have imployed in gathering of certaine heades or places', work that has been undertaken for their profit, for the 'ease' (A3) with which readers can now put these heads to use. This is hard, specialist work, but 'If happily these my labours please, I will with the painfull husbandman gather more against the next impression, because my harvest was so fruitfull' (A3v). The transition from bee to husbandman within the repertoire of *florilegia* metaphors concentrates attention on the workmanship of the publisher in a simultaneously manual and intellectual sense. Ling's account of the editorial work undertaken on *Englands Helicon* continues to draw on commonplacing principles, although more attention is given to the processes involved in producing a poetry anthology, especially in relation to gathering and selecting poems. The story of his editorial labours he provides in his preface begins with procuring poems: 'The travaile that hath beene taken in gathering them from so many handes, hath wearied some howres, which severed, might in part have perished, digested into this meane volume, may in the opinion of some not be altogether unworthy the labour' (A4). The term used to describe the agent undertaking this activity is 'Collector'. Like Tottel and Disle before him, he sets out the ethical foundations for publication. Ling has rescued these worthy poems from the vagaries of manuscript circulation, motivated by his civic concern to benefit the reader and a wider commonwealth of learning. Given most of the poems in *Englands Helicon* came from previously printed, rather than manuscript, sources, Ling is not necessarily describing the conditions in which verse was

---

[30] Nicholas Ling, *Politeuphuia, Wits Commonwealth* (1597), A2–2v.

160 *Englands Helicon*

collected, but instead deploying a well-rehearsed rhetoric of publication available from the early years of print to credit the publisher's work in anthology compilation.[31] When Ling defends his editing practices, he once again combines the principles of common profit with the practice of commonplacing, this time in relation to the trade practices of the Stationers' Company:

> if any Stationer shall finde faulte, that his Coppies are robd by any thing in this Collection, let me aske him this question, Why more in this, then in any Diuine or humaine Author? From whence a man (writing of that argument) shal gather any saying, sentence, similie, or example, his name put to it who is the Author of the same. (A4)

Perhaps not surprisingly, given so much of *Englands Helicon* is borrowed, Ling seems defensive on the subject of ownership of copy; indeed St Clair claims this passage as evidence for a 'clamp-down' by the Stationers' Company on the publication of previously printed material in antholo-gies.[32] Yet, as we have seen, there is no evidence that any stationers brought complaints before the Company or, indeed, that there was any clamp-down: anthologies published after 1600 continued to reprint poems from titles owned by others. What instead might be the purpose of raising this issue? Ling asks the stationer who thinks his ability to profit from his copy might be curtailed through such practices to recognise he is operating under a false logic. Stationers should not act like Tottel's 'ungentle hoarders', restricting the profitable circulation of texts.[33] Instead, anthol-ogies offer publishers creative and commercial opportunities since such small parcels of text – a 'saying, sentence, similie, or example' – cannot be 'owned' in any definitive sense. Rather, this moveable textual material is part of the profitable commerce of the book trade, available to all for the gathering. Ling is providing his fellow stationers with a rationale for producing anthologies that is informed by a civic humanist model of literary reproduction. Publishers and printers have an extra-commercial, ethical imperative to put books and other textual matter into circulation to benefit the commonwealth, and not simply to act in their own economic interests to protect copy from competitors.[34] Publishers, in Ling's account, are ethical agents, defined by their labour and skill, their 'travaile' in gathering textual material, which has then been 'digested into this meane volume', and their judicious negotiation of different interests in the

---

[31] See Tonry, *Agency and Intention*, and the discussion of these prefaces in Chapter 1, 22–7.
[32] St Clair, *Reading Nation*, 492.   [33] See Chapter 1, 25–6.
[34] Crane, *Framing Authority*, 169; Tonry, *Agency and Intention*, 24–5.

'Impos'd Designe': *the Work of Form*   161

'Collection', including those of the various authors (A4). Ling manipulated this ethos of print to imagine a cultural role for the publisher as a mediator of texts and maker of books alongside the humanist compiler. One place that various roles of the publisher were therefore being defined in this period was in these compilations, from commonplace books to poetry anthologies.[35]

Ling's critique of copyright coincides with the end of the trade wars between the Drapers and Stationers and the translation of *Englands Helicon*'s publisher, Flasket, to the Stationers' Company. This event marked the culmination of efforts to drive non-members from the bookselling and printing trade, thereby entrenching the Company's monopoly. Ling explicitly employs the language of common profit to challenge monopolistic practices. A. B.'s dedicatory verse shares this civic idealism, presenting the series of compilations, from 'Wits Common-wealth' to *Englands Helicon*, as a profitable publishing venture undertaken by citizens acting in the interests of the commonwealth. The civic humanism Kirk Melnikoff has identified in Ling's editing of *Politeuphuia* can therefore also be found in *Englands Helicon*. Melnikoff points to entries concerning authority, in which Ling argues against its centralisation in a monarch, instead advocating the commonwealth principle of *res publica* in which authority is shared among 'a number of possible "*Gouernours*," or . . . in a number of possible "offices"'.[36] The craft of compilation, for Ling and his partners, was therefore simultaneously a trade practice, conditioned by commercial interests and regulations governing the manufacture of books, and an expression of their civic identity, governed by an ethos of publication which fashions these senior members of their guilds as learned citizens within the commonwealth.

'*Impos'd Designe*': the Work of Form

Englands Helicon is a particularly well-crafted anthology. A. B.'s verse describes *Englands Helicon* as the culmination of a design that Bodenham is called upon to recognise as his own handiwork: '*Now comes thy* Helicon, *to make complete / And furnish vp thy last impos'd designe*' (A3). Here, '*impos'd design*' refers to the series of books produced under the aegis of Bodenham, yet it is equally applicable to the design of *Englands Helicon* as an instantiation of the wider project. Pastoral lends itself to anthologising.

---

[35] On playbooks and the publisher, see Lesser, *Renaissance Drama*.
[36] Melnikoff, *Elizabethan Publishing*, 160–61.

162   *Englands Helicon*

Its accretive formal properties are most evident in eclogue books, loosely combined in sequences designed to display the skilful incorporation of variety within order.[37] Pastoral's range of sub-genres meant that variety could readily be displayed within an elastic overarching scheme, while its stock characters and motifs and dialogic structures were particularly useful for organising lyrics into varied sequences and recombining lyric voices into new dialogues. Shepherds and shepherdesses previously unknown to each other, once excerpted and placed in new relationships with figures drawn from other lyrics, could thus be made to engage in new conversations. However, not all the poems included in *Englands Helicon* began life as pastorals and some instead required work to bring them into line with the organising schema of this anthology. When these poems are remodelled in pastoral form, the mechanical work of editing is made visible in the layout of verse on the page, providing visual and typographic evidence for the ways in which literary genres are crafted through the agency of the printing house.[38]

Editing in these cases proceeds through a process of recrafting that is alert to the power of generic markers. Two main methods are used for imposing a pastoral schema across the collection: reframing through titles and introducing stock pastoral figures into the poems. In the case of a lyric excerpted from *The Phoenix Nest*, it was both given a new title, '*The Sheepheards description of Love*', the first line changed from 'Now what is Love' (*Phoenix Nest*, N1v) to 'Sheepheard, what's Love' (L2v), and then turned into an eclogue through the addition of two speakers, Melibeus and Faustus, who now converse on the subject of love. Other markers are introduced, as Rollins despairs, by 'scatter[ing] four more uses of *Sheepheard* and one of *Nimph*' throughout the poem.[39] Melibeus and Faustus reappear later in the anthology in the titles given to a lyric excerpted from Yong's *Diana*, '*The Sheepheard* Faustus *his Song*' (M4–4v), and '*Olde Melibeus Song, courting his Nimph*' (O4v–P1), assigned to Greville. Given that Melibeus is not named in this poem, and technically it is anacreontic rather than pastoral, since its subject is an old man's love for a young woman, the title has been introduced both to pastoralise this lyric and to create an echo effect within the anthology through the repetition and reverberation of this pastoral name across the collection.

---

[37] Sukanta Chaudhuri, *Renaissance Pastoral and Its English Developments* (Oxford: Clarendon Press, 1989), 136–8.

[38] On this phenomenon in relation to the sonnet, see Wall, *Imprint of Gender*, 70–4; Juliet Fleming, 'Changed Opinion as to Flowers', in Smith and Wilson, eds., *Renaissance Paratexts*, 48–64.

[39] See Rollins in Bodenham, *Englands Helicon*, II, 64–5, for full details of this reframing.

'Impos'd Designe': the Work of Form   163

While Rollins was scathing in his assessment of the 'editor's' literary sensibility, he grudgingly admired his skill: 'The editor's care in giving titles shows that he was a careful and methodical worker to whom mechanical consistency was a jewel.'[40] The taint of labour runs through this judgement and illustrates how the work of those 'mechanicals' in the book trade has not merited adequate attention in comparison with the more reputable figures of authors, like Spenser, who engaged in editing or are credited with the composition of the printed book. J. Paul Hunter, in his essay 'Poetry on the Page: Visual Signalling and the Mind's Ear', is very alert to the properties of print textuality – how printing conventions, such as the disposition of page space, signalled the formal features of poetry and informed reading practices, including reading aloud. Yet, his brilliant analysis takes us not to those working in the printing house, but to the author as the primary compositor of literary texts.[41] The manual work of text production within the printing house is often viewed simply as a 'necessary function' and separate from poetic making – in other words, the creative and intellectual work of composing.[42] By bringing the mechanical craft of the printing house into focus, it is possible to see, not only the hands of authors at work in shaping poetic forms, but also those of compositors. The transformation of '*The Sheepheards description of Love*' into an eclogue exemplifies this type of creative interplay between literary form and the work of the printing press. The layout of this poem on the page resulted from decisions made by those who prepared the copytext and the compositor who set the type and made judgements about the use of quads – metal spacers – and different fonts. When set on the page in the source, *The Phoenix Nest*, the poem was laid out in six uniform stanzas with the last two lines indented. It was then recast in *Englands Helicon* in the conventional typographic format of the eclogue by incorporating dialogue markers: Melibeus and Faustus's names are set off from the main body of the poem in italics in the left margin, which both denotes their status as speakers and divides the lyric between two voices (see Figures 3 and 4).

---

[40] Rollins, in Bodenham, *Englands Helicon*, ii, 65.
[41] J. Paul Hunter, 'Poetry on the Page: Visual Signalling and the Mind's Ear', in Baumann and Burton, eds., *Work of Form*, 180–96; András Kiséry and Allison Deutermann's 'The Matter of Form: Book History, Formalist Criticism, and Francis Bacon's Aphorisms', is similarly author-centric (in *The Book in History, The Book as History: New Intersections in the Material Text*, edited by Heidi Brayman, Jesse M. Lander, and Zachary Lesser (New Haven: Yale University Press, 2016), 29–63).
[42] See Tonry's critique of this hierarchy of composition, in *Agency and Intention*, 3–4.

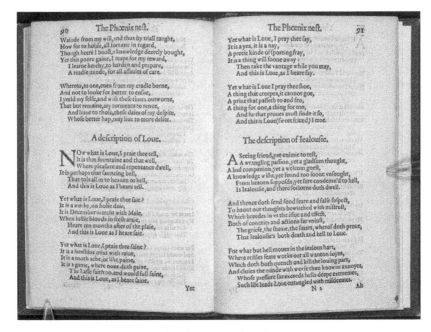

Figure 3   *The Phoenix Nest* (1593), pages 90–1.

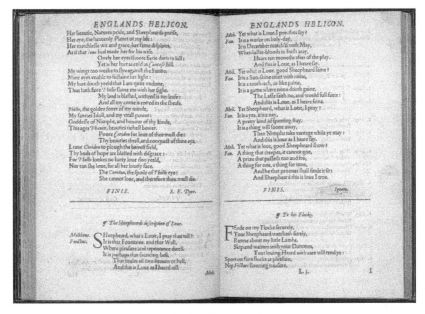

Figure 4   *Englands Helicon* (1600), sig. L3v–4r.

'Impos'd Designe': *the Work of Form*   165

These typographic and vocal properties are further enhanced in the setting in *Englands Helicon* by ending the first line of each stanza with a question mark throughout, whereas only the first lines of the second and third stanzas in *The Phoenix Nest* end in this way. Melibeus and Faustus are thereby firmly established as interlocutors. Attending to the differences between the settings of the poems across these two anthologies discloses the work of Rollins's mechanicals to provide a vivid illustration of how literary genres were crafted within the creative nexus of the printing house.

The work of form operates through the collective agencies of publishers and other non-authorial agents. Decisions were made about organisation and design on the basis of their careful reading of other books. Knowledge was thus tacitly acquired through observation, imitation, and practice. The *'impos'd design'* of *Englands Helicon* is expressed through the selection, organisation, and framing of poems which, in turn, respond to the wider literary field of the 1590s and the anthologising affordances of pastoral. The collection opens with a Sidney poem, a call to song, 'Onely joy, now heere you are' (B1–1v). A Sidneian opening is in keeping with other poetry anthologies produced in the 1590s that had established Sidney as the wellspring of an English lyric tradition.[43] By designing anthologies with Sidney as the point of origin, compilers made both a literary judgement and a commercial decision. Books appearing under Sidney's name were highly marketable and open to repackaging. As we have seen in the previous chapter, a Sidney poem was a prompt to textual gathering. Like other Sidneian compilations, the opening section of *Englands Helicon* is designed to place Sidney in dialogue with other living poets as part of a wider communal enterprise achieved through the craft of compilation.[44]

Intermixing dead with living poets defines the purpose of anthologising in terms of fabricating a living corpus of vernacular lyric poetry and performs several functions simultaneously: it puts in place schema, in which old and new, poetic fathers and sons, engage in dialogue; it makes a new literary property by redeploying material already in circulation alongside new texts and within new frames; and it provides a lesson in anthologising by offering a model of practice for subsequent excerpting and recombination. In the opening section, previously unpublished poems attributed to E. B. (Edmund Bolton), Drayton, Lodge, and Sheepheard Tonie (Anthony Munday) are carefully interspersed among lyrics drawn from the printed collections of Sidney and Spenser. Sidney's songs, 'Onely joy, now heere you are' (B1–1v), 'Ring out your belles' (B3v–4), and

---

[43] Alexander, *Writing after Sidney*, 66.   [44] Ibid., 32.

166 *Englands Helicon*

'Goe my flocke' (c1–1v), taken from *The Countesse of Pembrokes Arcadia* (1598–9, zz5–6, ss5, Aaa3v–4), alternate with E. B.'s '*Theorello. A Sheepheards Edillion*' (b2–3v) and '*A Palinode*' (b4v), before Spenser is brought into the conversation with 'Hobbinolls *Dittie in prayse* of Eliza Queene of the Sheepheards' (c1v–3v), from his *The Shepheardes Calendar*, which is then placed alongside Drayton's as yet unpublished '*The Sheepheards* Daffadill' (c3v–4). E. B. comes in again with '*A Canzon Pastorall in honour of her Majestie*' (c4v), followed by Greene's 'Melicertus *Madrigale*' (d1), extracted from his pastoral romance *Menaphon* (1599, f2v–3); a new verse by Lodge, '*Olde* Damons *Pastorall*' (d1v), introduces Spenser's 'Perigot *and* Cuddies *Roundelay*', again from *Shepheardes Calender* (1597, h3–12), which is followed by Breton's 'Phillida *and* Coridon', taken from *The Honorable Entertainement gieven to the Queenes Majestie in Progesse* (1591, d2v), before Sheepheard Tonie first enters the collection with his song, excerpted from his prose romance *Primaleon of Greece* (*c.* 1596?), given the Spenserian title '*To* Colin Cloute'.[45]

Intermixing is not only generational. Ling in his epistle sets out a method for compiling verse that values the social mixing of authors in civic terms. Voicing the possibility that some may complain that a poet considered 'a far meaner man in the eye of the world' has been placed alongside others of higher 'birth or fortune' allows Ling to argue that literary culture is customarily meritocratic, that 'the names of Poets … have beene placed with the names of the greatest Princes of the world, by the most autentique and worthiest judgements, without disparagement to their soveraigne titles' (a4v). The decision to place courtier-poets, like Sidney, Dyer, and Fulke Greville, alongside, for example, Munday and Greene, writers of ballads and popular prose romances, was therefore ideologically charged. Literary culture, argues Ling, should be socially diverse and the space of the anthology must be open to a mixed audience. One of the properties of anthologies is that they are incorporative; hence the gathering of poems is typically justified in terms of the principle of variety. In earlier anthologies, such as *Songs and Sonettes* and *Paradyse of Daynty Devises*, ballads are collected alongside courtly lyrics, illustrating how the variety at the heart of anthologising can result in formal and social hybridity. Anthologies could also be used as a space to set out social distinctions. When *Englands Helicon* is compared with *The Phoenix Nest*, an anthology from which poems are borrowed, then its compilers'

---

[45] Only one copy of the 1596 edition, a fragment, survives; however, this song is present in Book ii, chapter 27 of the 1619 edition.

'Impos'd Designe': *the Work of Form* 167

approach to social mixing becomes clearer. *The Phoenix Nest* is framed through epistles that express its aristocratic allegiances and the social status of its authors is consistently recorded in 'gentle' terms. When Lodge and Breton appear in its pages, their gentlemanly status is clearly identified – '*T. L.* Gent.' and '*N. B.* Gent.'. *Englands Helicon* does not use 'Gent.' after the names of any of its authors, hence Lodge is simply '*Thom. Lodge*'. The anthology has been designed on civic humanist principles to cater to the interests of diverse reading publics that are understood to be capable of making literary judgements of merit.

The principle of social mixing is evident in the way poems are organised into sequences. The collection is certainly not anti-monarchical – Spenser and Bolton's poems in praise of Elizabeth take prime position in the opening section. Instead, it operates by setting in play a dialogue between a courtly and a native rustic poetics. Because Drayton's '*The Sheepheards Daffadill*' immediately follows Spenser's 'Hobbinol's *Dittie*', it is framed as an imitation of the preceding poem in a lower, more homely key. Spenser writes '*in prayse of* Eliza *Queene of the Sheepheards*', who is

> Yclad in scarlet, like a mayden Queene,
> And Ermines white.
> Upon her head a crimson Coronet,
> With Daffadils and Damaske Roses set,
> Bay leaves betweene,
> And Primeroses greene:
> Embellish the sweet Violet.
>
> (c2)

Compared with the mythopoetic proportions of Spenser's Eliza, the mistress of Drayton's ballad 'Daffadill' is more homely and metonymically grounded in a native, domestic landscape, since she is, in a sense, her name:

> Shee's in a frock of Lincolne greene,
> The colour Maydes delight,
> And never hath her Beauty seene
> But through a vayle of white.

Both poems are open to recreational readings in which audiences are invited to share visual and other sensory pleasures. And both are made up of flower lists that function as meta-*florilegia*, in that they reflect on the process of anthologising, gathering, and making literary garlands at times of leisure; hence Drayton's shepherd is 'making (as he fed his sheepe), / A wreath of Daffadillies' (c3). Where they differ is in their mistresses, in

168   *Englands Helicon*

that one is courtly and the other rustic. Pastoral had long provided a space for the 'coded performance' of such modes of recreation.[46] The type of recreation and poetic making offered by these songs may differ, in that Spenser's lyric is royal and courtly and Drayton's ballad rustic and homely, but when read and heard alongside one another within the anthology, they express the anthologistic principle of variety, resulting in a socially hybrid soundscape. Lodge's '*Olde* Damons *Pastorall*', a pastoral commonplace poem possibly written for this collection, is prompted by the mean estate proverb that 'true peace with Sheepheards dwelleth', and similarly reflects on a more 'Homely' reading experience – 'feede gentle Lambs while I sit reading' – that teaches the meritocratic civic virtues of the mean estate: 'What to other seemeth sorrie, / abject state and humble biding: / Is our joy and Country glorie' (D IV).[47] This is not to argue that *Englands Helicon* is at all anti-courtly; there are certainly many lyrics that advertise their origins in royal and aristocratic entertainments, such as 'Apollos *Love-Song for faire* Daphne', a '*Dittie* . . . *sung before her Majestie, at the right honourable the Lord* Chandos, *at* Sudley *Castell, at her last being there in prograce*' (Q2v). Instead the design of this anthology offers socially hybridised models of recreation to its readers that can travel between the households of the aristocracy and those of citizens.

Not surprisingly, the Sidney who emerges from *Englands Helicon* is primarily a love poet, who sings of courtship and is identified with pastoral's more domestic recreational forms – a Sidney that we are familiar with from the 1590s anthologies discussed in the preceding chapter. The Sidney lyric that opens *Englands Helicon*, 'Onely joy, now heere you are', in some ways, is a strange choice. For one thing, it is not a pastoral, but a seduction song set at night when 'Dumbe sleepe holdeth all the house' (D IV). The youthful male speaker tries to persuade his beloved to 'Take me to thee, and thee to me', to which she replies 'No, no, no, no, my Deere, let be' – these lines constitute the song's refrain. What makes the poem pastoral in the anthology is the framing title, '*The Sheepheard to his chosen Nimph*'; otherwise there are no other distinguishing markers, except perhaps the flowers on the bed's coverlet: 'These sweet flowers on fine bed too, / Us in their best language woo' (B1r). Why then begin with this poem and not something more recognisably pastoral? The answer lies in a number of its features: it is a dialogue poem in which not only men

---

[46] Montrose, 'Of Gentlemen and Shepherds'.
[47] Four lines from this poem, assigned to D. Lodge, were printed in *Englands Parnassus* (1600, 39), also published by Ling.

'Impos'd Designe': *the Work of Form*   169

converse, as is the case in the opening Sidneian elegies of *The Phoenix Nest*, but male and female voices engage in patterns of response that will be reiterated across the anthology; it is a love poem set within a domestic space and so advertises the usefulness of this anthology for household recreation; and finally it is a song, and a popular one at that, and so alerts readers to the suitability of the lyrics within this anthology for musical performance. The household properties of Sidney's lyric are encapsulated in the embroidered coverlet. Textiles provide a recurrent trope for describing literary fabrications, particularly compilations that are pieced and woven together, while needlework was both a household craft and a particularly feminine mode of agency.[48] Within this song, the embroidered bedspread is part of a complexly gendered soundscape that gives voice to a female interlocutor, but in a form deliberately constrained by the vocal and physical presence of the male speaker; hence her voice is confined to the reiterative refrain. The song ends in troubling discord. Sidney's lyric is illustrative of the contradictory position of women in songs of this period. Women were participating in song culture as 'patrons, consumers, instrumentalists, and vocalists', but often on male terms that they must negotiate.[49]

Other types of books offered compilers models for designing anthologies. The sheer number of lyrics excerpted from prose romances – Greene's *Menaphon*, Lodge's *Rosalynde*, and Bartholomew Yong's translation of Montemayor's *Diana* – illustrates the significance of the lessons this genre offered when selecting material for recreational reading and performance. The prose romances published in the 1590s were designed to appeal to the varied reading practices of an audience made up of the middling sort. These 'pleasant histories', with their stories of love and courtship, offered alternative modes of 'reading for pleasure' to the more exclusive Petrarchan sonnet sequences of the 1590s.[50] What made the prose romance particularly attractive to anthology-makers was its multimodal and generically hybrid form. The incorporation of inset songs, verse letters, and other types of lyrics advertised these books as suitable sources for excerpting texts and provided those compiling *Englands Helicon* with examples of narrative craftsmanship – lessons in how to knit individual lyrics into the fabric of a longer work. The dynamic, varied structure of romance illustrated how poems could function as self-contained lyrics, divisible from the main text and capable of being read on their own, and at the same time readily

---

[48] Frye, *Pens and Needles*, 116.   [49] Trudell, 'Performing Women', 29.
[50] Newcomb, *Reading Popular Romance*, 1–10; Mentz, *Romance for Sale*, 17–45.

170   *Englands Helicon*

integrated within the wider narrative structure of the prose romance. In other words, prose romances provided lessons in how to fabricate an anthology. The titles given to the lyrics excerpted from prose romances illustrate how the compilers of *Englands Helicon* read and manipulated their multimodality. The titles are of two main types: either they identify the speaker or singer and genre – 'Rosalindes *Madrigall*' (s1–1v) – or, more commonly, they point to the wider prose narratives from which lyrics were excerpted by identifying characters and situations – '*The Sheepheard* Eurymachus *to his faire Sheepheardesse*' (N1v–2v), 'Alanius *the Sheepheard, his dolefull Song, complayning of* Ismeniaes *crueltie*' (o2–3), 'Faustus and Firmius sing to their Nimph by turnes' (R1–1v), or 'A Song betweene Taurisius and Diana aunswering verse for verse' (R2–2v). The inclusion of numerous lyrics drawn from the pastoral romances means that characters recur and recombine throughout the collection, setting in place ongoing dialogues across the anthology that draw characters from other literary sources into the conversation: Selvagia and Silvanus, Silvanus and Syrenus, Astrophel and Stella, Amintas and Phillis, Faustus and Firmius, Taurisius and Diana, Syrenus and Diana, Philistus and Clorinda, and so on. These are desiring subjects and their various invitations to love and complaints against faithless lovers, abandonment, and unrequited love result in a flexible, reverberating structure that is endlessly digressive and reiterative. Voices break off only to be answered or echoed and resumed in another key by another set of characters.

These loose, flexible formal properties of romance demonstrate how lyrics drawn from different sources can be compiled into new sequences and accrue new meanings.[51] A song from Sidney's *Astrophil and Stella* is placed between two lyrics from Yong's *Diana*.[52] The first, '*The Sheepheard* Arsilius, *his Song to his Rebeck*', taken from Yong's *Diana* (M2v–3), uneasily balances the enjoyment of love with lament. The song captures the passing moment and rapidly shifting emotions as Arsilius, caught in the throes of desire, waits anxiously for his beloved to arrive: 'O stay not time, but passe with speedie hast, / And Fortune hinder not her comming now, / O God, betides me yet this greefe at last?' (T2). The title given to the following poem, '*Another of* Astrophel *to his* Stella', at first seems slightly disjunctive since it refers to another source text – *Astrophil and Stella* – and to Sidney's other Astrophel poems in the anthology. And yet, this title reads Sidney's

---

[51] On this phenomenon in manuscript miscellanies, see Eckhardt, *Manuscript Verse Collectors*, 1–21.
[52] It is taken from *The Countesse of Pembroke's Arcadia* (Aaa2–3v); a shorter version of this lyric is in *Syr P. S. His Astrophel and Stella* (1591).

'Impos'd Designe': *the Work of Form*   171

poem in relation to the preceding poem, in the sense that it is offering another, similar type of lyric to the one before, which indeed it does. These lyrics are loosely conjoined by the forms of temporal and spatial deixis running across these individual poems that turns them into a sequence. The first song explores the emotional temporality of waiting: the presence of the object of desire is eagerly anticipated and endlessly deferred. Whereas in Yong's lyric, the lovers are just at the point of meeting, in Sidney's song the lovers 'Did for mutuall comfort meete / Both within them-selves oppressed, / But each in the other blessed' (T2–2v). However, at the end of the song, Stella departs 'Leaving him to passion rent: / With what she had done and spoken, / That there-with my Song is broken' (T3v). What then follows is a 'broken' song, 'Syrenus *his Song to* Dianaes *Flocks*', again taken from Yong's *Diana* (M1v), in which the shepherd recalls and then dismisses his 'Passed contents', since 'Now my joyes are dead and dombe' (T3v, T4). The reiterative refrain to the song, 'O leave me then, and doo not wearie me', reinforces this reverberating, echoic acoustic patterning within the anthology.

Those involved in compiling *Englands Helicon* were reading and studying books in a commercial sense, not only to assess and predict 'the likely readings of their customers', but also to learn how to manipulate textual matter and to fabricate compilations.[53] The various forms of design on display in *Englands Helicon*, from the layout of poems on the page to the use of titles and the choices made when selecting poems and arranging them into sequences within the overarching schema of the pastoral anthology, blur the distinctions between the manual, mechanical work of book production and the creative and intellectual work of composing. Framing this work are the prefaces before *Englands Helicon*, penned by A. B. and Ling, which take responsibility for the anthology and its production, and invite their readers to witness the craft displayed in its form. The experiential language used to describe the '*paines*' they have taken '*heerein*' (A3) and the '*travaile that hath been taken in gathering*' (A4r), alongside the '*impos'd design*' of *Englands Helicon*, results in a language of book production that is embodied and practised, situated in environments in which things are made. Taken together, they are part in the 'historical shaping of print' described by Adrian Johns – those claims made and strategies employed to persuade authors and readers to credit the work undertaken by publishers and within the printing house on their behalf.[54]

---

[53] The quote is from Lesser, *Renaissance Drama*, 8.   [54] Johns, *Nature of the Book*, 3.

172   *Englands Helicon*

Assigning Authorship

Attribution practices in *Englands Helicon* have attracted critical interest thanks to the range of ascriptions used on its pages – names, initials, pseudonyms, 'Anomos', and 'Ignoto' – and, most notably, the use of cancel slips to alter earlier attributions.[55] What interests me is how questions of attribution are acted upon in this anthology thus making the work of editing visible. Ling acknowledges he bears some responsibility for verse attribution in the anthology, but he is also careful to point out that he necessarily relied on attributions made by others in 'some especiall coppy comming into his handes' (A4). Assigning poems to authors is acknowledged by Ling to be an uncertain process, reliant on the quality of sources and the vagaries of transmission. In cases of misattribution, Ling advises the author that he is able 'freely to challenge his owne in publique, where els he might be robd of his proper due' (A4). The printed book is understood to be beset by the same uncertainties as the manuscript sources on which it sometimes relies. Error was accepted as part and parcel of the process of making books.[56] What appears to be important to Ling is not accuracy *per se*, but the moral responsibility of publishers to authors to ensure good practice. An intriguing feature of Ling's address to disgruntled authors is that it is couched in terms of a bargain or contract: he has done his best to ensure correct attribution, but 'If any man hath beene defrauded of any thing by him composed, by another mans title put to the same', then he is free to challenge it; if he is offended that his name has been 'published to any invention of his', then he should be 'satisfie[d]' he is in good company (B4–4v). Ling's main concern here, arguably, is not even with authors, as such, but rather with responsible editorial procedures. Editorial notes in the anthology address the task of attribution by announcing the impossibility of doing so in a number of cases, pointing out that '*the Authors name unknowne to me*' (Q1v), or '*The Author thereof unknowne*' (Q2v), or that this information is missing from the source text, '*the Authors names not there set downe, & therefore left to their owners*' (X2). In the preface, the claim that only limited knowledge was available provides an opportunity to display judgement and outline methods. Efforts to acquire authoritative information may have resulted in some cases of misattribution, so Ling invites authors to become correcting

---

[55] Rollins, in Bodenham, *Englands Helicon*, II, 66; Sir Walter Raleigh, *Selected Poetry and Prose* (London: Athlone Press, 1965), 24; North, *Anonymous Renaissance*, 75–7.

[56] See Smyth on error, in *Material Texts*, chapter 3.

Assigning Authorship 173

readers.[57] It is an approach shared with Disle's errata list from the 1577 edition of *Paradyse*, which similarly engaged the reader in the book's production. The publisher offered readers a contract, in which he has granted them the authority and responsibility to correct faults in the text, with the assistance of the list he helpfully provided. When Disle praises the 'curious eye' of this reader, he is attributing expertise, defining their reading practices as studious and attentive to detail.[58] It is this skilful reader who is invited into the printing house to observe and to participate in its practices.

Francis Davison was this type of correcting reader envisioned by Ling and Disle. Soon after the publication of *Englands Helicon*, he compiled a table listing the first line of the poems it gathered along with their authors.[59] Davison was, of course, a very specialised reader, who by this stage was probably in the process of compiling his own anthology for publication. One of the ways in which he read this anthology was for authorship. For the most part, Davison provided straightforward transcriptions of attributions in *Englands Helicon*. In other cases, he expanded initials, particularly S. E. D. which becomes E. Dier: he too is prone to misinformation, mistakenly expanding I. D. to 'I. Davis' (fol. 99), rather than John Dickenson, the author of *The Shepheard's Complaint* (*c.* 1596), from which the poem derives, possibly because John Davies was known to him and more collectable than the lesser known Dickenson. Davison could also draw on privileged knowledge not available to the compilers of *Englands Helicon*. Whereas an editorial note following a set of three lyrics stated '*These three ditties were taken out of Maister* John Dowlands *booke of tableture for the Lute, the Authors names not there set downe, & therefore left to their owners*' (x2), Davison's list supplied the missing attributions for two of the lyrics: beside 'Away with these self loving lads' he writes 'F. Grevill', and 'Earle of Cumberland' beside 'My thoughts are wingd wth hope, my hope wth love' (fol. 100). Other alterations are made: one of the Lodge poems from *Rosalynde*, 'Alas how I wander amidst these woods', is correctly attributed to 'T. Lodge', not Dyer (fol. 100), although he replicates the misattribution of the other Lodge poem, 'When ye dog', which he too ascribes to 'E. Dier' (fol. 100).

When it comes to interpreting the cancel slips, Davison's practices are quite revealing. Five cancel slips were pasted over names or initials and took two forms: either the cancel slip replaces the name of one author with

---

[57] See Massai on perfectibility in editing and the role of correcting readers, in *Shakespeare*, 199.
[58] *OED*, 1a, 2c. These meanings are now obsolete.   [59] BL, Harley MS 280, fols. 99–101.

174 *Englands Helicon*

another or substitutes a name with Ignoto. Apart from the slip printed with 'N. Breton' pasted over 'S. Phil. Sidney', all others cover the names of two authors, Raleigh and Fulke Greville, or rather their initials, S. W. R. and M. F. G, with cancel slips on which 'Ignoto' is printed. At what point in the book's production did this activity take place? The pages were already printed, so this intervention occurred either before the sheets reached the booksellers, or after only a few copies were sold and the remaining stock then were amended, or it may have been an even earlier intervention in the printing house, when cancel slips were put in place after the main body of the text was printed, but before the preliminaries (sig. A), given this sheet was typically left to the end. The expense and labour involved points to the involvement, at some level, of the printer, Roberts, and the publisher, Flasket. Ling's epistle also suggests his part in the process, given he is so concerned with misattribution. More particularly, he berates those disgruntled authors who 'in prizing of [their] owne birth or fortune, shall take it in scorne, that a far meaner man in the eye of the world, shal be placed by him' (B4v). Ling's ire appears targeted and may have been prompted by men of 'birth or fortune', who objected to being named in the anthology: only Raleigh's and Fulke Greville's names are replaced with 'Ignoto'. Davison's copy must have had cancel slips. For the song, 'Fayre in a morne', Davison follows the cancel slip in attributing the lyric to 'N. Bretton' (99v) and not Sidney. The initial mistaking of a Sidney song for that of Breton reminds us of how intimately these songs were circulating alongside each other in manuscript channels in the 1590s.[60] In all other cases, he has clearly removed the slip to reveal the initials it covers, which he takes as authoritative: S. W. R. is then listed as S. W. Rawly and M. F. G. is identified as F. Grevill. Whereas Davison interpreted the first cancel slip as a correction of a misattribution, presumably based on knowledge of other sources, he seems to have understood the others as a form of censorship, in which the Ignoto slips mask the identity of the actual author who has been subject to name suppression. In other words, he employed different reading practices according to how he assessed the evidence. These cancel slips demonstrate that authorship mattered, and it mattered differently. Their use in *Englands Helicon* vividly illustrates the complex agencies at work in the business of assigning authorship, disclosing the various negotiations between publishers, printers, authors, and readers.

---

[60] See Chapter 3, 121–4.

Assigning Authorship 175

Authors are given prominence in *Englands Helicon*. Whereas other printers' prefaces, as we have seen, utilise the trope of the absent author, placing this figure at some distance from the printing house, Ling speaks to authors directly, inviting them to credit his labours on their behalf. There are authors who can be placed near the printing house, even amongst those publishers and printers producing these compilations. Munday, one of those involved in editing *Bel-vedére*, contributes six poems to *Englands Helicon* under the pastoral pseudonym 'Sheepheard Tonie': only two are excerpted from his previously printed books, the others are new to this anthology. The same is the case for Drayton's poems: all are new, apart from 'Rowlands *Song*', which first appeared in *Idea. The Shepheards Garland* (1593), although it is substantially revised in *Englands Helicon*. While there is some evidence to place Munday and Drayton close to the scene of production, in other cases, it is difficult to pin down the precise nature of an author's involvement in the anthology. Rollins floated the possibility that Thomas Lodge was involved in editing, arguing that the careful revisions to his poems were probably undertaken by Lodge himself, particularly given his publishing relationship with Ling, thereby locating this author in the printing house correcting copy.[61] The differences between *Englands Helicon*'s version of 'Coridons *Song*' and the earlier text in *Rosalynde* are substantive: words are changed to complete rhymes and four lines added to complete the octet (P2). Yet, Lodge also suffers from misattribution that went unchanged. 'Like desert woods' and 'Oh woods unto your walks' were first published in *The Phoenix Nest* (1593) where they were attributed to 'T. Lodge, gent.', but in *Englands Helicon* they are attributed to S. E. D. and Ignoto respectively; similarly 'When the dog' (S2–2v), 'Alas, how I wander amidst these woods' (X2–2v), both taken from Lodge's *Rosalynde* (P1–1v), which Ling had published, are also misattributed to S. E. D. The available evidence is not only inconclusive, but inconsistent in ways that illustrate the often makeshift practices of book production.

Sheepheard Tonie, by comparison, is an example of how authors could use the space of the anthology to fashion literary reputations. Munday was long practised in anthology production, having worked with Proctor, Jones, and others on *Gorgious Gallery, of Gallant Inventions*.[62] Given that Munday was a prolific author in print, the fact that the majority of his poems were published in *Englands Helicon* for the first time suggests they

---

[61] Rollins, in Bodenham, *Englands Helicon*, II, 62.   [62] See Chapter 2, 96–9.

176   *Englands Helicon*

were composed in order to make up this anthology.[63] Pseudonyms were an established print convention and could provide an opportunity to establish an authorial 'brand'.[64] The use of a pseudonym gives Sheepheard Tonie a cultural value that permits his participation within the charmed circle of shepherd-poets represented within pastoral collections like Spenser's *Colin Clouts*/*Astrophel*. The seven lyrics under the signature Sheepheard Tonie are dispersed throughout the anthology and place him in the company of Sidney-Astrophel, Spenser-Colin Clout, and Drayton-Rowland. Editorial work undertaken in framing and placing Sheepheard Tonie's lyrics within sequences capitalises on the signifying power of the Sidney name by fabricating social and cultural proximities: a Sheepheard Tonie poem is given the title '*Countess of Pembroke's Pastorall*' (Y1–2v) and is paired with a Sidney song ('The nightingale so soone as Aprill bringeth'), given the title '*Another of* Astrophell' (Y2v), to make up a very familiar co-creative Sidneian sequence, bringing brother and sister into recreative dialogue through song. Methods for compiling poems within anthologies are key to this fabrication of a literary identity. Sequences are stitched together through titles and poems are turned into dialogues through shared characters and *topoi* to create a loose narrative structure.

A Sheepheard Tonie poem performs this crucial role of stitching together a sequence of three lyrics that all feature the shepherdess Phillida. Breton's '*A sweete Pastorall*' (E4v–F1v), in which '*Phillida* the faire hath lost, / the comfort of her favour' (F1), is followed by Surrey's pastoral, '*Phillida* was a faire mayde' (F1v–3), with the narrative title it is given in *Songes and Sonettes* (with minor variants), 'Harpalus *complaynt on* Phillidaes *love bestowed on* Corin, *who loved her not, and denyed him that loved her*'. Finally, Munday's lyric, 'On a goodly Sommers day', is given the title '*An other of the same subject, but made as it were in aunswere*' (F3–4v). This last Munday poem, as its title announces, has been carefully designed as a sequel to Surrey's poem. Whereas Surrey's shepherd complains to his sheep and curses his fate, his mistress, and his rival, Corin, Munday's Harpalus addresses Phillida directly, warning her of Corin's infidelity and that he courts another, Phillis. Her response promises a further instalment to the lyric:

---

[63] '*To* Colin Clout' was printed in *The Second Booke of Primaleon of Greece* (1596 (fragment), 1619), Book 2, chapter 27, and 'Montana *the Shepherd, his love to* Aminta' in *Fedele and Fortunio* (1585).
[64] North, *Anonymous Renaissance*, 3.

Re-creating Poetry 177

Harpalus, I thanke not thee,
For this sorry tale to mee.
Meete me heere againe to morrow,
Then I will conclude my sorrow
mildly, if may be.
(F4v)

The verse quite deliberately puts in place a pattern for dialogic reading and a model of compilation that encourages an expectation of sequentiality across the anthology, in other words, that other poems can be expected to respond meaningfully on the same theme. The subsequent lyrics that feature Phillida and Corin, or Coridon, such as Breton's 'Astrophell *his song of* Phillida *and* Coridon' (G4–H1), Ignoto's 'Phillidaes *Love-call to her* Coridon, *and his replying*' (I4–K1), and all the other Phillidas that appear in lyrics – Breton's '*A Sheepheards Dreame*' (K3v–4) and the song '*Of* Phillida' (V2) – are thereby loosely affiliated within the fabric of the anthology, while retaining their status as separate lyrics and so open to subsequent excerpting and recombination. Munday's '*An other of the same subject, but made as it were in aunswere*' was therefore consciously crafted by this author with the process of anthologising in mind.

Re-creating Poetry

The remodelling of the poem taken from *The Phoenix Nest* into a pastoral dialogue in *Englands Helicon* illustrates how literary forms are crafted through the work of the printing house. Juliet Flemings's recent work on the printer of *Englands Helicon*, James Roberts, similarly asks us to consider how 'poetic making' incorporated not only authorial, but also non-authorial and non-human agencies, 'both the labour of the technicians and the operations of the machines that constituted the work of the press'.[65] Poetic making, in these terms, allows us to understand how the layout of poems on the page not only moulds poems within genres, but was also deliberately designed to accentuate the recreational, acoustic properties of the printed book. *Englands Helicon* is distinguished by the skill of its presswork, which is noteworthy for the varied patterns of lineation displayed in the collection. This feature correlates with the musicality of *Englands Helicon*, evident in the way that lyrics travelled to

---

[65] Fleming, 'Changed Opinion as to Flowers', 57–8.

178   *Englands Helicon*

and from this anthology via printed songbooks.[66] The layout of poetry on the page marks out the multimedia uses of these lyrics; it not only operates at the visual level, but also points to their acoustic properties, thereby realising the musical soundscape of the anthology through the technologies of print. At the same time, the availability of many of these poems for musical performance is advertised in editorial notes which direct readers to the printed music books in which settings can be found. Music and poetry are mutually implicated in poetic making within *Englands Helicon*, in keeping with the recreative properties of performance cultures.

A key aspect of the *mise-en-page* was the block of text. Care was taken with the layout of poems in Roberts's printing house and extensive use was made of quads to mark out indentations when setting lines of verse.[67] To create varied lineation, the compositor interpreted the lineation provided in the copytext from which he worked, under instruction from the master printer, as well as drawing on knowledge gained through the experience of setting other texts. Using his judgement, and taking into account the design of the *mise-en-page* as a whole, the compositor built the line inserting quads and carefully adjusting the spaces as required.[68] The lineation of a poem was the work of numerous individuals at different points in production: authors, compilers, the publisher, master printer, compositor, and others. The case of a multi-author anthology like *Englands Helicon* is particularly complicated given that poems are coming from a variety of sources. For some lyrics, the layout follows the setting in the book from which it was excerpted; in the case of others, lineation has been altered; and for those first printed in the anthology, we cannot be certain who was responsible for layout in the copytext. What is distinctive about the *mise-en-page* of *Englands Helicon* is not the fact that varied lineation is used, since this is present in many of the books from which these poems are taken, but rather the impressive variety of lineation displayed in the layout of the poems across the anthology as a whole.[69]

---

[66] See the discussion of music and poetry in *Englands Helicon* in Maynard, *Elizabethan Lyric Poetry*, 56–70; Pomeroy, *Elizabethan Miscellanies*, 93–115; and more recently Larson, *Matter of Song*, 114–15.

[67] Philip Gaskell, *A New Introduction to Bibliography* (1972; Delaware: Oak Knoll Press, 1995), 45.

[68] Joseph Moxon, *Mechanick Exercises on the Whole Art of Printing (1683–4)*, edited by Herbert Davis and Harry Carter (Oxford University Press, 1968), 203–19. See Mark Bland's discussion of how 'a text is filled and pieced together, rather than filled in' by compositors, in *A Guide to Early Printed Books and Manuscripts* (Oxford: Wiley-Blackwell, 2010), 117–18.

[69] Little has been written about the lineation of poetry: Hunter's 'Poetry on the Page' and Rosenberg's 'Point of the Couplet' focus on the couplet. M. B. Parkes briefly discusses layout, but is more interested in punctuation (see *Pause and Effect*, 110–11), as is Ros King in 'Seeing the Rhythm: an Interpretation of Sixteenth-Century Punctuation and Metrical Practice', in *Ma(r)king the Text: the*

Re-creating Poetry 179

There is no instance of more than two consecutive poems with the same layout and many patterns of indentation are pronounced and intricate. What is clear from *Englands Helicon* is that one of the editorial decisions made was to emphasise variety, rather than uniformity, in the layout of poetry on the page, in order to visualise the formal variety of the poetry collected and, hence, the idea of the anthology as a *mixtum compositum*. Layout, however, not only operated at the visual level, but also had acoustic properties that advertised the musicality of this anthology.

The distinctiveness of *Englands Helicon* becomes apparent when it is compared with earlier anthologies. The metre of poems gathered in *Songes and Sonettes* was carefully regularised into iambs, but there was less attention to metrical features in the layout of the poetry, which was printed in blocks as a 'simple stichic structure'.[70] In other words, lineation was not used to teach its readers how to read the printed text as poetry by pointing up prosodic features, such as rhyme and metrical variation. *Paradyse of Daynty Devises* similarly printed most of its poems in uniform blocks, with the first line indented, although with some variation. The triple rhymed lines, made up of tri- and dimeters, that follow a pair of fourteeners in Francis Kinwelmarsh's '*For Whitsunday*' (A3v) are indented, as is the exclamation – a dimeter – that closes each stanza and is set in alignment with the end of the line above:

> And loe, whose hope of better day,
> Is overwhelmd with long delay.
>   Oh hard mishap.
>
>   (E2r)

The result is a phenomenalising of print, in which the visual, typographic layout of the line on the page expresses its emotional import, its choric sound of despair. And yet, the varied metrical structure of its stanzas, with its eight lines of poulter's measure, followed by four tetrameter lines, is otherwise set uniformly. Unlike *Englands Helicon*, in *Paradyse* there is no evidence that prosodic features are being pointed out to readers consistently through the layout on the page. Tellingly, the anthology that does incorporate comparatively varied patterns of lineation that correlate with the rhythmic features of stress verse is *A Handefull of Pleasant Delites*, typically in those ballads that are closely related to carols, dance songs.[71]

Presentation of Meaning on the Literary Page, edited by Joe Bray, Miriam Handley, and Anne C. Henry (Aldershot: Ashgate, 2000), 235–52.
[70] Parkes, *Pause and Effect*, 101.   [71] See Chapter 2, 81.

180   *Englands Helicon*

The musical properties of the ballads gathered in this anthology are marked up as such on the page, both through varied lineation and through the tunes identified in the headnotes.

Many of the poems collected in *Englands Helicon* retain the layout from the books from which they were excerpted. Compilers reading through these books for material must have kept an eye out for poems not only because they were pastoral, but also because they were metrically varied and so had a visually distinctive presence on the page. The poems excerpted from the prose romances by Lodge and Greene and those from Yong's translation of *Diana* retained the layout of the source texts because it was already complex.[72] Variety of lineation identifies these inset lyrics within the wider narrative of these prose romances and breaks up the uniformity of the blocks of printed prose, helping readers to identify lyrics visually and generically from the surrounding prose text. Since these lyrics are described as songs in the framing narrative, layout provides pointers for their performative properties. The dialogue song given the title 'Faustus *and* Firmius *sing to their Nimph by turnes*' (R1–1v) in *Englands Helicon* was excerpted from Yong's translation of Montemayor's *Diana* (320–1), and is made up of septets rhyming abbaacC – the last line is the refrain:

> *Firmius.*   Of mine owne selfe I doo complaine,
>   And not for loving thee so much,
>   But that in deede thy power is such:
>   That my true love it dooth restraine,
>   And onely this dooth giue me paine,
>   For faine I would
>   Love her more, if that I could.
>
>   (R1)

Varied lineation draws attention to rhyme, given that the verse lines making up the quintet are all octosyllabic, and to the refrain, an iambic dimeter, followed by a longer, lingering trochaic line. The layout on the page gives typographic expression to the vocal properties of the song, to what is meant in Yong's text when it is written that Firmius 'began thus to tune his voice' (*Diana*, 320); in other words, how he adapts his voice to express emotions and thoughts, here represented through the modulations of rhyme and metre and the printed lines on the page.

Changes made to the lineation of poems from their layout in their sources allow us to see this attention to the acoustic, performative

---

[72] Roberts printed Lodge and Greene's romances in 1604 and 1605, after *Englands Helicon*.

Re-creating Poetry 181

properties of print at work. While the elaborate lineation of Sidney's song 'Ring out your belles' is retained from Ponsonby's *The Countesse of Pembrokes Arcadia* (1598–9, ss5), the layout of other of his songs is altered in *Englands Helicon*. The songs 'Onely joy' and 'Goe my flocke' in the Ponsonby edition are set in uniform blocks with no identation. For 'Onely joy' the change is relatively minor but telling: the last two lines of the sextain, the refrain, are now indented. Typographic pointing here identifies the form – a song – and marks up the lyric for performance, functioning as a visual and generic cue for how it is to be vocalised. Pointing introduced in *Englands Helicon* for 'Goe my flocke' is more complex because of the rhyme scheme, ababb, and its rhythmic patterning – the indented lines now mark up and enhance the vocal properties of a feminine rhyme, the cadence of the falling hypermetric stress:

> Goe my flocke, goe get yee hence,
> > Seeke a better place of feeding:
> Where yee may have some defence
> > From the stormes in my breast breeding,
> > And showers from mine eyes proceeding.
>
> (c1)

Sidney composed many of his lyrics with musical settings in mind and a number were printed in songbooks.[73] 'Onely joy, now here you are' was later reprinted with a madrigal setting composed by Giovanni Giacomo Gastoldi (*c.* 1554–1609), suggesting that it had an earlier musical life, while the beautiful 'The nightingale so soone as Aprill bringeth' (y2v) was first printed with its tune identified, 'Non credo gia che piu infelice amante', in *The Countesse of Pembrokes Arcadia* (1598–9, rr3–3v), and later printed with a madrigal setting in Thomas Bateson's *The First Set of English Madrigals* (1604, 11).

Some of the most dramatic instances of lineation are found in the numerous dance songs gathered in the collection. There are roundelays, including Spenser's 'Perigot *and* Cuddy's *Roundelay*' (d2r–3r), Greene's 'Menaphons *Roundelay*' (e2r–v), and Drayton's '*A Roundelay between two shepherds*' (l3v–4r). A roundelay or round has its origins in a circle dance song, in which the song structure guides the movement of the dancers.[74] Another prominent form is the jig: Wootton's 'Damaetas *jig in praise of his love*' (g1v–2r), Greene's 'Dorons *Jigge*' (g3v–4), and, relatedly, Sidney's

---

[73] Gavin Alexander, 'The Musical Sidneys', *John Donne Journal*, 25 (2006), 65–105.
[74] Karl Reichl, 'Plotting the Map of Medieval Oral Literature, in *Medieval Oral Literature*, edited by Karl Reichl (Berlin: De Gruyter, 2012), 45.

182   *Englands Helicon*

'*The Sheepheards braule, one halfe aunswering the other*' (M3v). The brawl or branle was a dance of French origin, in which couples linked arms either in lines or in circles. Its simple, rustic style meant that the dance moved between non-elite and elite performance cultures.[75] These rustic communal dance songs bring to the fore the ways in which song is expressed through the movement of the body. Roundelays and other dance songs are marked out in the collection through typographic pointing which expresses the motion of the dance through the spatialised form of the poem on the page. This embodied mode of print textuality is evident in the setting of Breton's '*A Report Song in a dreame, between a Sheepheard and his Nimph*', in which the dynamic movement of the verse lines on the page is mimetic of the physical actions described in the dance song:

> Shall we goe daunce the hay?   The hay?
> Never pipe could ever play
>   better Sheepheards Roundelay.
> Shall we goe sing the Song?   The Song?
> Never Loue did ever wrong:
>   faire Maides hold hands all a-long.

This dance song, 'The Hay', is a branle or brawl, in which dancers interweave towards the close of the dance. The words provide physical instructions for the dance song: in the branle, participants hold hands like the 'faire Maides' who 'hold hands all-along, and then

>   at the base they run,   They run.

Lineation here marks out the physical movements of this dance song, turning the printed line into a flexible mode of embodiment, materialising voice and bodies in motion on the page. And yet, this dance, as the title announces, is '*a dreame*' from which the speaker 'wakt, and all was done' (BB1v). The dream calls attention to the ephemerality of dance song as sound and movement and, relatedly, the complex processes of imaginative approximation required to relate the dance fleetingly embodied in time and space to the dance experienced on the page.[76]

The layout of songs on the page contributes to the mutually constitutive dialogue with printed songbooks in this anthology. Poetry and music anthologies, of course, have different properties. Music books required specialist type and printing; this substantial initial investment was then

---

[75] Winerock, '"Mixt" and Matched', 39–40.
[76] See Trudell on music and evanescence, in *Unwritten Poetry*, 11–12.

Re-creating Poetry 183

protected through a monopoly on printing music books, hence certain publishers and printers necessarily specialised in these books.[77] Musical notation clearly marked out a song for performance and identified the setting to which it should be performed. However, not only was the practice of providing musical notation inconsistent, and hence early modern songbooks did not always include scores for every song they collected; the setting printed in the book also did not fully determine the song's performance, since lyrics underwent an ongoing 're-creation' through performance.[78] As we have seen in previous chapters, anthologies capture these inconsistencies and fluid practices, even as they facilitate the musical transmission of poetry through re-creation. The layout of songs on the page in *Englands Helicon* obviously does not perform the specialist function of musical notation; nonetheless it does guide the reader to the performance properties of these lyrics.

The performativity of lyrics is also pointed out in those editorial notes in *Englands Helicon* which advertise where readers can find the musical setting for these songs: '*Out of M.* Morleyes *Madrigalls*' (s1; see also v4, bb4v); '*Out of M.* Birds *set Songs*' (s3v; see also t4, v2, b4); '*These three ditties were taken out of Maister* John Dowlands *booke of tableture for the Lute*' (x2); and finally, '*Out of Maister* N. Young *his* Musica Transalpina' (z2v).[79] Other unacknowledged borrowings from music books include Byrd's *Songs of Sundrie Natures* (1589) and Thomas Weelkes's *Cantus Primus. Madrigals to 3.4.5.&6. Voyces* (1597). In the 1590s, the production of printed music books had advanced rapidly.[80] *Englands Helicon* captures this moment in the history of the printed music book through the selection and framing of the lyrics it excerpts. Printed music and poetry anthologies share lyrics and recreational cultures of use. Rather than competing, these books complemented each other, hence the eagerness of the compilers of *Englands Helicon* to advertise their musical sources. The professional musicians compiling these printed music books were putting together their own anthologies, often by harvesting texts from printed

---

[77] D. W. Krummel, *English Music Printing, 1553–1700* (London: Bibliographical Society, 1975), 13–16.
[78] Larson, *Matter of Song*, 114; Toft, *With Passionate Voice*, 1, 20.
[79] Thomas Morley's *Madrigals to Four Voices* (1594), William Byrd's *Psalmes, Sonets, & Songs of Sadness and Pietie* (1588–9), John Dowland's *The Firste Booke of Songes or Ayres* (1597–1600), and Nicholas Yonge, *Musica Transalpina* (1588).
[80] Joseph Kernan, 'Elizabethan Anthologies of Italian Madrigals', *Journal of the American Musicological Society*, 4 (1951), 122–38.

184   *Englands Helicon*

poetry anthologies. Readers sent to these songbooks to find the settings therefore would also find other lyrics in *Englands Helicon* set to music in their pages.

Announcing that an anthology drew on lyrics shared with printed music books advertised its availability for amateur performance within the early modern household. A copy of *Englands Helicon*, now held in the British Library, was once owned by a seventeenth-century gentlewoman, Frances Wolfreston, who left her mark of ownership at the front of the anthology: 'frances wolfreston hor book' (C.39.e.48). Her library is distinguished by the number of books of plays, poetry, and collections of jests and riddles, and so provides a notable example of collecting and reading for recreation within the early modern gentry household (see Figures 5 and 6).[81] In her copy of *Englands Helicon,* Wolfreston made notes beside two lyrics which show that one of the uses to which she put this anthology was amateur performance. Written beside the title of the first lyric, '*Faire* Phillis *and her Sheepheard*' (Y3r), is the direction, 'tune of crimson velvet', and beside the title of the following poem, '*The Sheepheards Song of* Venus *and* Adonis' (Y4v), the prompt 'same tune'.[82] 'Crimson Velvet' was a popular tune to which ballads were sung from at least the mid-sixteenth century to the second half of the seventeenth. Both lyrics were available for singing to the same tune since they share the same complex twenty-line stanza, with minor variations in metre.[83] And both were printed for the first time in *Englands Helicon,* where care was taken with their layout. As one might expect from the complex stanza, the lineation on the page is intricate. Since the rhyme and metre of the two poems vary at points, the layout is not identical. The annotations to this copy of *Englands Helicon* reveal that Wolfreston marked her copy specifically for performance and comprehended these lyrics as song that could be re-created through performance; when Frances read these lyrics, she heard and experienced them voiced to the tune 'Crimson Velvet'. The acoustic properties of the lyrics gathered in the anthology are amplified by the company they keep. These 'Crimson

---

[81] On her library, see Paul Morgan, 'Frances Wolfreston and "Hor Bouks": a Seventeenth-Century Woman Book-Collector', *The Library*, 11 (1989), 197–218; Sarah Lindenbaum, 'Frances Wolfreston Hor Bouks', https://franceswolfrestonhorbouks.com/.
[82] BL C.39.e.48. This is also the copy microfilmed for *Early English Books Online*.
[83] Claude M. Simpson, 'Crimson Velvet', in *British Broadside Ballad*, 141–2. See Alexander's discussion of these lyrics in 'On the Reuse of Poetic Form: the Ghost in the Shell', in Baumann and Burton, eds., *Work of Form*, 124–7.

Re-creating Poetry 185

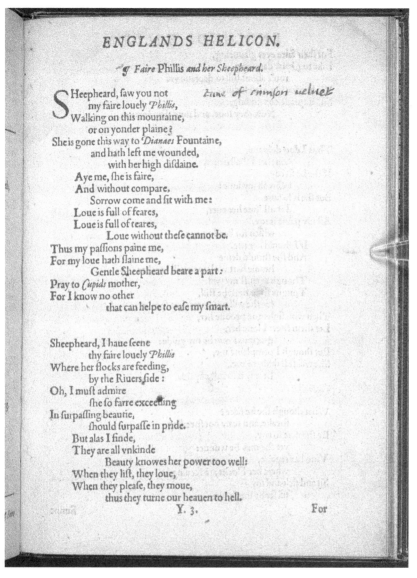

Figure 5 *Englands Helicon* (1600), sig. Y3r.

'Velvet' lyrics are part of a sequence of verse known to have been set to music: they follow Sidney's Nightingale lyric and are themselves followed by a set of three lyrics excerpted from Yonge's *Musica Transalpina* (z2v–3) and the ballad 'In Pescod time, when Hound to horne' (z3r), the opening

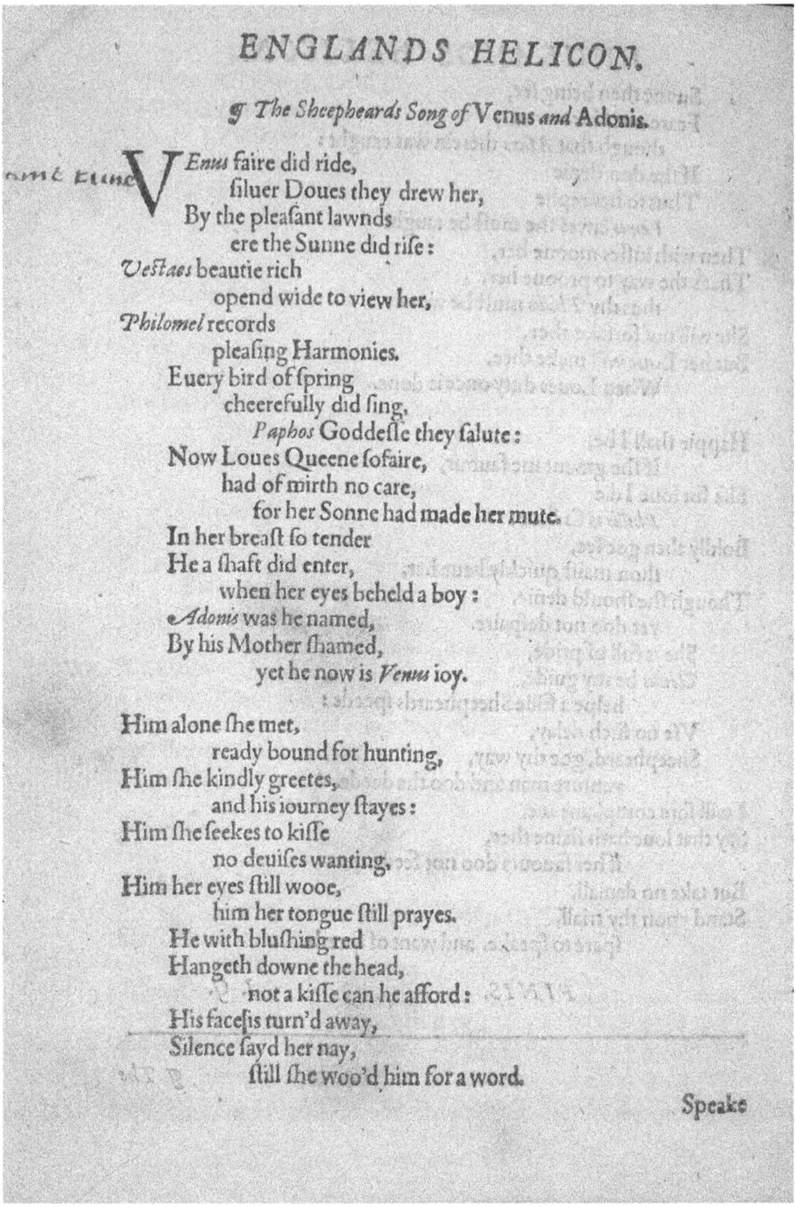

186   *Englands Helicon*

ENGLANDS HELICON.

¶ *The Sheepheards Song of* Venus *and* Adonis.

Venus faire did ride,
    filuer Doues they drew her,
By the pleafant lawnds
    ere the Sunne did rife :
Veſtaes beautie rich
    opend wide to view her,
Philomel records
    pleafing Harmonies.
Euery bird of fpring
    cheerefully did fing,
        Paphos Goddeſſe they falute :
Now Loues Queene fofaire,
    had of mirth no care,
        for her Sonne had made her mute.
In her breaſt fo tender
He a ſhaft did enter,
    when her eyes beheld a boy :
Adonis was he named,
By his Mother ſhamed,
        yet he now is Venus ioy.

Him alone ſhe met,
    ready bound for hunting,
Him ſhe kindly greetes,
    and his iourney ſtayes :
Him ſhe feekes to kiſſe
    no deuifes wanting,
Him her eyes ſtill wooe,
    him her tongue ſtill prayes.
He with bluſhing red
Hangeth downe the head,
    not a kiſſe can he afford :
His faceſis turn'd away,
Silence fayd her nay,
        ſtill ſhe woo'd him for a word.

                                        Speake

Figure 6   *Englands Helicon* (1600), sig. Y3v.

Re-creating Poetry 187

phrase of which gave its name to a tune to which other ballad lyrics were sung throughout the seventeenth century.[84]

One of the most popular songs collected in *Englands Helicon* is Munday's 'Beauty sate bathing by a Spring' (D3v–4). This lyric was set to different musical settings in quick succession over five years in Francis Pilkington's *First Booke of Songs or Ayres* (1605), Robert Jones's *Ultimum Vale* (1605), and William Corkine's *Ayres to Sing and Play* (1610). As a compiler of his own anthology of 'ayres', Pilkington was a specialised reader of *Englands Helicon* and so read this anthology with musical settings in mind. Along with Munday's 'Beauty sate bathing', he set three other lyrics from its pages to music: Henry Constable's '*Diaphenia* like the Daffadown-dillie' (N1v), Watson's 'With fragrant flowers we strew the way' (F4v–G1r), and Lodge's 'When love was first begot' (H3v–4r). Munday was similarly an experienced maker of lyrics for amateur performance. In 1588, his *Banquet of Daintie Conceits* appeared, an anthology of ballads comparable to *A Handefull of Pleasant Delites* and similarly intended for household recreation. Many of the printed music books, such as Yonge's *Musica Transalpina*, also published in 1588, advertised the professional skills of the compiler, often drawing attention to their expertise in continental musical styles.[85] By contrast, Munday markets himself and his songbook very deliberately in terms of amateur performance within the household, professing 'that I have no jote of knowledge in Musique, but what I have doone and doo, is onely by the eare'.[86] The ability to read written notation was increasing across the period; nonetheless the majority, like Munday, learnt tacitly and performed music by ear, through hearing and imitating others' singing and playing.[87] Lyrics, such as those sung to the tune of 'Crimson Velvet', could be performed by ear and so were open to re-creation within a range of soundscapes, both elite and non-elite. The verses collected in *Banquet of Daintie Conceits*, as Munday explained in his preface, were composed specifically for performance by those who had learnt music tacitly. When these lyrics are read with poetic metre in mind, then they 'will seeme very bad stuffe in reading', since they were composed with an ear to the musical properties of specific tunes, and so 'wyll delight thee, when thou singest any of them to thine Instrument'. 'Beauty sate bathing' is composed in simple ballad measure and, like the ditties

---

[84] The musical setting for this ballad was available in Anthony Holborne, *The Cittharn Schoole* (1597), sig. C1v–2; Simpson, *British Broadside Ballad*, 369–71.
[85] Nicholas Yonge, *Musica Transalpina* (1588), A2r–v.
[86] Munday, *Banquet of Daintie Conceits* (1588), A3v.   [87] Marsh, *Music and Society*, 6–7.

188   *Englands Helicon*

Munday describes in *Banquet*, lines are not set in regular accentual syllabic metre, but 'rise and fall, in just time and order of Musique'.[88] The flexible musicality of this lyric meant that it could be re-created through different cultures of musical performance by amateurs and, when set to music in songbooks compiled by professional musicians, those able to read music. As Simon Smith explains, we can 'think of the various producers and consumers of printed music books in early modern England as a broad group, not just in size but also in the range of social and professional backgrounds represented on demand and supply sides of the market'.[89]

'Beauty sate bathing by a Spring' is excerpted from the second book of Munday's prose romance, *Primaleon of Greece* (1596). Here it is framed within a dialogue between Princess Florida and her lover, Prince Edward. Responding to her request that he sing to her 'in a pleasanter key', Prince Edward looks among his papers and finds a 'Canzonet, which, how blunt or rude soever it be, I will commit it to your gracious hearing'.[90] This multimodal fiction of composition and performance moves freely between the written and textual and the spoken and aural. The place of performance is the garden, a leisured space, in which the male singer and female auditor engage in courtship rituals. When excerpted in *Englands Helicon*, the garden is re-created in the anthology itself, a leisured meeting place with its soundscape of pastoral songs. In musical composition and performance, as in reading, the aim was to match the matter of the words in order to move the affections of the audience.[91] Munday's song is an erotic dream in which the male speaker is a type of Actaeon, who imagines his mistress 'bathing by a spring' and desires 'to see what was forbidden', but his 'vaine Desire' is chastised by 'better Memory'. Falling asleep, his 'fond imagination: / Seemed to see, but could not tell / her feature or her fashion', and the speaker claims the idle innocence of 'Babes' for his own erotic dream (D3–3v). The song is self-consciously tantalising, encouraging the performer to move his or her audience towards the sensory states of desire described in the lyric, and to maintain the languorous quality of the dream state in which the speaker, singer, and audience are suspended in the moment of performance, between dreaming and waking. The leisured

---

[88] *Banquet of Daintie Conceits* (1588), A3r.
[89] Simon Smith, *Musical Response in the Early Modern Playhouse, 1603–1625* (Cambridge University Press, 2017), 12.
[90] The 1596 edition of *The Seconde Book of Primaleon* exists in a single, fragmentary copy of which only the A, Ll, Mm, and part of the Nn signatures survive; *The Famous and Renowned Historie of Primaleon of Greece*, chapter 27, 207–8
[91] Toft, *With Passionate Voice*, 10–14.

Re-creating Poetry 189

time evoked through the performativity of the lyric is figured as intensely pleasurable.

The sensory acoustics of desire voiced in Munday's lyric echo across other songs in the collection. The two Thyrsis madrigals, for example, composed by Alfonso Ferrabosco and excerpted from Yonge's *Musica Transalpina*, which follow the 'Crimson Velvet' ballads, are erotic pastoral songs. The first, '*Thirsis* to die desired', puns on 'to die' in order to figure the lovers' movement towards sexual consummation. Like Munday's song, this lyric heightens the sensory, harmonising sight, sound, and taste: Thyrsis 'Thinking it death while hee his lookes maintained, / full fixed on her eyes, full of pleasure, / and lovely Nectar sweet from them he tasted' (z2v). Once again, the performance is caught in the sensual moment, the repetition of 'full' expressing the *jouissance* in which the audience is invited to partake. These amorous pastoral songs set in play across the anthology an acoustics of leisured time and space. Readers and performers are invited to experience and so participate in these forms of recreation in which the company of women is a defining feature of their complexly mixed-gender performance. Tellingly, the auditor of 'Beauty sate bathing' in Munday's romance is a woman. Watson's song, 'With fragrant flowers we strew the way' (F4v–G1) was composed for female voices and performed by women at an entertainment for Queen Elizabeth. Other female-voiced songs include '*A Pastorall Song betweene* Phillis *and* Amarillis' (x4–4v) and Lodge's 'When love was first begot' (H3v–4). The latter comes from his pastoral romance, *Rosalynde*, in which it is sung by Phoebe in response to Montanus (M1–1v). 'Coridon, *arise my* Coridon', as specified in its title in *Englands Helicon*, is 'Phillidaes *Love-call to her* Coridon, *and his replying*' (14–K1) and thus a dialogue between female and male voices.[92]

Books of ayres, like those of Dowland, Morley, and Pilkington, Trudell argues, 'were specifically designed for household performance by amateurs, including women', because the settings were relatively simple to master.[93] The part song, in particular, was open to mixed-gender singing within the household and music books were printed to allow the performers to face each other and read from the same book. Scores for the different parts were printed vertically and horizontally, which meant that the notation and lyrics could be read by the performers gathered at the four corners of the

---

[92] 'Coridon, arise my Coridon' is set to music in John Lilliat's miscellany, Bod. MS Rawl. poet. 148, 88v–90, which dates from *c.* 1592–1602.
[93] Trudell, 'Performing Women', 19–20.

190   *Englands Helicon*

book.[94] The material form of the book, the spatiality of the printed page, in a very physical sense, thus could bring male and female performers together within the private space of the household and allowed for the embodiment of the scenes of dialogue and response set out in the lyrics. Female musical performance was frowned upon in public, and yet encouraged within the household as a display of civility and cultivation.[95] Lodge's 'Phoebe's *Sonnet*' is set as an ayre in four parts. It opens with a refrain that identifies it as a woman's song, lamenting the fickleness of love. When performed within the early modern household, it is available for mixed-gender singing. This is also the way that it is framed in Lodge's *Rosalynde*, since it is part of a scene of communal singing among the shepherds and shepherdesses, when they come together at times of leisure to sing songs of love and courtship.

All these books – poetry and music anthologies and prose romances, with their inset songs – in various ways are designed for amateur household performance. Taken together, they suggest the ways in which men and women, from a range of social backgrounds, engaged with the recreational affordances of anthologies. The producers of *Englands Helicon* recognised the recreative and musical possibilities of a pastoral anthology, effectively capitalising on the markets for printed music books in the 1590s. The result is not 'courtly' pastoral, but a more domesticated mode open to being 'differently inhabited or used' through reading and in performance.[96] A full engagement with the recreative properties of *Englands Helicon*, as is the case with other poetry anthologies studied here, requires an embodied model of material culture, – one that analyses the forms of material textuality through a mode of reading that can address their recreative, performative, and affective capacities and account for the ways in which they are made and remade through the work of hands, voices, and bodies in motion.

Coda: *Englands Helicon. Or The Muses Harmony* (1614)

Englands Helicon changed hands in late 1613 when Richard More acquired the copy from Flasket on 20 December 1613.[97] The network that had proved so effective in the late 1590s was no more; by 1610, the majority of

---

[94] Ibid., 18–19. For a manuscript example, see the discussion of BL, Add. MS 4900 in Chapter 1, 69–70.
[95] Trudell, 'Performing Women'.   [96] Fumerton, *Unsettled*, 54.
[97] Flasket stopped entering copy in the *Stationers' Register* in 1607.

Coda: Englands Helicon. Or The Muses Harmony 191

those involved in the production of the compilations affiliated with Bodenham were either dead or had left the trade.[98] The late sixteenth century also saw the decline of one of the most prolific producers of Elizabethan anthologies, Richard Jones, who sold his printing shop in 1598. The choices made in the production of the second edition of *Englands Helicon* are instructive because they point to the formative role of those in the business of making books in the history of anthology production. When he took over *Englands Helicon*, More concentrated his energies on replacing all the original paratext. All connection with the Bodenham series of compilations was removed: Bodenham's arms, A.B.'s sonnet to Bodenham, the epistle to Bodenham's kinsmen, and Ling's epistle to the reader. Instead, More asserted his own creative agency over the anthology, adding a sonnet dedicating the volume to Lady Elizabeth Cary. Whereas the original dedication presented *Englands Helicon* as the culmination of the Bodenham's '*impos'd design*', More's sonnet gives credit to his own assessment of its value as a pastoral anthology:

> . . . *bright* Apollo *to these layes hath given*
> *So great a gift, that any favouring*
> *The* Shepheards *quill, shall with the lights of Heaven*
> *Have equall fate*. . .
>
> (sig. A2r)

More offers a critical reading, setting out his literary judgement of the quality of the verse, and advertising the anthology's re-creative openness to those readers '*favouring / The* Shepheards *quill*' and so looking for models of pastoral lyrics for their own compositions.

More was well positioned to capitalise on the market for pastoral in 1614. The years 1613 to 1615 saw the reinvigoration of a mode of political pastoral, identified with Sidney and Spenser, in the volumes of eclogues authored by William Browne, Christopher Brooke, and George Wither – *The Shepheards Pipe* (1614) and *The Shepherds Hunting* (1615).[99] More had previously published Brooke and Browne's *Two Elegies Consecrated to the never-dying Memorie of . . . Henry Prince of Wales* in 1613, and these are the only new poets represented in the 1614 edition of *Englands Helicon*.[100]

---

[98] Bodenham died in 1610, Ling and Flasket in 1607, and Roberts sold his printing materials to William Jaggard in 1606.

[99] On the 1614 edition of *Englands Helicon* and Spenserian pastoral, see Jane Tylus, 'Jacobean Poetry and Lyric Disappointment', in *Soliciting Interpretation: Literary Theory and Seventeenth-Century Poetry*, edited by Elizabeth D. Harvey and Kathleen Eisaman Maus (Chicago University Press, 1990), 182–3; O'Callaghan, *Shepheards Nation*, 26–31.

[100] The other poems added to this edition are taken from the 1611 edition of *A Poetical Rapsodie*.

192   *Englands Helicon*

The new tag on the title-page of *Englands Helicon* – '*The Courts of Kings heare no such straines, / As daily lull the Rusticke Swaines*' – when read together with More's sonnet, summons a community of poets independent from the court, gathered in the memory of Sidney and Spenser, whose poems open the collection. The new dedicatee, Elizabeth Cary, had recently published her closet drama, *The Tragedie of Mariam* (1613), an event which cast this learned, 'truly vertuous and honourable Lady' as a fit successor to Mary Sidney, Countess of Pembroke, the guardian of a Sidneian cultural tradition.

The creative and material investments made by More in this second edition of *Englands Helicon* did not translate into a set of ongoing practices. From available evidence, the 1614 edition of *Englands Helicon* is the first and only time that More authored a preface.[101] Why was *Englands Helicon* an exception, and what was it that encouraged More to assert his own agency so visibly? The answer, I would suggest, has to do with the affordances of the anthology. Other texts published by More which include epistles or dedicatory verse are the work of either a single author or translator, and it is they who use the preface to advertise their own role in the volume's production. An anthology is not authored but compiled; because of this, a space is left open for the publisher to fashion his agency. More used this space in the book to present *Englands Helicon* as critically dependent on his own literary labours, removing all trace of the earlier publishing network. In doing so, he took on the cultural role of the stationer that Ling had advocated in his epistle before the first edition of *Englands Helicon*. Through the front matter, particularly his dedicatory sonnet, More embraced this role, acting as a cultural arbiter, who guides readers in their engagement with the anthology, including its further uses. His own engagement with *Englands Helicon* is a reminder that these compilations were books in process that relied on the investments of publishers, printers, and other non-authorial agents in their production.

---

[101] Gervase Markham was commissioned by More to enlarge and correct the 1631 edition of Conrad Heresbach's *The Whole Art of Husbandry* (1631, STC 13201), and he, not More, supplied the new dedicatory epistle, sig. A2r–v. The epistles from the 'Book to the Reader' and from the 'Printer to the Reader' before John Day's *Law-trickes* (1608, STC 6416) and John Donne's *Ignatius his Conclaue* (1611, STC 7027) are written by the authors, not More.

CHAPTER 5

A Poetical Rapsody
Francis Davison, the 'Printer', and the Craft of Compilation

A Poetical Rapsody, first published in 1602, is said to be the 'last' of the Elizabethan poetry anthologies.[1] This anthology, however, like others studied here, has a much longer afterlife, and continued to be published in revised editions until 1621. The publication history of *A Poetical Rapsody*, along with that of *Englands Helicon*, highlights some of the problems with the limits imposed by the terminus points of conventional periodisation. Instead, the history of anthologies in print in large part depended on publishers, their careers, how they read the market. Like other anthologies, the story of the compilation of *A Poetical Rapsody* also extends well before its first appearance in print, thus bringing in other collaborations along the way. *A Poetical Rapsody* provides a valuable case study for understanding this aspect of anthology-making because, fortuitously, manuscript lists put together by Francis Davison survive that allow us to glimpse at least some of the stages of compilation before the book was printed. Davison, as we have seen in the previous chapter, was a studious reader of anthologies. *A Poetical Rapsody* differs from earlier multi-authored poetry anthologies in that, rather than the publisher, it is the gentleman compiler, Francis Davison, who takes command of the front of the book. We may remember that *The Phoenix Nest* was said to be the work of a gentleman compiler, identified only by his initials, R. S., yet, unlike Davison, he is otherwise absent from the book. Davison is often exclusively credited with compiling this anthology. That said, even the account he provides in his preface situates this anthology within overlapping networks of production, from friends and kin to the printing house. Davison's surviving manuscripts, which take the form of various catalogues and lists of textual material, reveal well-developed habits of record-keeping and systems for organising textual material.[2] Recent studies have drawn much-needed attention to the labour and skill involved in organising

---

[1] Pomeroy, *Elizabethan Miscellanies*, 27.   [2] See Chapter 4, 173–4.

193

194 *A Poetical Rapsody*

material into compilations, from commonplace books to miscellanies.[3] Scribal cultures fostered manual crafts and relied on systems of assembly that reveal shared cultures of compilation across manuscript and print. Davison's catalogues provide evidence for systematic practices of textual assembly and the dynamic processes of compilation, during which skills were learnt and put into use.

The term 'rhapsody' in the title of this anthology was used in the sixteenth century to describe the humanist *compilatio*. Pierre Boaistuau explained that 'Rapsody' was another word for the 'collation or gathering togither of divers authorities'.[4] Rhapsody aptly describes the structure of this anthology, which gathers together discrete, yet interrelated collections, complete with their own title-pages: 'Pastorals and Eglogues'; 'Sonnets, Odes, Elegies, and Madrigalls. By Francis Davison and Walter Davison, Brethren'; 'Sonnets, Odes, Elegies and other Poesies ... by Anomos'; and 'Divers Poems of Sundry Authors'. Poems have been conjoined, Davison writes, 'to make the booke grow to a competent volume', an explanation that sets out both a material understanding of how poems have been gathered together to make up the physical book, and a conceptual understanding of *compilatio*, that the sundry parts brought together fit together appropriately, gaining meaning in relation to each other. Running alongside is an account of composition that is materially embodied, peopled by kin, family, and friends. Davison explains in his preface how he gathered his own poems along with those of his brother and his unnamed friend. These relationships are then carried across the different collections in the first edition, binding the anthology loosely together. If we compare the narrativising of compilation in *A Poetical Rapsody* with Isabella Whitney's *Sweet Nosgay* then instructive distinctions emerge that help to locate and distinguish these anthologies within wider recreational cultures. The story of the writing life of 'Is. W. gent' in *A Sweet Nosgay*, a collection of her 'owne gathering and making' (A4v, C5r), is situated in familiar relationships, made up of textual exchanges between family and friends, resulting in a rich vernacular poetics that speaks to the unsettled domestic worlds of the middling sort. The composition of *A Poetical Rapsody*, by contrast, is styled as a distinctly courtly production, especially in the first edition, the proper occupation of gentlemen, and located within an elite milieu. Of all

---

[3] See Vine, *Miscellaneous Order*; Marcy North, 'Amateur Compilers, Scribal Labour, and the Contents of Early Poetic Miscellanies', *English Manuscript Studies, 1100–1700*, 16 (2017), 82–111.
[4] On rhapsody, see also Brown, 'Donne, Rhapsody', 41–55; Pierre Boaistuau, *Theatrum Mundi the Theatre or Rule of the World* (1566), A6v–7.

the anthologies studied here, it provides the clearest example of how a socially exclusive poetics of private recreation is given cultural purchase.

'Manuscripts to gett'

Scribal practices are often characterised as unstructured and highly perso-nalised, contingent upon occasion and the individualised reading experi-ence of the compiler.[5] Of course, this is the case in some circumstances, but not all. Practices of compiling collections of textual material in manuscript varied considerably. In certain locales, scribal practices were far from unstudied. The humanist education system in which elite men, and some elite women, were schooled provided training in hand-copying and inculcated methods for compiling – how to select, excerpt, and recombine textual materials within a range of formats. These were as much manual as intellectual skills that relied on training, practice, and experience in order to calculate the time, labour, and other resources required to transcribe and organise textual materials. 'By the time that they reached the university,' Marcy North writes of humanist-educated young men, 'they were well-equipped to measure and organise the practical effort of manuscript production.'[6] These skills were not necessarily restricted to university-educated men, and humanist practices of manuscript compila-tion were also fostered within mercantile communities.[7] This chapter, however, will concentrate on the work of compiling undertaken by a young gentleman trained for court service. In doing so, it will shed light on a different type of household as a site for textual production and transmission – the elite household with its gentlemen secretaries and private recreations.

Francis Davison left behind catalogues and lists that provide evidence for the craft, both intellectual and manual, involved in compiling a poetry anthology. His scribal practices cut across the distinctions Harold Love made between the amateur, responding to occasion and motivated by sociability, and the professional or entrepreneurial compiler, who looked to wider constituencies and markets and for whom this activity was an occupation.[8] Davison was an assiduous collector of manuscripts and printed books, who habitually recorded and tracked the transmission of

---

[5] See, for example, Wall, *Imprint of Gender*, 8–10; Marotti, *Manuscript, Print*, 135–47.
[6] North, 'Amateur Compilers', 84.   [7] Vine, *Miscellaneous Order*, chapter 4.
[8] Harold Love, *Scribal Publication in Seventeenth-Century England* (Oxford: Clarendon Press, 1993), 46–80.

196   *A Poetical Rapsody*

textual material within social networks. He compiled an index of *Englands Helicon*, listing first lines and authors, that methodically digested this anthology's contents, and provided a useful tool for subsequent reference and study.[9] Given that *A Poetical Rapsody* was published just two years after *Englands Helicon*, this study aid suggests more than an occasional interest in this anthology. Instead, his index demonstrates how this book had become an object of careful study. John Chamberlain, in a letter dated 8 July 1602, wrote that Davison was no longer pursuing a post in a secretariat, but had turned his attention to another occupation: 'it seems young Davison meanes to take another course, and turne poet, for he hath lately turned out certain sonets and epigrams'.[10] Davison's scribal practices reveal that the work of the poet and that of secretary were not so distinct.

Davison was trained in humanist methods of manuscript production in preparation for a career in court service and he brought these skills to anthology-making. He also was well positioned to access elite scribal channels when collecting verse because of his impressive set of family connections. Born into the middle ranks of the bureaucratic class at court, epitomised by families such as the Bacons and Cecils, his father, William, was secretary to Francis Walsingham, before taking the post of ambassador to the Netherlands in the late 1570s. Here, he was an agent of Robert Dudley, Earl of Leicester, a kinsman of Davison through his wife, Catherine Spelman; William served Sir Philip Sidney in 1586, the year of Sidney's death. Soon after his return, William was made Secretary of State, and is now best known for the role he played in the execution of Mary, Queen of Scots, which brought about his downfall.[11] He was restored to Elizabeth's favour, if not his court post, through the intercession of Robert Devereux, Earl of Essex, who also took an interest in Francis. Francis was educated to serve a similar role to his father at court. He attended Emmanuel College, Cambridge, and entered Gray's Inn in 1593, the inn of Walsingham, Burghley, and Bacon, and the training ground for court service. Gray's Inn held spectacular grand revels in 1594–5, an entertainment that included songs by Thomas Campion and speeches by Francis Bacon, and Davison was given the honour of creating the final

---

[9] London, British Library, Harley MS 280, 99–100v.
[10] John Chamberlain, *The Letters of John Chamberlain*, ed. Norman Egbert McClure, 2 vols. (Philadelphia: American Philosophical Society, 1939), I, 156.
[11] Paul Hammer, *The Polarisation of Elizabethan Politics: the Political Career of Robert Devereux, Second Earl of Essex, 1585–97* (Cambridge University Press, 1999), 60, 101–2, 183.

'*Manuscripts to gett*' 197

entertainment performed in front of Elizabeth, 'The Masque of Proteus'.[12] Soon after the revels, in May 1595, Essex sponsored Davison's tour of Europe, accompanied by William Temple, who had been Sidney's secretary, and a fellow student at Gray's Inn, Robert Wroth, who would marry Sidney's niece, Mary.[13] One of the aims of travel was to learn statecraft by observing European courts and Davison duly sent Essex's secretary, Anthony Bacon, a treatise on the state of Saxony. Davison's year in Europe failed to bear further fruit; surviving documents report quarrels, with his own tutor, Temple, and with Essex's agent in Venice. Back in England, Davison struggled to secure a position in a secretariat.[14] Any further hope of Essex's patronage ended with the earl's execution in 1601. In May 1602, Davison was briefly taken on by Sir Thomas Parry, one of his 'leash of Secretaries', along with one Gosnall, who had been Essex's secretary in Ireland, but both were dismissed with Parry's appointment as ambassador to France.[15]

Davison may have been unsuccessful in his efforts to secure a place in a secretariat, but the catalogues he compiled stand testimony to his humanist training for this role. One set of skills was the preparation and management of documents, from letters to treatises, tasks that required the development of systems of record-keeping, cataloguing, and archiving.[16] Davison recorded titles of books and papers through systematised practices that are marked by a practical efficiency in organising time and labour. Cataloguing his books and papers clearly functions, in part, as record management, keeping track of material that has been lent or is held by another. Davison gives a short title indicative of contents and sometimes the name of the author or subject; in the case of his poetry catalogue, he also consistently notes the size of the book as a further identifying and organising system, for example, 'In folio' or 'In the loose Papers in 4°' (see Figure 7). It points to a system of storage according to the material properties of the object – size – which takes us to the physical organisation of his library or other places where he stored and used his books. Other lists record the processes of textual transmission, with marginal notes

---

[12] Richard McCoy, *The Rites of Knighthood: the Literature and Politics of Elizabethan Chivalry* (Berkeley: University of California Press, 1989), chapter 10.

[13] See 'A Note of all the ye Relations wch I caried into France both mine own & Mr Wroathe' (BL Harley MS 298, 154r). Wroth entered Gray's Inn in November 1594, and may have also known Davison at Cambridge.

[14] John Considine, 'Francis Davison', *ODNB*.   [15] Ibid.; Chamberlain, *Letters*, I, 142.

[16] Woudhuysen writes that 'The secretary's principal official duties lay in organising his employer's correspondence, writing and transcribing letters, memorandums, and other documents, keeping notes of his business, and reminding him of his affairs'; *Sir Philip Sidney*, 83.

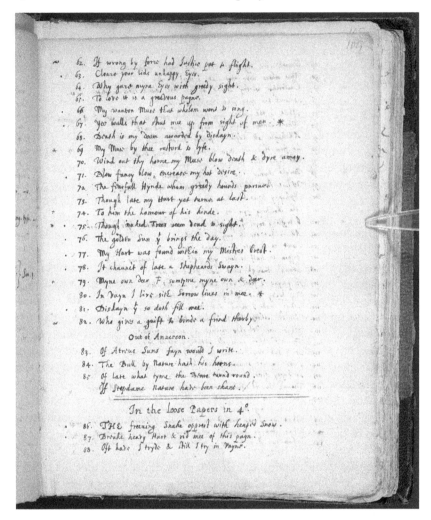

Figure 7 British Library, MS Harley 280, fol. 104r.

added identifying who has the material in their possession, as well as further lists of 'Papers sent' and 'Manuscripts to gett' (BL Harley MS 298, fols. 159r–v).

Davison's lists recording the traffic in textual material take us to the various scribal networks in which he participated. Moving in court, university, and Inns of Court circles gave him privileged access to elite scribal channels. He capitalised on this situation by acting as an agent in

'*Manuscripts to gett*' 199

the transmission of manuscripts and books.[17] His lists outline patterns of transmission that map scribal networks. He made a catalogue of the treatises he took on his European travels – 'A Note of all ye Relations wch I caried into France both mine own & Mr Wroathe' (154r) – and a list of 'Written Bookes, Discourse' (160r), which includes tracts relating to Mary, Queen of Scots and Henry Saville's translations of Tacitus, that were compiled when he was in the service of Essex. These lists describe the world of service and political milieu of Davison, father and son, at Elizabeth's court. The exchange of books and manuscripts, alongside that of letters, builds social alliances that are hierarchical, in the case of social superiors, as well as vertical, marking out the consanguinity of kinship networks. Many lists record familial connections: on a small slip of paper is a list of 'Remembrances' that records 'All my Bookes & Papers wch my Brother Duncomb hath' (158r).[18] 'Papers sent' records books sent to Lord Edward Zouche, John Bridges, Bishop of Oxford, and Sir John Constable, Bacon's brother-in-law and a fellow student of Gray's Inn in the mid-1590s (159r).[19] Davison lent Henry Bing, who had been his contemporary at Cambridge and Gray's Inn, a tract relating to Robert Cecil's negotiations with France, presumably his discussions with Henry IV in 1598. He sends a copy of a letter from Essex to a Monsieur de la Faille, who shares his name with a family of Antwerp merchants with extensive business in England. Intriguingly, Davison sends a copy of 'Grayes In Sportes under Sr Henry Helmes' to a 'Eleaz. Hodgson', who is also named as one of the agents, alongside Ben Jonson, through which he might acquire Donne's poems. Who was 'Eleaz. Hodgson'? A headnote to one of Davison's sonnets in *A Poetical Rapsody* claims it was occasioned by 'presenting' his mistress 'with the speech of Grayes-Inne Maske at the Court 1594. consisting of three partes, The Story of Proteus Transformations, the wonders of the Adamantine Rocke, and a speech to her Maiestie' (D3r).

Davison's 'Catalog of all ye Poëms in Ryme & Measured Verse by A. W.', many of which were printed in *A Poetical Rapsody*, illustrates how catalogues can operate as a type of early modern database, recording texts, information, and their location efficiently for future uses.[20] The

---

[17] See British Library, Harley MS 298, 156–60. On the different collections in which Davison kept verse, see Woudhuysen, *Sir Philip Sidney*, 155.

[18] William Duncombe had entered Gray's Inn the year after Davison and married his sister, Catherine.

[19] Zouche was one of the peers who tried Mary, Queen of Scots, and so presumably was acquainted with William Davison.

[20] Harley MS 280, 101–5v. H. R. Rollins provides a full transcription of this catalogue in his 'A. W. and "A Poetical Rhapsody", *Studies in Philology*, 29 (1932), 239–51.

200   *A Poetical Rapsody*

different physical formats in which poems are stored is used as an organisational tool: Davison records those copied into a large manuscript book, 'In folio, written wth ye Authors own hand', 'In the Loose Papers in 4°', a set of 'imperfect Fragments', and other poems 'In the Paper Book bound wth ye Shepheards Calender'.[21] These catalogues record the material organisation of physical resources – paperbooks, loose sheets, and scraps of paper – on which the activity of compilation relies. What we are witnessing in these catalogues is an aspect of the craft of anthology-making. The decisions made when assembling these catalogues, however, are not always self-explanatory. The question arises, for example, as to why all the poems listed in the catalogue are attributed to A. W., when some will be identified as those of other authors in *A Poetical Rapsody*. And who is A. W.? Rollins rightly concluded that the initials A. W. refer not to an individual, but to a category – the 'anonymous writer' – that can be inhabited by many poets.[22] Even if 'anonymous writer', as Rollins worried, sounds too modern, we can understand these initials as not signifying a person, but rather acting as a designation or place that is itself a function of collecting verse. The question remains, however, as to why Davison suppressed names in this catalogue, especially when he took care with attribution in his catalogue of the poems in *Englands Helicon*. Perhaps it is a feature of scribal practices – names are not assigned to poems because authors are known to the compiler, or indeed unknown, lost in transmission. One of the titles given to a sub-list within the catalogue, 'In folio, written with ye Authors hand', might mean these are copies of autograph manuscripts or have a known provenance. But, if so, why then use the initials A. W. in the catalogue's title? One possibility is that these catalogues were compiled not only for personal reference, as an *aide memoire*, but for use in the printing house, hence the name suppression.

Systems – through numbering, headings, and other divisional markers – are employed to organise, order, and divide poems into units that, in turn, act as material and conceptual frames. Poems listed by first line in the catalogue with the headings 'In folio, written wth ye Authors own hand' (103) and 'In the loose Papers in 4°' (104; see Figure 7) are throughnumbered from 1 to 121. Numbers identify the poem's place within a

---

[21] The poems listed in this catalogue are rare: 'Perin areed' is shared with Bod. MS Rawl. poet. 85, 93v–8; 'It chaunc't of late' with Bod. MS Add. B. 105, 79v; 'My heavy heart with grief and torment', with BL Harley MS 2127, 23–25v; 'The bull by nature', with BL Harley MS 6910, 145v–6; and 'Breake heavy heart', in BL Harley MS 6910, 153–3v; BL MS Add. 15227, 78r; Harley MS 2127, 25v.
[22] Rollins, 'A. W.', 247–51.

'Manuscripts to gett' 201

wider system and so are a finding aid that sets in place structures and sequences that can facilitate further use, including reorganisation into new sequences. The catalogue is dynamic and malleable: the folio book and quarto collection of loose papers are both distinct units and in the process of being reconstituted as a larger repository of verse. Subdivisional markers are used to add granularity to the classification of these repositories. A further heading added to the list of poems from the folio book introduces a sub-category that groups this verse according to literary type – 'Out of Anacreon'. Double-ruled lines followed by the heading 'In the loose Papers in 4°' mark the threshold between the two collections. Yet, since it is through-numbered, another system of organisation is simultaneously at work that merges the two repositories (see Figure 7). Added to these collections in folio and quarto, within the larger catalogue, are an unnumbered list of 'Imperfect Fragments' and 'Translations', and an index to the poems 'In the Paper book bound wth ye Shepheards Calender'.

The lists of poems on the verso of this leaf demonstrate the various iterations and recombinations that are part of the process of anthology-making (see Figure 8). These new lists repeat and renumber many of the first lines that identify poems in previous lists. The shortened first lines used in these secondary lists are signs of economy, necessitated by drafting and redrafting of lists that will provide the foundations of the anthology. The first list on the left of the page largely corresponds to the poems that will be printed in the opening section of 'Pastorals and Eglogs' in *A Poetical Rapsody* (1602). These have been selected from the paperbook bound with *Shepheardes Calender* – '2 Eglog. upon the death of S^r Ph: Sidney, / Perin aread what new mischance betide' and '3 Eglog. a fragment, concerning ould Age. / For when thou are not as thou wont of yore' (105r) – and 'It chaunct of late a Shepheards Swayn' taken from the folio book (104r). Other poems are coming from sources outside those listed in this catalogue – Sir Philip Sidney's 'Joyne Mates in mirth to mee' and 'Walking in bright Phoebus blaze', Mary, Countess of Pembroke's 'I sing devine Astreas Prayse', and 'Come gentle heardgroom sitt by mee', attributed to 'Ignoto' in *A Poetical Rapsody*.[23] At some point between this list and the

---

[23] There are no extant manuscript witnesses of Mary and Philip Sidney poems; 'Come gentle heardgroom' is attributed to Sir Philip Sidney in Berkshire Record Office, Gen. Ser. Misc. Papers 31/6, s.sh. It is also attributed to Sir Arthur Gorges: Cambridge Dd.5.75, *c.* 1592, fols. 39v–40; British Library MS Egerton 3165, fols. 101v–4v, Add. MS 15117, fols. 10v–11. Woudhuysen speculates that Davison may have acquired these poems from his tutor, Temple, Sidney's former secretary, or from the Herbert family, given the dedication of the anthology to William Herbert, Earl of Pembroke; *Sir Philip Sidney*, 291–2

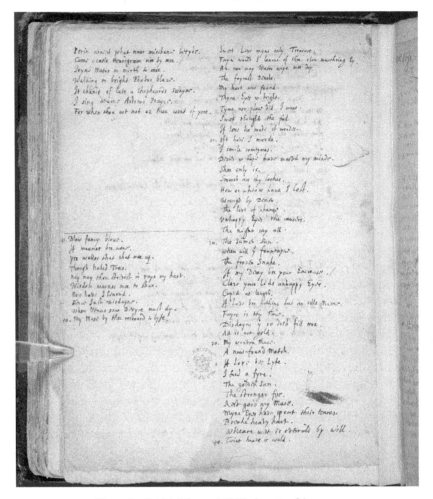

Figure 8   British Library, MS Harley 280, fol. 105v.

published anthology, poems were once again reordered and further pastorals, notably those of Walter and Francis Davison, were added. The second list, which consists of a column on the right, then a half-column on the left, is numbered in groups of ten, and largely correlates with the sequence of 'Sonets, Odes, Elegies and other Poesies' attributed to 'Anomos' in *A Poetical Rapsody* (see Figure 8). This new list takes poems from the papers 'In folio' (103r–4r), in 'loose Papers' (104r), and 'Imperfect fragments' (105r), reorganising them into a new sequence. Once again, the

Francis Davison and 'the Printer' 203

differences between this list and 'Sonets, Odes, Elegies and other Poesies' in *A Poetical Rapsody* reveal further, albeit minor, changes: two further poems were taken from the folio papers and moved to the front of this section, and a couple of poems from the loose papers were also added.

The changing order of the poems in these lists, as they go through different iterations, captures the inherent flexibility of compilations, their capacity for recombination and reframing. Davison was not the only compiler at work here. His catalogue points to sets of papers put together by others at earlier stages that take different forms, like the paperbook. What I would also want to emphasise is that this activity necessarily required time and effort and so relied on the work of compilers in the manual, intellectual, and experiential sense – the type of work that we have seen described by Nicholas Ling in his prefaces before *Politeuphuia* and *Englands Helicon*. Davison's catalogues put into practice technical skills, acquired through humanist training in hand-copying and compilation, alongside other methods that were more improvised and responded to the situation at hand. The craft of anthology-making relied on shared cultures of compilation that travelled across manuscript cultures and the printing house. As we shall see, Davison wanted to distinguish his work from that of the 'Printer', but the two had more in common than he cared to admit.

Francis Davison and 'the Printer'

The story Davison tells in his preface to *A Poetical Rapsody* puts forward a very familiar narrative of gentlemanly publication. Persuaded 'by some private reasons, and by the instant intreatie of speciall friendes', he collected his own poems together with those of his brother, Walter, and an unnamed friend, 'Anomos', 'to be published'. This is only part of the story, Davison explains, since certain decisions about the anthology's organisation were taken by the 'Printer'. Davison wants to put in place a clear demarcation between the work of the book trade and his own gentlemanly and amateur act of publication. To do so, he brings into play the 'bad printer', a convention often used to distance the writer from the work of the printing house. Decisions about the organisation of the contents, for example, were said to have been taken by this 'Printer':

> If any except against the mixing (both at the beginning and ende of this booke) of diverse thinges written by great and learned Personages, with our meane and worthles Scriblings, I utterly disclaime it, as being done by the Printer, either to grace the forefront with Sir *Ph. Sidneys*, and others names, or to make the booke grow to a competent volume. (A3r)

204 *A Poetical Rapsody*

Davison's manipulation of the 'bad printer' convention, as North explains, 'blaming the printer for his graver indiscretions but accepting enough guilt to take credit' for the inclusion of Sidney and other worthies, means that is difficult to disentangle from his account who precisely was responsible for what in terms of content, organisation, and attribution.[24] As a consequence, the distinction between the role assumed by Davison and that he assigns to the printing house is blurred. The poems of his brother and unnamed friend, Davison explains, were printed 'without their consent': his brother 'being in the low Country Warres' and his friend 'utterly ignorant thereof'. While he was able to conceal the latter's name, the 'Printer' 'put in, without my privity' (A2v), both brothers' names, although this implies that Davison had already supplied the printer with the information to make these attributions or, relatedly, he was working so closely with the printer that knowledge was shared as a matter of course.[25]

Davison is consciously manipulating print conventions, used to define an elite publication, to mark out his place in relation to the work undertaken in the printing house. Here, he is working with a version of the 'absent author' trope typically used by publishers to make a space to formulate their publishing practices. In this case, Davison uses this trope to cast himself in the role of the gentleman compiler who naturally has an ambivalent relationship to publication, preferring instead the genteel discretion of anonymity. Yet, by his own admission, he publishes the poems of his friend and brother without their consent or knowledge, since they are both absent, which means his own role in the anthology's production approximates that of the 'bad printer'. Such slipperiness around issues of consent and intent illustrates some of the difficulties in determining who undertook specific tasks in anthology production, especially in relation to attribution and compilation, given these activities were shared in piecemeal fashion. The contradictions in Davison's story and the resulting uncertainties also have the effect of implicating this gentleman compiler alongside the printer in the process of publication, even as he insists that he has maintained a respectable distance from this business.

Who does Davison mean by the 'Printer'? Marta Straznicky notes the term was 'used with "masterly imprecision" and had at least five distinct meanings: the actual printer, the bookseller, the editor, the provider of the manuscript, and occasionally even the author'.[26] Rather than take us to an

---

[24] North, *Anonymous Renaissance*, 85.   [25] I am grateful to Andrew Gordon for this latter point.
[26] Straznicky, 'Introduction', in Marta Straznicky (ed.), *Shakespeare's Stationers: Studies in Cultural Bibliography* (Philadelphia: University of Pennsylvania, 2013), 307 n. 2.

Francis Davison and 'the Printer' 205

individual, the very motility of this term, with its oscillation between these various agents, points to a more collaborative and accretive process of book production. The 'Printer' invoked by Davison can usefully be understood as a location, rather than as an individual, a conceptual category that that can be inhabited, at any one point, by the publisher-bookseller (John Bailey), the printer (Valentine Simmes), and Davison. The publisher, John Bailey the younger, appears to have had a very brief career, publishing perhaps only five works between 1601 and 1603.[27] Simmes, a printer-bookseller, printed two of these volumes: the first edition of *The Passion of a Discontented Mind* (1601) and *A Poetical Rapsody* (1602). In 1601, the year before he worked on *A Poetical Rapsody*, Simmes printed Samuel Daniel's *Works* for Simon Waterson, a publication event to which Davison responds in 'To Samuel Daniel *Prince of English Poets*' (E9v–10r).[28] Simmes was a very experienced printer, who specialised in printing high-quality literary books. *A Poetical Rapsody* was put out as a little duodecimo book, with care taken to ensure its quality, so that the *mise-en-page* remains spacious and not over-crowded, even though this anthology is small enough for a pocket. Poems therefore start on new pages and much use is made of subdivisional title-pages and ornaments to mark out divisions. The hexameter poems, dedicated to Sidney's experiments in quantitative meter, for example, are printed vertically, both advertising their novelty and ensuring that the hexameter line is displayed fittingly and not broken (18v–10v).

Davison's 'Printer' is a figure in which the interests of the gentleman compiler and the print trade coincide to the extent that they cannot be easily disentangled. If, as Davison claimed, the decision to place Sidney's poem at the front of the collection was taken by the 'Printer', then his own dedication of the volume to William Herbert, Earl of Pembroke, and constant references to Sidney in the preface collude with this marketing decision.[29] Fealty is declared to the Sidney–Herbert family to whom Davison 'humbly dedicates, his owne, his Brothers, and *Anomos* Poems, both in his owne, and in their names' (A2r). The framing of *A Poetical*

---

[27] The *Short-Title Catalogue* lists two John Baileys, the second of whom is identified as the publisher of *A Poetical Rhapsody* and whose shop was near or at the door of the Office of the Six Clerks.

[28] Craig W. Ferguson, *Valentine Simmes: Printer to Drayton, Shakespeare, Chapman, Greene, Dekker, Middleton, Daniel, Jonson, Marlowe, Marston, Heywood, and Other Elizabethans* (Charlottesville: Bibliographical Society, University of West Virginia, 1968), 5–6, 13–19, 26. Simmes writes prefaces before M. B.'s *The Triall of True Friendship* (1596, STC 1053) and R. T.'s *Two Tales, Translated out of Ariosto* (1597, STC 749).

[29] See also North, *Anonymous Renaissance*, 85.

206   *A Poetical Rapsody*

Rapsody is overtly Sidneian.[30] The decision to publish an anthology of lyric poetry is justified through his example. Davison rehearses the arguments made by Sidney in *An Apologie for Poetrie* that the composition of poetry is a fit and manly accomplishment for statesmen, soldiers, lawyers, and divines. Even amorous poetry possesses a moral seriousness: if 'thou mislike the Lyricall, because the chiefest subiect thereof is Love; I reply, that Love being virtuously intended, & worthily placed, is the Whetstone of witt, and Spurre to all generous actions' as the example of 'the everpraise worthy *Sidney*' testifies (A3r). As we have seen in the poetry anthologies of the 1590s, Sidney's example underpins the framing of a recreational poetics. Yet, the Sidney invoked by Davison is a very different literary property to Nashe's Ovidian love poet or the lighter, recreational lyric poet of Jones's Breton anthologies.[31] The mode of recreational poetry elaborated here is aligned not with the feminised idle courtier, but with the more manly soldier-poet, embarked on a military career or other professional duties, and hence a proper gentlemanly occupation at those times of leisure. This is how Davison casts his own and his brother's poems: in the case of his brother, who 'is by profession a Souldier', these are his juvenilia, since he 'was not 18. yeeres olde when hee writt these Toyes'; similarly, Francis's were written 'at idle times as I journeyed up and downe during my Travails' (A3v). With *Brittons Bowre* and *Arbor of Amorous Devices*, Jones had similarly sought to market these anthologies to the 'gentleman reader', and in doing so identify a class of book buyers reading for recreation. Davison is in the business of marketing exclusivity and advertising the quality of the poetry collected. As a consequence, his relationship with the 'gentleman reader' is certainly not that of Jones's deferential 'poore Printer', since he is of their class and, as his preface implies, probably better connected.

Court connections are prominently on display in the opening section, 'Pastorals and Eglogues', which begins with 'Two Pastoralls, made by Sir *Philip Sidney*, never yet published' – the first new poems of Sidney's to appear in print for a decade. Davison may have blamed the organisation of this section on the printer, but it is here that the constellation outlined in his dedication and preface – the Davison brothers, Anomos, and the Sidney family – has its fullest expression and the court connections of the Davison family are placed on show. The quality of the gathering is mirrored in the quality of the *mise-en-page*. At its core, this first edition of

---

[30] See Alexander, *Writing after Sidney*, 32–5; Marotti, *Manuscript, Print*, 235–36.
[31] See Chapter 3, 114–38.

Francis Davison and 'the Printer' 207

A Poetical Rapsody was a familial collection of poems by the Davison brothers and Francis's 'deere friend', around which are intermixed at the beginning and end, as Davison claimed, poems by Sidney and others. The ordering of poems in 'Pastorals and Eglogues' means that the Sidney poems, those of Philip and Mary, Countess of Pembroke, are placed alongside and in dialogue with those of Davison and 'Anomos' to produce a Davison family romance that charts the highs and lows of court service. The dialogues, occasional verse, and eclogues that make up this section are handy forms for conjoining poems into sequences, giving scope for the fabrication of spaces with the anthology.

Starting with Sidney poems to 'grace the forefront' of the book was strategy of the earlier 1590s anthologies, *Brittons Bowre* and *The Phoenix Nest*, whose opening elegies remembering Sidney set in place mourning communities that framed the collection. At some point in the compilation history of this anthology, it seems an elegiac opening was considered. Heading the list in Davison's catalogue that correlates with 'Pastorals and Eglogues' is 'Perin areed what new mischance betyde' (see Figure 8), an elegy for Sidney: in *A Poetical Rapsody*, this elegy is placed towards the end of this section. Instead, the Sidneian opening chosen is a song. *Englands Helicon* had also opened with a Sidney song; however, this is where the similarity ends, since these songs put in place very different acoustic fields. The song at the front of *Englands Helicon*, 'Onely joy, now heere you are' (B1r–v), belongs to a recreational poetics located in the household and in the company of women.[32] The scene of performance of the Sidney song in *A Poetical Rapsody*, 'Joyne Mates in mirth to mee', is set among an exclusively male company, as the sub-title relates: 'Upon his meeting with his two worthy Friends and fellow-Poets, Sir Edward Dier, and Maister Fulke Grevill'. The song promises privileged access to this Sidney circle:

> Welcome my two to me,   E.D. F.G. P.S.
> The number best beloved,
> Within my heart you be
> In friendship unremoved.
> *Joyne hands, &c.*

This address to two friends is given material, visual form on the printed page through the setting of the initials of Dyer, Greville, and Sidney in the margin against the text of the poem. The *mise-en-page* operates in concert

---

[32] See Chapter 4, 168–9.

208 *A Poetical Rapsody*

with the song's acoustics to perform a reanimation of this Sidney circle within the pages of the anthology.[33] Apostrophe, as we have seen, belongs to the rhetoric of performativity. Through its mode of address, the singer, Sidney, gives life and form to his addressees, his 'Mates', bodying them forth. Their silence on the page is not final, but rather promises a response. The scope of this pastoral meeting place, in which Sidney, Dyer, and Fulke Greville 'recreate them selves', to use Jones's phrase, is defined through the manly homoerotics of virtuous male friendship. The moral seriousness of this mode of friendship is elaborated in its companion poem in *A Poetical Rapsody*, 'Disprayse of a courtly life'. Sidney's poem is in the tradition of Wyatt's satiric mean estate poems, gathered in *Songes and Sonettes*. Whereas the falseness of the 'servile Court' (B2r) in Wyatt is opposed to the liberty of virtuous mind at home on the country estate, here, Sidney concentrates the virtues of the mean estate in the certainties and love of male friendship:

> Only for my two loves sake,   *Sir Ed. D. and M. F. G.*
> In whose love I pleasure take,
> Only two do me delight
> With their ever-pleasing sight.
>
> (B3r)

Once again, the visual properties of the page enhance the poem's meaning. The setting of initials in relation to the text insists that the abstract virtues and love announced in the poem are embodied in these men. Gathered at the front of the book, these Sidney pastorals set in place a politicised pastoral world whose the manly recreations and poetic exchanges are in tension with court service.

Placed alongside this homosocial world of male friendship, populated by Sidney, Dyer, and Fulke Greville, is the Countess of Pembroke's estate, Wilton, the site of the performance of 'A DIALOGUE *betweene two shepheards*, Thenot, *and* Piers, *in praise of* ASTREA, *made by the excellent Lady, the Lady* Mary *Countesse of* Pembrook, *at the Queenes Maiesties being at her house at Anno 15.*' As was the case with Spenser's *Astrophel*, the pairing of these two Sidney poems provides further evidence for how Philip Sidney's memory, and indeed authorship, was shaped relationally through his sister, Mary – a Sidneian dyad that Davison picked out in his dedication of *A Poetical Rapsody* to her son, William Herbert, Earl of Pembroke: '*Thou Worthy Sonne, vnto a peerelesse MOTHER, / Thou Nephew to great SIDNEY of renowne*' (A2r). Ostensibly a panegyric, Mary

---

[33] On intermediation, see Trudell, *Unwritten Poetry*, 10–16.

Francis Davison and 'the Printer' 209

Sidney's dialogue wittily exploits the reversibility of praise and dispraise within the epideictic mode to entertain the possibility that royal panegyric is but flattery. Once placed alongside Philip Sidney's 'Disprayse of a courtly life', a dialogue is established that does not necessarily disprove its accusation that the court is 'servile', but potentially augments its complaint. Through this pairing, Wilton, presided over by the countess, is fashioned as a virtuous alternative to Elizabeth's court. Piers, the archetypal plain-speaking Protestant shepherd, is a *parrhesiastes*, and there-fore hostile to flattery and eager to speak truth to power. He responds to Thenot's praise of Astraea–Elizabeth by pointing out repeatedly that he is a liar. The premise is that Astraea is more glorious than any comparison Thenot can muster, since 'Above conceit her honour flies'. Yet the closing line, 'But silence, nought can praise her', is double-edged, given the implicit association between praise and flattery throughout, and seems to want to close down the panegyric mode. The priority given to Piers in this dialogue aligns the countess with the *parrhesiastes* who is licensed to speak plainly to monarchs and elegantly articulates the critical role of the aristocracy within the state.

The arrangement of poems in this section means that the Davison family are affiliated with the Sidney family through the textual and social proximities allowed within anthology which permit the mixing of 'diverse things written by great & learned personages, with our meane and worth-lesse scriblings' (A3r). The effect is to present the Davisons as inhabiting the same courtly milieu and sharing Sidneian values. Mary Sidney's Wilton entertainment is followed by pastorals attributed to Walter and Francis, each with elaborate headnotes that want to give the impression they are part of the countess's entertainments for Elizabeth. Walter's pastoral is formally innovative in Sidney fashion, a '*Roun-de-lay in inverted Rimes, between the twoo friendly Rivals*, Strephon *and* Klauis, *in the presence of* URANIA, *Mistris to them both*', and has its sequel in Francis's 'Strephons Palinode', the lengthy headnote to which tells a story of Urania's jealousy, which causes her to banish Strephon from her court, until he '*humbly craves pardon*' and is received '*into greater grace and favour than before*' (B8r). What follows is Davison's *prosopopoeia* of Urania–Elizabeth, 'Ura-niaes *Answer in inverted Rimes, Staffe for Staffe*', a type of wish-fulfilment in which the male subordinate speaks in the voice of a powerful woman, who does not offer erotic consolation, but instead tells a story of virtue rewarded. Inverted rhymes mean that Urania takes her cue from Strephon, repeating his words and taking his prompts. Urania acknowledges that 'Too long thou hast felt tormenting, / Too great paines / So great Love and

210   *A Poetical Rapsody*

Faith sustaines' and promises him 'Fuller pardon then you crave' (B9v). This act of *prosopopoeia* puts words in Urania–Elizabeth's mouth to fabricate a reversal of fortunes.

The sequencing of poems in 'Pastorals and Eglogues' puts in place dialogues, setting scenes, and describing scenarios that take advantage of the accretive and dialogic form of the eclogue to build a narrative that articulates the misfortunes of the Davison family. It is a politicised mode of compilation that recalls not only Spenser's pastoral collections, both *The Shepheardes Calender* and *Colin Clouts/Astrophel*, but also sections of *Songes and Sonettes* where the sequencing and framing of Surrey's and Wyatt's verse gives the topic of the dangers of court life a particular relevance to the fates of these men.[34] The eclogue following Davison's Urania poems, 'A Shepheard poore, *Eubulus*, call'd he was', tells another story of an honest and loyal shepherd who has been brought low through '*Astreas* burning-hot Disdaine / That parched hath the roote of all my blis' (B11v). His fate repeats that of Strephon before he was returned to Urania's favour and had many resonances in 1602. Some readers may have recalled the punishment meted out to William Davison by Urania–Astraea–Elizabeth for his part in the execution of Mary, Queen of Scots. Others, given the recent fall and execution of the Earl of Essex, may have drawn other conclusions about the dangers of losing Astraea's favour. The withdrawal of Astraea's 'heavenly beames, which were mine only light', and the coming of the night is 'Tirant-like' since it usurps the proper flow of favour to subjects, disregarding 'all my service, faith, and patient minde' (B12r). Eubulus's emblem from Penelope's epistle in Ovid's *Heroides* both recalls the emblems of *Shepheardes Calender* and casts his eclogue in the form of Ovidian complaint: 'uni mihi pergama restant' ('for me alone [Pergamum] still stands') (C3r).[35] Eubulus is a constant Penelope, keeping faith despite the cruelty of his situation, whose 'sad plaints' fall on deaf ears, and whose 'Woes in mournfull inke arraide' (C2r) Astraea refuses to read, reversing the earlier *prosopopoeia* of Urania–Elizabeth in 'Strephons Palinode'. In this winter eclogue, Eubulus in his old age is feminised, becoming an Ovidian heroine who endlessly plains to herself, with no hope of response or redress.

When *A Poetical Rapsody* is compared with Davison's catalogue, it is possible to trace at least some of the recombinations of poems made during

---

[34] See Peter C. Herman, '*Songes and Sonettes*, 1557', in Hamrick, ed., *Tottel's Songes*, 122–30.
[35] Ovid, *Heroides. Amores*, trans. Grant Showerman, rev. G. P. Goold (Cambridge, MA: Harvard University Press, 1977), 14–15, l. 51,

Francis Davison and 'the Printer' 211

the process of compiling the anthology. Anthologies, in print and manuscript, share this capacity for textual reassembly. A set of three eclogues close 'Pastorals and Eglogues': the elegy for Sidney, 'Perin, areed what new mischance betide', attributed to A. W., Ignoto's eclogue between a shepherd and a herdsman, 'Come gentle Heard-man, sit by mee', and finally, an eclogue '*Concerning olde Age*', assigned to Anomos, 'For when thou art not as thou wont of yore' (C3v–12r). The first two head the list in Davison's catalogue, while the last eclogue concludes it (see Figure 8). What Davison's catalogue also tells us is that the two eclogues that feature Perin – 'Perin areed' and 'For when thou art' – were taken from the paperbook bound with a copy of Spenser's *The Shepheardes Calender* (Harley 280, fol. 105r); the other two eclogues copied in this paperbook, 'A little Heard-Groom for hee was no bett.' and the 'Sestine of 8', 'Yee gastly Groves that heare my wofull cryes', will later be added to the second, 1608 edition of *A Poetical Rapsody*. The paperbook bound with *The Shepheardes Calender* is particularly intriguing because it suggests how books that are themselves composite prompted subsequent acts of compilation. This paperbook uses Spenser's book as a practical guide in how to assemble an eclogue book. The material form of the paperbook itself facilitates assembly. Since they were either bought pre-bound from a stationer or bound by the compiler, the underlying 'integrity' of the book, with its 'regular structure', is 'established at the outset'.[36] At the same time, the eclogue provides a generic model for how to conjoin poems into a sequence. The paperbook bound with the copy of *The Shepheardes Calender* engages in a dialogue with its 'fore' text, reading Spenserian pastoral as an invitation to collaborative composition.[37] The first eclogue, 'A little Heard-groom for hee was no bett*er*', imitates Spenser's January and June eclogues, heightening the mode of complaint since summer's lively warmth cannot dispel the winter's 'frost of could Despaire', laying the ground for the elegiac second eclogue. Spenser's shepherds return in these new eclogues: Cuddy, the 'little heardgroom', Willy, the name given to Sidney, is the youthful shepherd from the 'March' eclogue, Thenot and Wrenock are Spenser's wise old shepherds, while Perin of the second and

---

[36] Bland, *Guide*, 68. On the paperbook, see also Woudhuysen, *Sir Philip Sidney*, 49–50; Jonathan Gibson, 'Casting Off Blanks: Hidden Structures in Early Modern Paper Books', in *Material Readings of Early Modern Culture: Texts and Social Practices, 1580–1730*, edited by James Daybell and Peter Hinds (Basingstoke: Palgrave Macmillan, 2010), 210–11.
[37] Intriguingly, the Latin verses of Robert Mill, when a student at Cambridge around 1583, were 'wrytten one the backsyde of the sheephards kalender'; see Woudhuysen, *Sir Philip Sidney*, 260.

212   *A Poetical Rapsody*

third eclogues seems to be the counterpart of Colin, the character of the author. Finally, the variant on the sestina – 'A Sestine of 8', 'Yee gastly Groves that heare my wofull cryes' – closely imitates Spenser's sestina, 'Ye wastful woods bear witness of my Woe' from the August eclogue of *The Shepheardes Calender*.

The eclogues in the paperbook are disaggregated and reassembled in both Davison's catalogue and in different editions of *A Poetical Rapsody* in varying combinations. For the first edition, only the second and third are incorporated into the 'Pastorals and Eglogues' section. The choice of the third eclogue to end this section is particularly apposite. This eclogue is entitled 'a fragment, concerning ould Age' in the paperbook, and given the explanatory title in *A Poetical Rapsody*, 'IIII. Eglogue. *Concerning olde Age. The beginning and the end of this Eglogue are wanting*' (c10v), where it is attributed to Anomos. Its inclusion in its unfinished state adds veracity to Davison's story of the absence of his friend, 'Anomos', from the scene of publication, acting as a reminder of the errancy of textual transmission: texts are lost, destroyed, either wholly or partially, and then circulate in fragmentary states. Davison's catalogue has a section listing poems that are 'Imperfect fragments'. This self-consciously fragmentary eclogue introduces a rhetoric of incompleteness into the compilation that functions on many levels. The eclogue features Wrenock, the 'good olde shephearde' named by Colin in Spenser's December eclogue, and places him in conversation with Perin, who featured in 'III. Eglogue', '*Made long since vpon the death of Sir Phillip Sidney*'. The numbering in this section is haphazard since 'II. Eglogue' comes not before, but after 'III. Eglogue'. Read relationally, the incomplete 'III. Eglogue' sets in place ongoing dialogues moving across poems and publications that intimate that this 'recovered' fragment is part of a wider corpus of Spenserian texts, some of which are now missing. In doing so, it prefigures the textual strategies of later 'discovered' texts of long dead authors: in 1609, Spenser's *Two Cantos of Mutabilitie*, fragments of a longer work, will be printed in his *Works*. When read in relation to the politicised language of loss in these eclogues, epitomised by Eubulus's complaints that go unanswered and the elegy for Sidney, the fragment also invites readers to consider more disorderly histories of production resulting from the political uncertainties shadowed in these pastorals. More pragmatically, coupled with the seemingly out of sequence eclogues at the end of this section, it discloses the makeshift practices, contingent upon changing circumstances, that accompany more organised methods of compilation when making anthologies.

Private Recreations

'Sonnets, Odes, Elegies, and Madrigalls' by the Davison brothers follows the family drama played out in 'Pastorals and Eglogues' and is coupled with 'Sonets, Odes, Elegies and other Poesies' attributed to Anomos. All are variants on the sonnet sequence that take Sidney's *Astrophil and Stella* as their model. The sonnet sequence, presided over by a desiring writing subject, provides spaces for fabricating variant fictions of authorship within the 'multiple paradigmatic frames' of the anthology.[38] The first edition of this anthology employs genres – eclogues and sonnet sequences – that lend themselves to constructing sequences and put in place fictions of association. Whereas in 'Pastorals and Eglogues' shepherd-poets converse across the section, in these sonnet sequences Sidneian love poets address their mistresses, who speak back, Spaces are thereby fashioned for private recreations that are defined by their social exclusivity and so can be distinguished from the more socially mixed recreational spaces we have seen in other anthologies. Private recreation takes place among mixed company, bringing together men and women in rituals of courtship and within milieux that are explicitly courtly.[39]

Francis's collection has been carefully crafted. Descriptive titles to the poems set in play fictions of authorship and narrate a story of courtship that begins with the poet's wooing of his first mistress, and then his second. The narrative style of the titles demonstrates a keen awareness of how the sonnet sequence can be turned into a dramatic lived space. The sequence opens with a consciously first, framing sonnet, given the title *'Dedication of these Rimes, to his first love'*. Like Sidney's first sonnet, it is an invitation to love as an invitation to read, productively dogged by interpretive and amorous uncertainty: 'My lines your eies, my love your hart displeasing, / Breed hate in you, and kill my hope of easing; / Say with your self, how can the wretch amend it?' *Gradatio* does not build up hope but rather records disappointment, compounded by the falling hypermetric stress, conveying the lover's fears that he will fail to persuade, and prompting his plea to his mistress to find a solution. The closing couplet puts thoughts into his mistress's head: 'I wondrous faire, he wondrous deerely loving, / How can his thoughts but make his pen be moving?'

---

[38] Wall, *Imprint of Gender*, 93–7.
[39] On private recreation, see Paul L. Faber, 'Ophelia's Songspace: Elite Female Musical Performance and Propriety on the Elizabethan and Jacobean Stage', in *Shakespeare, Music and Performance*, edited by Bill Barclay and David Lindley (Cambridge University Press, 2017), 59–70.

214   *A Poetical Rapsody*

(D2r). Walter's section similarly is a sonnet sequence interspersed with inset odes and an elegy, with its own opening invitation to love and to read that echoes not only Sidney, but his brother's sonnet with its play on eyes, lines, and love: 'Since eies, love, lines, erre then by your direction; / Excuse mine Eies, my Lines, and my Affection' (E12). There is a consanguinity here in which Sidneian imitation becomes a family affair.

Both sequences foreground acts of writing and reading within poems. Yet, it is the sequence attributed to Francis that demonstrates a high degree of craft through the way titles are formulated, acting very effectively as frames that dramatise physical encounters, locating the composition of sonnets within social situations and places where gifts have been given, kisses have been begged, and 'a Kisse received' (Madrigals III and IIII, D6v), and verse letters have been sent (Elegie, D8–11). Poems are not simply texts but physical and embodied objects circulating within the world these poems figure forth and are replete with details that point to events in Francis's life, putting in play fictions of an elite writing life. The lengthy headnote to Sonnet IIII describes a crowning moment in Davison's career and locates it within the ongoing amorous transactions of the sonnet sequence: '*Upon presenting her with the speech of Grayes-Inne Maske at the Court 1594. consisting of three partes, The Story of Proteus Transformations, the wonders of the Adamantine Rocke, and a speech to her Maiestie*'. His mistress is invited to 'Accept then of these lines, though meanely pend, / So fit for you to take, and me to send' (D3v). His mistress is not silent. Sonnets VI and VII are a pair of answering sonnets, as the title points out: '*Her Answere, in the same Rimes*' (E1v). On the one hand, it is a device that demonstrates the male poet's virtuosity, with the same rhymes and rhetorical formula deployed from contrary speaking positions. On the other, it is a *prosopopoeia* in which the mistress may take her cue, but it is to resist his definition of her words and actions, paradoxically disrupting, while exhibiting, the male poet's ability to speak for his mistress. Poetic composition and transmission in this sequence takes place primarily in the company of women: this is Sidneian recreational verse. The male lover and his mistress are writers and readers, constantly interpreting and responding to poems sent and received. The ode given the title '*Upon her giving him backe the Paper wherein the former Song was written, as though it had beene an answere thereunto*', conjoins poems, in this case, the preceding '*A Prosopopoeia: Wherein his Hart speakes to his second Ladies breast*' (E2v), requiring that they be read relationally, in sequence, to appreciate their meaning. Referring to this *prosopopoeia* written on a 'paper' that 'into your

Private Recreations 215

sweet Bosome I delivered' (E2v), he explains the bodying forth this rhetorical figure enacts:

> Thought you it nothing else contain'd,
> But written words in Ryme restraind?
> O then your thought abused was,
> My Hart close wrapt therein, into your Brest infused was.
>
> (E3r)

The heart wrapped in paper may verge on the grotesque, but this image effectively sets out the textual and extra-textual properties of his sonnet. His paper is a material text that bodies forth his desire and figures the desired physical proximity of his body to hers, describing a process of osmosis, in which his love becomes part of her through an act of emotional and bodily union. Davison here sets out an agentive model of compilation that insists that readers actively make connections between the poems, and through these acts of relational, contextualising reading turn sundry sonnets, odes, elegies, and madrigals into a miscellaneous sequence.

Anomos is named as the author of the third major section of *A Poetical Rapsody* and emerges from this anthology as one of its most significant authorial characters. *A Poetical Rapsody*, like *Englands Helicon*, uses an array of terms to signify suppressed authorship: Anomos, Ignoto, Incerto, and the mysterious A. W. Like A. W. we can perhaps view Anomos as a designation, rather than an individual; as Rollins points out, in the preface to the 1608 edition, 'my deere friend Anomos' is turned from singular to plural: 'my deere friends Anonymoi'.[40] On the one hand, Anomos exemplifies the early modern type of the composite author, identified by Todd Knight as 'less a subject or an agent of literary production in the modern sense than a location'.[41] On the other, this figure is also the subject of stories of authorial individuation. Anomos is a place where stories of composition converge. Davison's preface introduces Anomos to readers as a poet of substance: he is an author in whom readers should be interested. Anomos is individuated: he is a close friend, who began writing poetry 'almost twentie years since' (A3v) in the 1580s, some of which he addressed to Sidney while he lived and others after his death, and an entire section within anthology is devoted to his poetry. Yet, what then are readers to make of the other occurrences of name suppression – Ignoto, Incertus, or even A. W. – who appear in 'Pastorals and Eglogues'? Are these also to be identified with this unnamed friend? Other alternatives are

---

[40] Davison, *A Poetical Rhapsody*, ed. Rollins, II, 95.   [41] Knight, *Bound to Read*, 166.

216   *A Poetical Rapsody*

put into circulation, but all do not necessarily coalesce in the Anomos of 'Sonets, Odes, Elegies and other Poesies'. As in other anthologies, there is a very mixed economy of naming, with a variety of author functions in play across the collection.

In the collection gathered 'under the Name of *Anomos*' (A3r), once again we are presented with the writing subject of the sonnet sequence. It is an avowedly Sidneian compilation: 'Sonets, Odes, Elegies and other Poesies. / *Splendidis longum valedico nugis.* / ANOMOS.' The tag comes from Sidney's motto at the end of *Certain Sonnets* and translates as 'I bid a long farewell to splendid trifles'. Sidney's motto frames and organises the following miscellany – the long farewell to love – which ends with the pattern poem, '*An Altare and Sacrifice to Disdaine, for freeing him from love*'. The closing motto comes from Ovid's *Amores*: '*Vicimus & domitium pedibus calcamus amorem*' ('Victory is mine, and I tread under foot my conquered love' (3.9a.5).[42] The collection showcases Sidneian metrical experimentation by including verse composed in quantitative measure, each type clearly identified in the title: four poems are composed in phaleuciacs, one in sapphic metre, and a set of hexameter poems that are appropriately elegies for Sidney. There is ample evidence for crafted compilation in this collection. If we can credit the account that Davison gives in his preface, then one might assume that Anomos's collection came to him in the form in which it is published, with no further intervention: he claims that his friend was 'utterly ignorant' of his plans and so at a considerable distance from the scene of publication (A2v). The reader is therefore encouraged to interpret the 'Sonets, Odes, Elegies and other Poesies' gathered 'under the Name of *Anomos*' (A3r) as having their origins in this writing subject. Yet, when Davison's catalogue of the poems of A. W. and *A Poetical Rapsody* are compared, then an ongoing process of selection and reorganisation is made visible that extends well beyond the authorial story told by Davison. The Anomos who is said to author this section is a more composite character than Davison's account of his friend admits. Anomos's set of poems in *A Poetical Rapsody* opens with an introductory section, 'III. Sonnets for a Proeme to the Poems following', which is accompanied by a headnote that explains the integral authorial relationship of this introduction to the following collection: '*That Love onely made him a Poet, and that all sortes of Verses, both in Rime and Measure, agree with his Lady*' (G1v). However, none of the poems in this

---

[42] Ovid, *Heroides. Amores*, trans. Grant Showerman, rev. G. P. Goold (Cambridge, MA: Harvard University Press, 1914), LCL 41: 494–5

Private Recreations 217

proem are listed in Davison's catalogue, which is a surprising omission since all the poems that follow these first three sonnets are listed in order in the far left and bottom right column of Davison's second list (see Figure 8), beginning with 'Sweet love myne only treasure' and ending with 'My muse by thee restor'd to life'. If Davison's friend was as absent from the process of compilation as he claims, then this collection was the work of other hands.

The 'Certaine other Poems upon diverse Subjects, by the same Author', again attributed to Anomos, is more obviously a multi-, rather than single-authored collection. The first set of poems, '*Three Odes translated out of* Anacreon, *the Greeke Lyrick Poet*', can be found on Davison's list attributed to A. W.[43] However, added to this group are two further translations of Anacreon's second and third odes – 'Nature in her worke doth give' and 'Cupid abroad, was lated in the night' – assigned to T. S. (Thomas Spelman) and R. G. (Robert Greene), respectively (15v–6r). These additional translations of Anacreon's odes would appear to accord with Davison's complaint that the 'Printer' was 'mixing' at the 'ende of this book' poems of 'others names . . . to make the booke grow to a competent volume' (A3r). Hence, the final section of 'Diverse Poems of Sundry Authors', none of which is attributed to Francis or Walter Davison or to Anomos, and instead bear the initials and names of John Davies, Thomas Campion, Henry Wotton, Sir Walter Raleigh, Joshua Sylvester, Edmund Spenser, and Henry Constable. It suggests a history of compilation, often apparent in manuscript miscellanies, in which later owners take over a collection put together by an earlier compiler and add their own material, thus turning it into 'something much more miscellaneous'.[44] However, as we have seen, it is impossible to disentangle Davison from this 'later' work that he attributes to the 'Printer'. Assigning responsibility for the anthology's compilation to any one individual is fraught with difficulties. What makes *A Poetical Rapsody* distinctive is the fact that detailed, and often contradictory, fictions are told about its composition. These stories fashion a figure of the gentleman compiler, who gathers the poems of his well-connected family and friends, to promote the value of an anthology that has its origins in the privileged milieu of the elite, even though this fiction cannot quite remove itself from the work of the 'Printer' and the business of making anthologies.

Central to these fictions of gentlemanly composition are the various songs gathered throughout which identify the anthology with the private

---

[43] 'Out of Anacreon', BL Harley MS 280, 104r.   [44] Vine, *Miscellaneous Order*, 19.

218   *A Poetical Rapsody*

recreations of gentlemen and gentlewomen. Like *Englands Helicon*, *A Poetical Rapsody* publishes songs from court entertainments and from printed music books.[45] The final collection, 'Diverse Poems of Sundry Authors', is primarily a collection of songs, signalled by its opening lyric, John Davies's *'A Hymne in prayse of Musicke'*, followed by his sonnet sequence addressed to his mistress, Philomela, the nightingale, in which he takes the name 'Melophilus', playing on the association of music with the sweet sounds of birdsong. Next are a set of Thomas Campion songs, two of which had been published in Philip Rosseter's *A Booke of Ayres* (1601).[46] The difference to *Englands Helicon* is that, rather than advertising their sources in printed music books, these songs are typically contextualised within *A Poetical Rapsody* in ways that advertise the cultural milieu in which Davison participated. Hence, Campion's 'Of Neptunes Empyre let us sing' is published with the editorial note that it was sung in the 'Grayes-Inne Maske, at the Court. 1564 [*sic*]', which included entertainments authored by Davison. Madrigals, a newly fashionable song form in printed music books, feature prominently in the collections attributed to the Davison brothers and Anomos. Here, songs are advertised as part of the acoustic world of gentlemen and gentlewomen as they engage in rituals of courtship. In Francis's sequence, an ode declares that only his mistress's beauty and singing voice please the poet, 'since her Notes charmde mine Eare, / Even the sweetest Tunes I heare, / To mee seem rude harsh noyses' (D5v), which is then followed by two madrigals, 'Love, if a God thou art' and 'In health and ease am I' (D6r–7v). The first of these was later printed by Robert Jones in his *Cantos. The First Set of Madrigals* published in 1607.[47]

   Jones set at least four madrigals from *A Poetical Rapsody* to music in this songbook and would set two more in his *Ultimum Vale* (1608). In his preface to *The First Booke of Songes & Ayres* (1600), Jones relates how certain gentlemen 'were earnest to have me apparel these ditties for them;

---

[45] 'A Dialogue betwixt the Lover and his Lady' ('Lady, my flame still burning') and 'Her Answere' ('Sweet lord, your flame still burning') (K1or) are translations of Ferrabosco's madrigals, 'Donna, l'ardente fiamma' and 'Signor, la vostra fiamma', previously printed in the second volume of Yonge's *Musica Transalpina*, and John Farmer's *First set of English Madrigals* (1599), B2v–3v; 'Faustina hath the fairer face' in Michael Cavendish's *14. Ayres in Tabletorie ... And 8. Madrigalles* (1598); 'Absence heare thou my Protestation' in Morley's *The First Book of Ayres* (1600); 'Her face, her tongue, her wit, so fair, so sweet, so sharp', in William Barley, *A New Book of Tablature*, (1596), A4v; 'And would you see my Mistres face' in Rosseter, *Book of Ayres* (1601),

[46] 'Blame not my Cheeks, though pale with loue they bee' and 'When to her Lute Corinna sings'.

[47] *Cantus the First Set of Madrigals, of 3.4.5.6.7.8. parts: for viols and voices, or for voices alone, or as you please* (1607), Song 5. Both madrigals are translations of lyrics by Luigi Groto, known for his songs; 'Love, if a God' was also set as a lute-song in Bod. MS Mus. Sch., fol. 575.

'*Newly augmented and corrected*' 219

which though they intended for their private recreation, never meaning they should come into the light, were yet content upon intreaty to make the incouragements of this my first adventure'. The sources of these lyrics have not been traced. While it might be tempting to propose the Davison brothers and their unnamed friends as their authors, there is a wider point to be made about how musical composition is depicted as a skill to be cultivated by gentlemen, part of their 'private recreation'; hence these are 'idle ditties (as they will needes have me call them)'.[48] The term 'private recreation', as employed by Robert Jones, refers to an exclusive social space, not to 'isolated or sequestered activity but to musical production within one's private *circle*', as Paul Faber explains – those occasions when 'wealthy families, taking cues from royals, performed music for each other as an everyday part of "the good life"'.[49] This modelling of recreational culture can be distinguished from the more socially open performance cultures, and affordances of the songbook, that Munday set out in *Banquet of Daintie Conceits*, as we have seen in Chapter 4. This is not to say that either Jones's songbooks or *A Poetical Rapsody* emerge out of 'a single milieu of production', or that they 'disseminate a previously existing performance culture'.[50] Rather, both compilations are in the business of marketing elite models of composition and a culture of leisure defined through the socially exclusive terms of private recreation.

'Newly augmented and corrected'

A Poetical Rapsody had a longevity in print of around twenty years, rivalling that of *Songes and Sonettes*, *A Paradyse of Daynty Devises*, and *A Handefull of Pleasant Delites*. Three further editions were published in 1608, 1611, and 1621. With each new iteration, poems were added, removed, and reorganised, and paratext altered. Alongside Davison's catalogue, these editions supply valuable evidence for the various organisational practices involved in producing an anthology, even if there will be other stages of compilation that have left no trace. These editions provide some insight into the working practices of the new publisher, Roger Jackson, who in 1603 acquired the title from John Bailey and financed and oversaw new editions. In 1603, Jackson was just starting out as a bookseller, having entered his first title in 1601; he would go on to have a successful publishing career until his death in 1625. Jackson's prefaces before the

[48] *The First Booke of Songes & Ayres of Foure Parts with Tableture for the Lute* (1600), A3r.
[49] Faber, 'Ophelia's Songspace', 65, 67. [50] Trudell, *Unwritten Poetry*, 74.

220   *A Poetical Rapsody*

books he published direct attention to his partnerships with authors, editors, and unnamed 'friends' when preparing texts for publication. In the preface before Thomas Gainsford's commonplace book, *The Rich Cabinet* (1616), Jackson set out a publishing scenario which foregrounds the partnerships he formed and sets out the rationale for reorganising an earlier edition (now apparently lost), that was:

> (I must ingeniously confesse:) neither so orderly disgested [*sic*] by the Penne, nor so exactly corrected at the Presse (by reason of some unseasonable hast:) as both the Author and my selfe have since seriously wished. Now therefore, at better leasure (for your greater delight in reading, and ease in finding:) I have here (with the helpe of a skilfull and industrious friend) Methodically reduced all into this *Rich Cabinet*; doubly furnished with ample Addition of newe Treasures of divers kinds.[51]

Jackson explains his role as that of a critical reader and a practised maker of commonplace books.[52] Like Nicholas Ling before him, Jackson introduces the reader to a hermeneutics of editing which draws on the humanist principles of commonplacing, directing the reader's attention to the technical skill involved and pointing to a system for organising intellectual matter. The preface asks its readers to credit the editorial labour of those involved in producing this volume – Jackson, Gainsford, and the unnamed 'skilful and industrious friend'. This is a handy book 'Methodically reduced' for readers' 'greater delight in reading, and ease in finding'.[53] It is possible to discern publishing choices emerging across Jackson's output – books of poetry, including *A Poetical Rapsody*, commonplace books, and didactic manuals. These books are framed, both materially and conceptually, in terms of their use and incorporate tools for training readers in methods of knowledge acquisition.[54]

One feature linking the poetry books and didactic manuals Jackson published is the table of contents.[55] When he took over *A Poetical Rapsody*, an alphabetical table of contents was added, a finding aid training readers in how to use the book.[56] The table allows for different ways of comprehending and making use of the poems collected in an anthology. To an extent, the formal subdivisions of the first edition of *A Poetical Rhapsody*

---

[51] T. G., *The Rich Cabinet* (1616, STC 11522), A2–2v.   [52] Lesser, *Renaissance Drama*, 36, 47
[53] Francis Davison, *Davisons Poems, or, A Poeticall Rapsody* (1621).
[54] Sarah Pennell and Natasha Glaisyer, 'Introduction', in *Didactic Literature*, 2–3.
[55] See, for example, the Jackson publications: Simon Latham, *Lathams Falconry* (1614, STC 15267; 1618, STC 15268.3); Arthur Saul, *The Famous Game of Chesse-play* (1614, STC 21772; 1618, STC 21773); Robert Record, *Records Arithmeticke* (1615, STC 20806.5).
[56] On tables of contents, see Blair, *Too Much to Know*, 135–44; Chapter 1, 31–2.

'Newly augmented and corrected' 221

were simply turned into an alphabetically organised table – eclogues, elegies, madrigals, odes, pastorals, poems, and sonnets – with new categories added – epitaphs, epigrams, and hymns – gleaned from the titles. Also included were poems' titles typically phrased in the form of topics, drawing on the organisational structure of commonplace books, and often cross-referenced to genre. Those using the table could therefore move flexibly between form and topic as ways of reading, identifying, understanding, and using these poems and the anthology itself. So, for example, listed under the letter 'L' were a series of poems on the topic of 'Love' where the reader was also directed to 'See Son.' or 'See Ode'. Both anthologies and manuals were produced in order to sustain a variety of reading practices, from the close reading of texts to excerpting, all governed by an understanding that, above all, these books must be usable and reusable.

When Jackson republished the anthology for the first time in 1608, there is textual evidence he worked with others. Of the sixty-four new poems added to this edition, thirty-six are printed under Davison's initials, F. D., and six also appear in his catalogue of poems. Among the new Davison poems added to this edition are a set of epigrams translated from Martial, a genre that was just coming into vogue in these years.[57] Davison's papers record his continued systematic collection of poems and other textual material from scribal channels after 1602. The list of 'Manuscripts to gett' he compiled dates from after 1607, since he refers to Sir John Constable, who was knighted that year. This list is organised under broadly generic headings: 'Letters of all sorts. Especially by ye late E. of Essex'; 'Orations. Apologies. Instructions. Relations'; 'Sports/masks & Entertaynments'; 'Emblems & Impresaes/q. Those in white-hall/Gallery'; and 'Anagrams'. The next lists 'POEMS of all sorts' via genre and author: the psalms of Mary Sidney, Countess of Pembroke (on the proviso that 'they shall Not bee printed'), Joshua Silvester, Sir John Harington, and Joseph Hall; Donne's satires, elegies, and epigrams; Jonson's poems; and Henry Constable's sonnets. If a second anthology was planned, it was not printed. It is possible, however, that some of these poems made their way into the 1608 edition.[58] The provenance of much of the new verse added to this edition points to collectors with privileged access to elite scribal networks. In 1608, the set of court entertainments attributed to Sir John

---

[57] James Doelman, *The Epigram in England, 1590–1640* (Manchester University Press, 2016), 167–8.
[58] BL Harl MS 298, 159v. Rollins argues that Davison acted as one of the correctors, since his poems and those of his brother have been extensively revised, yet there is very little evidence of substantive revision to poems by other authors; in Davison, *Poetical Rhapsody*, II, 74–8.

222   *A Poetical Rapsody*

Davies had not yet appeared in print and had limited manuscript circulation; they might well have been among the 'Sports/masks & Entertaynments' Davison gathered.[59]

Most of the new poems added to the 1608 edition are mixed among the
first nine poems of the first edition, with eight new poems reserved for the
end. The result is a pronounced miscellaneity to the opening section, with
priority given to what is new, as the title-page announces: 'For Varietie and
Pleasure, the like never yet published'. While the court associations at the
front of the book remain, the Davison family romance that shaped
'Pastorals and Eglogues' is much attenuated. The ample white space and
printers' emblems that marked out the quality and integrity of this
Sidneian selection have also disappeared; instead the *mise-en-page* is
cramped, with comparatively little use of borders. 'Pastorals and Eglogues'
has been interspliced with sections of new poems, many non-pastoral: the
sestina from the paperbook bound together with *The Shepheardes Calender*
(C4–5), a set of epigrammatic 'Inscriptions', an epitaph for Henry III
(C5–6), a Horatian dialogue in praise of Elizabeth (C6v–7), and a series
of sonnets, madrigals, and epigrams all attributed to F. D. and closed off
by a printer's ornament and a blank page (C7v–11v). 'Ten Sonnets by
T. W.', excerpted from Thomas Watson's *The Hekatompathia*, follow,
with their own divisional title-page, and these are conjoined to the set of
sonnets attributed to 'C[harles]. B[est].' (C11v–D4v). The 'Pastorals and
Eglogues' section then resumes with 'Strephons Palinode' (D5–5v).
Whereas the front of the 1602 edition had been graced 'with Sir *Philip
Sidneys* and others names', this 1608 edition is now graced with the name
of Sir John Davies, putting in place new interpretive frames.[60]

The set of Davies's entertainments, the '12. wonders of the world', and
'A Lotterie' have their sources in official forms of recreation designed for
Elizabeth's court, and are a more courtly example of the type of ornamen-
tal poetry we have seen gathered in *The Phoenix Nest*: Nicholas Breton's
'Riddles', a game performed by 'ladies' for their entertainment, and 'The
Chesse Play'.[61] These poems are crafted multimodal objects that accrue

---

[59] The only extant copies that can be dated before 1608 are to be found in a miscellany compiled in
late 1606 by someone with close connections to the court and Inns of Court; see Maria Reardon,
'The Manuscript Miscellany in Early Stuart England: a Study of British Library Additional
22601 and Related Texts' (unpublished PhD dissertation, Queen Mary, University of London,
2007), 25–6, 36–7.
[60] The second edition of Davies's *Nosce Teipsum* was also published in 1608 with the attribution on
the title-page to 'Sir Iohn Davis, his Maiesties Atturney generall in Ireland'.
[61] See the discussion in Chapter 3, 145–8.

'Newly augmented and corrected'

meaning through the part they play in elaborate performances. The headnote and glosses to 'A Lotterie presented before the *late Queenes Majestie* at the Lord Chancellors House. 1601.' give details of this entertainment, from the mariner entering in costume with the box containing the lottery, the song he performs, to his address to the assembled ladies to try their fortune in the lottery, and its rules. The '12. wonders of the world' is also surprisingly multimodal, designed for recirculation and recreation. The entertainment consists of a dozen roundels that were once painted on trenchers and presented by Davies as a New Year's gift to Thomas Sackville, Earl of Dorset. Once published in *A Poetical Rapsody* in 1608, they were then available to trencher makers: a set made around 1620 is now part of the collections in the Victoria and Albert Museum.[62] These roundels were also set to music by John Maynard and published in *The XII. Wonders of the World Set and Composed for the Violl de Gambo, the Lute, and the Voyce*, in 1611 (STC 17749). Presumably these songs can be sung to accompany the presentation of the trenchers during a banquet. Davies's 'A Lotterie' similarly consists of a set of 'Lots', made up of 'portable epigrammes', like the roundels, designed 'to be carried away', thereby enacting their own processes of transmission.[63] These *'never yet published'* (B1r) entertainments are markedly novel. Their inclusion at the front of the collection advertises to the buyer not only that this edition included substantial new material, as indeed it did, but also that the contents of this anthology can be put to further novel recreational uses in a variety of contexts.[64]

The third 'Newly corrected and augmented' 1611 edition has once again been rearranged, in part, to bear out the claims on its title-page, but also, arguably, to ensure that it is now more 'orderly digested' for 'greater delight in reading and ease in finding', in the words of Jackson's preface before *The Rich Cabinet*. This third edition has been reorganised to reinstate the authorial and formal structures put in place by the first edition. Those ornamental court entertainments, which opened the second edition, have been retained – this is the year, after all, that Maynard's settings of 'The 12. wonders' appeared. The new groups of poems, assigned to Francis Davison, Watson, and Best, which were spliced into the 1608 'Pastorals and Eglogues', have been removed. Francis's 1608

---

[62] Victoria and Albert Museum, British Galleries, Room 56, The Djangoly Gallery, case 8: http://collections.vam.ac.uk/item/O78997/twelve-wonders-of-the-world-set-of-roundels-unknown/.

[63] On this type of verse, see Fleming, *Graffiti*, 19–20.

[64] Rollins says of this editorial strategy: 'This skilful rearrangement should have convinced any prospective buyer that the edition was actually new'; *Poetical Rhapsody*, II, 12.

224   *A Poetical Rapsody*

poems are now in the section assigned to the Davison brothers in the anthology, while the 'Ten Sonnets by T. W.' and those of Best open the section of 'Sonnets, Odes, Elegies, and other Poesies'. Contents are also reorganised to make literary sense of the eight new poems added to the collection. Davison's 1608 'An Epitaph upon the hart of Henry the third, late King of France & Poland' has been moved from the middle of the volume to the final section, where it is placed so that it faces its 'pair' across the opening of the page – Charles Best's 'An Epitaph on *Henry* the fourth *the last French King*' (111v–12) newly added in 1611. In fact, all the new poems for this edition were penned by Charles Best.[65] This new section of Best's verse in *A Poetical Rapsody* is made up of an epitaph on Elizabeth I, followed by a series of panegyrics addressed to the royal family – James, Henry, and Elizabeth – finishing with a pair of Latin devotional poems with their English translations. Given the divisional title, '*Addit. per Cha. Best. Arm.*', it is presented as a little anthology of Best's poetry that has been willingly contributed by the author to complete *A Poetical Rapsody* and stands alongside the collections of the Davison brothers and Anomos, adding to the gathering of gentlemen authors in the anthology.

The fourth and final 1621 edition was extensively redesigned. With its new title, *Davisons Poems, or, A Poeticall Rapsody*, and substantially restructured into 'sixe Bookes', the anthology, which had now been in print for almost two decades, was given a new shelf-life. By 1621, redesigning previously printed books by dividing them into books had become a distinctive feature of Jackson's publishing practice. Revisions to Jackson's 1616 edition of Shakespeare's *Rape of Lucrece*, as has been well documented, involved subdividing this narrative poem into books, each with an argument, which were then listed on a contents page, and was a means of making this long narrative poem, as Jackson said of *The Rich Cabinet*, more 'orderly digested'.[66] Similarly, the title-page to *A Poetical Rapsody*, listing the six books, assures readers that this edition offers a new, improved reading experience: 'The fourth Impression, Newly corrected and augmented, and put into a forme more pleasing to the reader.'

---

[65] Little is known of Best. He was admitted to the Middle Temple in 1590, and took the role of the Orator in the Prince of Love in the 1597/8 Christmas revels; see, G. C. Moore Smith, 'Charles Best', *Review of English Studies*, 1 (1925), 454–6. John Davies of Hereford in his 1611 epigram addressed to Best, published the same year as this edition of *A Poetical Rapsody*, presses him to publish rather than 'be mute' (*The Scourge of Folly* (1611), 216).

[66] See Sasha Roberts, *Reading Shakespeare's Poems in Early Modern England* (Basingstoke: Palgrave Macmillan, 2003), 122–6; Katherine Duncan-Jones, 'Ravished and Revised: the 1616 *Lucrece*', *Review of English Studies*, 52, (2001), 516–23.

'Newly augmented and corrected' 225

The redesign of the 1621 edition necessarily required methods and systems of organisation since poems had to be classified and redistributed among the set of new books listed on the title-page: *'Poems and Devises'*, *'Sonets and Canzonets'*, *'Pastoralls and Elegies'*, *'Madrigalls and Odes'*, *'Epigrams and Epitaphs'*, and *'Epistles, and Epithalamions'*.[67] What collaborations were necessitated by this work, which involved devising new conceptual and physical categories, reading through the poems, and making decisions about their formal affiliations? Perhaps, as was the case with *A Rich Cabinet*, Jackson worked with a 'skilfull and industrious friend' or employed a writer, as was his practice in the case of the second 1620 edition of John Dennys's *The Secrets of Angling*, when he commissioned William Lawson to write additional material since Dennys had died many years earlier in 1609.[68]

Work on the 1621 edition was not uniform. Different methods were put into practice, some requiring more technical skills than others. For most of the 1621 categories – sonnet, pastoral, madrigal, ode, epigram, and epitaph – verse could be easily identified by the titles and headings provided in the previous editions. Since poems were transposed into these new categories in the same order that they appeared in the previous edition, it seems those responsible for this work read through the 1611 edition seriatim, systematically extracting verse according to its title. That said, sonnets not identified as such in their titles must have been selected through an assessment of their formal properties. New categories introduced in this 1621 edition – *'Devises'* and *'Canzonets'* – similarly required a more considered poetic assessment.[69] Poems selected for *'Devises'* indicate that this category was formulated with concepts of design and ingenuity in mind. Poems gathered in this section are examples of ornamental poetry and display a crafted materiality or technical virtuosity. Hence, the section opens with Davies's '12. wonders of the world' (D5v–8). Also included are the set of *'Inscriptions'* (D8–E1v), a pattern poem (E4v), dialogue poems that are examples of *prosopopoeia*, for example, the *'Dialogue betweene the Soule and the Body'* (E4v–F2v), or demonstrate other types of technical skill, such as those Sidneian experiments in quantitative metre, the phaleuciac and sapphic poems (E2v–3v, E5), and Best's Latin verses with their

---

[67] Compare Rollins's lists of contents for the 1611 and 1621 editions for the extent to which the 1621 edition has been 'completely rearranged'; Davison, *Poetical Rhapsody*, ed. Rollins, II, 17, 22.

[68] John Dennys, *The Secrets of Angling* (1620, STC 6611.5), A4.

[69] Here, I would depart from Piers Brown's reading that 'this is a pragmatic rather than a poetic re-ordering: the poems in each section appear in the same order as in the previous edition' ('Donne, Rhapsody', 53), which does not take into account these new categories.

226   *A Poetical Rapsody*

English translations (E6v–8). The new section of '*Canzonets*' similarly
required some judgement of form. Those working on this section read
through the anthology carefully selecting verse identified as songs or hymns
in their titles, or on the theme of music, or extracted verse composed in
sextains, variants of the sextilla, a Spanish ballad form.

While the level of knowledge of poetic form required for this work may
be open to question, nonetheless poetic assessments were made alongside
more pragmatic choices when selecting verse for the new books introduced
in the 1621 edition. Other aspects of this edition are less systematic and
instead illustrate the everyday contingencies of book production making
their way into the form of the anthology. The only new poems, two
epithalamia, added to the 1621 edition were printed on the last page of
the table of contents (A8v), before the 'First Booke of *Poems and Devises*',
even though the title-page informs the reader that it is the sixth and last
book that contains '*Epistles, and Epithalamions*'. By way of correction, a
further table is added below the epithalamia, 'A short Contents of all the
sixe Bookes contained *In this volume &c*', which lists at the end 'And
Epithalamions begins before folio 1' (A8v). The likely reason why these
epithalamia are not found at the end of the book is that they were a late
addition, probably acquired after printing had begun, and so squeezed into
available space at the front of the book, on a sheet that had not yet been
printed. This editorial decision was pragmatic, and also had the advantage
of making these new poems more visible, lending some credibility to the
claim on the title-page that this edition was 'Newly . . . augmented', when
there was, in fact, so little new verse in comparison with previous editions.

Discussions of *A Poetical Rapsody* have tended to focus on its gentleman
compiler, often describing the volume as 'Francis Davison's miscellany'.[70]
To an extent, this is justified. The 1621 edition, after all, is renamed
Davisons Poems, or, A Poeticall Rapsody, and this is how its fictions of
compilation operate, especially in the first edition, to fashion a gentleman
compiler and to locate the book within an elite performance culture of
private recreation. The story of its compilation, as we have seen, however,
is more entangled in the work of others than this fiction allows. When
looking across Davison's catalogues and the different editions of *A Poetical
Rapsody* put out across the first two decades of the seventeenth century, a
varied constellation of actors emerges, some identifiable, others unknown
or anonymous, deliberately so in the case of Anomos, or is it Anonymoi?
The publication of *A Poetical Rapsody* in 1602 did not bring the history of

---

[70] Wall, *Imprint of Gender*, 209.

'Elizabethan' anthologies to a close.[71] Instead, if we focus on publishers and other compilers, then this anthology, like others, makes visible an alternative history of publication. Questions then emerge of why certain publishers chose to invest in anthologies, what kind of publishing decisions they were making, and how they read the market for these books. In Jackson's case, his output and the prefaces he appends to books point to an interest in the craft of compilation and in handy books so that *A Poetical Rapsody* takes its place in his stock alongside practical manuals addressed to the gentry. What these anthologies offer, in their various iterations, is a rich history of book production and use, across a range of locales in early modern England.

[71] Pomeroy, *Elizabethan Miscellanies*, 119.

Conclusion

This book argues that using craft as a tool of analysis in the study of poetry anthologies means that it is possible to conceptualise processes of production, from compilation to poetic making and remaking, as embodied practices. The craft of anthology-making involved people, objects, and environments, from printing houses and bookshops to households in all their social diversity, and allows this study to attend to the microsocialities created through shared practices, textual material, and performances. Craft offers an incorporative model of literary history that brings together authors, compilers, publishers, printers, readers, and performers from across the social spectrum and tells stories of cultural formation that are alert to its hybridity. The form of the poetry anthology is itself incorporative, gathering a variety of poems that often have travelled and will travel widely, moving between the elite and non-elite, placing gentleman and gentlewomen alongside citizens, servants, and anonymous others, and capturing within their pages the heterogeneity of vernacular literary cultures. Attending to the crafting of anthologies therefore allows us to account for the variety of early modern recreational cultures and modes of poetic making that travel across the social spectrum and are constitutive of a domestic Renaissance that is always thoroughly heteroglot.

Craft intersects with the multivalent term 'recreation', which both refers to acts of remaking, especially through performance, and takes us to the recreational cultures of early modern England. A recreational poetics engaged these books and the poems they collect in processes of intermediation as they travelled within performance cultures, in which such ditties were read, sung, and used in games. Recent work on musical cultures of poetry and drama, such as that of Scott Trudell, Katherine Larson, and Simon Smith, has meant that we are now well placed to appreciate the recreative, performative properties of poetry anthologies. Bringing performance into the frame allows us to think about how the pleasures of the text are constitutive of genres and acoustic communities and to think about

Conclusion 229

poetic making in ways that are alert to poetry's sensory and affective properties. The resulting model of materiality moves away from the book-as-artefact to bring into play its extra-textual properties, how it is embodied, practised, experienced, and open to uses and performances that are contingent upon occasion and locale. If we look to the recreative affordances of the anthology, then it takes us to other types of books and textual materials. One of the most productive exchanges that has emerged from this study is the dialogue between poetry anthologies and ballads and songbooks, both in manuscript and in print. The popularity of the ballad anthology continued across the sixteenth and seventeenth centuries.[1] With the publication of printed songbooks in increasing numbers from the 1590s, this exchange becomes very audible and visible in the form of the poetry anthology. Elizabeth Pomeroy speculated that 'song collections may well have replaced the poetical miscellanies in popular appeal': 'Their great vogue, lasting to the 1630s, helps to explain the rather sudden end of the lyric miscellanies with *A Poetical Rhapsody* in 1602.'[2] While this sense of ending is overstated, as I have argued, the role of printed songbooks in shaping recreational cultures in the seventeenth century is a fruitful area for study that has begun to be explored by a new generation of scholars.[3]

Crafting Poetry Anthologies in Renaissance England turns attention to the ballads, ditties, and the idle forms of ornamental poetry that make up these books. In doing so, the aim has been to bring into focus the role of non-elite poetic cultures and alternative 'minor' traditions in shaping the history of English lyric poetry. Along the way, canonical authors, Wyatt, Surrey, Sidney, and Spenser, also make an appearance. However, the aim of this study is always to shift the focus off-centre and to look at traditions aslant. The incorporative form of the anthology allows me to locate these major authors in relation to minor poets, both male and female – Whitney, Munday, Breton, and the anonymous authors of ballads and other ditties – and others who are difficult to place, such as Mary Sidney, Countess of Pembroke. Mary Sidney was acknowledged as a creative force in literary culture by her contemporaries, yet, until relatively recently, has had an uncertain place in the literary canon. The reason I have returned to the generative trope of the company of women throughout this study is to

---

[1] Richard Johnson is credited with compiling ballad anthologies that were in print until the end of the seventeenth century; see Allan G. Chester, "Richard Johnson's *Golden Garland*', *Modern Language Quarterly*, 10 (1949), 61–7.
[2] Pomeroy, *Elizabethan Miscellanies*, 105–6.
[3] See, for example, the work of Katherine Larson and Scott Trudell.

230   Conclusion

open the poetry anthology to women, as authors, readers, performers, and makers of texts and compilers of books. It is a resonant trope that is variously articulated across the anthologies in this study, performing diverse functions, from shaping a concept of a civic and domestic Renaissance through the mother tongue to models of recreative poetic making embodied in an ornamental poetics.

The poetry anthology is both distinctive and intersects with other forms of compiled books. This study, therefore, has been necessarily selective, rather than providing as exhaustive survey. Anthologies are grouped chronologically and by publisher to allow variant expressions of anthology-making, poetic craft, and cultures of recreation to be explored. The study sets out phases of anthology production, tracing changes across the output of publishers like Jones, in order to chart patterns of response and innovation. This book may end with *A Poetical Rapsody*, but by tracking further editions of this and other anthologies my purpose is to disrupt any sense of a clear end to a phase of anthology production in 1603 with the passing of the Elizabethan era. Instead, other avenues for exploration emerge, including the role of publishers in making other types of compilations, evident in the vogue for anthologies of madrigals, airs, and other song forms in the seventeenth century. Above all, what I have aimed to bring to the study of the poetry anthology is an appreciation of its re-creative capacities

Bibliography

Manuscripts
Bodleian Library (Bod.), Oxford

MS Add. B. 105
MS Ashmole 48
MS Douce e.16
MS Rawl. poet. 85
MS Rawl. poet. 108
MS Rawl. poet. 148

British Library (BL)

Add. MS 4900
Add. MS 15117
Add. MS 15227
Add. MS 36526A
Add. MS 38599
Harley MS 280
Harley MS 298
Harley MS 2127
Harley MS 6910
Egerton MS 3165

Folger Shakespeare Library

MS v.a.149

Royal College of Music (RCM)

MS 722
MS 2111

232   *Bibliography*

Printed Primary Sources

Since anthologies do not necessarily have a single author or compiler, I have followed the naming in *The English Short-Title Catalogue* for ease in finding. Unless otherwise stated, the place of publication is London.

Allott, Robert. *Wits Theater of the Little World.* James Roberts for Nicholas Ling, 1599.
Englands Parnassus. Nicholas Ling, Cuthbert Burby, and Thomas Hayes, 1600.
Balthorpe, Nicholas. *A Newe Balade Made by Nicholas Balthorp which Suffered in Calys the .xv. Daie of Marche.* John Waley, 1557.
Barley, William. *A New Booke of Tabliture.* John Danter for William Barley, 1596.
Bellot, Jacques. *La Maistre d'Escole Anglois.* Thomas Purfoote for Henry Disle, 1580.
Becon, Thomas, *A Pleasaunt Newe Nosegaye Full of Many Godly and Swete Floures, Lately Gathered by Theodore Basille.* John Mayler for John Gough, 1542.
Boaistuau, Pierre. *Theatrum Mundi, the Theatre or Rule of the World.* Henry Denham for Thomas Hacket, 1566.
Bodenham, John. *Bel-vedére or the Garden of the Muses.* [Felix Kingston] for Hugh Astley, 1600.
Englands Helicon. James Roberts for John Flasket, 1600.
Englands Helicon. Or the Muses Harmony. Thomas Snodham for Richard More, 1614.
England's Helicon, edited by H. R. Rollins, 2 vols. Cambridge, MA: Harvard University Press, 1935.
Breton, Nicholas. *The Arbor of Amorous Deuices.* Richard Jones, 1597.
The Arbor of Amorous Devices: 1597, edited by H. R. Rollins. Cambridge, MA: Harvard University Press, 1936.
Brittons Bowre of Delights. Richard Jones, 1591.
Brittons Bowre of Delights. Richard Jones, 1597.
Floorish vpon Fancie. [William How] for Richard Jones, 1577.
Floorish vpon Fancie. Richard Jones, 1582.
Floorish vpon Fancie. Richard Jones, c. 1585.
The Historie of the Life and Fortune of Don Frederigo. John Charlewood for Richard Jones, 1590.
The Pilgrimage to Paradise, Ioyned with the Countesse of Penbrookes Loue. Oxford: Joseph Barnes, 1592.
A Smale Handfull of Fragrant Flowers. Richard Jones, 1575.
The Workes of a Young Wyt, Trust up with a Fardell of Pretie fancies. Thomas Dawson and Thomas Gardiner, 1577.
Brinsley, John. *Ludus Literarius.* [Humphrey Lownes] for Thomas Man, 1612.
Byrd, William. *Psalmes, Sonets, & Songs of Sadnes and Pietie.* Thomas Este, 1588–9.
Cavendish, Michael. *14. Ayres in Tabletorie.* Peter Short, 1598.

Bibliography   233

Chamberlain, John. *The Letters of John Chamberlain*, ed. Norman Egbert McClure, 2 vols. Philadelphia: American Philosophical Society, 1939.

Corkine, William. *Ayres, to Sing and Play*. William Stansby for John Brown, 1610.

Davison, Francis. *Dauisons Poems, or, A Poeticall Rapsody*. Bernard Alsop for Roger Jackson, 1621.

A Poetical Rapsody. Valentine Simmes for John Bailey, 1602.

A Poetical Rapsodie. Nicholas Okes for Roger Jackson, 1608.

A Poetical Rapsodie. William Stansby for Roger Jackson, 1611.

A Poetical Rhapsody, edited by H. R. Rollins, 2 vols. Cambridge, MA: Harvard University Press, 1931.

Day, John. *Law-trickes*. Edward Allde for Richard More, 1608.

Dennys, John. *The Secrets of Angling*. Roger Jackson, 1620.

Donne, John. *Ignatius his Conclaue*. Nicholas Okes for Richard More, 1611.

Dowland, John. *The Firste Booke of Songes or Ayres*. Peter Short, 1597, 1600.

Edwards, Richard. *The Excellent Comedie of Two the Moste Faithfullest Freendes, Damon and Pithias*. [William Williamson] for Richard Jones, 1571.

The Paradyse of Daynty Deuises. [Richard Jones?] for Henry Disle, 1576.

The Paradyse of Daynty Deuises. [Richard Jones?] for Henry Disle, 1578.

The Paradyse of Daintie Deuises. [Richard Jones?] for Henry Disle, 1580.

The Paradise of Daintie Deuises. Robert Waldegrave for Edward White, 1585.

[The Paradise of Daintie Deuises.] [Edward Allde?] for Edward White, 1590?.

The Paradice of Dainty Deuises. Edward Allde for Edward White, 1596.

The Paradice of Dainty Deuises. [James Roberts] for Edward White, 1600.

The Paradise of Daintie Deuises. [John Windet] for Edward White, 1606.

The Paradise of Dainty Devices (1576–1606), edited by H. R. Rollins. Cambridge, MA: Harvard University Press, 1927.

The Works of Richard Edwards: Politics, Poetry and Performance in Sixteenth Century England, edited by Ros King (Manchester University Press, 2001).

Farmer, John. *The First Set of English Madrigals*. William Barley, 1599.

Forster, Richard. *Ephemerides meteora graphicae*. John Kingston for Henry Disle, 1575.

Fulwood, William. *A New Ballad against Vnthrifts*. John Allde, 1562.

A Supplication to Eldertonne. John Allde, 1562.

Gascoigne, George. *A Hundreth Sundrie Flowres Bounde up in One Small Poesie*. Henry Bynneman and Henry Middleton for Richard Smith, 1573.

Greene, Robert. *Greene's Neuer Too Late*. James Roberts for Nicholas Ling, 1600.

Menaphon. Valentine Simmes for Nicholas Ling, 1599.

Hall, John. *[The Courte of Vertue]*. Thomas Marshe, 1565.

The Court of Virtue (1565), ed. Russell A. Fraser. Routledge and Kegan Paul, 1961.

Psalmes of Dauid Drawen into English Metre by Tomas Sterneholde. Edward Whitchurch, 1551.

Harington, John. *The Arundel Harington Manuscript of Tudor Poetry*, edited by Ruth Hughey, 2 vols. Columbus: Ohio State University Press, 1960.

Heresbach, Conrad. *The Whole Art of Husbandry*. Thomas Cote for Richard More, 1631

234   *Bibliography*

Heywood, Thomas. *The Dramatic Works*, 6 vols. J. Pearson, 1874.

Holborne, Anthony. *The Cittharn Schoole*. Peter Short, 1597.

Holland, Philemon. *The Philosophie, Commonlie Called the Morals Written by the Learned Philosopher Plutarch*. Arnold Hatfield, 1603.

Hollyband, Claudius. *The Frenche Schoolemaister*. William How for Abraham Veale, 1573.

Howard, Henry, Earl of Surrey. *An Excellent Epitaffe of Syr Thomas Wyat with Two Other Compendious Dytties*. John Herford for Robert Toy, 1545.

The Fourth Boke of Virgill, Intreating of the Love betweene Aeneas & Dido, Translated into English, and Drawne into a Strauge Metre by Henrye Late Earle of Surrey. John Day for William Awen, 1554.

Songes and Sonettes, Written by Henry Haward Late Earle of Surrey, and Other. Richard Tottel, 1557 [STC 13860, Q1].

Songes and Sonettes, Written by Henry Haward Late Earle of Surrey, and Other. Richard Tottel, 1557. [STC 13861, Q2; STC 13862]

Songes and Sonettes, Written by Henry Haward Late Earle of Surrey, and Other. Richard Tottel, 1559.

Songes and Sonettes, Written by Henry Haward Late Earle of Surrey, and Other. Richard Tottel, 1565.

Songes and Sonettes, Written by Henry Haward Late Earle of Surrey, and Other. Richard Tottel, 1567.

Songes and Sonettes, Written by Henry Haward Late Earle of Surrey, and Other. Richard Tottel, 1574.

Songes and Sonettes, Written by Henry Haward Late Earle of Surrey, and Other. John Windet, 1585.

Songes and Sonettes, Written by Henry Haward Late Earle of Surrey, and Other. Richard Robinson, 1587.

Tottel's Miscellany, edited by H. R. Rollins, 2 vols., 1928; Cambridge, MA: Harvard University Press, 1966.

Tottel's Miscellany, edited by Amanda Holton and Tom McFaul. Penguin, 2011.

Howell, Thomas. *The Arbor of Amitie*. Henry Denham, 1568.

I. P. *A Meruaylous Straunge Deformed Swyne*. William How for Richard Jones, 1570.

Jones, Robert. *Cantus: the First Set of Madrigals*. John Windet, 1607.

The First Booke of Songes & Ayres. Peter Short, 1600.

Vltimvm Vale. John Windet for Simon Waterson, 1605.

Ling, Nicholas. *Politeuphuia, Wits Common Wealth*. James Roberts for Nicholas Ling, 1597.

Littleton, Thomas. *Lyttylton Tenures Newly Revised and Truly Corrected with a Table*. William Powell, 1553.

Lloyd, Lodowick. *An Epitaph vpon the Death of the Honorable, Syr Edward Saunders Knight*. Henry Singleton for Henry Disle, 1576.

Bibliography   235

Lodge. *Thomas Margarite of America.* Abel Jeffes for John Busbie,1596.
Phillis. James Roberts for John Busbie, 1593.
Prosopopeia: The Teares of the Holy, Blessed, and Sanctified Marie, the Mother of God. Thomas Scarlett for Edward White, 1596.
Rosalynde. Abel Jeffes for Nicholas Ling and Thomas Gubbins,1596.
Rosalynde. Valentine Simmes for Nicholas Ling and Thomas Gubbins,1598.
A Treatise of the Plague. Thomas Creede and Valentine Simmes for Edward White and Nicholas Ling, 1603.
M. B., *The Triall of True Friendship.* Valentine Simmes, 1596.
Morley, Thomas. *The First Booke of Ayres.* Henry Ballard for William Barley, 1600.
Madrigalls to Fovr Voyces. Thomas Este, 1594.
Mulliner, Thomas. *The Mulliner Book,* ed. John Caldwell. Stainer and Bell, 2011.
Munday, Anthony. *A Banquet of Daintie Conceits.* John Charlewood for Edward White, 1588.
Fedele and Fortunio. John Charlewood? for Thomas Hackett, 1585.
The Mirrour of Mutability. John Allde for Richard Ballard, 1579.
The Second Booke of Primaleon of Greece. John Danter for Cuthbert Burby, 1596.
Nichols, Josias. *A Spirituall Poseaye Contayning Most Godly and Fruictfull Consolations and Prayers.* William Williamson for John Harrison, 1572.
Partridge, John. *The Widowes Treasure.* John Kingston for Henry Disle, 1582.
Pilkington, Francis. *The First Booke of Songs or Ayres.* Thomas Este, 1605.
Proctor, Thomas. *A Gorgeous Gallery of Gallant Inventions* (1578), edited by H. R. Rollins. Cambridge, MA: Harvard University Press, 1926.
A Gorgious Gallery of Gallant Inuentions. [William How] for Richard Jones, 1578.
The Triumph of Trueth. Yareth James, 1585?.
Puttenham, George. *The Art of English Poesy: a Critical Edition, Edited by Frank Whigham and Wayne Rebhorn.* Ithaca: Cornell University Press, 2007.
R. S. *The Phoenix Nest.* John Jackson [Eliot's Court Press], 1593.
The Phoenix Nest, ed. H. E. Rollins. 1931; Cambridge, MA: Harvard University Press, 1969.
R. T. *Two Tales, Translated out of Ariosto.* Valentine Simmes, 1597
Rich, Barnabe *A Right Exelent and Pleasaunt Dialogue between Mercury and an English Souldier.* John Day for Henry Disle, 1574.
Robinson, Clement. *[A Handefull of Pleasant Delites].* [W. How? for Richard Jones, c. 1575].
A Handefull of Pleasant Delites. Richard Jones, 1584.
[A Handefull of Pleasant Delites]. [John Danter for Richard Jones, c. 1595].
A Handful of Pleasant Delights by Clement Robinson and Divers Others, edited by H. R. Rollins. Massachusetts, MA: Harvard University Press, 1924.
Shakespeare, William. *The Passionate Pilgrime.* Thomas Judson for William Jaggard, 1599.

236 *Bibliography*

Sidney, Philip, Sir. *An Apologie for Poetrie.* [James Roberts] for Henry Olney, 1595.

The Countesse of Pembrokes Arcadia. [John Windet] for William Ponsonbie, 1590.

Syr P. S. His Astrophel and Stella. [John Charlewood] for Thomas Newman, 1591.

Spenser, Edmund. *Colin Clouts Come Home Againe.* [Thomas Creede] for William Ponsonby, 1595.

The Shorter Poems, edited by Richard McCabe. Penguin, 1999.

T. F. *Newes from the North.* John Allde, 1579.

T. G. *The Rich Cabinet.* John Beale for Roger Jackson, 1616.

Tusser, Thomas. *Fiue Hundreth Points of Good Husbandry.* Richard Tottel, 1573.

A Hundreth Good Pointes of Husbandry. Richard Tottel, 1557.

A Hundreth Good Pointes of Husbandry. Henry Denham for Richard Tottel, 1570.

Twyne, Thomas. *The Schoolemaster, or Teacher of Table Philosophie.* Richard Jones, 1576.

Weelkes, Thomas. *Cantus Primus. Madrigals to 3.4.5. & 6. Voyces.* Thomas Este, 1597.

Whetstone, George. *The Rocke of Regard Diuided into Foure Parts.* Henry Middleton for Robert Waley, 1576.

Whitney, Isabella. *The Copy of a Letter, Lately Written in Meeter, by a Yonge Gentilwoman.* Richard Jones, 1567?

[A Sweet Nosgay, or Pleasant Posye]. [Richard Jones, 1573?]

Thomas Whythorne, *The Autobiography of Thomas Whythorne: a Modern Spelling Edition,* edited by James M. Osborn. Oxford University Press, 1962.

Triplex, of Songs, for Three, Fower, and Five Voyces. John Day, 1571.

Nicholas Yonge, *Mvsica Transalpina.* Thomas Este, 1588.

Selected Secondary Sources

Alexander, Gavin. 'The Musical Sidneys', *John Donne Journal,* 25 (2006), 65–105.

'*Prosopopoeia' in Renaissance Figures of Speech,* edited by Sylvia Adamson, Gavin Alexander, and Katrin Ettenhuber. Cambridge University Press, 2007. 107–9.

Writing After Sidney: The Literary Response to Sir Philip Sidney, 1586-1640. Oxford University Press, 2006.

Anderson, Randall. 'Metaphors of the Book as Garden in the English Renaissance', *Yearbook of English Studies,* 33 (2003), 248–61.

Arber, Edward, ed. *Transcript of the Registers of the Company of Stationers of London, 1554–1640,* 5 vols. London: Stationers Company, 1875-7.

Bibliography 237

Arcangeli, Alessandro. *Recreation in the Renaissance: Attitudes towards Leisure and Pastimes in European Culture, c. 1425–1675*. Basingstoke: Palgrave Macmillan, 2003.

Auslander, Leora. 'Beyond Words', *American Historical Review*, 110 (2004), 1015–45.

Bates, Catherine. *Masculinity, Gender and Identity in the English Renaissance Lyric.* Cambridge University Press, 2007.

Baumann, Elizabeth Scott and Ben Burton, eds. *The Work of Form: Poetics and Materiality in Early Modern Culture*. Oxford University Press, 2014.

Blair, Ann. *Too Much to Know: Managing Scholarly Information before the Modern Age.* New Haven: Yale University Press, 2010.

Bland, Mark. *A Guide to Early Printed Books and Manuscripts*. Oxford: Wiley-Blackwell, 2010.

Boffey, Julia. 'Early Printers and English Lyrics: Sources, Selections and Presentations of Texts', *Papers of the Bibliographical Society of America*, 85 (1991), 11–26.

Brooks, Christopher. 'Apprenticeship, Social Mobility and the Middling Sort, 1500–1800', in *The Middling Sort of People: Culture, Society and Politics in England, 1500–1800*, edited by Jonathan Barry. Basingstoke: Palgrave, 1994. 52–83.

Brown, Piers. 'Donne, Rhapsody and Textual Order', in Eckhardt and Smith, eds., *Manuscript Miscellanies*. 39–55.

Burke, Peter. 'The Invention of Leisure in Early Modern Europe', *Past and Present*, 146 (1995), 136–50.

Burns, E. Jane. 'Sewing like a Girl: Working Women in the Chanson de Toile', in *Medieval Women's Song: Cross-Cultural Approaches*, edited by Ann Klinck and Ann Marie Rasmussen. Philadelphia: University of Pennsylvania Press, 2002. 98–124.

Butler, Shane. *The Ancient Phonograph*. New York: Zone Books, 2015.

Child, H. H. 'The Song Books and Miscellanies', in *The Cambridge History of English Literature*, edited by A. W. Ward and A. R. Waller, 15 vols. (New York: G. P. Putnam's Sons, 1907–17), IV, Chapter 6.

Cohen, Matt. *The Networked Wilderness: Communicating in Early New England.* Minneapolis: University of Minnesota Press, 2010.

Coldiron, Ann. *English Printing, Verse Translation, and the Battle of the Sexes, 1476–1557*. Farnham: Ashgate, 2009.

Cooper, Lisa H. *Artisans and Narrative Craft in Late Medieval England*. Cambridge University Press, 2011.

Craik, Katharine. *Reading Sensations in Early Modern England*. Basingstoke: Palgrave Macmillan, 2007.

Crane, Mary Thomas. *Framing Authority: Sayings, Self, and Society in Sixteenth-Century England*. Princeton University Press, 1993.

Eckhardt, Joshua. *Manuscript Verse Collectors and the Politics of Anti-Courtly Love Poetry*. Oxford University Press, 2009.

238 *Bibliography*

Eckhardt, Joshua and Daniel Starza Smith, eds. *Manuscript Miscellanies in Early Modern England*. Farnham: Ashgate, 2014.

Faber, Paul L. 'Ophelia's Songspace: Elite Female Musical Performance and Propriety on the Elizabethan and Jacobean Stage', in *Shakespeare, Music and Performance*, edited by Bill Barclay and David Lindley. Cambridge University Press, 2017. 59–70.

Ferguson, Craig W. *Valentine Simmes: Printer to Drayton, Shakespeare, Chapman, Greene, Dekker, Middleton, Daniel, Jonson, Marlowe, Marston, Heywood, and Other Elizabethans*. Charlottesville: Bibliographical Society, University of West Virginia, 1968,

Ferry, Anne. *Tradition and the Individual Poem: an Inquiry into Anthologies*. Stanford University Press, 2001.

Fleming, Juliet. 'Changed Opinion as to Flowers', in Smith and Wilson, eds., *Renaissance Paratexts*. Cambridge University Press, 2011, 48–64.

Graffiti and the Writing Arts of Early Modern England. Cambridge: Reaktion Books, 2001.

'How to Look at a Printed Flower', *Word and Image*, 22 (2006), 165–87.

'The Ladies' Man and the Age of Elizabeth', in *Sexuality and Gender in Early Modern Europe: Institutions, Texts, Images*, edited by James Turner. Cambridge University Press, 1993, 158–81.

Frye, Susan. *Pens and Needles: Women's Textualities in Renaissance England*. Philadelphia: University of Pennsylvania Press, 2013.

Fumerton, Patricia. 'Remembering by Dismembering: Databases, Archiving, and the Recollection of Seventeenth-Century Broadside Ballads', in *Ballads and Broadsides in Britain, 1500–1800*, edited by Patricia Fumerton, Anita Guerrini, and Kris McAbee. Farnham: Ashgate, 2010.

Unsettled: the Culture of Mobility and the Working Poor in Early Modern England. University of Chicago Press, 2006.

Gadd, Ian. '"Being like a field": Corporate identity in the Stationers' Company, 1557-1684', unpublished DPhil. thesis, Oxford University, 1999.

Gibson, Jonathan. 'Casting Off Blanks: Hidden Structures in Early Modern Paper Books', in *Material Readings of Early Modern Culture: Texts and Social Practices, 1580–1730*, edited by James Daybell and Peter Hinds (Basingstoke: Palgrave Macmillan, 2010), 208–28.

Gillespie, Alexandra. 'Poets, Printers, and Early English Sammelbände', *Huntingdon Library Quarterly*, 67 (2004), 189–214.

Gordon, Andrew. *Writing Early Modern London: Memory, Text and Community*. Basingstoke: Palgrave Macmillan, 2013.

Greg, W. W. and E. Boswell, eds. *Records of the Stationers' Company, 1576 to 1602 from Register B*. London: Bibliographical Society, 1930.

Hamling, Tara and Catherine Richardson. *A Day at Home in Early Modern England: Material Culture and Domestic Life, 1500–1700*. New Haven: Yale University Press, 2017.

Hamrick, Stephen, ed. *Tottel's Songes and Sonettes in Context*. Farnham: Ashgate, 2013.

Bibliography 239

Heale, Elizabeth. 'Misogyny and the Complete Gentleman in Early Printed Poetry Miscellanies', *Yearbook of English Studies*, 33 (2003), 233–47

Wyatt, Surrey, and Early Tudor Poetry. London: Longman, 1998.

Hebel, William J. 'Nicholas Ling and *Englands Helicon*', *The Library*, 5 (1924), 153–60.

Heffernan, Megan. 'Gathered by Invention: Additive Forms and Inference in Gascoigne's Poesy', *Modern Language Quarterly*, 76 (2015), 413–45.

Holton, Amanda. 'An Obscured Tradition: the Sonnet and its Fourteen-Line Predecessor', *Review of English Studies*, 62 (2001), 389–91.

Hunter, Paul J. 'Poetry on the Page: Visual Signalling and the Mind's Ear', in Baumann and Burton eds., *Work of Form*. 180–96.

Johns, Adrian. *Nature of the Book: Print and Knowledge in the Making*. Chicago University Press, 1998.

Johnson, Gerard. 'Nicholas Ling, Publisher 1580–1607', *Studies in Bibliography*, 38 (1985), 203–14.

'The Stationers versus the Drapers: Control of the Press in the Late Sixteenth Century', *The Library*, 10 (1988), 1–16.

Jowett, John. 'Henry Chettle: "Your Old Compositor"', *Text*, 15 (2003), 141–61.

Kalas, Rayna. *Frame, Glass, Verse: the Technology of Poetic Invention in the English Renaissance*. Ithaca: Cornell University Press, 2007.

Kernan, Joseph. 'Elizabethan Anthologies of Italian Madrigals', *Journal of the American Musicological Society*, 4 (1951), 122–38.

King, Ros. 'Seeing the Rhythm: an Interpretation of Sixteenth-Century Punctuation and Metrical Practice', in *Ma(r)king the Text: the Presentation of Meaning on the Literary Page*, edited by Joe Bray, Miriam Handley, and Anne C. Henry. Aldershot: Ashgate, 2000. 235–52.

Kiséry, András and Allison Deutermann. 'The Matter of Form: Book History, Formalist Criticism, and Francis Bacon's Aphorisms', in *The Book in History, the Book as History: New Intersections in the Material Text*, edited by Heidi Brayman, Jesse M. Lander, and Zachary Lesser. New Haven: Yale University Press, 2016. 29–63.

Knight, Jeffrey Todd. *Bound to Read: Compilations, Collections, and the Making of Renaissance Literature*. Philadelphia: University of Pennsylvania Press, 2013.

Krummel, D. W. *English Music Printing, 1553–1700*. London: Bibliographical Society, 1975.

Larson, Katherine. *The Matter of Song in Early Modern England: Texts in and of the Air*. Oxford University Press, 2019.

Lesser, Zachary. *Renaissance Drama and the Politics of Publication*. Cambridge University Press, 2004.

Lesser, Zachary and Peter Stallybrass, 'The First Literary *Hamlet* and the Commonplacing of Professional Plays', *Shakespeare Quarterly*, 59 (2008), 371–420.

Levine, Caroline. *Forms: Whole, Rhythm, Hierarchy, Network*. Princeton University Press, 2015.

Bibliography

Livingston, Carole Rose. *British Broadside Ballads of the Sixteenth Century: a Catalogue of the Extant Sheets and an Essay.* New York: Garland, 1991.

Love, Harold. *Scribal Publication in Seventeenth-Century England.* Oxford: Clarendon Press, 1993.

McCoy, Richard. *The Rites of Knighthood: the Literature and Politics of Elizabethan Chivalry.* Berkeley: University of California Press, 1989.

McKerrow, R. B. *Printers' and Publishers' Devices in England and Scotland, 1485–1640.* London: Bibliographical Society, 1913.

Marotti, Arthur. *Manuscript, Print, and the English Renaissance Lyric.* Ithaca: Cornell University Press, 1995.

Marquis, Paul. 'Printing History and Editorial Design in the Elizabethan Version of Tottel's *Songes and Sonettes*', in Hamrick, ed., *Tottel's Songes.* 13–36.

Marsh, Christopher. *Music and Society in Early Modern England.* Cambridge University Press, 2010.

Massai, Sonya. *Shakespeare and the Rise of the Editor.* Cambridge University Press, 2007.

Matz, Robert. *Defending Literature in Early Modern England: Renaissance Literary Theory in Social Context.* Cambridge University Press, 2000.

May, Steven. *The Elizabethan Courtier Poets: Their Poems and their Contexts.* 1991; Asheville, NC: Pegasus Press, 1999.

'Popularizing Courtly Poetry: Tottel's Miscellany and its Progeny', in *The Oxford Handbook of Tudor Literature, 1485–1603,* edited by Mike Pincombe and Cathy Shrank. Oxford University Press, 2009. 418–31

'William Hunnis and the 1577 Paradyse of Dainty Devices', *Studies in Bibliography,* 28 (1975), 63–80.

May, Steven and William Ringler, *Elizabethan Poetry: a Bibliography and First-Line Index of English Verse, 1559–1603,* 3 vols. London: Thoemmes Continuum, 2004.

Maynard, Winifred. *Elizabethan Lyric Poetry and Its Music.* Oxford: Clarendon Press, 1986.

Melnikoff, Kirk. *Elizabethan Publishing and the Makings of Literary Culture.* University of Toronto Press, 2018.

Mentz, Steve. *Romance for Sale in Early Modern England: the Rise of Prose Fiction.* Aldershot: Ashgate, 2006.

Miller, Jacqueline T. 'Mother Tongues: Language and Lactation in Early Modern Literature', *English Literary Renaissance,* 27 (1997), 177–96.

Montrose, Louis Adrian. 'Of Gentlemen and Shepherds: the Politics of Elizabethan Pastoral Form', *English Literary History,* 50 (1983), 415–59.

Morgan, Paul. 'Frances Wolfreston and "Hor Bouks": a Seventeenth-Century Woman Book-Collector', *The Library,* 11 (1989), 197–218.

Nebeker, Eric. 'Broadside Ballads, Miscellanies, and the Lyric in Print', *English Literary History,* 76 (2009), 989–1013.

Nelson, Katie. 'Love in the Music Room: Thomas Whythorne and the Private Affairs of Tudor Music Tutors', *Early Music,* 40 (2012), 15–26.

Bibliography

Newcomb, Lori Humphrey. *Reading Popular Romance in Early Modern England.* New York: Columbia University Press, 2002.

North, Marcy. 'Amateur Compilers, Scribal Labour, and the Contents of Early Poetic Miscellanies', *English Manuscript Studies, 1100–1700*, 16 (2017), 82–111.

The Anonymous Renaissance: Cultures of Discretion in Tudor–Stuart England. University of Chicago Press, 2003.

O'Callaghan, Michelle. 'Collecting Verse: "Significant Shape" and the Manuscript Book in the Early Seventeenth Century', *Huntington Library Quarterly*, 80 (2017), 309–24.

'"Good Ladies be Working": Singing at Work in Tudor Women's Song', *Huntington Library Quarterly*, 82 (2019), 107–26.

'"my printer must, haue somwhat to his share": Isabella Whitney, Richard Jones, and Crafting Books', *Women's Writing* 26 (2019), 15–34.

The 'Shepheards Nation': Jacobean Spenserians and Early Stuart Political Culture, 1612–1625. Oxford: Clarendon Press, 2000.

Parker, Patricia. '"Rude Mechanicals": A Midsummer Night's Dream and Shakespearean Joinery', in *Shakespeare from the Margins: Language, Culture, Context.* University of Chicago Press, 1996.

Parkes, M. B. *Pause and Effect: an Introduction to the History of Punctuation in the West.* Aldershot: Scolar, 1992.

Scribes, Scripts and Readers: Studies in the Communication, Presentation and Dissemination of Medieval Texts. London: Hambledon Press, 1991.

Pender, Patricia. *Early Modern Women's Writing and the Rhetoric of Modesty.* Basingstoke: Palgrave Macmillan, 2012.

Pennell, Sarah and Natasha Glaisyer, eds. *Didactic Literature in England, 1500–1800: Expertise Constructed.* Aldershot: Ashgate, 2003.

Pincombe, Mike, and Cathy Shrank, eds. *The Oxford Handbook of Tudor Literature, 1485–1603.* Oxford University Press, 2009.

Pomeroy, Elizabeth W. *The Elizabethan Miscellanies: their Development and Conventions*, University of California English Studies 36. Los Angeles: University of California Press, 1973.

Powell, Jason. 'The Network Behind "Tottel's Miscellany"', *English Literary Renaissance*, 46 (2016), 193–224.

Reid, Lindsay Ann. *Ovidian Bibliofictions and the Tudor Book: Metamorphosing Classical Heroines in Late Medieval and Renaissance England.* Farnham: Ashgate, 2014.

Roberts, Sasha. *Reading Shakespeare's Poems in Early Modern England.* Basingstoke: Palgrave Macmillan, 2003.

'Women's Literary Capital in Early Modern England: Formal Composition and Rhetorical Display in Manuscript and Print', *Women's Writing*, 14 (2007), 246–69.

Robson, Mark. *The Sense of Early Modern Writing: Rhetoric, Poetics, Aesthetics.* Manchester University Press, 2006.

242 *Bibliography*

Rollins, H. R. 'A. W. and "A Poetical Rhapsody"', *Studies in Philology*, 29 (1932), 239–51.

Rosenberg, Jessica. 'The Point of the Couplet: Shakespeare's *Sonnets* and Tusser's *A Hundreth Good Pointes of Husbandrie*', *English Literary History*, 53 (2016), 1–21.

St Clair, William. *The Reading Nation in the Romantic Period*. Cambridge University Press, 2004.

Sherman, William. 'On the Threshold: Architecture, Paratext and Early Print Culture', in *Agent of Change: Print Culture after Elizabeth L. Eisenstein*, edited by Sabrina Alcorn Baron, Eric Lindquist, and Eleanor Shevlin. Amherst: University of Massachusetts Press, 2007. 67–81.

Shrank, Cathy. '"Matters of Love as Discourse": the English Sonnet, 1560–1580', *Studies in Philology*, 105 (2008), 30–49.

Simpson, Claude M. *The British Broadside Ballad and Its Music*. New Brunswick: Rutgers University Press, 1966.

Smith, Bruce. *The Acoustic Worlds of Early Modern England: Attending to the O-Factor*. University of Chicago Press, 1999.

Smith, Helen. *Grossly Material Things: Women and Book Production in Early Modern England*. Cambridge University Press, 2012.

Smith, Helen and Louise Wilson, eds. *Renaissance Paratexts*. Cambridge University Press, 2011.

Smith, Pamela H. 'In the Workshop of History: Making, Writing, and Meaning', *West 86th*, 19 (2012), 4–31.

Smith, Simon. *Musical Response in the Early Modern Playhouse, 1603–1625*. Cambridge University Press, 2017.

Smyth, Adam. *Material Texts in Early Modern England*. Cambridge University Press, 2018.

'*Profit & Delight*': Printed Miscellanies in England, 1640–1682. Detroit: Wayne State University Press, 2004.

Stallybrass, Peter. '"Little Jobs": Broadsides and the Printing Revolution', in *Agents of Change: Print Culture Studies after Elizabeth L. Eisenstein*, edited by Sabrina Alcorn Baron, Eric Lindquist, and Eleanor Shevlin. Amherst: University of Massachusetts Press, 2007, 315–41.

Stevens, John. *Music and Poetry in the Early Tudor Court*. Cambridge University Press, 1961.

Straznicky, Marta, ed. *Shakespeare's Stationers: Studies in Cultural Bibliography*. Philadelphia: University of Pennsylvania Press, 2013.

Sullivan, Ceri. *The Rhetoric of Credit: Merchants in Early Modern Writing*. London: Associated University Presses, 2002.

Swann, Elizabeth. '"To dream to eat Books": Bibliophagy, Bees and Literary Taste in Early Modern Commonplace Culture', in *Text, Food and the Early Modern Reader: Eating Words*, edited by Jason Scott-Warren and Andrew Zurcher. New York: Routledge, 2018. 69–88.

Toft, Robert. *With Passionate Voice: Re-creative Singing in 16th-Century England and Italy*. Oxford University Press, 2014.

Bibliography 243

Tonry, Kathleen. *Agency and Intention in English Print, 1476–1526.* Turnhout: Brepols, 2016.

Trudell, Scott. 'Performing Women in English Books of Ayres', in *Gender and Song in Early Modern England,* edited by Leslie C. Dunn and Katherine Larson. Farnham: Ashgate, 2014. 15–29.

Unwritten Poetry: Song, Performance, and Media in Early Modern England. Oxford University Press, 2019.

Vine, Angus. *Manuscript Culture and the Early Modern Organization of Knowledge.* Oxford University Press, 2019.

Wall, Wendy. *The Imprint of Gender: Authorship and Publication in the English Renaissance.* Ithaca: Cornell University Press, 1993.

Recipes for Thought: Knowledge and Taste in the Early Modern Kitchen. Philadelphia: University of Pennsylvania Press, 2016.

Staging Domesticity: Household Work and English Identity in Early Modern Drama. Cambridge University Press, 2002.

Ward, John. 'Music for "A Handefull of pleasant delites"', *Journal of the American Musicological Society,* 10 (1957), 151–80.

Warner, J. Christopher. *The Making and Marketing of Tottel's Miscellany, 1557: Songs and Sonnets in the Summer of the Martyrs' Fires.* Farnham: Ashgate, 2013.

Winerock, Emily F. '"Mixt" and Matched: Dance Games in Late Sixteenth- and Early Seventeenth-Century Europe', *Playthings in Early Modernity: Party Games, Word Games, Mind Games,* edited by Allison Levy. Kalamazoo: Medieval Institute Publications, 2017. 29–48.

Withington, Philip. *The Politics of Commonwealth: Citizens and Freemen in Early Modern England* (Cambridge University Press, 2005).

'Two Renaissances: Urban Political Culture in Post-Reformation England Reconsidered', *Historical Journal,* 44 (2001), 239–67.

Woudhuysen, Henry. *Sir Philip Sidney and the Circulation of Manuscripts, 1558–1640.* Oxford: Clarendon Press, 1996.

Zarnowiecki, Matthew. *Fair Copies: Reproducing the English Lyric from Tottel to Shakespeare.* University of Toronto Press, 2014.

Zumthor, Paul. 'The Vocalization of the Text: the Medieval "Poetic Effect"', *Viator,* 19 (1988), 273–82.

Electronic Resources

Fumerton, Patricia. ed., *English Broadside Ballad Archive.* http://ebba.english.ucsb.edu.

Lindenbaum, Sarah. 'Frances Wolfreston Hor Bouks'. https://franceswolfrestonhorbouks.com.

O'Callaghan, Michelle and Alice Eardley, eds. *Verse Miscellanies Online: Printed Poetry Collections of the Sixteenth and Seventeenth Centuries.* http://versemiscellaniesonline.bodleian.ox.ac.uk/.

Index

Alexander, Gavin, 114
Allott, Robert, 153–4
Arbor of Amorous Devices, The, 8, 13, 114–15,
   130–1, 144, 149, 206
'A Lovers Farwel to his Love and Joy', 142
acrostics, 144
authors, 13–14, 37, 100–1, 120–2
   absent author, 10, 119, 175, 204
   anonymity, 109–10, 172, 200, 204, 215
   as artificer, 46, 106, 108, 113
   attribution, 37, 39, 47, 66–7, 100, 172–5, 200
   as compilers, 14, 105, 134–5
   gentleman, 104, 106, 120, 132, 142
   gentlewoman, 105, 109–12
   pseudonyms, 13, 38, 109, 172, 175–6
Awen, William, 23–4, 27

Bacon, Anthony, 197
Bacon, Sir Francis, 196, 199
ballads, 5, 16–17, 21, 41, 48–9, 58–9, 79–80,
   111, 142–3, 149
   ballad anthology, 75, 79, 187, 229
   Bod. MS Ashmole 48, 66–9, 82
   Canand, John
     'By fortune as I lay in bed', 63
     'O evill tounges, which clap at everie wynd',
      63
   Elderton, William, 67–8
     'Ye gods of Love that sit above', 143
   Fulwood, William
     'A New Ballad against unthrifts',
      68, 69
     'A supplication to Eldertonne', 68
   minstrels, 67, 69, 72
   moralising, 60, 80, 93
   Newe Balade Made by Nicholas Balthorp,
     65–6
   re-creative, 63–72, 78, 93, 104, 143
   Sheale, Richard, 67, 72
     'O god what a world ys this now to se', 67
   Spooner, Henry, 67, 82

'I wyll not paynt to purchase prayse', 68
'When Ragyng dethe doth drawe his darte',
   68–9
   tunes, 51, 80–2, 87–8, 92–3, 100, 142, 184
Barley, William, *New Booke of Tabliture, A*,
   148
Bateson, Thomas, *The First Set of English
   Madrigals*, 181
Becon, Thomas, *A Pleasaunt Newe Nosegaye*, 9
Bel-vedére or the Garden of the Muses, 9, 151,
   153–6, 175
Best, Charles, 222, 224
Bing, Henry, 199
Blount, Richard, 119
Bodenham, John, 150, 152–4, 161, 191
Boleyn, Anne, 55
Bolton, Edmund, 165–6, 167
book trade, 11, 111
booksellers
   Astley, Hugh, 154, 156
   Bailey, John, the younger, 205, 219
   Ballard, Richard, 98
   Burby, Cuthbert, 154
   Busby, John, 154
   Flasket, John, 154, 156–8, 161, 174
   Gubbins, Thomas, 154
   Hayes, Thomas, 154
   James, Yareth, 98
   Smethwicke, John, 154
   common profit, 10, 22–7, 75, 119, 140, 155,
     159–61
   copyright, 157–8, 160–1
   craft, 9–10, 18, 35, 95, 138, 151, 155–6,
     158–65, 171, 177–8
   credit of, 24, 27
   cultural domain, 29, 95, 97–8, 119,
     155–61
   drapers, 97–8, 154, 156–7, 161
   editing. See *compilatio*
   grocers, 156
   printers, 10, 178, 203–7

Index

Allde, John, 68, 97–8, 105
Barnes, Joseph, 120
Charlewood, John, 156–7
Kingston, Felix, 154–6
Roberts, James, 154–8, 174, 177
Simmes, Valentine, 205
Waldegrave, Robert, 158
publishers, 9–10, 12, 18, 20–1, 23–7, 43, 80,
161, 192
women
Allde, Margaret, 105
Breton, Nicholas, 13, 101, 113, 118–24, 142,
145–6, 151, 166–7, 174, 176, 182, 229
'Amoris Lachrimae', 123
'Deepe lamenting loss of tresure', 123
'Oh dear love when shall it be' (*Astrophil and
Stella*), 123
'Phillida and Coridon', 166
Floorish upon Fancie, A, 73, 118
*Historie of the Life and Fortune of Don
Frederigo, The*, 119
Pilgrimage to Paradise, The, 120
Smale Handfull of Fragrant Flowers, A, 9, 73,
118
Workes of a Young Wyt, The, 92, 118
Bridges, John, Bishop of Oxford, 199
Brittons Bowre of Delights, 8, 114, 116, 118–21,
123–7, 131, 133, 141–4, 149, 206–7
acrostics, 144
'Amoris Lachrimae', 123–4, 128, 144
'Sweet birds that sit and sing', 143
'Good Muse rocke me asleepe', 125
Brooke, Christopher, *Two Elegies Consecrated
to. . . Henry Prince of Wales*, 191
Browne, William
The Shepheards Pipe, 191
*Two Elegies Consecrated to. . . Henry Prince of
Wales*, 191
Bryskett, Lodowick
'The Mourning Muse of Thestylis', 134, 136
'A pastorall Aeglogue upon the Death of Sir
Phillip Sidney Knight', 136
Butler, Shane, 55
Byrd, William, 151
Songs of Sundrie Natures, 183

Campion, Edmund, 41
Campion, Thomas, 129, 196,
217–18
Carr, Henry, 80
Cary, Lady Elizabeth, 191–2
Cavendish, Anne or Elizabeth, 144
Cecil, Robert, Earl of Salisbury, 199
Chamberlain, John, 196
Cheney, Patrick, 134

Child, H. H., 152
Churchyard, Thomas, 111
compilatio, 2, 6–9, 48, 85–6, 95, 105–8, 128–9,
135–6, 156
anthology, 6–10, 13, 98, 113, 116, 131,
136–7, 149, 159–60, 166, 179, 192,
203, 216, 226, 228–9
elegiac, 115–18, 121, 133–4, 136–7, 207
manuscript, 122–3
multimodality, 77–8, 169–70, 177–90,
228
pastoral, 151, 161–2
commonplace books, 6, 32, 44, 53, 95, 113,
128, 154, 158–60, 220
commonplace poems, 43–5, 52, 101,
168
editing, 11–13, 30–1, 33–4, 38–9, 42, 153,
158–84, 219–26
miscellaneous order, 7, 122, 215
motifs, 7–8, 77, 95, 106, 108, 127, 133, 137,
144, 152, 159, 194
Constable, Henry, 187, 217, 221
Constable, Sir John, 199, 221
Corkine, William, *Ayres to Sing and Play*, 187
Court of Venus, The, 7, 18, 21, 23, 59–61, 78
craft, 1–2, 8, 10, 12, 28, 33, 42, 70, 95–6,
228
poetic, 16, 44–5, 48, 74, 95, 98–106, 130,
137, 222–3
scribal, 122, 194–203
women, 105, 169
Crane, Mary Thomas, 11

Daniel, Samuel, 138, 205
Delia, 129
'Go wayling verse the infant of my love',
129–30
Davies, Sir John, 173, 217–18,
222–3
Davison, Francis, 12, 18, 173–4, 193–219,
221–3, 226
'The Masque of Proteus', 197, 199
Davison, Walter, 194, 202–4, 206, 209, 214,
217
Davison, William, 196, 199, 210
Dennys, John, *The Secrets of Angling*, 225
Devereux, Robert, Earl of Essex, 196–7, 199,
210
Dickenson, John, *The Shepheard's Complaint*,
173
Digges, Leonard, 30
Digges, William, 30
Disle, Henry, 17, 20, 26–30, 38–40, 43, 51, 75,
96, 119, 132, 155, 173
Donne, John, 221

246   *Index*

Dowland, John, 151, 173
Drayton, Michael, 157, 166, 175–6, 181
   Englands Heroicall Epistles, 157
   Idea. The Shepheards Garland, 175
   Ideas Mirrour, 157
   Owle, The, 157
Dudley, Ambrose, third Earl of Warwick, 121
Dudley, Robert, Earl of Leicester, 121, 132, 196
Duncombe, William, 199
Dyer, Sir Edward, 121–2, 124, 151, 173, 207

Edwards, Richard, 11, 20–1, 29–30,
   50
   Damon and Pithias, 29
Eliot's Court printing house, 131
Elizabeth I, Queen, 132, 167, 189, 197, 210,
   222, 224
   'When I was fayre and younge', 122
Elizabeth, Princess, 224
Englands Helicon, 8–9, 12, 18, 97, 126, 131, 138,
   149–93, 196, 215, 218
   'A Canzon Pastorall in honour of her
      Maiestie', 166
   'A Palinode', 166
   'A Pastorall Song betweene Phillis and
      Amarillis', 189
   'A Report Song in a Dreame', 182
   'A Roundelay between two shepherds', 181
   'A Song betweene Taurisius and Diana', 170
   'A sweete Pastorall', 176
   'Alanius the Sheepheard, his Dolefull Song',
   170
   'Alas, how I wander amidst these woods', 175
   'An Other of the Same Subject', 176–7
   'Beauty sate bathing by a spring', 187–9
   'Damaetas Jig in Praise of his Love', 181
   'Diaphenia like the Daffadown-dillie', 187
   'Doron's Jigge', 181
   'Faire Phillis and her Sheepheard', 184
   'Faustus and Firmius Sing to their Nimph by
      Turnes', 170, 180
   'Goe my flocke', 166, 181
   'Harpalus complaynt on Phillidaes love
      bestowed on Corin', 176
   'Hobbinolls Dittie in Prayse of Eliza Queene
      of the Sheepheards', 166–8
   'In Pescod time, when Hound to horne', 185
   'Like desert woods', 175
   'Melicertus Madrigale', 166
   'Menaphons Roundelay', 181
   'Oh woods unto your walks', 175
   'Olde Damons Pastorall', 166, 168
   'Onely joy, now heere you are', 165, 168–9,
      181, 207
   'Perigot and Cuddies Roundelay', 166, 181

'Phillidaes Love-call to her Coridon', 189
'Phoebe's Sonnet', 190
'Ring out your belles', 165
'Rosalindes Madrigall', 170
'Syrenus his Song to Dianaes Flock', 171
'The Sheepheard Arsilius, his Song to his
   Rebeck', 170
'The Sheepheard Eurymachus to his faire
   Sheepheardesse', 170
'The Sheepheards Daffadill', 166–8
'The Sheepheards Description of Love', 162–5
'The Sheepheards Song of Venus and Adonis',
   184
'The Shepherd's Brawl', 182
'Theorello. A Sheepheards Edillion', 166
'Thirsis to die desired', 189
'To Colin Cloute', 166
'When love was first begot', 187, 189
'When the dog', 175
'With fragrant flowers we strew the way', 187,
   189
Englands Parnassus, 9, 154

Faber, Paul, 219
Faille, Monsieur de la, 199
Faucet, George, 152
Fehrenbach, R. J., 109
Ferrabosco, Alfonso, 189
Finett, John, 121
Fleming, Juliet, 128, 177
Fraunce, Abraham, 137

Gainsford, Thomas, *The Rich Cabinet*, 220,
   223–4
Garret, Elizabeth, 144
Gascoigne, George, *A Hundreth Sundrie Flowres*,
   14, 105
Gastoldi, Giovanni Giacomo, 181
Gordon, Andrew, 14
Gorgious Gallery, of Gallant Inventions, A, 1, 3, 5,
   8, 12, 17, 73, 95–105, 112, 119, 130,
   133, 143, 159, 175
   'A Letter sent from beyond the Seaes to his
      Lover', 112
   'A Letter written by a yonge gentilwoman',
      112
   'A short Epistle written in behalf of N. B. to
      M. H.', 101
   'An other loving Letter', 112
   'The Lady beloved exclaimeth of the great
      untruth of her lover', 105
   'The lamentable lover abiding in the bitter
      bale of direfull doubts', 102–3
   'The Lamentacion of a Gentilwoman', 74,
      101, 105, 109–12

Index

'The Lover complayneth of his Ladies unconstancy', 103–4
Greene, Robert, 158, 180–1, 217
  Menaphon, 154, 166, 169
Greville, Fulke, 133, 173–4, 207
Grimald, Nicholas, 30, 34
Gunter, Edward, 92
Gunter, Elinor, 92

Hall, John, *The Courte of Vertue*, 21, 59–64, 68, 88
Hall, Joseph, 221
Hamling, Tara, 82
Handefull of Pleasant Delites, A, 5, 8, 11, 15, 17, 73, 75–83, 87–8, 92, 96, 100–1, 121, 148, 179, 187, 219
  'A proper new Song made by a Studient in Cambridge', 83
  'A proper wooing Song', 88
  'An answer as pretie to the scof of his Lady', 83
  'Attend thee, go play thee', 82–3, 87, 100
  'Dame Beauties replie to the Lover late at libertie', 103
  'Faine would I have a pretie thing', 95
  'Maid wil you marry?', 87–8, 92
  'Maide wil ye love me?', 87
  'The Complaint of a Woman Lover', 59, 83–6
  'The painefull plight of a Lover', 105
Harington, Sir John, 30, 221
Harvey, Elizabeth, 52
Hastings, Sarah, 144
Heale, Elizabeth, 55, 104
Henry IV, of France, 199
Henry, Prince of Wales, 224
Herbert, William, Earl of Pembroke, 205, 208
Heywood, Jasper, 37, 41–2
Heywood, John, 45, 51
Heywood, Thomas, *Fair Maid of the Exchange*, 143
Hodgson, Eleaz., 199
Hollyband, Claudius, *The Frenche Schoolmaister*, 50–1
household, 4–5, 22, 47–8, 82, 107–8, 112, 146, 148–9
  elite, 56
  godly, 48, 61, 66
  humanist, 46, 51
  maternal, 52–4
  poetics of, 16, 47, 63, 74, 78, 89–91, 169, 207
  recreation, 5, 16, 18, 49, 63, 69–70, 151, 184–90
Howard, Thomas, Earl of Norfolk, 23
Howell, Thomas, *The Arbor of Amitie*, 101–2
Hunnis, William, 38–9, 61

Jackson, John, 132
Jackson, Roger, 219–27
Jaggard, William, *The Passionate Pilgrime*, 13, 142
James I and VI of Scotland, King, 224
Johns, Adrian, 9
Jones, Richard, 14, 17, 27–9, 73–7, 79–81, 93, 105–6, 108–9, 115, 118–21, 124, 130–1, 149, 175, 191, 206, 208
Jones, Robert, 218–19
  Cantus. The First Set of Madrigals, 218
  The First Booke of Songes & Ayres, 218
  Ultimum Vale, 187, 218
Jones, William, 28
Jonson, Ben, 221

Kay, Dennis, 134
Kinwelmarsh, Francis, 37, 179

Lacy, Andrew, 63
Larson, Katherine, 228
Lawson, William, 225
Leche, John, 47
Leland, John, *Naeniae in mortem Thomæ Viat equitis incomparabilis*, 116–17, 133
Lesser, Zachary, 151, 154
Levine, Caroline, 4
Ling, Nicholas, 12, 153–5, 157–61, 166, 172–5, 191, 220
Littleton, Sir Thomas, *Tenures*, 31
Lloyd, Lodowick, 39
Lodge, Thomas, 40–2, 151, 157, 165–8, 175, 180, 187
  Rosalynde, 154, 169, 173, 175, 189–90

Mackwilliams, Elizabeth, 144
Mainwaring, George, 106
Malone, Edward, 98
Marbury, Francis, *The Marriage of Wit and Wisdom*, 82
Marlowe, Christopher, 73
Marotti, Arthur, 116
Marsh, Thomas, 60
Mary, Queen of Scots, 196, 199
materiality, 1, 229
  embodied, 4, 14–15, 49, 70, 78, 84, 92, 95, 104, 136, 144–5, 155, 171, 179, 182, 190, 214–15, 228–9
May, Steven, 39
Maynard, John
  The XII. Wonders of the World, 223
Melnikoff, Kirk, 76
More, Richard, 192
Morley, Thomas, 151
Mulliner, Thomas, 51–2, 57

248 Index

Munday, Anthony, 41, 98, 154, 157, 187–9, 229
  Banquet of Daintie Conceits, 187–8, 219
  Primaleon of Greece, 188
  'Sheepheard Tonie', 165–6, 175–7
music, 15, 21, 45, 49–52, 81, 148, 228–9
  dance songs, 56–7, 82, 87, 92–3, 142, 179,
    181–2
  music books, 6, 9, 18, 50–1, 70, 142, 148,
    178, 184, 187–9, 217–19, 223, 229
  musical literacy, 49, 51, 61, 148, 187–8
  and poetry, 15, 49, 64, 69, 103, 124, 137, 178
  re-creative, 57, 59–60, 64, 66, 72, 84, 136–7,
    143, 178

Nashe, Thomas, 125–9
  Syr P. S. His Astrophel and Stella, 124
Newman, Thomas, 116, 130, 132
  Syr P. S. His Astrophel and Stella, 124–30
Nichols, Josias, *A Spirituall Poseaye*, 9
Noel, Henry, 122
North, Marcy, 109, 195, 204
Norton, Thomas, 30

Ovid
  Amores, 127, 216
  Ars Amatoria, 85, 127–8
  Heroides, 56, 85, 110, 210
  Tristia, 111
Oxford, Earl of, Edward de Vere, 29, 37, 122

Paradyse of Daynty Devises, The, 3, 8–9, 11,
    17–18, 20–2, 26–30, 34–5, 37–43,
  · 46–7, 50–4, 75, 96, 100–1, 148, 166,
    173, 179, 219
  'An Epitaph upon the death of syr William
    Drury, Knight', 40
  'An Epitaph upon the death of the honorable,
    syr Edward Saunders', 39
  'For Whitsunday', 179
  'In goyng to my naked bedde', 52–4, 63, 130
  'Mine owne good father thou art gone', 39–40
  'My lucke is losse', 38, 109
  'O Soveraigne salve of sinne', 41
  'The wandering youth, whose race so rashlie
    runne', 47
paratext, 7, 106, 109, 171, 191, 219
  cancel slips, 173–4
  errata list, 27, 39, 173
  lineation, 81
  mise-en-page, 99, 135, 163, 178–9, 206–7, 222
  prefaces, 10, 121, 126, 132, 153, 158–61,
    203, 220
  table of contents, 32, 220–1, 224, 226
  title-pages, 7, 37–8, 79, 98, 121, 155, 192,
    194, 222–3, 225

titles, 32–3, 162, 168, 170, 221, 225
typography, 34–5, 100, 123, 134–6, 145, 165,
    177–82
Parker, Anne, 144
Parker, Patricia, 99
Parry, Sir Thomas, 197
Passionate Pilgrime, The, 114, 149
Peele, George, 122
Pender, Patricia, 130
Phoenix Nest, The, 8, 12, 114, 116, 131–4, 136,
    145–9, 153, 166, 175, 177, 193, 207
  'An Elegie, or friends passion, for his
    Astrophill', 133
  'An Epitaph upon the right Honorable sir
    Philip Sidney knight', 133
  'An Excellent Dreame of Ladies and their
    Riddles', 145–6
  'The Chesse Play', 147, 222
  'Her face, her tongue, her wit', 147
  'Most Rare, and Excellent Dreame', 146–7
  'The Preamble to N. B. his Garden plot', 145
  'The Description of Love', 162–5
Pilkington, Francis, *First Booke of Songs or Ayres*,
    187
Plat, Hugh, *The Floures of Philosophie*, 105, 108
Poetical Rapsody, A, 8, 18, 193–6, 199–227
  '12. Wonders of the World', 222–3, 225
  'A Dialogue Betweene Two Shepheards',
    208–9
  'A Hymne in prayse of Musicke', 218
  'A little Heard-Groom', 211
  'A Lotterie', 222–3
  'A Prosopopoeia', 214
  'A Shepheard poore, Eubulus, call'd he was',
    210
  'An Altare and Sacrifice to Disdaine', 216
  'An Epitaph on Henry the Fourth', 224
  'An Epitaph upon the Hart of Henry the
    Third', 224
  'Anomos', 202–3, 206, 211–12, 215–17, 224,
    226
  'Come gentle Heard-man, sit by mee', 201,
    211
  'Cupid abroad, was lated in the night', 217
  'Dedication of these Rimes, to his First Love',
    213
  'Dialogue between the Soul and the Body',
    225
  'Disprayse of a Courtly Life', 208–9
  'For when thou art not as thou wont of yore',
    211
  'Hee Demaunds Pardon, for Looking, Loving,
    and Writing', 214
  'Her Answere, in the same Rimes', 214
  'In health and ease am I', 218

Index

'Joyne Mates in mirth to mee', 206–8
'Love, if a God thou art', 218
'My muse by thee restor'd to life', 217
'Nature in her work doth give', 217
'Perin areed what new mischance betyde', 207, 211
'Roundelay in Inverted Rimes', 209
'Strephons Palinode', 210, 222
'Sweet love myne only treasure', 217
'Ten Sonnets by T. W.', 224
'Three Odes Translated out of Anacreon', 217
'Upon her Giving him Backe the Paper', 214
'Upon Presenting her with the Speech of Grayes-Inne Maske', 214
'Uraniaes Answer in Inverted Rimes', 209
'Yee ghastly Groves that heare my wofull cryes', 211
Politeuphuia, 13, 150, 154–5, 158–9
Pomeroy, Elizabeth, 6, 229
Ponsonby, William, 121, 134, 158, 181
Powell, Jason, 30
Powell, William, 31
Proctor, John, 97
Proctor, Thomas, 12, 96–8, 100, 175
Puttenham, George, *Art of English Poesy*, 64, 69, 101, 122, 141–3

Radcliffe, Bridget, Countess of Sussex, 148
Raleigh, Sir Walter, 133, 174, 217
Ratcliff, Katharine, 144
readers, 21, 179, 191
  as book buyers, 76
  as citizens, 25, 108
  correcting, 27, 172–3
  gentlemen, 97, 118–19, 121, 126, 141–2, 149, 206
  gentlewomen, 118
  servants, 90
  women, 85–6, 128
recreation, 3–5, 8, 14–17, 21–2, 73, 88, 115, 144, 168–9, 228
  garden, 7, 145–7, 188
  godly, 60–3, 66, 69
  multimodality, 15, 49, 63, 77, 143, 148, 151, 190, 223
  poetics of, 16–17, 115, 124–5, 138–48, 206–7, 228
  private, 140–1, 148, 194–5, 213–19
  reading for pleasure, 115, 124–5, 127–8, 145–8, 169, 189
renaissance, 43
  civic, 21, 25, 90, 95, 155, 230
  domestic, 46, 52–3, 81, 112, 230
Reshoulde, James, 'An Echo made in imitatione of Sr P Sidneys echo', 123

rhetorical figures
  anaphora, 'the dancing figure', 142
  apostrophe, 55, 84, 136–7, 208
  beau semblant, 140, 143, 146–7
  ploche, 103
  prosopopoeia, 52, 55, 58, 101, 137, 209, 214
Rich, Barnabe, 40
Richardson, Catherine, 82
Richardson, Thomas, 83
Richmond, Duchess of, Mary Howard (Fitzroy), 55
Roberts, Sasha, 141
Robinson, Clement, 12
Rollins, H. R., 131, 150, 175, 200, 215
Rosseter, Philip, *A Booke of Ayres*, 218
Roydon, Matthew, 133
Roydon, Owen, 97

Sackville, Thomas, Earl of Dorset, 223
St Clair, William, 157, 160
Saville, Henry, 199
Shakespeare, William, 5, 73
  Hamlet, 72
  Merry Wives of Windsor, The, 148
  Passionate Pilgrime, The, 13, 142
  Rape of Lucrece, 224
Sheale, Richard, 82
Shepherd, John, 57
Sherman, William, 127
Sherry, Richard, *A Treatise of Schemes and Tropes*, 23
Sidney, Mary, Countess of Pembroke, 120, 130, 134–5, 138–9, 192, 207–9, 221, 229
  'I sing devine Astreas Prayse', 201
Sidney, Sir Philip, 5, 17, 73, 99, 113–18, 124–7, 132–4, 138–9, 146, 151, 165–6, 168–9, 174, 176, 181, 191, 196–7, 204–9, 213–16, 222, 229
  An Apologie for Poetrie, 138, 206
  Astrophil and Stella, 114, 116, 124, 126–30, 134, 170–1, 213
  Countesse of Pembrokes Arcadia, The, 114, 121, 126, 134, 138–9, 166, 181
  'In a grove most riche of shade', 123
  'Joyne mates in mirth to mee', 201
  'Walking in bright Phoebus blaze', 201
Sidney, Sir Robert, 122
Silvester, Joshua, 221
Smith, Helen, 2, 105
Smith, Pamela H., 28
Smith, Simon, 188, 228

250   *Index*

Songes and Sonettes, written by the ryght honorable Lorde Henry Haward late Earle of Surrey, 2, 5, 17, 20–6, 28, 30–7, 45, 48, 51, 59–61, 65, 75, 81, 86, 100–1, 108, 116–18, 133, 148–9, 166, 176, 179, 210, 219
'By fortune as I lay in bed', 63
'Dyvers thy death doe diversly bemone', 116, 124
'Girt in my giltles gowne as I sit here and sow', 36
'Good ladies, ye that have your pleasures in exile', 54–8, 84–5, 112
'I lothe that I did love', 63
'My mothers maides when they do sowe and spinne', 46–7, 52
'O evill tounges, which clap at everie wynd', 63
'O happy dames, that may embrace', 54–8, 84, 112
'Of thy life, Thomas, this compasse wel mark', 46, 117
'The lady prayeth the return of her lover', 112
'The lyfe long that lothsumly doth last', 69
'The restlesse rage of depe devouryng hell', 44
'When Cupid first scaled the fort', 69
'When ragyng love', 63–8, 80, 83–4
'Wrapt in my carelesse cloke', 36
'Wyatt resteth here', 116–17
Southwell, Elizabeth, 144
Spelman, Thomas, 217
Spenser, Edmund, 5, 73, 151, 165–6, 168, 181, 191, 217, 229
Astrophel, 116, 131, 137, 145
Colin Clouts Come Home Againe, 134, 176, 210
Shepheardes Calender, The, 46, 166, 200–1, 210–12, 222
Two Cantos of Mutabilitie, 212
Stallybrass, Peter, 154
Sternhold, Thomas, 61
Stevens, John, 66
Straznicky, Marta, 204
Surrey, Countess of, Frances de Vere, 54
Surrey, Earl of, Henry Howard, 5, 20, 23, 34, 46, 69, 114, 116–18, 210, 229
Certaine Bokes of Virgiles Aenæis, 23
The Fourth Boke of Virgill, 23
'When ragyng love', 63–6, 68–9, 84, 86
'Wyat resteth here', *An excellent Epitaffe of syr Thomas Wyat*, 116
Surrey, Henry Howard, Earl of, 176
Sylvester, Joshua, 217

Temple, William, 197
Throckmorton, Elizabeth, 144
Thynne, Francis, *Newes from the North*, 98
Tibullus *Elegies*, 155
Todd Knight, Jeffrey, 215
Tottel, Richard, 2, 7, 17, 22–31, 44, 46, 48, 96, 108, 119, 132, 155, 158, 160
Trentham, Elizabeth, 144
Trudell, Scott, 15, 189, 228
Tusser, Thomas, 78, 89–90
Five Hundreth Good Pointes, 90
Hundreth Good Pointes of Husbandry, A, 48, 90, 107

Vaux, Lord Thomas, 37
'I lothe that I did love', 50, 63, 69–72
'When Cupid first scaled the fort', 69
Vine, Angus, 7
Vives, Juan Lodovicus, *Introduction to Wisdom*, 61

Walsingham, Frances, 134
Walsingham, Sir Francis, 196
Wanton, Nicholas, 152
Warner, J. Christopher, 28
Waterson, Simon, 205
Watson, Thomas, 187, 189, 223
Amyntas, 123
Hekatompathia, The, 222
Weelkes, Thomas, *Cantus Primus. Madrigal s to 3.4.5.&6. Voyces*, 183
Whetstone, George, *The Rocke of Regard*, 86
White, Edward, 38, 40–2, 80
Whitney, Geoffrey, 89
Whitney, Isabella, 17, 72, 74–5, 88, 92, 229
'The Lamentacion of a Gentilwoman'. *See Gorgious Gallery*
Copy of a Letter, The, 17, 59, 73–7, 79, 83, 85–6, 96, 105–6, 121
Sweet Nosgay, or pleasant posye, A, 14, 17, 46, 73–4, 89–91, 94–5, 110, 130, 140, 194
Whythorne, Thomas, 45–6, 59, 107
Triplex, Of Songs, for three, fower, and five voyces, 51
Williams, R., 12, 96
Wilson, Louise, 3
Wither, George, *The Shepherds Hunting*, 191
Wits Theater of the Little World, 150–1, 154–5
Wolfreston, Frances, 184
women, company of, 4, 16, 18, 55–8, 77, 84–6, 125, 138–41, 144, 149, 168–9, 190, 207, 214–15, 229
idle courtier, 115
ladies' caskets, 128, 130

Index

mother tongue, 47, 52–3, 130, 139, 230
mother's song, 16, 54
parthenogenesis, 53, 130, 138
women at work, 47
Wotton, Henry, 217
Woudhuysen, Henry, 122, 123
Wroth, Lady Mary, 197
Wroth, Sir Robert, 197
Wyatt, Sir Thomas, the elder, 5, 20, 23, 34, 46, 61, 69, 114, 118, 210, 229
'Blame not my lute', 61–2

'My lute awake', 61
'My pen take pain', 61
Wyatt, Sir Thomas, the younger, 117

Yong, Bartholomew, *Diana*, 169–71, 180
Yonge, Nicholas, 151
Musica Transalpina, 185, 187, 189

Zouche, Lord Edward, 199
Zumthor, Paul, 15

Lightning Source UK Ltd.
Milton Keynes UK
UKHW020042031220
374536UK00004B/49